Best Wish

from

Jo at

Cooks Cottage

Franschhoek!

Come back soon and

try the

'Explorer's Club'

GREENWOOD

GUIDES

THE GREENWOOD GUIDE TO

SOUTH AFRICA

Hand-picked Things to Do and Places to Eat

A companion guide to the one you are holding.

This is a separate Greenwood Guide, detailing those places to eat and things to do across the whole of South Africa that sit most cosily with our professed likes and dislikes, i.e. a strong leaning towards the small, family-run, unusual, off-the-beaten track, and, above all, friendly and charming.

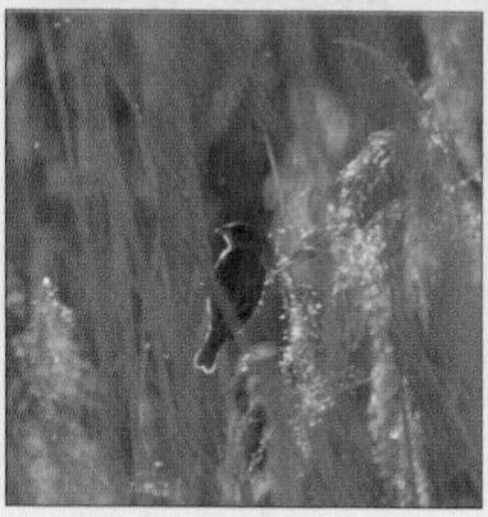

This book is designed for holiday-makers, both South African and from overseas, who want to travel independently, avoid mass tourism and meet friendly, humorous and hospitable people. To this end we have chosen small wineries, family-run restaurants where natural friendliness and character are as important as the food itself; wonderful walks and bird-watching excursions; small, even one-man or -woman, tour operators to lend expertise if you want it; we have included things to do with kids; we have found the best gardens, both private and municipal. Among establishments or activities that are already well known we have only included the truly worthy.

Basically if you like the sort of accommodation we have chosen, then you will find the new book a treat!

www.greenwoodguides.com

To order a copy

The Greenwood Guide to South Africa, Hand-Picked Things to Do and Places to Eat. If you would like to order a copy of this or any of our books, please fill in the coupon and send it with payment to Greenwood Guides, 12 Avalon Rd, London SW6 2EX. Payment can be made by UK cheque made out to 'Greenwood Guides Ltd', or by Visa/Mastercard. We will not process payments until the book is sent out.

Order form

	copy(ies)	price (each)	subtotal
THE GREENWOOD GUIDE TO SOUTH AFRICA **Hand-picked things to do and places to eat** (1ST EDITION)		£13.95	
THE GREENWOOD GUIDE TO SOUTH AFRICA **Hand-picked accommodation** (7TH EDITION)		£13.95	
THE GREENWOOD GUIDE TO NEW ZEALAND **Hand-picked accommodation, restaurants and activities** (5TH EDITION)		£13.95	
post and packing costs			

£2 per order in the UK or South Africa
£3 per order within Europe
£4 per order elsewhere

Total ....

Name ....

Address to send the book to ....

....

....

....

Payment is by UK sterling cheque made out to 'Greenwood Guides' or by VISA/Mastercard (only)

Card number

Expiry date M M Y Y

CCV number

Please send this coupon to

12 Avalon Rd, Fulham, London, SW6 2EX, UK

simon@greenwoodguides.com

First published in 2000 by Greenwood Guides,
12 Avalon Rd, London SW6 2EX, UK.

Seventh edition

ISBN 978-0-9551160-6-3

Printed in China through Colorcraft Ltd., Hong Kong.

The Team

Simon Greenwood on Stiffkey Marsh

Charlotte Turner in Argentina

Lily Yousry-Jouve in Namibia

Sarah Campbell-Pitt in Cape Town

Matt Hilton-Dennis in Fish Hoek

Dicken Gough somewhere above Fish Hoek

Kate Macwhanell in Fish Hoek

THE GREENWOOD GUIDE TO

SOUTH AFRICA AND NAMIBIA

with BOTSWANA and ZAMBIA

hand-picked accommodation

Including Phophonyane Lodge in Swaziland
and Malealea Lodge in Lesotho.

seventh edition

www.greenwoodguides.com

Acknowledgements

Series Editor: Simon Greenwood

Writing collaboration and inspections: Matthew Hilton-Dennis, Dickon Gough and Kate MacWhannell (South Africa), Lily Yousry-Jouve (Namibia), Sarah Campbell-Pitt (Zambia and Botswana). Thanks too to Susan McNaughton for her translations from Lily's French. Also to Tracy Woodland and Karoline Hanks for vital extra info on Southern Africa.

Map data provided by Collins Bartholomew Ltd.

Production, DTP and Design: Charlotte Turner, Tory Gordon-Harris and Jo Ekin

Printing: Colorcraft, Hong Kong

UK Distribution: Portfolio, London

SA Distribution: Quartet Sales and Marketing, Johannesburg

The cover image is of Belair, entry number 78. Cover design and digital manipulation by Tory Gordon-Harris.

Warren Johnson for his photos of Taita Falcon. Other incidental images as follows: title page courtesy of The Desert Homestead and Horse Trails, entry number 339; North West Province, KwaZulu Natal, Gauteng, Free State, Swaziland, Soweto and Mpumalanga by Tina Hillier; Western Cape, Northern Cape and Limpopo by Jamie Crawford; Namibia by Ollie Blackwell; Botswana and Zambia by Sarah Campbell-Pitt and Eastern Cape by Emily Dugan.

Symbols
and what they mean

 No credit cards accepted.

 Meals can be provided, often by prior arrangement.

 Rooms all have TVs.

 Stocked wild game can be seen. This does not include naturally occurring wild animals like springbok and waterbuck.

 Wireless Internet access

 Children are welcome without proviso.

 Working farm.

 Off-street car parking.

 Access only for wheelchairs.

 Full wheelchair facilities.

 Swimming available in pool, sea, dam or river.

 No smoking inside the buildings.

 Good hiking or walking direct from the house.

Contents

Introduction

Since we visit each place we feature each year and since we have to turn down so many applications from places that didn't quite appeal enough - or which, frankly, we just didn't like at all - I have been able to calculate that we have now made about 4,000 visits to Southern African places to stay over the past 9 years. I don't like to claim too much - and when I was young I didn't dream of this! – it looks very much as though we may have inadvertently become 'experts' in this area....

We are ever more stringent about whom we accept into the guide and I think long-standing GG-watchers will agree that the book has got better as well as bigger. I receive a great deal of mail from travellers, which I encourage. It gives us a good idea of how our choices are being received out there in the field. And since we live or die on the happiometer of our travellers, i.e. you, then this info is vital.

We have made genuine human hospitality our common denominator rather than the sterile but safe judgement of a place's worth according to its facilities. We do not give out stars or tiaras as a result. A place is either a lovely place to be or it isn't. Beyond that each traveller will need to look at location, rates and exactly what sort of place it is and make their own decisions.

We describe each place ourselves so I hope you will find the text accurate and appropriate as well as lively and at times even humorous.

The job of Greenwood Guides is first and foremost to assess the people running the accommodation and choose only those for whom looking after others, whether they be friends, family or paying guests, is a natural pleasure. Taste, furnishings, facilities, views, food, beds, bathrooms... all these things are important too, but only if they are provided by friendly people.

Thank you for choosing our guide. We do put in an enormous amount of effort each year, revisiting each place each edition, weeding out places that have lost their energy as often happens in the world of accommodation and sounding out all the new great, good and ordinary places that open each year. The standard rises continually in Southern Africa and this does mean that new places emerge at the top and old places drop off the bottom too. We seriously recommend therefore that you make sure that this is a latest edition of the guide. It is published annually in June.

As I always say, we would be delighted to hear from you when you get back from your travels.

NEW THINGS: WWW.GREENWOODGUIDES.COM

Our web site has been worthily fulfilling its role for many years, but at last we have found the time and energy to give it a make-over. We relaunched the site in March 2008 and, as well as our latest accommodation choices, it now also includes our recommendations for things to do, places to eat, information on travel to SA, maps and info for each province, text on history, animals and much else besides. Well worth a look even if you have bought this book.

THE GREENWOOD GUIDES APPROACH

There are essentially three types of place to stay. There are those that fulfil their obligations in a commercial way and leave you feeling throughout your stay like the paying customer that you are. And there are those few great places where you are welcomed in and treated as a friend, cliché though this may now have become, and where paying at the end of your visit is a pleasurable surprise. And of course there is a third category where paying for your stay is a disagreeable inevitability!

It is a particular irony of the accommodation world that no price is ever put on the essential qualities of a place – people, atmosphere, charm. These ideas are too woolly perhaps to quantify, but this is where one's real enjoyment of a place to stay stems from. You are asked to pay instead for tangible facilities like marble bathrooms and en-suite showers.

This is a fallacy that we try to dismantle in all our guides, which is why you will find places at all reasonable price levels. Expensive does not mean good. And nor does cheap (however appealing the word may sound!). If a place costs plenty then it will probably offer facilities in keeping with the price. But that does not mean you will have any fun. Some very expensive places forget that they are providing a service and look down their noses at their own guests. At the other end of the spectrum, the very cheapest places are often cheap for good reasons. Sometimes for spectacular reasons!

Character and genuine hospitality, the extra qualities we search for, are found spaced evenly across the price spectrum. Nowhere in this guide cuts corners at the risk of your displeasure. We give equal billing to each place we choose, no matter if it is a gorgeous lodge or a home-spun B&B.

At the top end, the most jewel-encrusted, nay 'boutique' places may drip with luxurious trimmings, but have retained their sense of atmosphere and humour, are friendly and informal and nearly all are still owned and managed by the same people. ('Boutique' always used to mean a 'small clothes shop in France', but it has sneaked into accommodation vocab somewhere along the line.)

Equally, there are places in the book that do not have much in the way of luxury, but easily compensate with unique settings, wonderful views and charming hosts.

We are hoping that those of you who normally only plump for luxury at a price will use this guide to vary their holiday a little and stay at a few of the wonderful family-run farms and B&Bs. And that those who usually go as cheap as possible will splash out once in a while on a more luxurious option. This book allows for great flexibility in terms of price and style of accommodation. We do not wish to divide the world into budget and luxury, only great and not great enough.

It is the quality of experience that draws us in and this is not determined by how much you pay. In the end I know that you will really like the owners in this book, many of whom we now count as friends. And you will certainly make friends yourselves if you stick to the Greenwood trail.

SOUTH AFRICA

(There is a separate introduction for Namibia before the start of the Namibian section; and for Zambia and Botswana before the start of that section.)

DRIVING

There is nowhere in South Africa that would make a 4-wheel drive a necessity. However make sure you confirm this issue if booking into other southern African places.

CAR HIRE

Make sure that you have considered the amount of daily mileage your car hire company gives you. 100km or even 200km a day is virtually nothing and the final cost can be far higher than you estimated. Try and work out roughly what distances you will be covering and ask for the correct daily allowance. Or ask for unlimited mileage. There is usually a surcharge for taking your car across the border from SA into other countries.

N.B. Also make sure you are insured to drive the car on dirt roads.

We highly recommend Allen's Car Hire, 417 Main Rd, Kirstenhof, Cape Town for local trips to and from Cape Town on 021-701-8844, abradley@mweb.co.za, www.allenscarhire.co.za. They are very friendly and helpful and we use them ourselves. Airport pick-ups and drop-offs no problem.

MOBILE/CELL PHONES

Airports all have shops that provide mobile phones. They are invaluable and we recommend that you get one. You can buy a cheap handset or just rent one for the duration of your stay and then pay for calls as you go with recharge cards.

TELEPHONE NUMBERS

The numbers printed for entries in SA or Namibia in the book are all from within South Africa or Namibia.
To call South Africa from the UK dial 0027 then drop the 0 from the local code.
To call Namibia from the UK dial 00264 then drop the 0 from the local code.
To call Botswana from the UK dial 00267 then drop the 0 from the local code.
To call Zambia from the UK dial 00260 then drop the 0 from the local code.
To call the UK from South Africa you now dial 0044 - it used to be 0944 but this changed recently.
Another change is when dialing a local number you now always have to dial the full number including the area code.

TORTOISES

Look out for tortoises. They are slow, but seem to spend a lot of time, completely against the tide of advice put forward for their benefit, crossing roads.

TIPPING

* In restaurants we tend to give 15%.
* At a petrol station my policy is to give no tip for just filling up, 3 rand for cleaning the windows, and 5 rand for cleaning the windows and checking oil and water. If you really don't want the attendant to clean your windows you need to make this a statement when you ask for the petrol… or they will often do it anyway.
• At a guest-house I would typically give R30 per person staying for up to two nights. If you are staying longer than two nights then you might feel like adding more. If there is obviously one maid to whom the tip will go then give it to her direct. If there are many staff members who will be sharing the tip then give it to your host.

THE GARDEN ROUTE

Many people imagine, not unreasonably, that the Garden Route is a bit like a wine route where you can go from garden to garden, smelling roses and admiring pergolas and rockeries. Not so. The Garden Route is so named for its lushness and greenery. The area is covered in forests and rivers which spill into the sea. And, although many people there surely do have lovely gardens, the name is a little misleading. A fantastic area for walking though.

TIME OF YEAR

I got in a bit of a tangle in the first edition trying neatly to package up what is really quite complicated. So I will limit myself to one observation. It seems to me that most Europeans come to South Africa in January, February and March to avoid their own miserable weather and write taunting postcards home from a sunny Cape.

However, the very best time of year to visit the Northern Cape, Mpumalanga, Limpopo, North West Province, KwaZulu Natal and the Karoo, i.e. the whole country except the southern Cape, is from May to October. The air is dry and warm, game viewing is at its best and there are fewer tourists keeping the prices higher. It's worth mentioning.

PAY FOR ENTRY

We could not afford to research and publish this guide in the way we do without the financial support of those we feature. Each place that we have chosen has paid an entry fee for which we make no apology. It has not influenced our decision-making about who is right or wrong for the guide and we turn down many more than we accept. The proof of this is in the proverbial pudding. Use the book and see for yourself. It is also very hard for us to write up a place that we are not enthusiastic about.

THE MAPS SECTION

The maps at the front of the book are designed to show you where in the country each place is positioned, and should not be used as a road map. There are many minor and dirt roads missing and we recommend that you buy a proper companion road atlas.

Each place is flagged with a number that corresponds to the page number below each entry.

Some have complained that it is hard to find detailed road maps of South Africa in the UK, so I suggest you buy one at the airport when you arrive in SA. Or try Stanfords in London on Long Acre in Covent Garden, 020-7836-1321.

CANCELLATION

Most places have some form of cancellation charge. Do make sure that you are aware what this is if you book in advance. Owners need to protect themselves against no-shows and will often demand a deposit for advance booking.

PRICES

The prices quoted are per person sharing per night, unless specifically stated otherwise. Every now and then complications have meant we quote the full room rate. Single rates are also given.

We have usually put in a range within which the actual price will fall. This may be because of fluctuating prices at different times of year, but also we have tried to predict the anticipated rise in prices over the book's shelf life. Obviously we cannot know what will happen to the value of the rand and prices might fall outside the quoted range.

Most game lodges quote an all-in package including meals and game activities.

Although South Africa has become substantially more expensive since the first edition of this guide came out 6 years ago, it is still great value on the whole. The value-for-money increases significantly the more off-the-beaten-track you wander.

CHILDREN

We have only given the child-friendly symbol to those places that are unconditionally accepting of the little fellows. This does not necessarily mean that if there is no symbol children are barred. But it may mean chatting with your hosts about their ages, their temperaments and how suitable a time and place it will be. Most owners are concerned about how their other guests will take to kids running wild when they are trying to relax on a long-anticipated holiday… from their own children. Places that are fully child-friendly are listed in the activities index at the back of the book.

DISCLAIMER

We make no claims to god-like objectivity in assessing what is or is not special about the places we feature. They are there because we like them. Our opinions and tastes are mortal and ours alone. We have done our utmost to get the facts right, but apologize for any mistakes that may have slipped through the net. Some things change which are outside our control: people sell up, prices increase, exchange rates fluctuate, unfortunate extensions are added, marriages break up and even acts of God can rain down destruction. We would be grateful to be told about any errors or changes, however great or small. We can always make these editions on the web version of this book.

DON'T TRY AND DO TOO MUCH. PLEASE.

It is the most common way to spoil your own holiday. South Africa and Namibia are huge countries and you cannot expect to see too much of them on one trip. Don't over-extend yourself. Stay everywhere for at least two nights and make sure that you aren't spending your hard-earned holiday fiddling with the radio and admiring the dashboard of your hire car.

PLEASE WRITE TO US

Our email address is simon@greenwoodguides.com for all comments. Although we visit each place each edition many of the places featured here are small, personal and owner-run. This means that their enjoyability depends largely on the happiness, health and energy of the hosts. This can evaporate in double-quick time for any number of reasons and standards plummet before we have had a chance to re-evaluate the place. So we are also very grateful to travellers who keep us up-to-date with how things are going. We are always most concerned to hear that the hosting has been inattentive.

OTHER GREENWOOD GUIDES

We also have a guide to New Zealand which is available in bookshops or by emailing us direct or mailing us the order form at the front of this book. The Greenwood Guides to Canada and Australia are available at www.greenwoodguides.com only.

THANKS

So that's about it for another year. My great thanks this time to Matt, Dickon, Kate, Lily and Sarah for all their efforts in researching and updating the guide. And a huge thank you to Charlotte who has, despite the arrival of Boris Greenwood right in the middle of the busiest period, ferried the guide through its publishing processes here in London without complaint.

I hope that this book will be seen as the main reason why you enjoyed your holiday as much as you did. Please feel free to write to me with praise or criticism for individual places that you visit at simon@greenwoodguides.com. And have a look at www.greenwoodguides.com before you set off.

Simon.

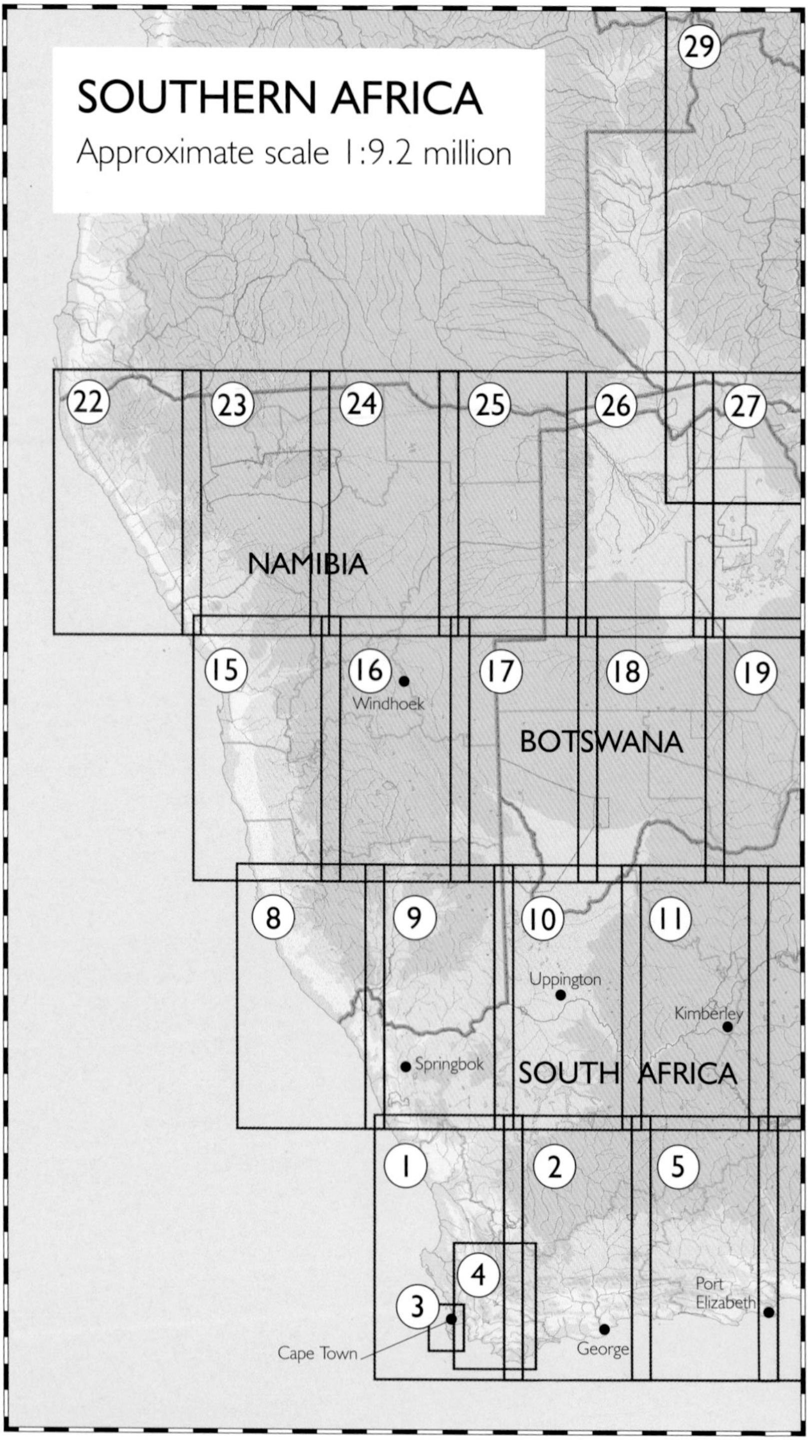

SOUTHERN AFRICA
Approximate scale 1:9.2 million
29
22
23
24
25
26
27
NAMIBIA
15
16
Windhoek
17
18
19
BOTSWANA
8
9
10
11
Uppington
Kimberley
Springbok
SOUTH AFRICA
1
2
5
4
3
Port Elizabeth
George
Cape Town

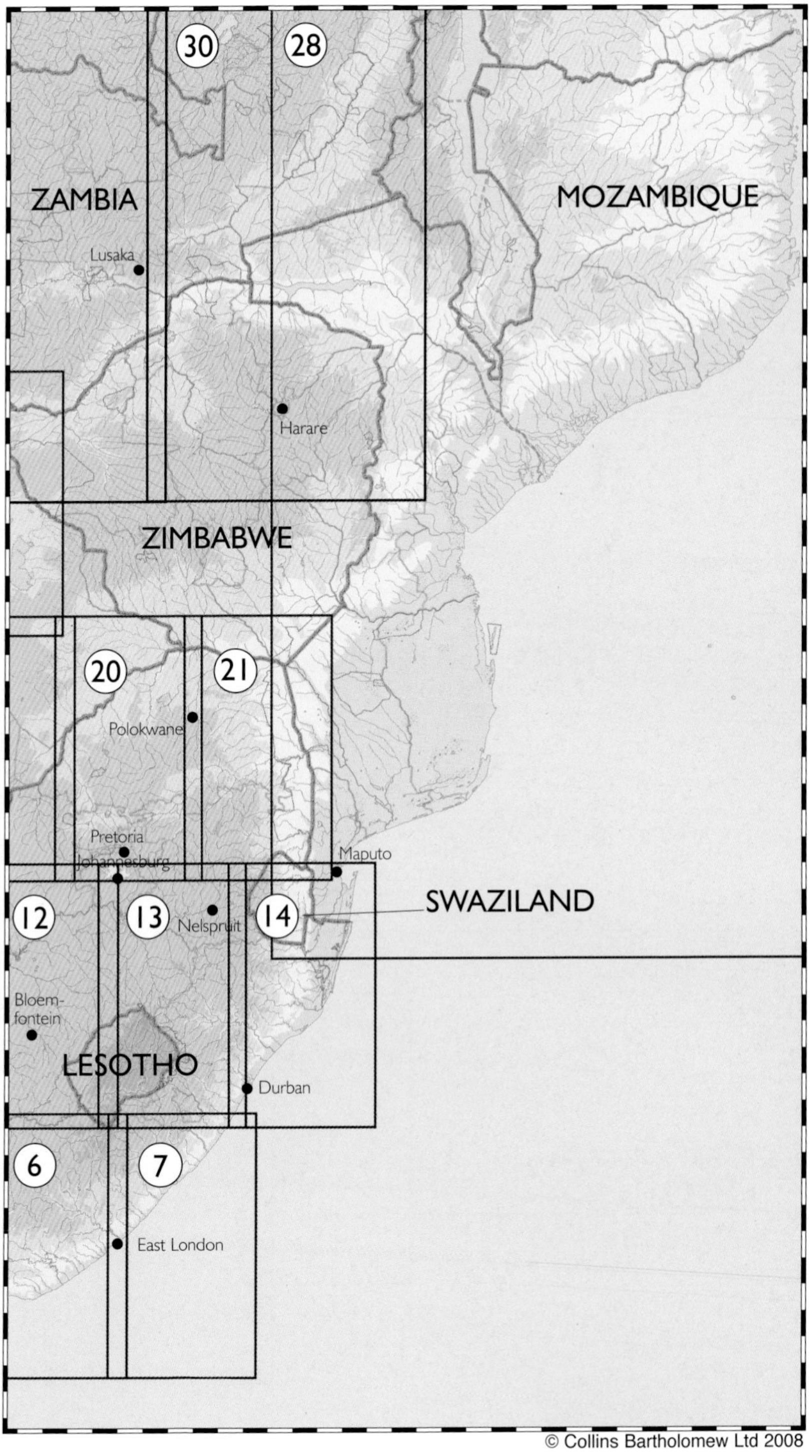
30
28
ZAMBIA
MOZAMBIQUE
Lusaka
Harare
ZIMBABWE
20
21
Polokwane
Pretoria
Johannesburg
Maputo
12
13
14
SWAZILAND
Nelspruit
Bloem-
fontein
LESOTHO
Durban
6
7
East London

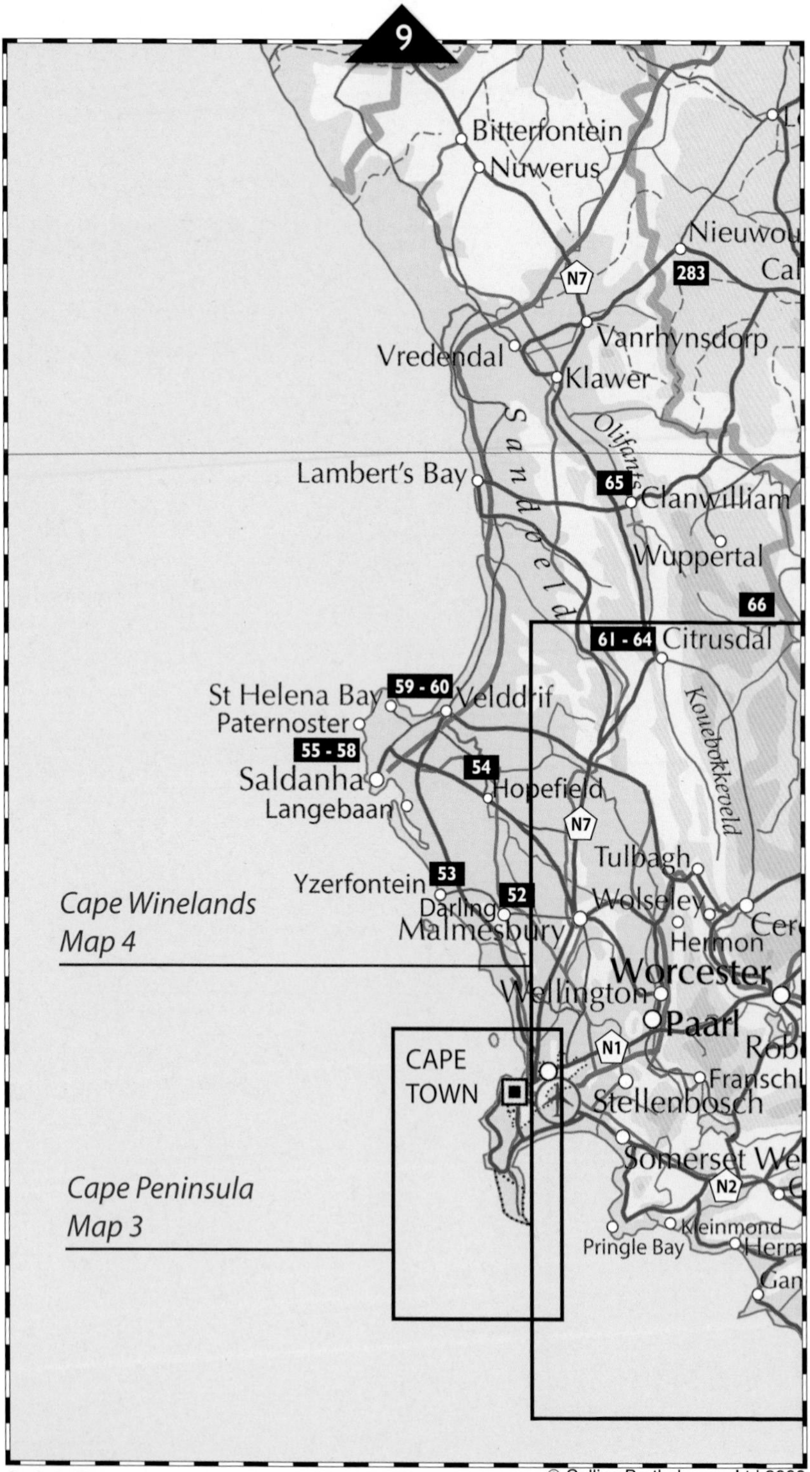
9
Bitterfontein
Nuwerus
283
N7
Vanrhynsdorp
Vredendal
Klawer
Sandveld
Olifants
Lambert's Bay
65
Clanwilliam
Wuppertal
66
61 - 64
Citrusdal
St Helena Bay
59 - 60
Velddrif
Paternoster
55 - 58
Koue bokkeveld
Saldanha
54
Hopefield
Langebaan
N7
Tulbagh
Yzerfontein
53
52
Darling
Wolseley
Cape Winelands
Map 4
Malmesbury
Hermon
Worcester
Wellington
Paarl
N1
CAPE
TOWN
Stellenbosch
Somerset
N2
Cape Peninsula
Map 3
Kleinmond
Pringle Bay

MAP 1

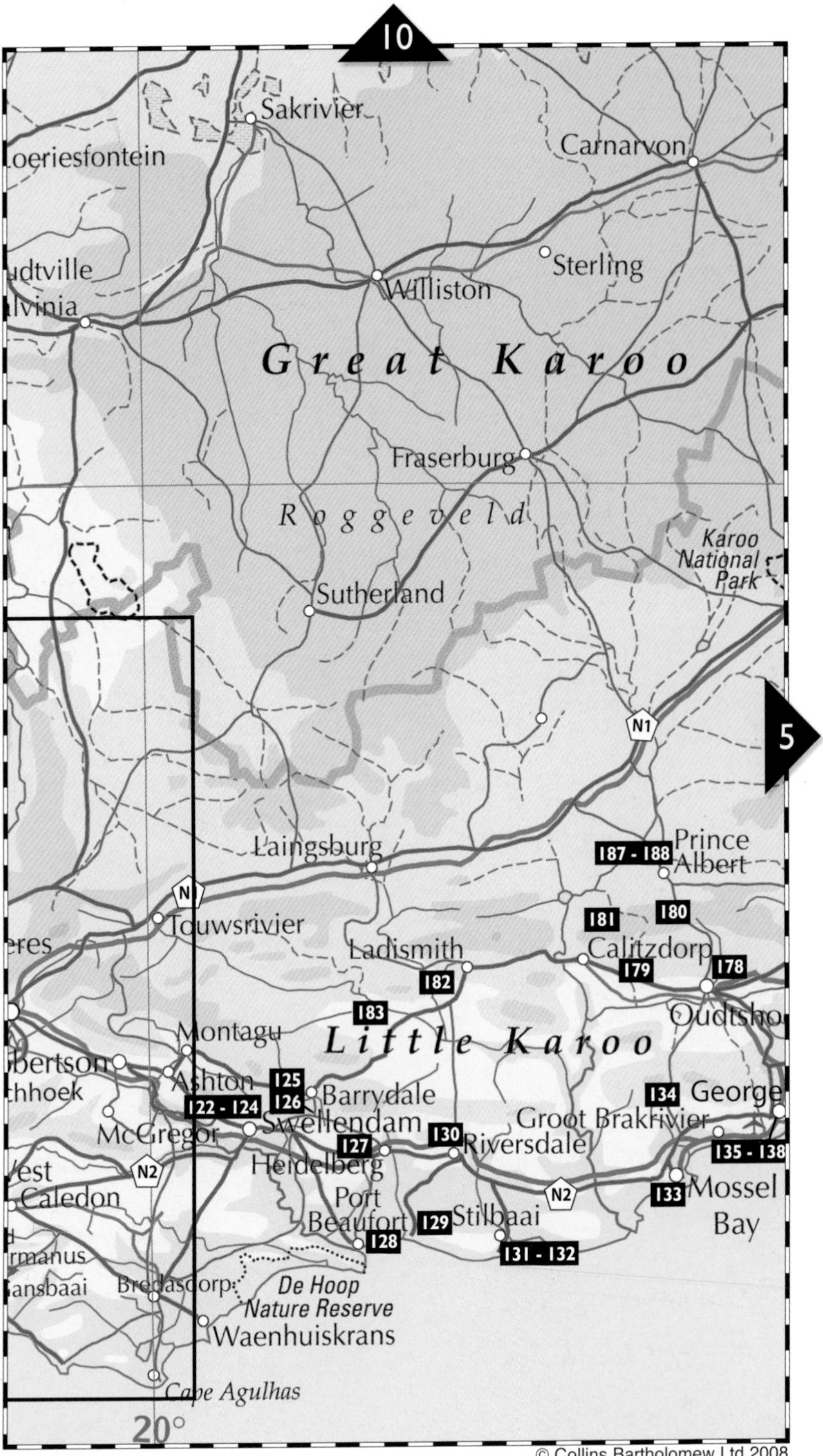
10
5
Sakrivier
Carnarvon
Loeriesfontein
udtville
lvinia
Sterling
Williston
Great Karoo
Fraserburg
Roggeveld
Karoo National Park
Sutherland
N1
Laingsburg
187 - 188
Prince Albert
181
180
Touwsrivier
eres
Ladismith
182
Calitzdorp
179
178
Oudtsho
183
Montagu
Little Karoo
bertson
Ashton
125
126
Barrydale
thhoek
122 - 124
Swellendam
134
George
Groot Brakrivier
McGregor
127
130
Riversdale
135 - 138
Heidelberg
West
N2
133
Mossel Bay
Caledon
Port Beaufort
129
Stilbaai
128
131 - 132
rmanus
ansbaai
Bredasdorp
De Hoop Nature Reserve
Waenhuiskrans
Cape Agulhas
20°

MAP 2

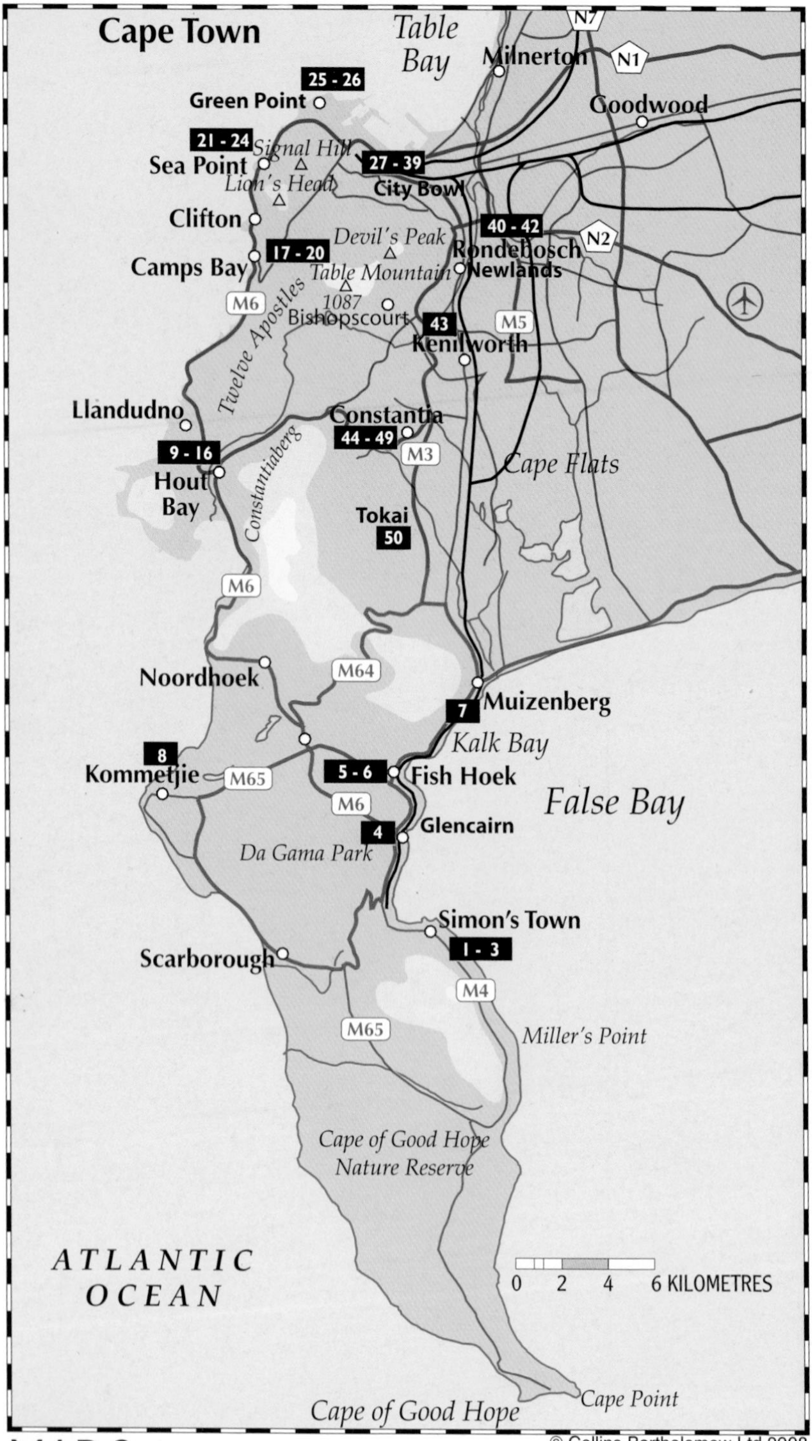
Cape Town
Table Bay
N7
Milnerton
N1
Goodwood
25 - 26
Green Point
21 - 24
Signal Hill
Sea Point
Lion's Head
27 - 39
City Bowl
Clifton
Devil's Peak
40 - 42
N2
Rondebosch
Newlands
17 - 20
Camps Bay
Table Mountain
1087
Bishopscourt
M6
Twelve Apostles
43
Kenilworth
M5
Llandudno
Constantia
44 - 49
M3
9 - 16
Hout Bay
Constantiaberg
Cape Flats
Tokai
50
M6
Noordhoek
M64
7
Muizenberg
Kalk Bay
8
Kommetjie
M65
5 - 6
Fish Hoek
False Bay
M6
4
Glencairn
Da Gama Park
Simon's Town
1 - 3
Scarborough
M4
M65
Miller's Point
Cape of Good Hope
Nature Reserve
ATLANTIC
OCEAN
0 2 4 6 KILOMETRES
Cape Point
Cape of Good Hope

MAP 3

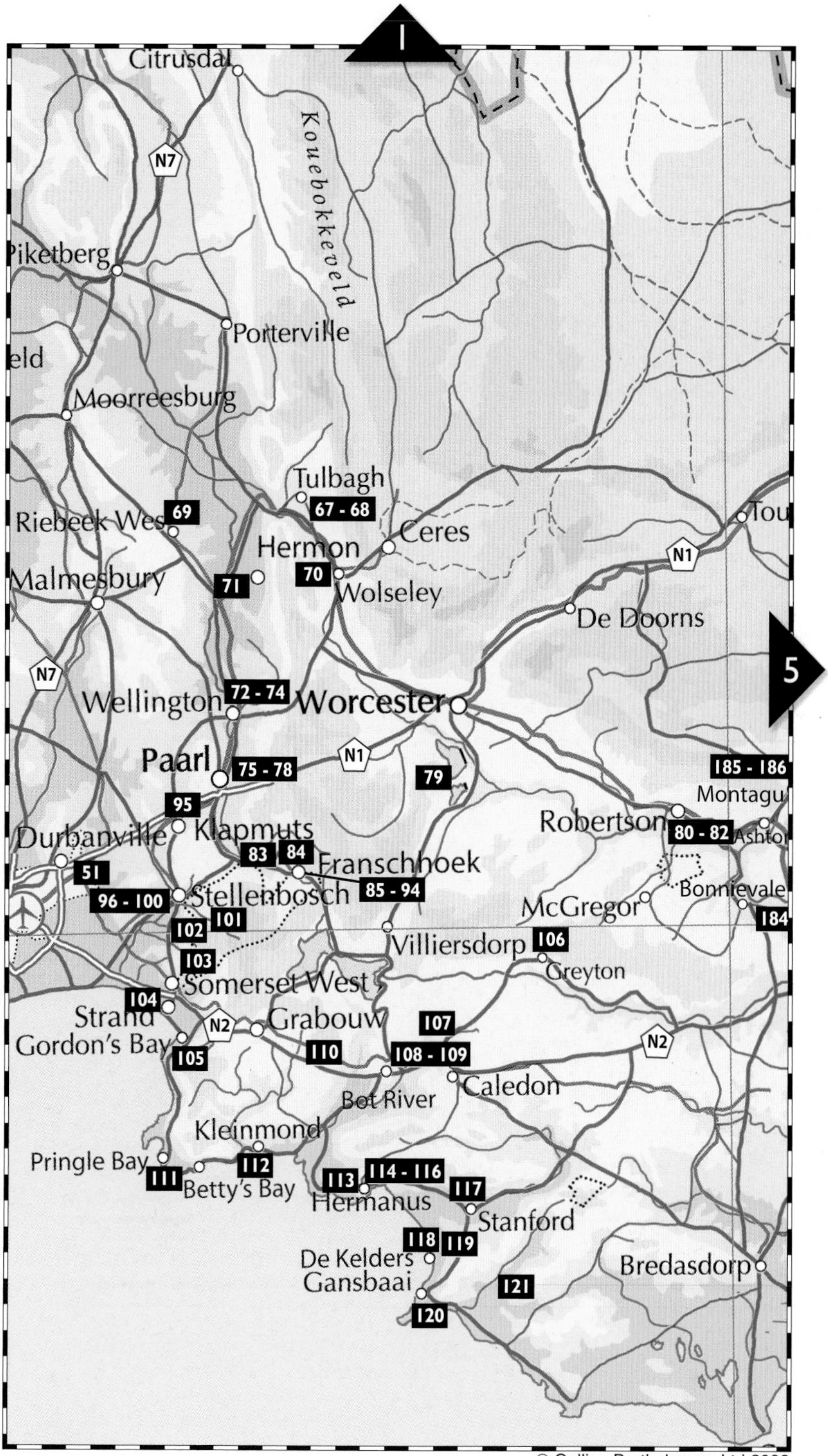
1
5
Citrusdal
N7
Kouebokkeveld
Piketberg
Porterville
eld
Moorreesburg
Tulbagh
67 - 68
69
Riebeek West
Hermon
Ceres
70
Wolseley
71
Malmesbury
N1
Tou
De Doorns
N7
72 - 74
Wellington
Worcester
N1
Paarl
75 - 78
79
185 - 186
Montagu
95
Klapmuts
Robertson
80 - 82
Ashton
Durbanville
83
84
Franschhoek
51
85 - 94
96 - 100
Stellenbosch
101
McGregor
Bonnievale
184
102
Villiersdorp
106
103
Greyton
Somerset West
104
Strand
Grabouw
107
N2
Gordon's Bay
105
110
108 - 109
N2
Caledon
Bot River
Kleinmond
Pringle Bay
112
111
Betty's Bay
113
114 - 116
Hermanus
117
Stanford
118
119
De Kelders
Gansbaai
Bredasdorp
121
120

MAP 4

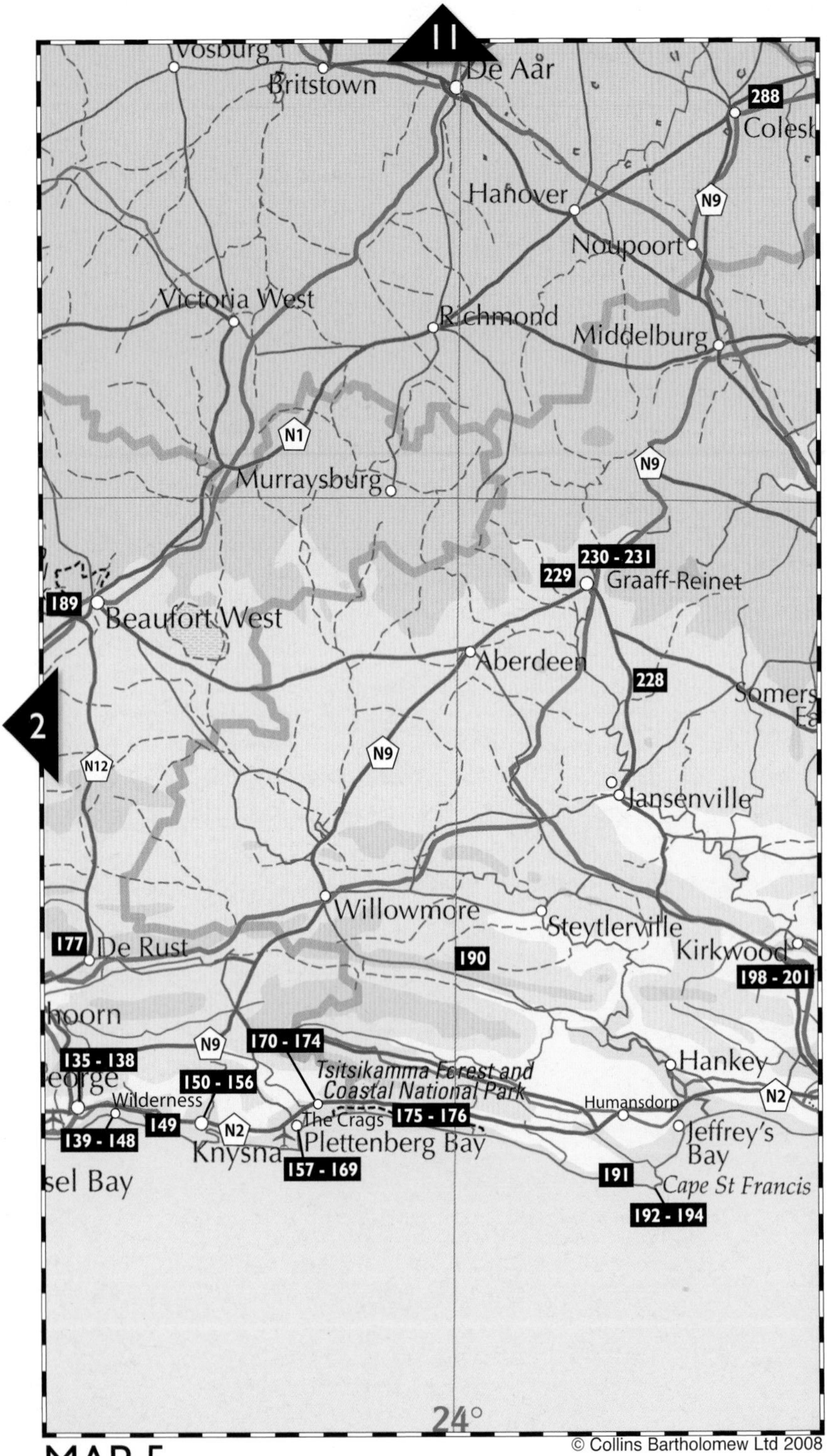
11
2
Vosburg
Britstown
De Aar
288
Hanover
N9
Noupoort
Victoria West
Richmond
Middelburg
N1
Murraysburg
230 - 231
229
Graaff-Reinet
189
Beaufort West
Aberdeen
228
N12
Jansenville
Willowmore
Steytlerville
177
De Rust
190
Kirkwood
198 - 201
170 - 174
135 - 138
150 - 156
Tsitsikamma Forest and
Coastal National Park
Hankey
N2
Wilderness
Humansdorp
149
The Crags
175 - 176
139 - 148
Knysna
Plettenberg Bay
Jeffrey's
Bay
157 - 169
191
Cape St Francis
192 - 194
24°

MAP 5

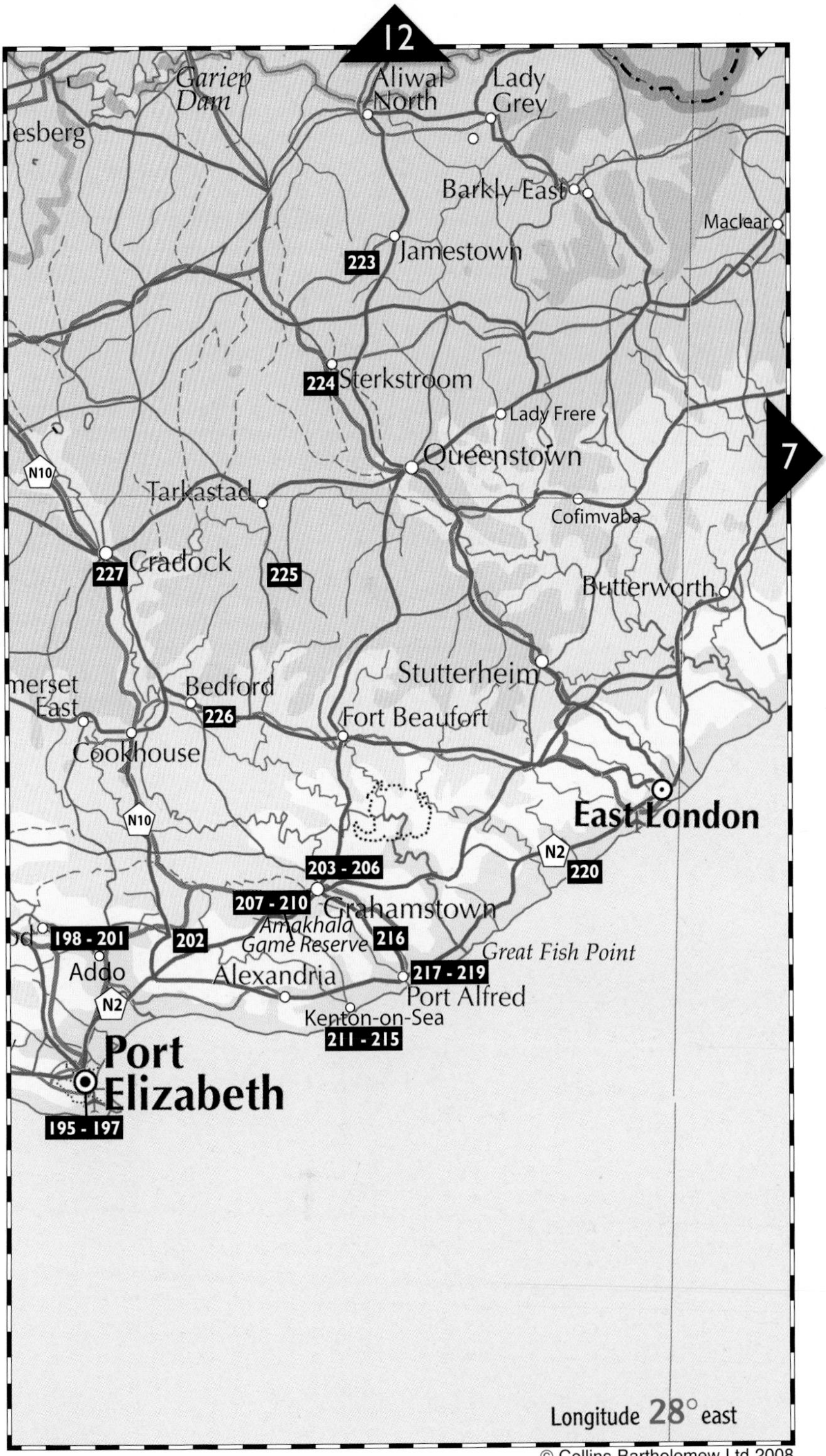
12
Gariep Dam
Aliwal North
Lady Grey
lesberg
Barkly East
Maclear
Jamestown
223
224
Sterkstroom
Lady Frere
7
Queenstown
N10
Tarkastad
Cofimvaba
Cradock
227
225
Butterworth
Stutterheim
merset East
Bedford
226
Fort Beaufort
Cookhouse
East London
N10
N2
220
203 - 206
207 - 210
Grahamstown
Amakhala Game Reserve
216
198 - 201
202
Great Fish Point
Addo
Alexandria
217 - 219
Port Alfred
N2
Kenton-on-Sea
211 - 215
Port Elizabeth
195 - 197
Longitude 28° east

MAP 6

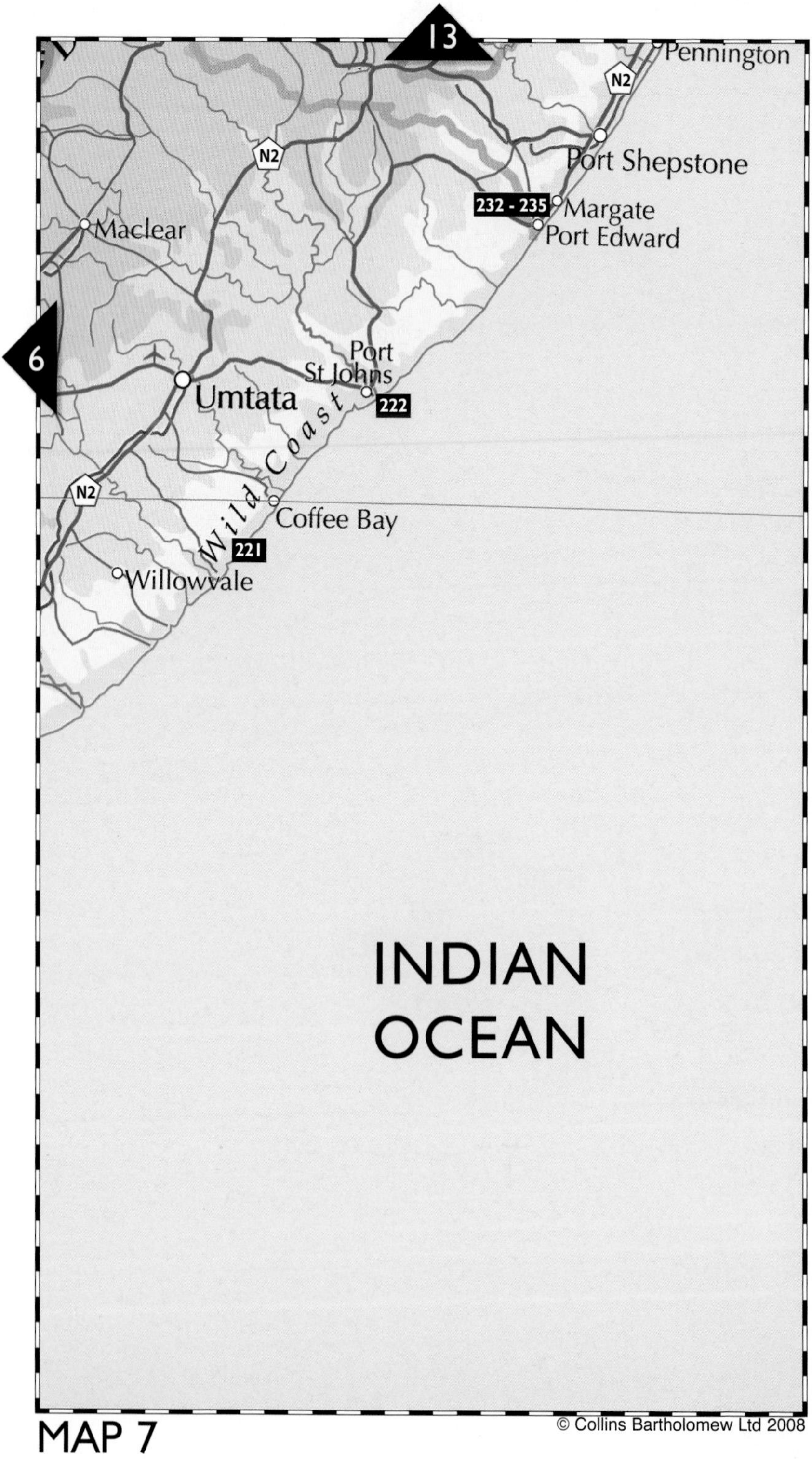
13
6
Pennington
N2
Port Shepstone
232 - 235
Margate
Port Edward
Maclear
N2
Port
St Johns
222
Umtata
Wild Coast
N2
Coffee Bay
221
Willowvale
INDIAN
OCEAN

MAP 7

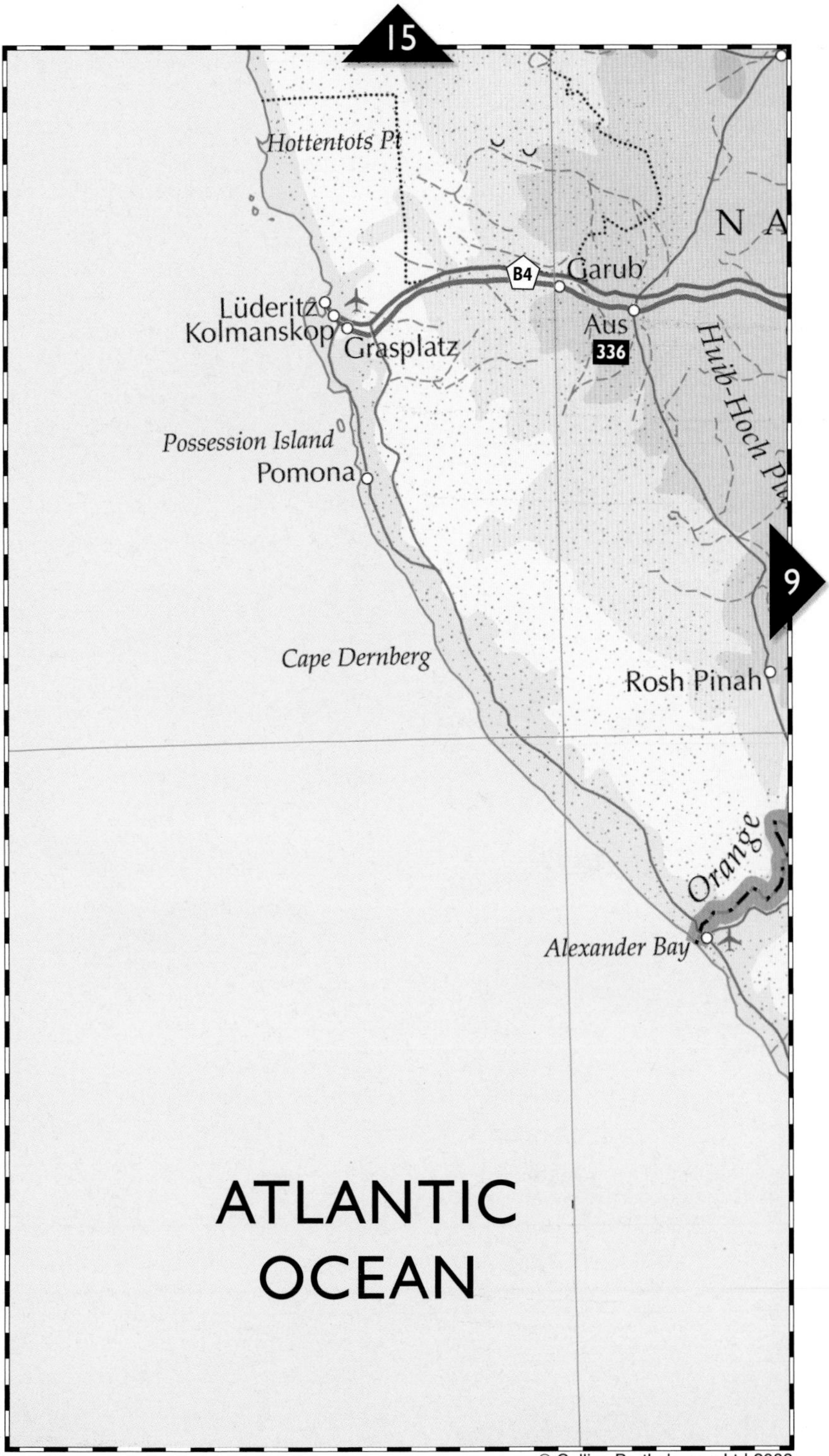
15
Hottentots Pt
N A
B4
Garub
Lüderitz
Kolmanskop
Grasplatz
Aus
336
Huib-Hoch Pl
Possession Island
Pomona
9
Cape Dernberg
Rosh Pinah
Orange
Alexander Bay
ATLANTIC
OCEAN

MAP 8

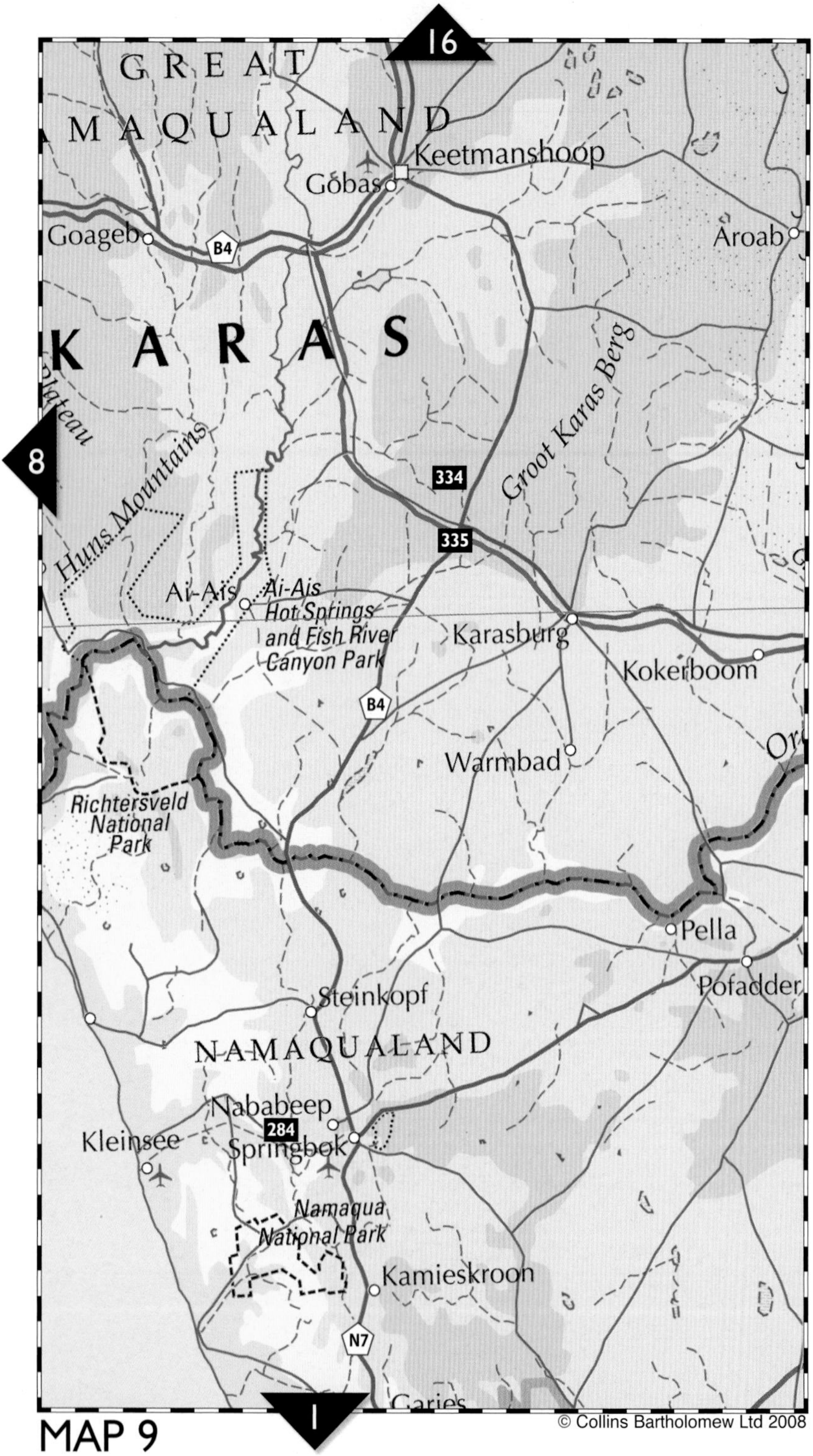
16
GREAT
NAMAQUALAND
Keetmanshoop
Gobas
Goageb
B4
Aroab
KARAS
Groot Karas Berg
Plateau
8
Huns Mountains
334
335
Ai-Ais
Ai-Ais Hot Springs and Fish River Canyon Park
Karasburg
Kokerboom
B4
Warmbad
Richtersveld National Park
Pella
Pofadder
Steinkopf
NAMAQUALAND
Nababeep
284
Kleinsee
Springbok
Namaqua National Park
Kamieskroon
N7
Garies
1

MAP 9

MAP 10

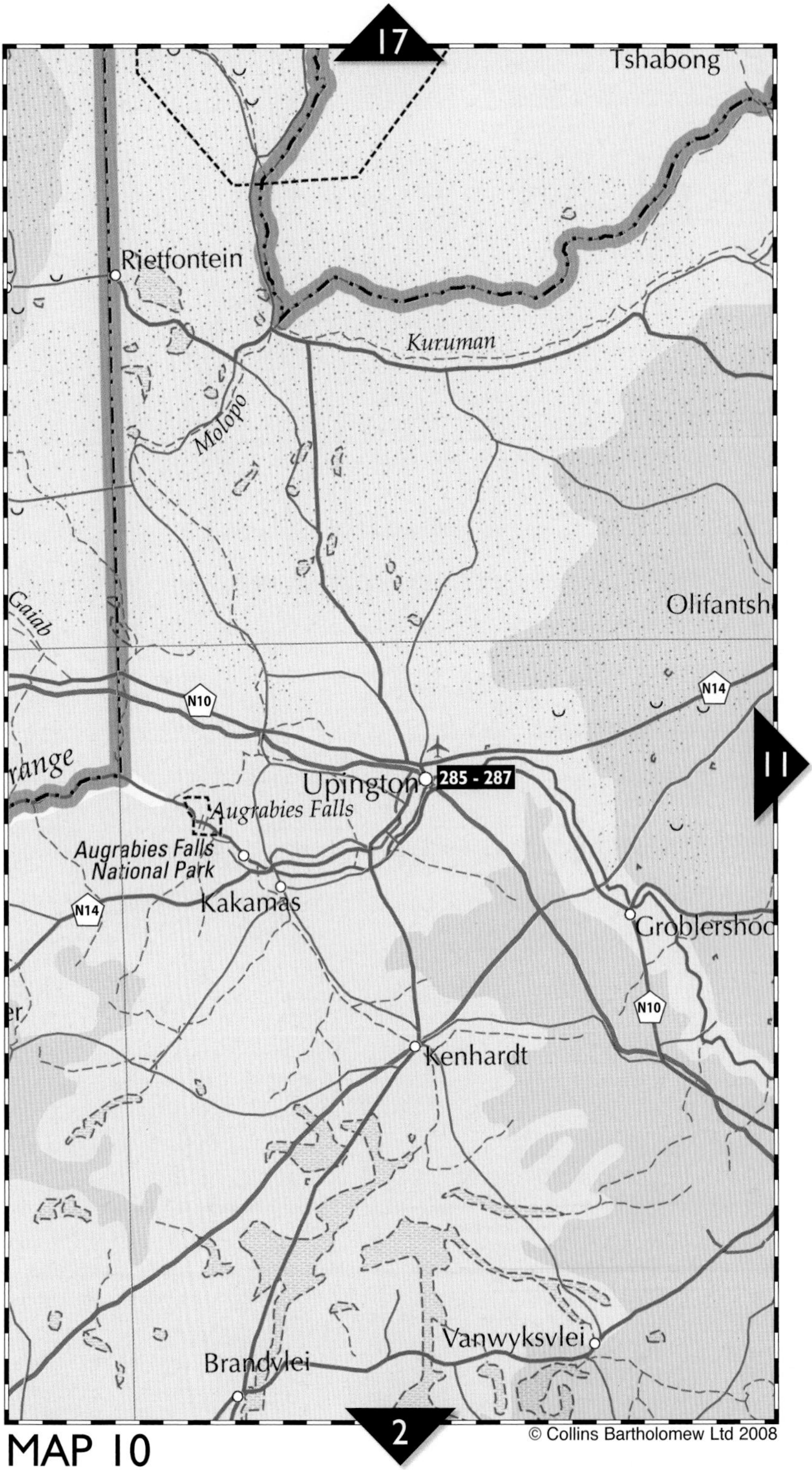
17
Tshabong
Rietfontein
Kuruman
Molopo
Olifantsh
Gaiab
N10
N14
range
Upington
285 - 287
Augrabies Falls
Augrabies Falls National Park
Kakamas
N14
11
Groblershoo
N10
er
Kenhardt
Vanwyksvlei
Brandvlei
2

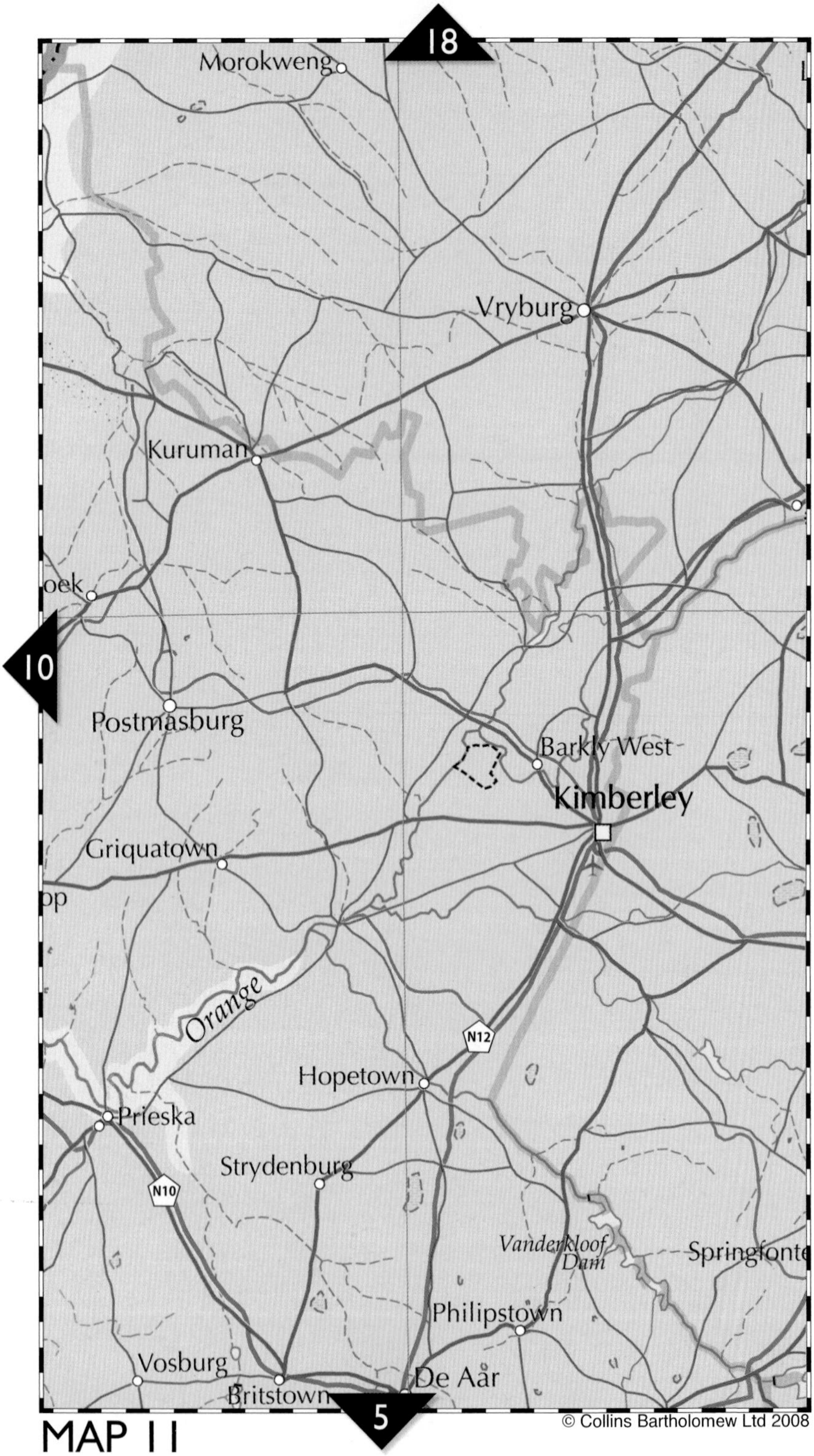
18
Morokweng
Vryburg
Kuruman
oek
10
Postmasburg
Barkly West
Kimberley
Griquatown
op
Orange
N12
Hopetown
Prieska
Strydenburg
N10
Vanderkloof Dam
Springfonte
Philipstown
Vosburg
De Aar
Britstown
5

MAP 11

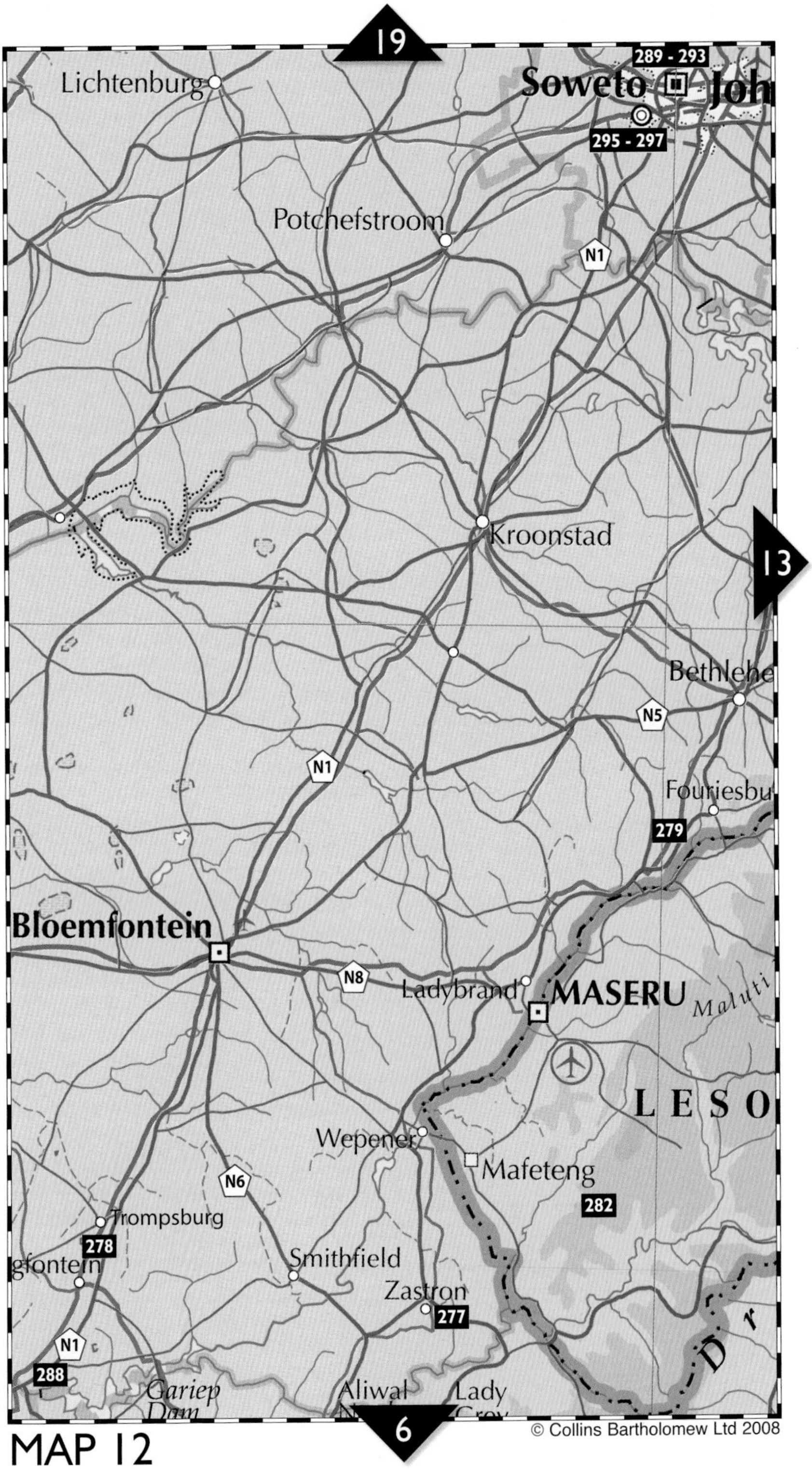
19
289 - 293
Soweto
Joh
295 - 297
Lichtenburg
Potchefstroom
N1
Kroonstad
13
Bethlehe
N5
N1
Fouriesbu
279
Bloemfontein
N8
Ladybrand
MASERU
Maluti
LESO
Wepener
Mafeteng
282
N6
Trompsburg
278
gfontein
Smithfield
Zastron
277
N1
288
Gariep
Dam
Aliwal
Lady
D
r
6

MAP 12

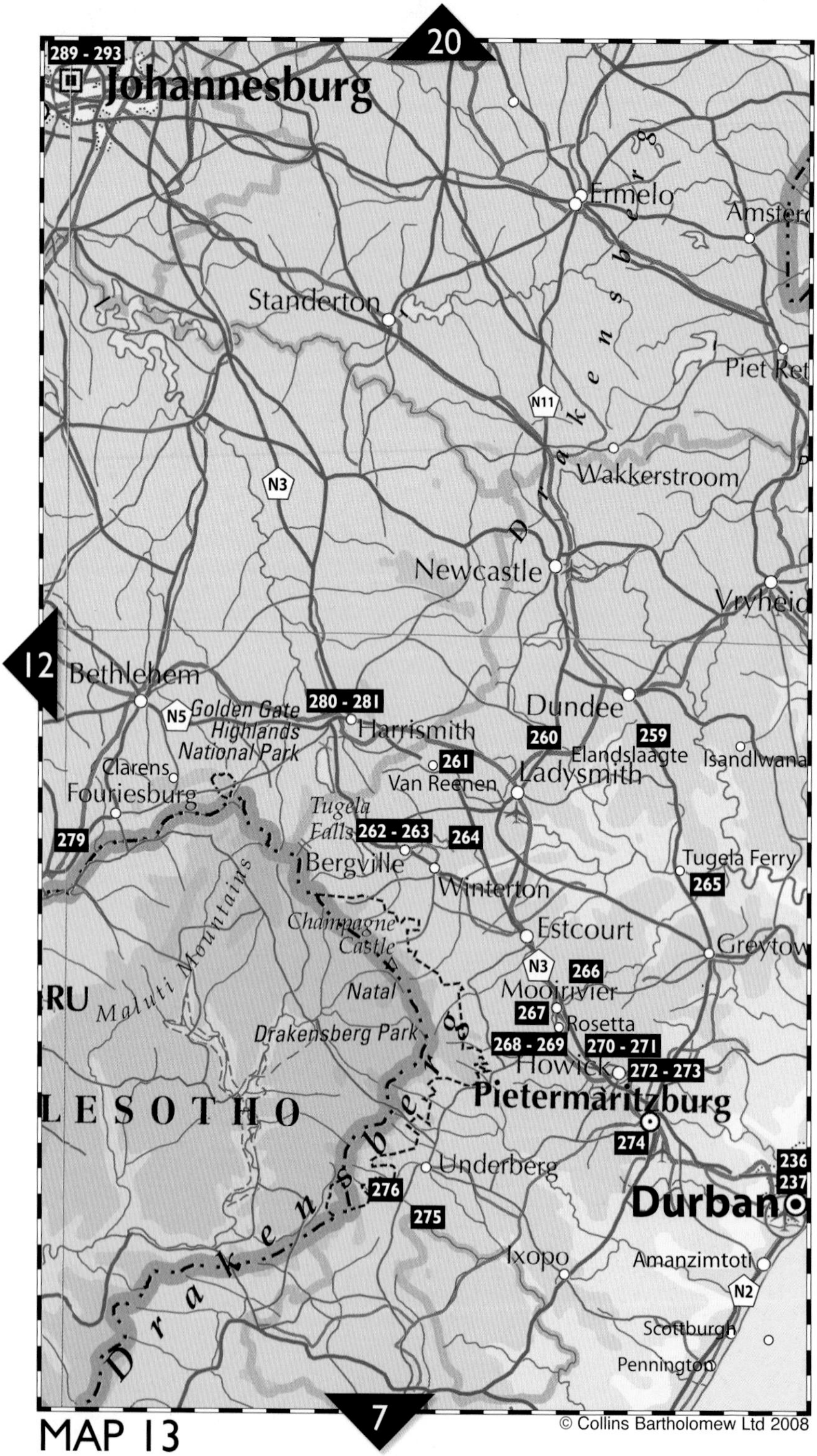
20
12
7
289 - 293
Johannesburg
Ermelo
Amsterd
Standerton
Piet Ret
N11
Wakkerstroom
N3
Drakensberg
Newcastle
Vryheid
Bethlehem
N5
Golden Gate Highlands National Park
280 - 281
Harrismith
Dundee
260
259
Elandslaagte
Isandlwana
261
Van Reenen
Ladysmith
Clarens
Fouriesburg
279
Tugela Falls
262 - 263
264
Bergville
Winterton
Tugela Ferry
265
Maluti Mountains
Champagne Castle
Estcourt
Greytow
N3
266
Mooirivier
RU
Natal
267
Rosetta
Drakensberg Park
268 - 269
270 - 271
Howick
272 - 273
Pietermaritzburg
LESOTHO
274
Underberg
236
237
276
Durban
275
Ixopo
Amanzimtoti
N2
Scottburgh
Pennington
Drakensberg

MAP 13

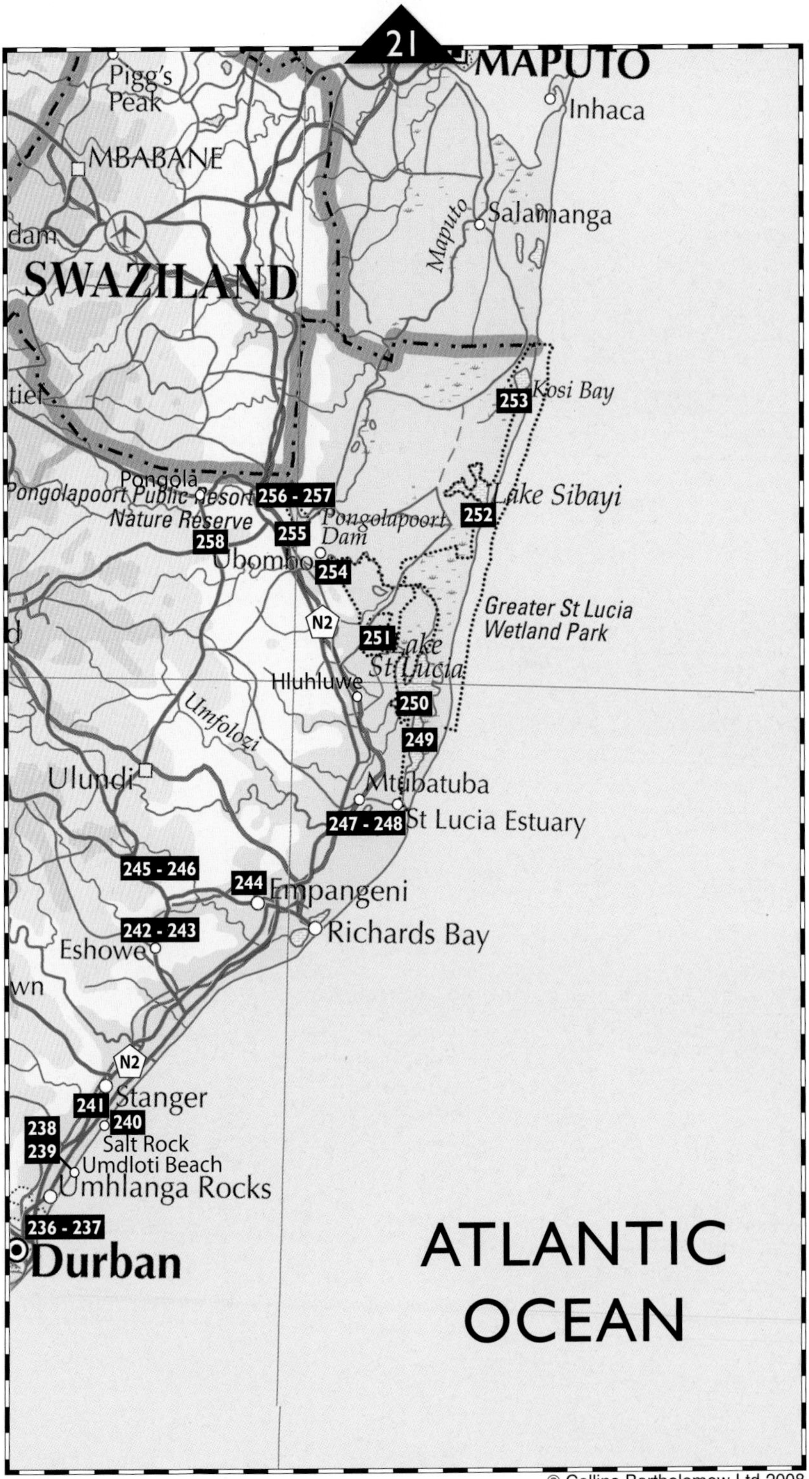
21
MAPUTO
Inhaca
Pigg's Peak
MBABANE
Salamanga
Maputo
SWAZILAND
Kosi Bay
253
Pongola
Pongolapoort Public Resort Nature Reserve
256 - 257
Lake Sibayi
252
Pongolapoort Dam
255
258
Ubombo
254
N2
Greater St Lucia Wetland Park
251
Lake St Lucia
Hluhluwe
250
Umfolozi
249
Ulundi
Mtubatuba
247 - 248
St Lucia Estuary
245 - 246
244
Empangeni
Richards Bay
242 - 243
Eshowe
N2
Stanger
241
240
238
239
Salt Rock
Umdloti Beach
Umhlanga Rocks
236 - 237
Durban
ATLANTIC OCEAN

MAP 14

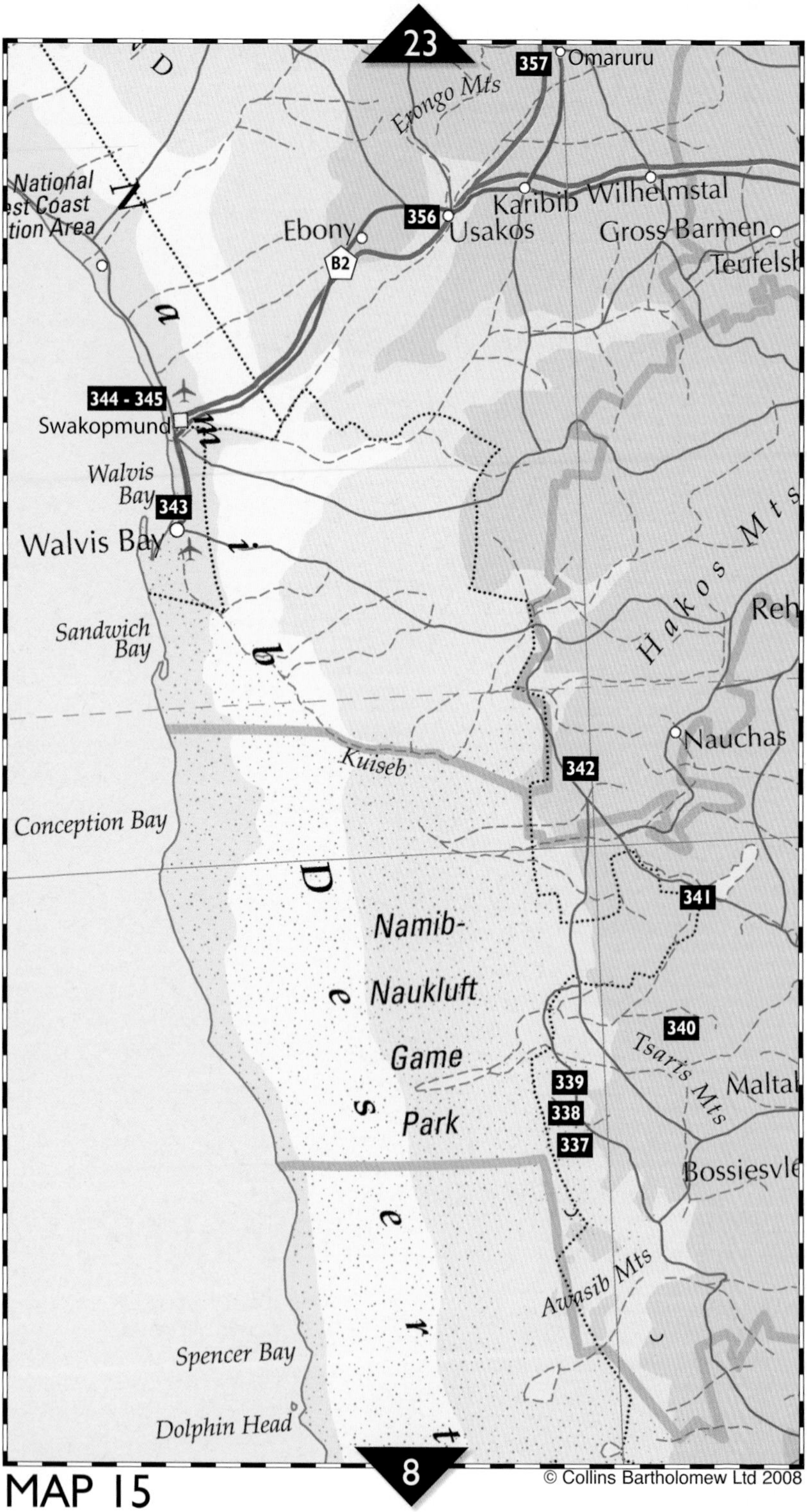
23
357
Omaruru
Erongo Mts
National
West Coast
tion Area
Ebony
356
Usakos
Karibib
Wilhelmstal
Gross Barmen
Teufelsb
B2
344 - 345
Swakopmund
Walvis
Bay
343
Walvis Bay
Sandwich
Bay
Hakos Mts
Reh
Nauchas
Kuiseb
342
Conception Bay
341
Namib-
Naukluft
Game
Park
Namib Desert
340
Tsaris Mts
Maltal
339
338
337
Bossiesvle
Awasib Mts
Spencer Bay
Dolphin Head
8

MAP 15

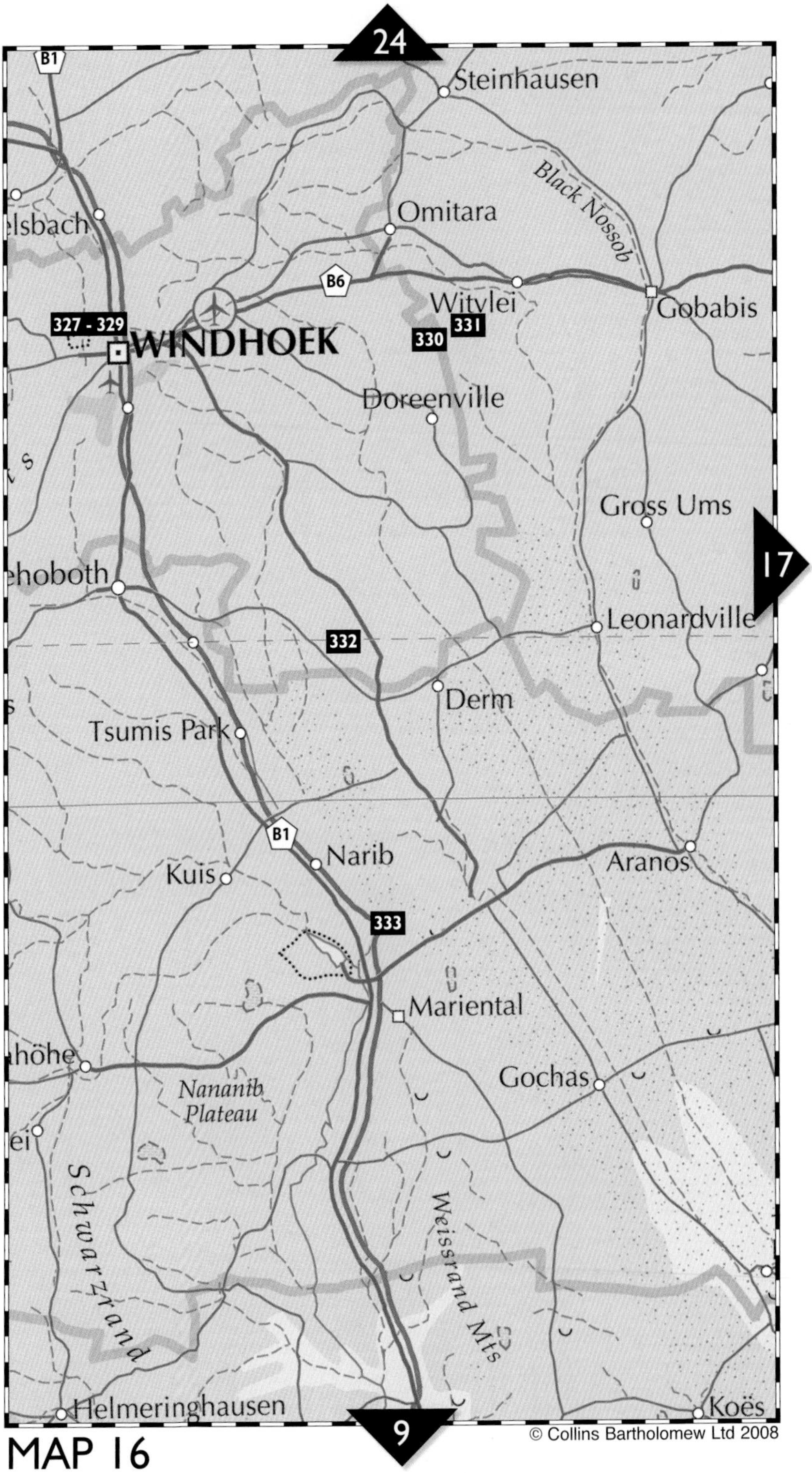
24
B1
Steinhausen
Black Nossob
Omitara
elsbach
B6
Witvlei
Gobabis
327 - 329
WINDHOEK
330
331
Doreenville
Gross Ums
17
ehoboth
Leonardville
332
Derm
Tsumis Park
B1
Narib
Kuis
Aranos
333
Mariental
ahöhe
Gochas
Nananib
Plateau
ei
Schwarzrand
Weissrand Mts
Helmeringhausen
Koës
9

MAP 16

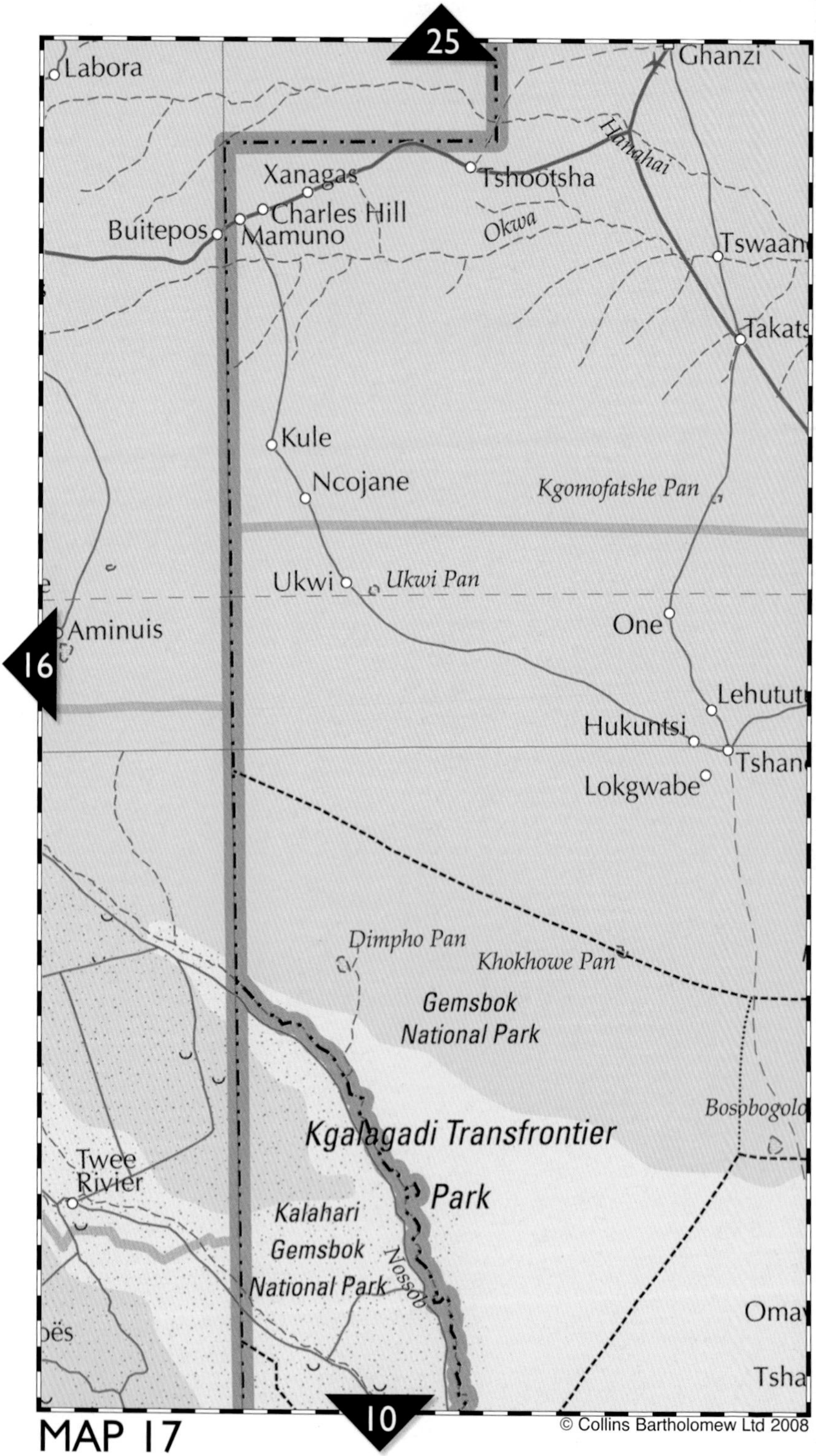
25
Labora
Ghanzi
Hanahai
Xanagas
Tshootsha
Charles Hill
Buitepos
Mamuno
Okwa
Tswaan
Takats
Kule
Ncojane
Kgomofatshe Pan
Ukwi
Ukwi Pan
One
Aminuis
16
Lehutut
Hukuntsi
Tshan
Lokgwabe
Dimpho Pan
Khokhowe Pan
Gemsbok National Park
Bosobogolo
Kgalagadi Transfrontier Park
Twee Rivier
Kalahari Gemsbok National Park
Nossob
Oma
Tsha
10

MAP 17

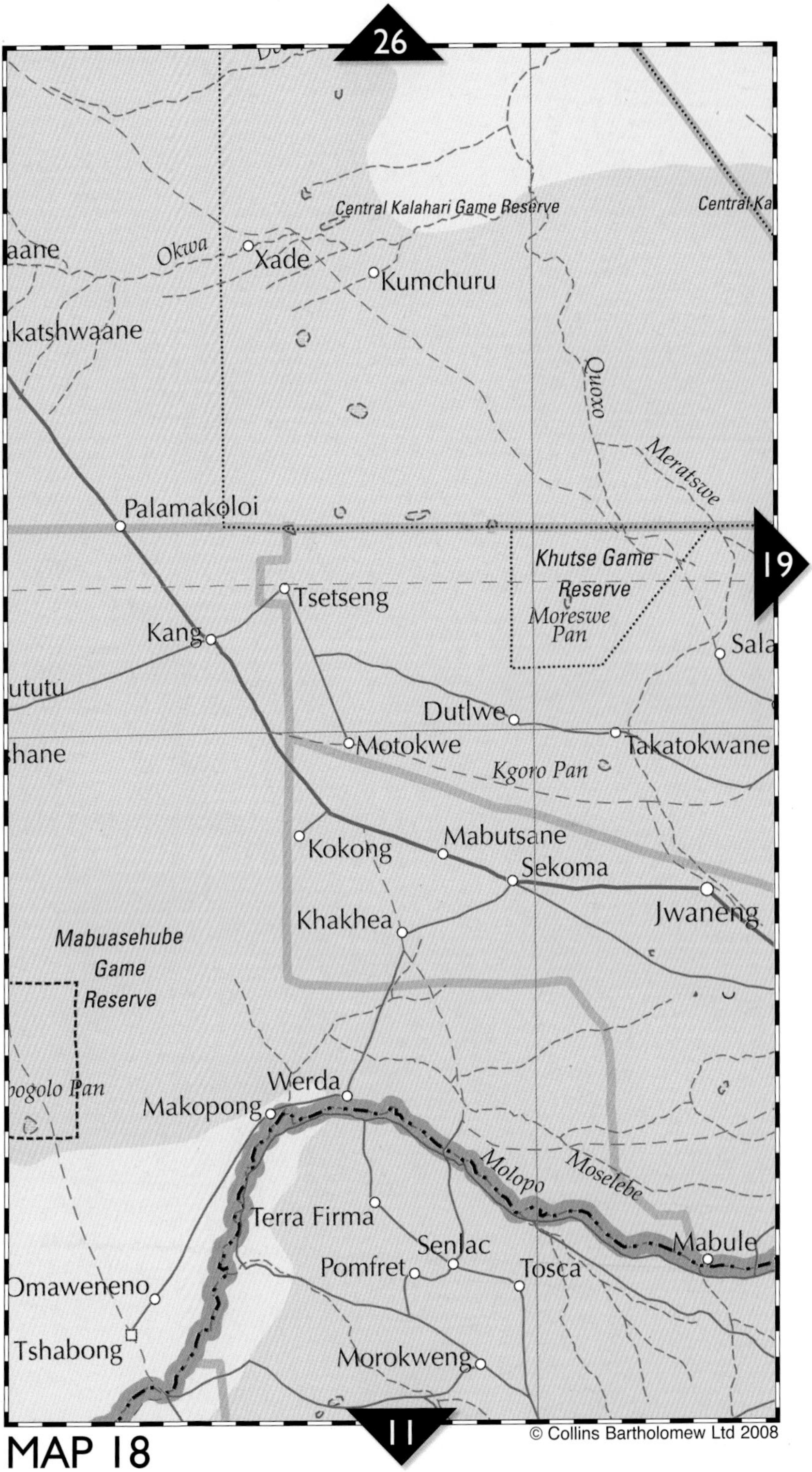
26
Central Kalahari Game Reserve
Central Ka
aane
Okwa
Xade
Kumchuru
katshwaane
Quoxo
Meratswe
Palamakoloi
Khutse Game Reserve
Moreswe Pan
19
Tsetseng
Kang
Sala
ututu
Dutlwe
Motokwe
Takatokwane
hane
Kgoro Pan
Mabutsane
Kokong
Sekoma
Jwaneng
Khakhea
Mabuasehube Game Reserve
Werda
bogolo Pan
Makopong
Molopo
Moselebe
Terra Firma
Mabule
Senlac
Pomfret
Tosca
Omaweneno
Tshabong
Morokweng
11

MAP 18

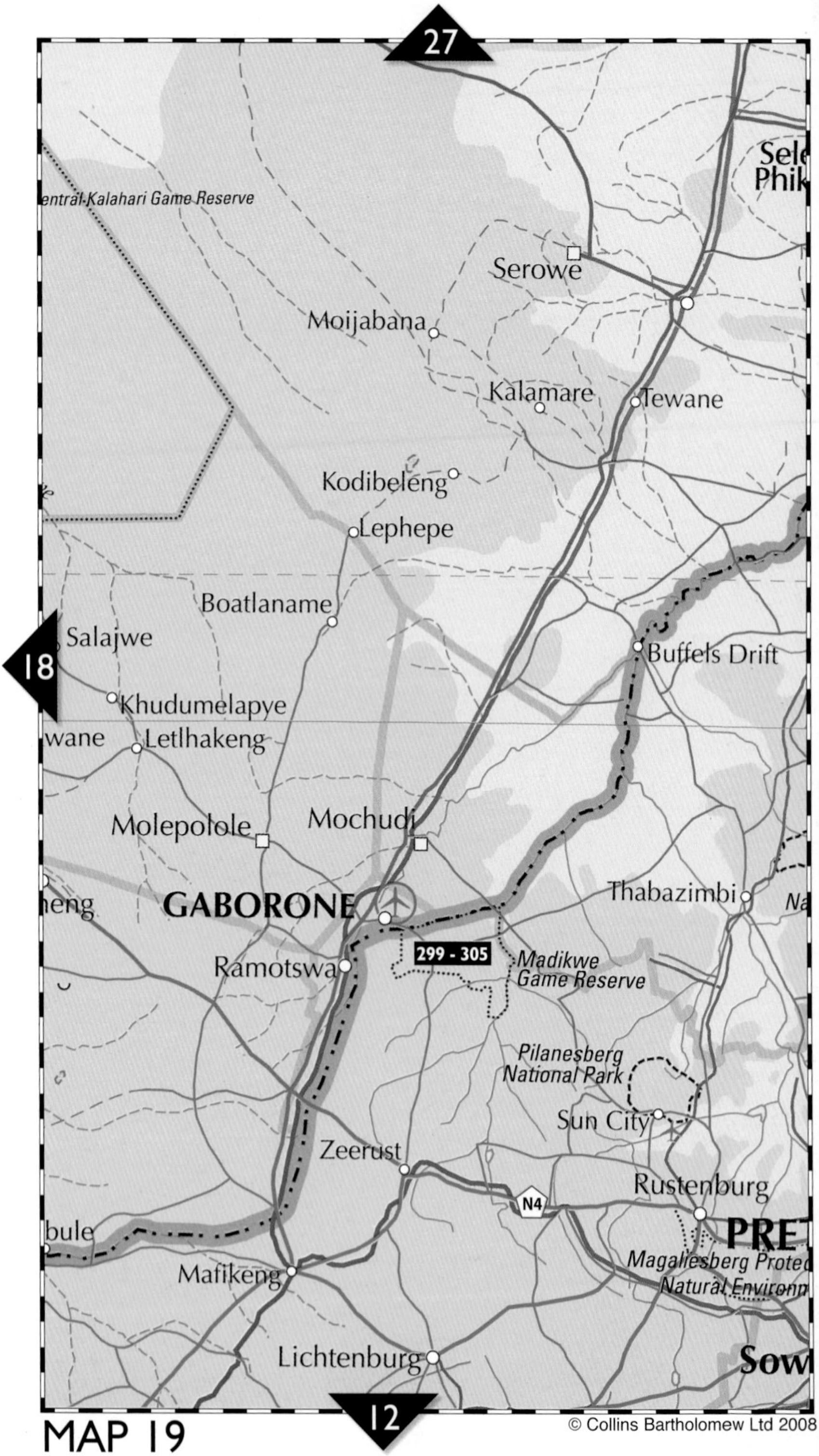
27
Sele
Phik
entral Kalahari Game Reserve
Serowe
Moijabana
Kalamare
Tewane
Kodibeleng
Lephepe
Boatlaname
Salajwe
18
Buffels Drift
Khudumelapye
wane
Letlhakeng
Molepolole
Mochudi
Thabazimbi
heng
GABORONE
Na
299 - 305
Ramotswa
Madikwe
Game Reserve
Pilanesberg
National Park
Sun City
Zeerust
Rustenburg
N4
bule
PRE
Magaliesberg Protec
Natural Environm
Mafikeng
Lichtenburg
Sow
12

MAP 19

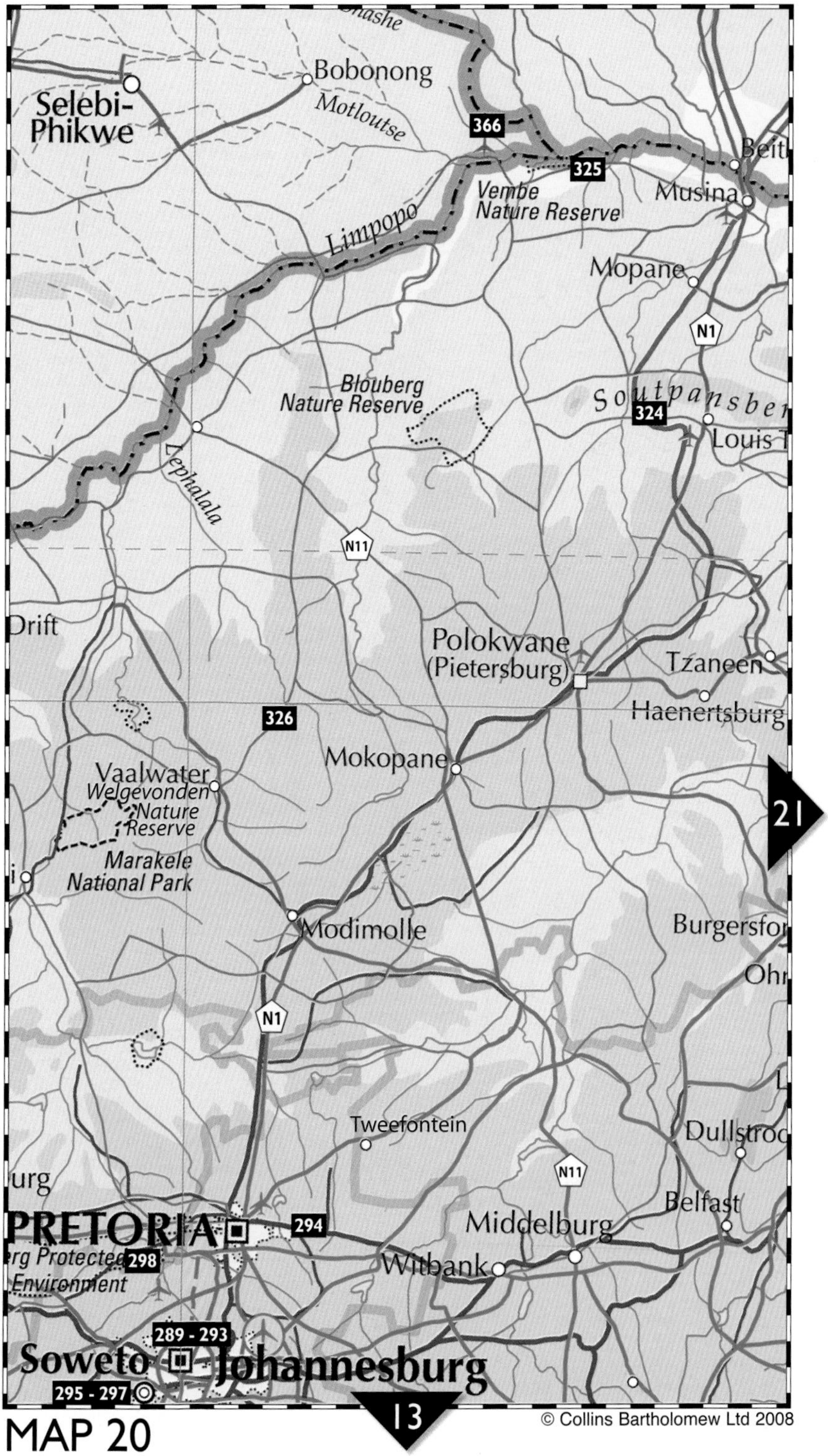

Shashe
Bobonong
Selebi-Phikwe
Motloutse
366
325
Beit
Musina
Vembe Nature Reserve
Limpopo
Mopane
N1
Blouberg Nature Reserve
Soutpansberg
324
Louis T
Lephalala
N11
Drift
Polokwane (Pietersburg)
Tzaneen
Haenertsburg
326
Mokopane
21
Vaalwater
Welgevonden Nature Reserve
Marakele National Park
Modimolle
Burgersfor
Ohr
N1
Tweefontein
Dullstroo
N11
urg
Belfast
PRETORIA
294
Middelburg
rg Protected Environment
298
Witbank
289 - 293
Soweto
Johannesburg
295 - 297
13

MAP 20

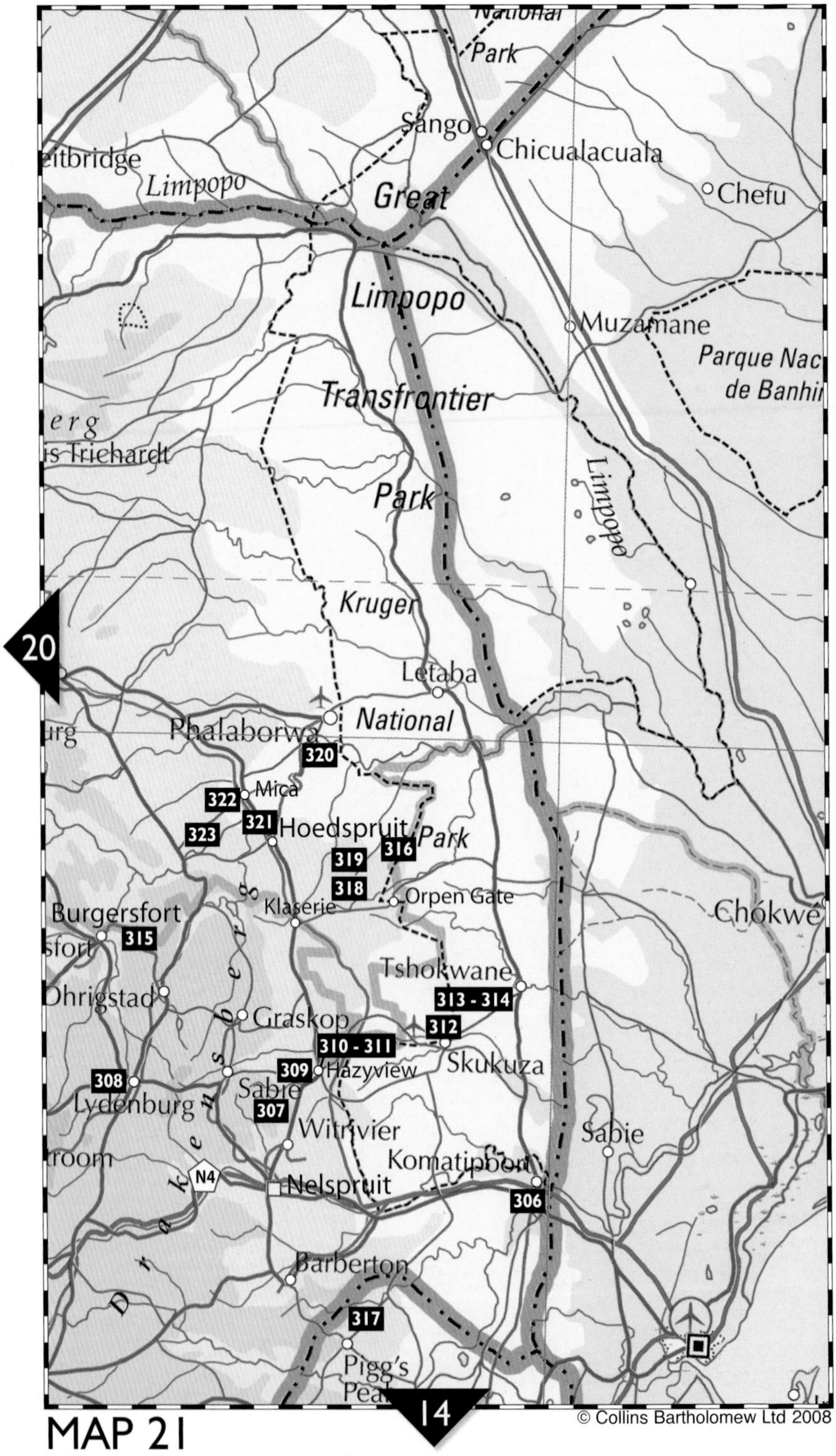
National
Park
Sango
Chicualacuala
eitbridge
Limpopo
Great
Chefu
Limpopo
Muzamane
Parque Nac
de Banhi
Transfrontier
erg
is Trichardt
Park
Limpopo
Kruger
20
Letaba
National
urg
Phalaborwa
320
322
Mica
321
Hoedspruit
Park
323
319
316
318
Orpen Gate
Chókwè
Burgersfort
Klaserie
315
sfort
Tshokwane
Ohrigstad
313 - 314
Graskop
312
310 - 311
308
309
Hazyview
Skukuza
Sabie
Lydenburg
307
Witrivier
Sabie
troom
Komatipoort
N4
Nelspruit
306
Barberton
317
Pigg's
Peak
14

MAP 21

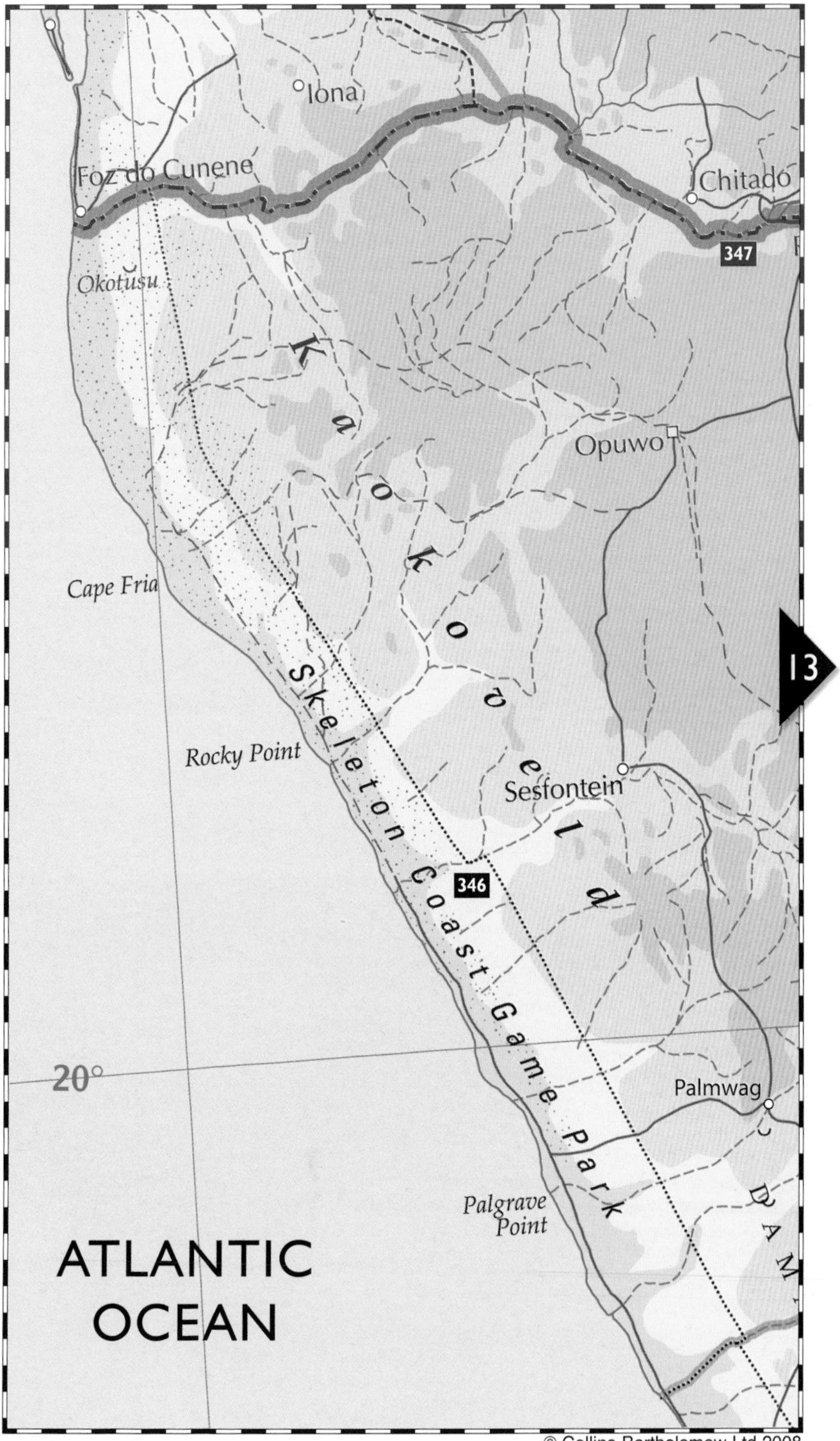
Iona
Foz do Cunene
Chitado
347
Okotusu
Kaokoveld
Opuwo
Cape Fria
13
Skeleton Coast Game Park
Rocky Point
Sesfontein
346
20°
Palmwag
Palgrave Point
ATLANTIC OCEAN

MAP 22

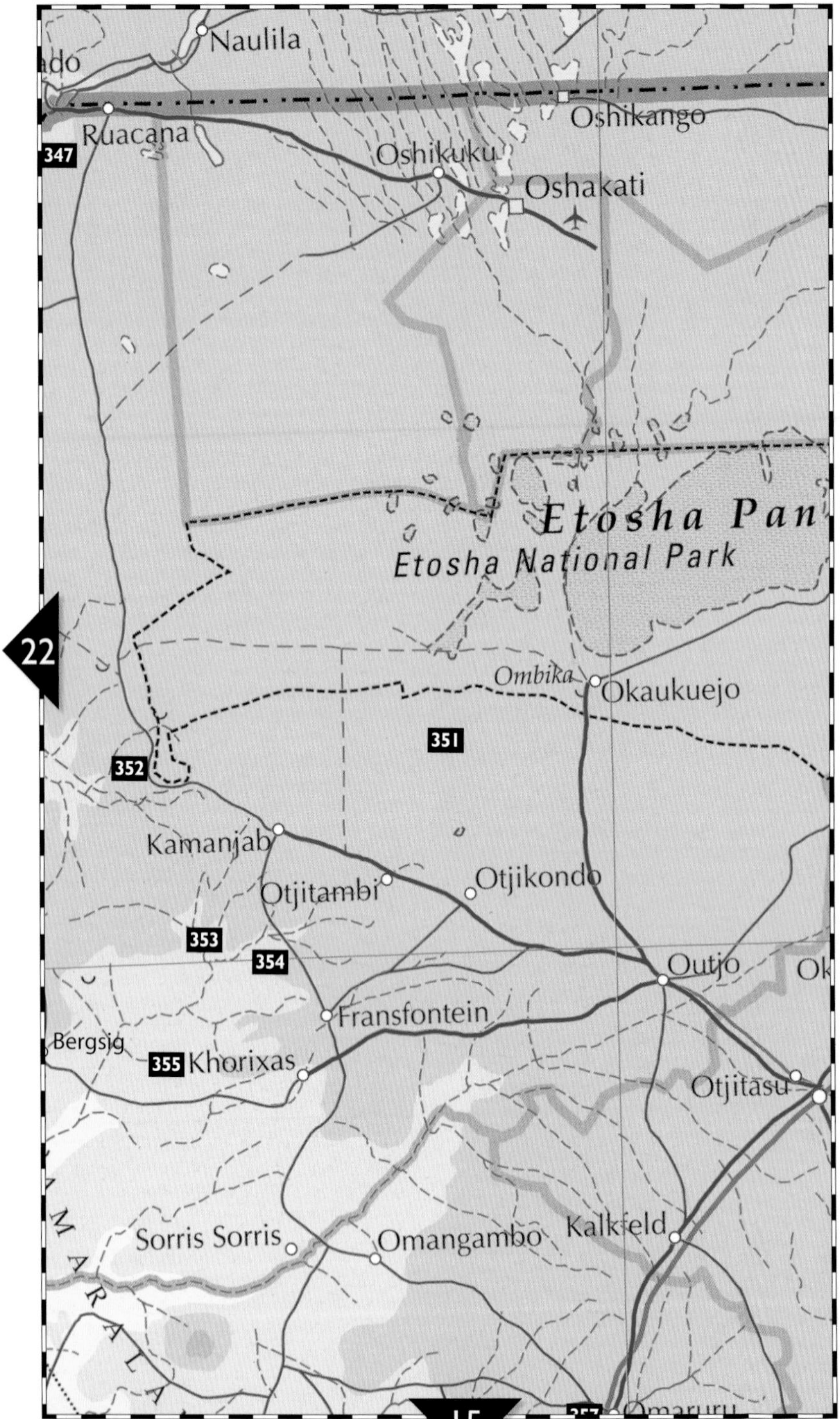

Naulila
Ruacana
347
Oshikuku
Oshikango
Oshakati
Etosha Pan
Etosha National Park
22
Ombika
Okaukuejo
351
352
Kamanjab
Otjitambi
Otjikondo
353
354
Outjo
Fransfontein
Bergsig
355
Khorixas
Otjitasu
Sorris Sorris
Omangambo
Kalkfeld

15

MAP 23

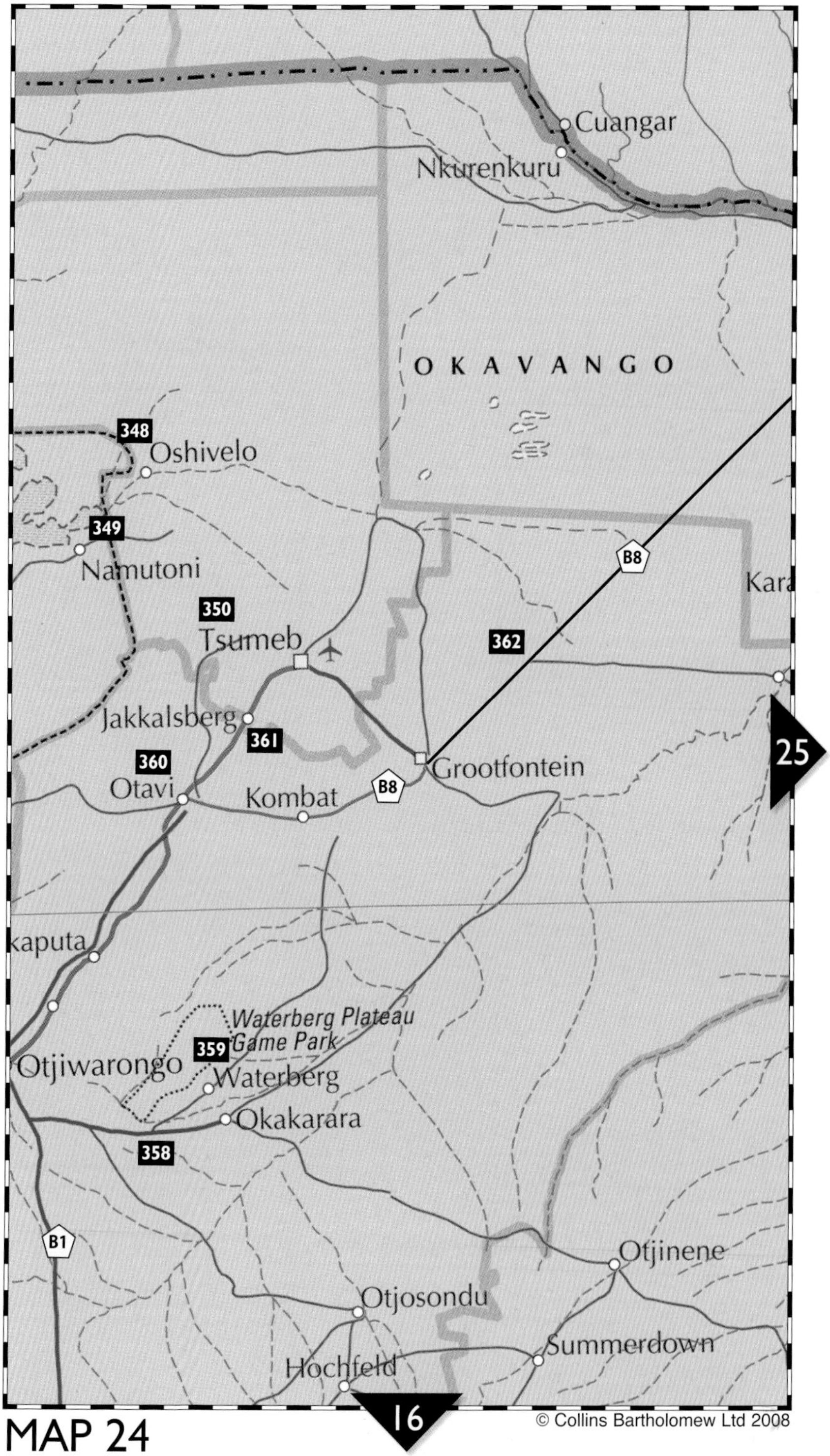
Cuangar
Nkurenkuru
OKAVANGO
348
Oshivelo
349
Namutoni
350
Tsumeb
B8
Kara
362
Jakkalsberg
361
360
Otavi
Kombat
B8
Grootfontein
25
kaputa
Waterberg Plateau Game Park
359
Otjiwarongo
Waterberg
Okakarara
358
B1
Otjinene
Otjosondu
Summerdown
Hochfeld
16

MAP 24

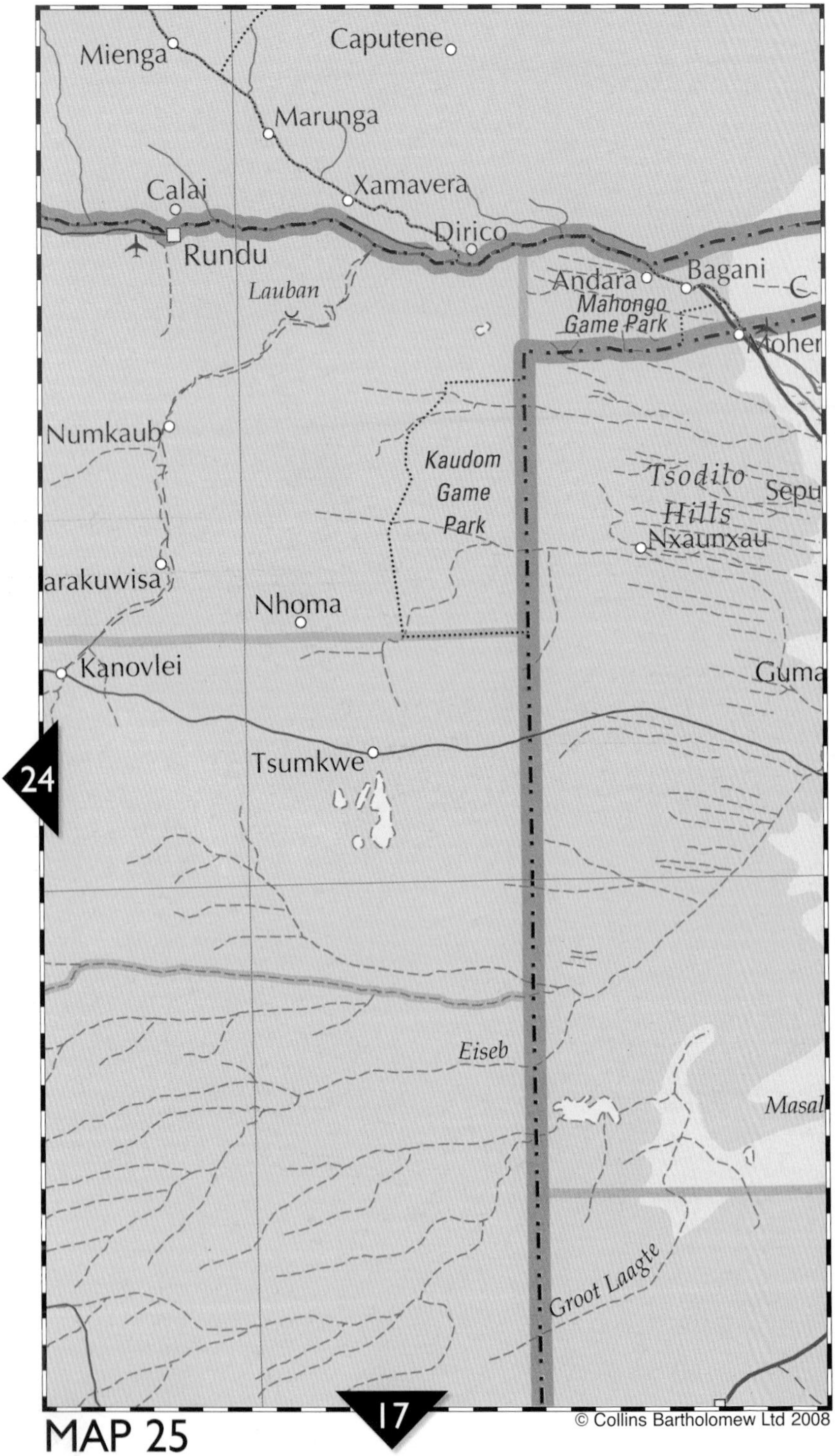
Caputene
Mienga
Marunga
Xamavera
Calai
Dirico
Rundu
Andara
Bagani
C
Lauban
Mahongo
Game Park
Moher
Numkaub
Kaudom
Game
Park
Tsodilo
Hills
Sepu
Nxaunxau
arakuwisa
Nhoma
Kanovlei
Guma
24
Tsumkwe
Eiseb
Masal
Groot Laagte
17

MAP 25

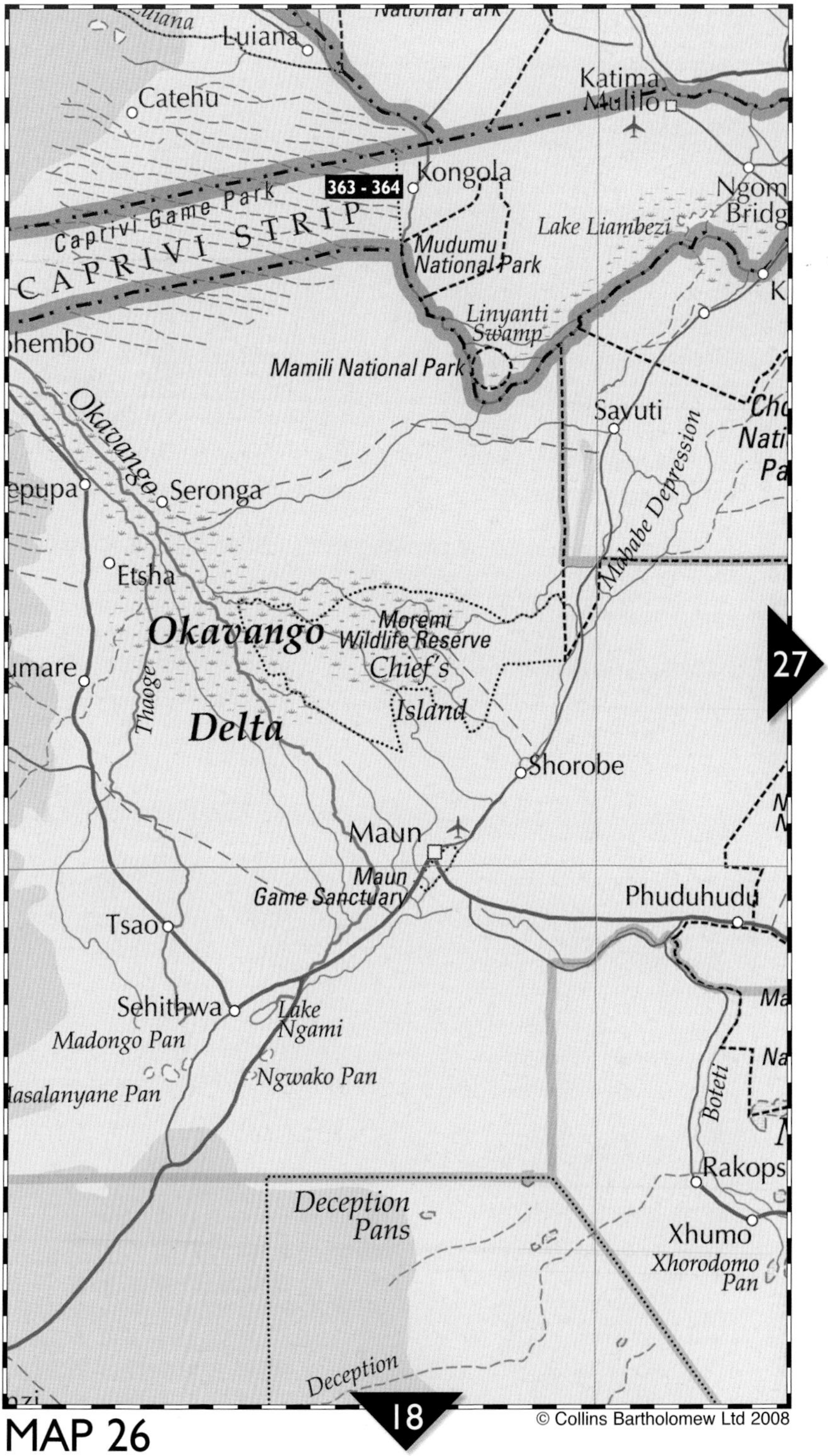
Luiana
Catehu
Katima Mulilo
363 - 364
Kongola
Ngom
Bridg
Caprivi Game Park
CAPRIVI STRIP
Lake Liambezi
Mudumu National Park
Linyanti Swamp
hembo
Mamili National Park
Savuti
Okavango
Mababe Depression
epupa
Seronga
Etsha
Okavango
Moremi Wildlife Reserve
Chief's Island
umare
Thaoge
Delta
Shorobe
Maun
Maun Game Sanctuary
Phuduhudu
Tsao
Sehithwa
Lake Ngami
Madongo Pan
Ngwako Pan
lasalanyane Pan
Boteti
Rakops
Deception Pans
Xhumo
Xhorodomo Pan
Deception
27
18

MAP 26

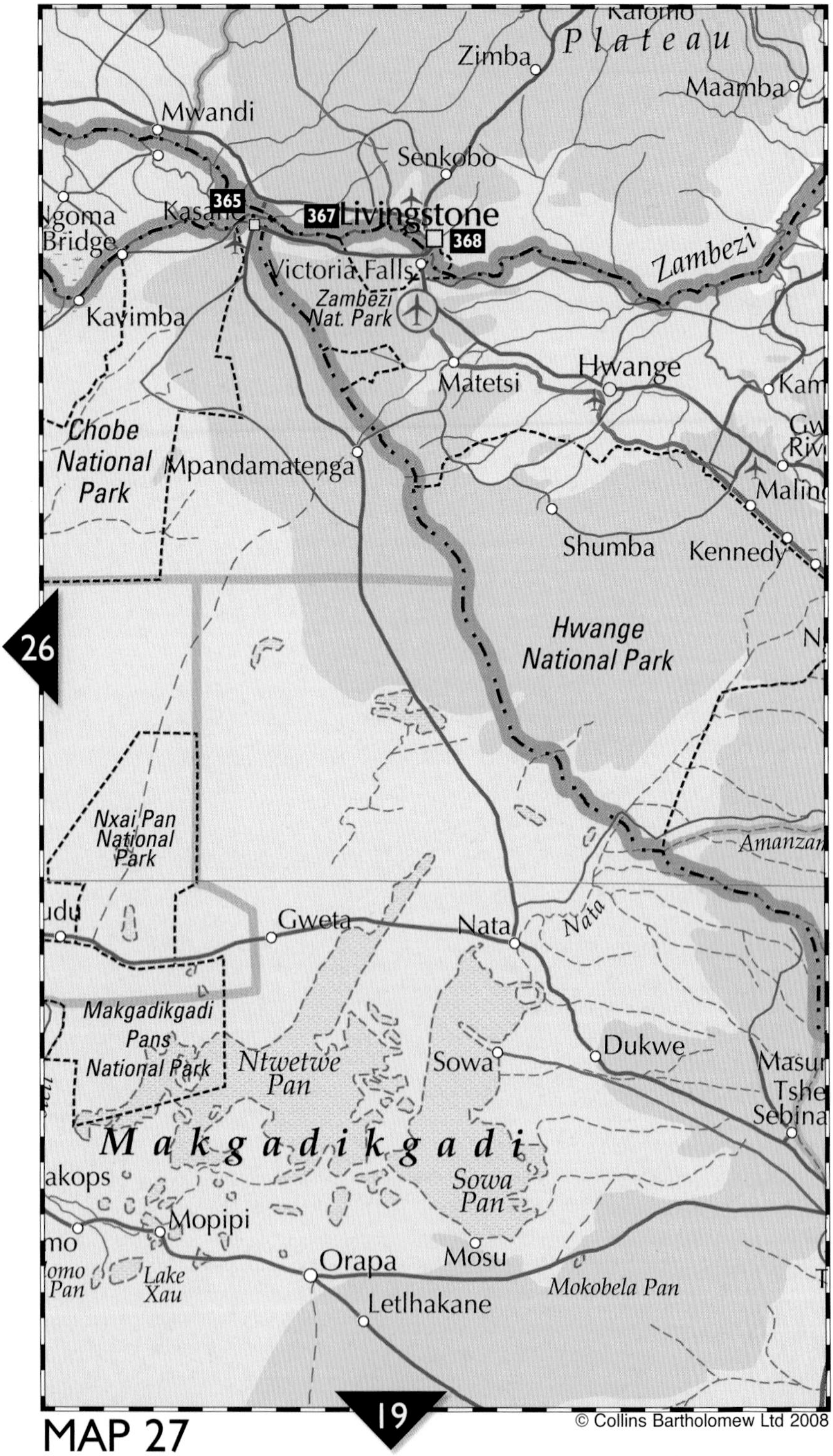
Kalomo
Plateau
Zimba
Maamba
Mwandi
Senkobo
365
Kasane
367
Livingstone
368
Ngoma
Bridge
Victoria Falls
Zambezi
Zambezi
Nat. Park
Kavimba
Hwange
Matetsi
Kam
Chobe
National
Park
Mpandamatenga
Gw
Riv
Malin
Shumba
Kennedy
26
Hwange
National Park
Nxai Pan
National
Park
Amanzam
udu
Gweta
Nata
Nata
Makgadikgadi
Pans
National Park
Ntwetwe
Pan
Sowa
Dukwe
Masur
Tshe
Sebina
Makgadikgadi
akops
Sowa
Pan
Mopipi
mo
Mosu
Orapa
omo
Pan
Lake
Xau
Mokobela Pan
Letlhakane
19

MAP 27

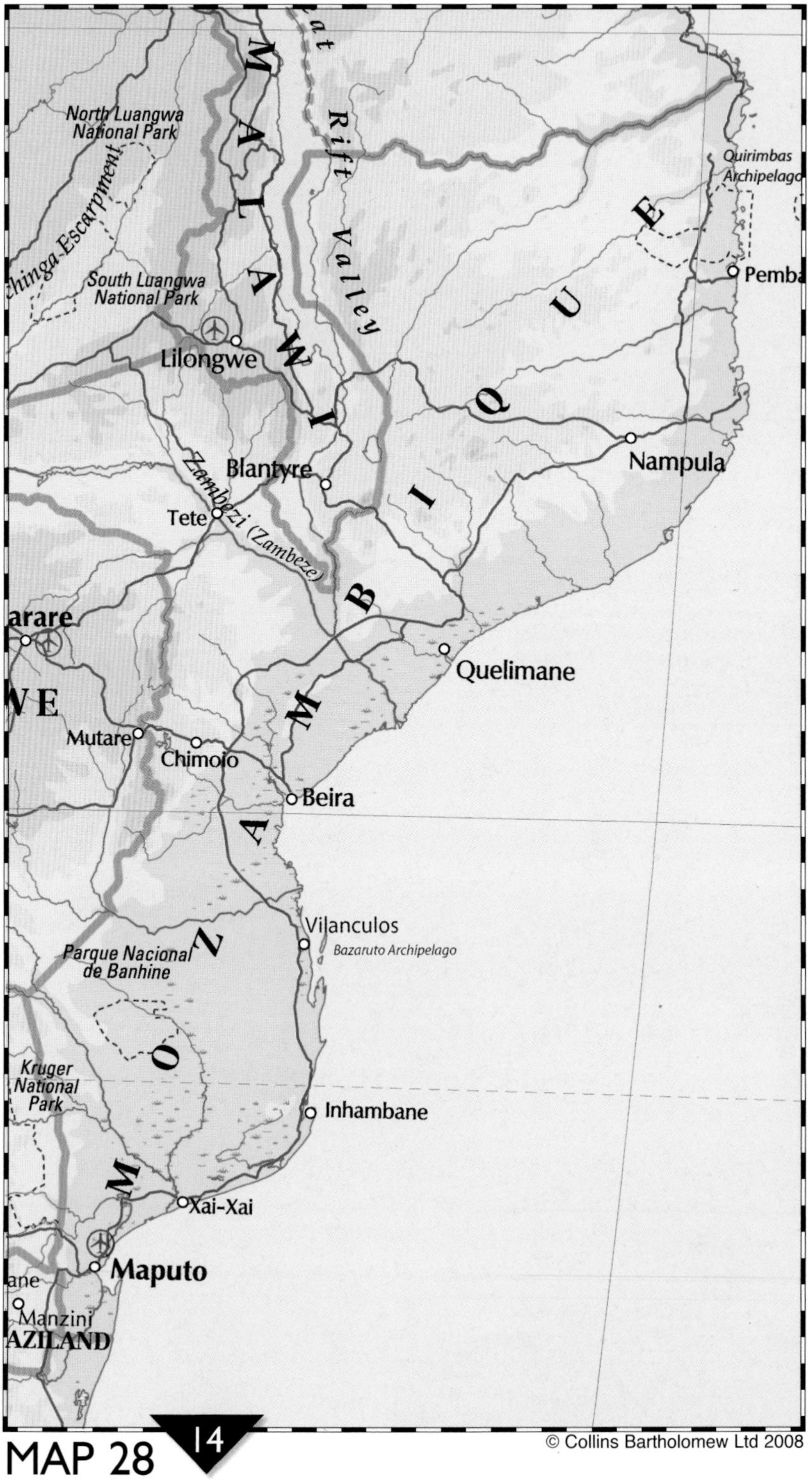

© Collins Bartholomew Ltd 2008

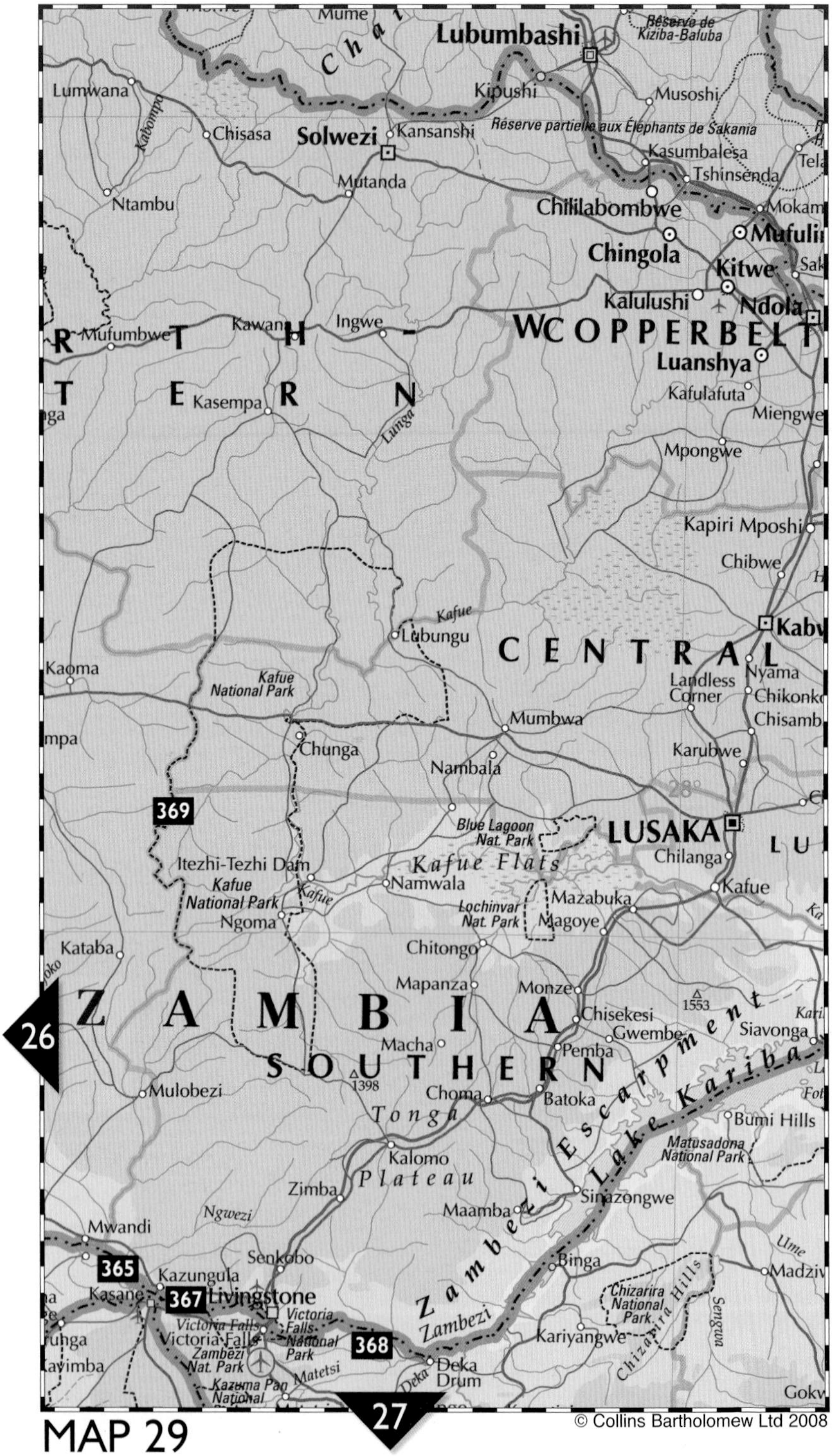
Lubumbashi
Réserve de Kiziba-Baluba
Mume
Lumwana
Kipushi
Musoshi
Kabompo
Chisasa
Solwezi
Kansanshi
Réserve partielle aux Éléphants de Sakania
Kasumbalesa
Tshinsenda
Mutanda
Ntambu
Chililabombwe
Chingola
Kitwe
Kalulushi
Ndola
Mufumbwe
Kawana
Ingwe
COPPERBELT
Luanshya
Kasempa
Lunga
Kafulafuta
Mpongwe
Kapiri Mposhi
Chibwe
Kafue
Lubungu
CENTRAL
Kaoma
Kafue National Park
Landless Corner
Nyama
Mumbwa
Chunga
Nambala
Karubwe
28°
369
Blue Lagoon Nat. Park
LUSAKA
Chilanga
Itezhi-Tezhi Dam
Kafue Flats
Namwala
Kafue
Kafue National Park
Lochinvar Nat. Park
Mazabuka
Ngoma
Magoye
Chitongo
Kataba
Mapanza
Monze
1553
ZAMBIA
Chisekesi
Gwembe
Siavonga
Macha
Pemba
SOUTHERN
1398
Choma
Batoka
Zambezi Escarpment
Lake Kariba
Mulobezi
Tonga
Bumi Hills
Kalomo
Matusadona National Park
Plateau
Zimba
Sinazongwe
Maamba
Ngwezi
Mwandi
Senkobo
Binga
365
Kazungula
Kasane
367
Livingstone
Chizarira National Park
Chizarira Hills
Sengwa
Victoria Falls National Park
Victoria Falls
Zambezi
368
Kariyangwe
Zambezi Nat. Park
Matetsi
Deka
Deka Drum
Kazuma Pan National
26
27

MAP 29

Avian Leisure

Marie-Louise and Patrick Cardwell
88 Dorries Drive,
Simon's Town
Tel: 021-786-1414
Fax: 021-786-1414
Email: enquiries@avianleisure.com
Web: www.avianleisure.com
Cell: 083-272-2455

The Cardwells have two smashing self-catering apartments under their Simon's Town home, but they offer so very much more than that. Patrick is a naturalist and there is nothing he doesn't know about his surroundings – and that's the whole of South Africa, not just Simon's Town. Whether it's a bird-watching tour from the Zambian border to the Garden Route coastline, or a detailed search for Northern Cape lizards, he's the man to organise your tour. Perhaps that is one of the reasons why the 'Planet Earth' crew stayed here while they were filming the whales that flop about in the bay below the house (in season only of course). High above Simon's Town, both flats have a wonderful position, gazing out across False Bay to the distant Overberg mountains. Your own mountain starts just across the road. It's a two-hour walk to the top of the 678m (roughly) Swartkop peak. We didn't have time to test the theory, but Marie-Louise assures us that the view from up there is even better. I don't doubt it. Both apartments are tiled throughout with massive airy bedrooms. Downstairs the glass wall slides back to give you a private wooden verandah overlooking the fynbos garden below. Upstairs, one wall of the vast lounge is taken up by a mini-library, the shelves bulging with natural history books – one guest had his nose buried in a bird book, ticking off his sightings before the next expedition... starting with the penguin, I imagine. *The Cardwells also run winery tours via six 4-star estates, all different settings and grape varieties. Towels, chairs etc provided for beach.*

Rooms: 2 apartments, one with 1 twin/king and 1 twin sharing separate bath and shower, the other with twin/king and a shower. Serviced twice a week.
Price: R295 - R395 pp sharing. Singles on request.
Meals: Continental breakfast basket by arrangement R70 pp. Full kitchen in lower apartment, kitchenette only in Watsonia. Weber for braais on the deck or full BBQ facility upstairs.
Directions: M3 from CT to Muizenberg, then Main Road through Fish Hoek to Simon's Town. Continue for 2km past golf course on L. Immediately after Oatlands Holiday Accomm turn R into Dorries Drive. House is 1km uphill on the R.

Fort Vic

Dr Lance Tooke

14 Victory Way, Simon's Town
Tel: Jeanette in SA: +27 (0)83-321-3651
Lance in UK: +44 (0)7986-557-652
Email: simonstown@btinternet.com Web: www.simonstown.net

I didn't get the pleasure of meeting Dr Lance who's based in London, but his friendly voice beaming down the phone was a reassuring start. And sure enough Fort Vic in Simon's Town, his second home, did not disappoint. The house was built by his neighbours and is entirely made of wood and stone dug from the mountain it sits upon. Inside is a forest of dense wood beams, bamboo ceilings, red stone walls and open-plan wooden staircases making it feel a bit like a bush lodge. The real drawcard here, however, is the view. You don't - can't! - get much more of a sea view than this and the best place to absorb it from is the huge master bedroom upstairs, although big sliding glass doors run throughout the house. Actually there are many places to enjoy the view from: the plunge pool, the sitting room or the smart kitchen lined with yellowwood cupboards and fitted with a central island, complete with gas cooker and fancy oven. The motto here is keep it simple with cream sheets, stylish free-standing showers and soft natural furnishings like basket lamps, wicker chairs and red cushions. The black cloth hanging in the kitchen covered in badges from all over the world is testament to Lance's travelling days prior to finding his favourite destination, Fort Vic. Although this is definitely a self-catering arrangement, Jeanette, the house manager, is available at all times to troubleshoot any problems, arrange trips or make bookings. Whales can be viewed (July - October) from the master bedroom and the pool.

Rooms: 1 self-catering house, 1 double room with victorian bath and shower in the room, 2 twins with showers in the rooms. Full kitchen and lounge area.
Price: R1,400 - R3,000 per day for the house, depending on season. Discounts of up to 50% for long stays.
Meals: Self-catering.
Directions: Detailed directions available on booking.

Moonglow Guest House

Gillian O'Leary
7 Bennett Close, Cairnside, Glencairn, Simon's Town
Tel: 021-786-5902 Fax: 021-786-5903
Email: seaview@moonglow.co.za Web: www.moonglow.co.za
Cell: 082-565-6568

"We've been here seven and a half years now but I still get goose-bumps every time I see the moon hanging over it," Gillian confides in me as we stare out over the smooth expanse of False Bay. I challenge you to find a better view of the bay than this one, and unsurprisingly most of the rooms at Moonglow take full advantage – even the ones that don't still get their own private seating areas round at the front. With Matty the dog dancing around my feet, and her friend Jess staring lovingly at the succulent blueberry muffin that was supplied with my tea, I could have happily stayed for an eternity ensconced on the sofa of the bar-lounge… but an ever-enthusiastic Gillian was keen to show me more and I had a job to do. Throughout this house you'll find original artworks everywhere, including a stunning leopard print and four-foot-high figurines honed from solid granite. If it catches Gillian's eye she's got to have it. Vibrant oil paintings add a splash of colour to creamy rooms, all drenched in sunlight from large picture windows or glass doors. Beds and tables have been individually designed, and a multitude of mohair blankets and the finest quality linens have had Gillian's hand-embroiderers busy detailing them with intricate dragonflies and bumblebees "... just so the colours match." Moonglow shines.

Rooms: 6: 4 queens all with shower only; 2 twins with bath and shower over.
Price: R350 - R475 pp sharing. Singles on request.
Meals: Full breakfast included. Lots of restaurants nearby.
Directions: Map on website or directions can be emailed on booking.

African Tides

Lance Bailey and Nicola Vlug
19 Mountain Road, Fish Hoek
Tel: 021-782-0277 Fax: 021-782-3950
Email: info@africantides.co.za Web: www.africantides.co.za
Cell: 084-298-5555

I was sold on Lance when I read his first email to us. This is the sort of guy you want to chat to over your toast in the morning: "Just to give you a bit of my background… uh... boring boring boring… then I sold my business and travelled with my family through Africa, overland in a converted Unimog for a year, came back home and decided to do what makes me happy, hence the guesthouse." And the best part is that it really does seem to have made him rather happy. Sitting on the balcony looking right out onto the bay, he has seen tuna, whales, seals and even dolphins. It was enough for me just to watch the fishermen bring in their catch of that day, while cradling a deliciously fresh coffee. Reminders of the trip that brought Lance here are all over the house. His wife Nicola, a snapper supreme, has had some of her best pictures blown up and framed, adding to the feeling that this is a hub for travel in the continent. The family room has a baby elephant to charm the kids (not a real one obviously), and in The Cape of Storms room, brooding skies and coastal landscapes take priority. But it would be a real shame to spend too much time in the rooms: a walk up Elsie's Peak is on your doorstep, Cape Town is just a short drive away and Lance can even take you crayfish diving. But those who feel that even the five-minute haul to the beach is a little strenuous, a good-sized pool teeters on the edge of the hill, and is perfect for whale-watching in style.

Rooms: 5: 1 family room with double, 2 singles and en-suite shower, 2 doubles with full bathrooms, 2 doubles with en-suite shower.
Price: R450 - R605 pp sharing. Under 12s on request. Different rates available to have the whole house as self-catering.
Meals: Full breakfast included. Other meals can be arranged on request.
Directions: From Kommetjie Road in Fish Hoek, turn into Highway Road, drive 100m and take the 2nd turn on the right. Continue straight up the road until dead end. African Tides is the last house on left.

Blue Yonder

Sally and Bruce Elliott
14 Hillside Rd, Fish Hoek
Tel: 021-782-0500 Fax: 021-782-0500
Email: info@blueyondercape.co.za Web: www.blueyondercape.co.za
Cell: 082-441-9589

For those of you on the self-catering trail this is a must. A three-storey house converted into flats, Blue Yonder is a luxury ocean liner of a place. When Sally opened the door to an invading GG team the sun was blasting through the wall-to-wall windows. She was keen to show me around, but I spent the first ten minutes standing out on the enormous silver-railed balcony, transfixed by the view. From all three apartments here you can watch the full arc of the sun, rising over a glittering False Bay, and finally sinking behind the red-tiled roofs of the Fish Hoek bungalows below. Excellent for whale-watching. Once the trance wears off (which it won't) head inside and polish off your complimentary drinks or make the most of the stainless steel and cream kitchens, complete with all mod cons (including my personal favourite: the dishwasher). Sally grew up in this house, but after a huge conversion job the Rhodesian teak floors are the only reminder of her family home. Now, gloriously indulgent queen-sized beds look out on the bay and cool, beige armchairs are just waiting to be lounged in. Once you summon the energy for a dip in the ocean, your own private steps lead down to the beach, just a stone's throw away. My advice? Bring the whole family, light up a braai on the balcony and settle in for at least a month. *5 mins to food shops. All apartments have braais.*

Rooms: 3 self-catering apartments: Upper: 1 queen with en-suite shower & 1 twin with en-suite bath & shower; Middle: 1 queen en-s b & sh, 2 twins en-s b & sh; Lower: 1 queen en-s sh only. Serviced every week day.
Price: R220 - R400 pp sharing.
Meals: In fridge on arrival: fruit juice, wine, tea, coffee, milk, sugar. Full kitchen.
Directions: Head to Muizenberg from Cape Town, continue south along main road through Fish Hoek. At roundabout at the end of FH main rd turn L towards Simon's Town. 1 km further take 1st R at traffic lights up Hillside Rd. Blue Yonder about 300m up on the R.

Kimberley House

Marsha Sanders

7 Kimberley Road, Kalk Bay
Tel: (UK)+44 208-348-5797 Cell: (UK)+44 790-430-3569
Email: marshasanders@blueyonder.co.uk
Web: www.cape-town-holiday-house.co.za

As soon as I had reached the top of the winding stair that began at the cobbled street below, I imagined this place buzzing with families and friends. Picture the scene. You make yourself at home in one of the bedrooms, all sea-light breezy and creaky on timber floors, before settling into a day on the stoep where the braai is stacked with fresh yellowtail from the Kalk Bay harbour market, slowly cooking with a dozen or so periperi prawns. Gradually you take in the fabulous view. Colourful St James houses descend to sea level, where False Bay begins and ripples along lines of perfect corduroy into the wild blue yonder. On the other side, faraway, the Hottentots Holland mountains seem weightless in the sea haze. Moving back indoors, the kitchen should be alive with activity and conversation that spills into the dining area and through concertina doors into a laid-back sitting room with a welcome fireplace. For a bit of quiet, try the patio out back. Tell-tale signs of 1875 origins include high ceilings and tall sash windows, but most of all in the very bones of the house, in the cellar, where the rocks of the mountainside itself form the foundations. It's also a great place to store the surf-boards. Unusual for the area, the house also keeps a surprisingly large walled garden with a lawn and vibrant flowerbeds, as well as a pleasantly-shaded bench and table. Kalk Bay is home to GG when we're in South Africa. We love the walks into the hills, the toothless fisherwomen and, of course, the peerless Olympia Café.

Rooms: 1 house with 3 bedrooms, all double and shower en-suite. There is a separate bathroom plus a TV room with sleeper couch.
Price: R2,000 - R2,500 for the house per night.
Meals: Self-catering.
Directions: Coming along the coast road from Muizenburg, as you approach Kalk Bay, 0.5 miles further on from St James railway station, turn right into Kimberley Road, a narrow cobbled street (easily missed). The house is half-way up the hill.

Sunset Beach Guest House

Kamala and Ingmar Petterson
73 Wireless Rd, Kommetjie
Tel: 021-783-4283 Fax: 021-783-4286
Email: info@sunsetbeach.co.za Web: www.sunsetbeach.co.za
Cell: 083-325-8321

I arrived at Sunset Beach in a thunderstorm, but even with wind and rain buffeting the windows, the house puts you in the mood for lazy summer days. The design is seaside inspired, but don't expect any cheap bucket and spade murals here: bleached wooden floorboards, plump furniture and white drapes make this a truly sophisticated coastal spot. Under the thatched eaves upstairs, the soft chairs and bookcase looked like the perfect place to spend a rainy day. And if home-made cookies in each room weren't enough to entice children in from outside, a toy box and bunk beds in the family room should do the job. There's a back garden with a swimming pool, but it's what's out the front that I got excited about. The house is so close to the sea that there is nothing between its large windows and the ocean but unspoilt beach. And the beach at Kommetjie really is unspoilt. With miles of white sand making me wish the rain would go away so I could explore, it's hard to believe you're just a short drive from Cape Town centre. But if you don't fancy moving (and there's a high chance you won't) the city will come to your table. A mouth-watering menu boasts fresh seafood dishes such as prawn and peach kebabs and mussels with sundried tomato sauce. This barefoot haven is perfect for young families and honeymooners alike, who come in droves for the guest house's relaxed philosophy that "sandy footprints are welcome reminders that guests are at home". *They also specialise in weddings with the ceremony taking place on the beach.*

Rooms: 5: 1 king, 1 queen, 1 twin; 1 king with bunk beds & 4-poster king; all rooms with en-s bath.
Price: R360 - R800 pp. Rates are seasonal. Singles plus R200 per night. Whole house R3,000 - R8,000.
Meals: Full breakfast incl'. Personal chef on site for lunches, gourmet picnics & dinners from R120 pp.
Directions: Take N2 from Cape Town or the airport. Join M3 towards Muizenberg and continue till road ends. Turn right at lights and take Ou Kaapse Weg over mountain to Noordhoek. Turn R into M64 towards Kommetjie then turn R again onto Wireless Road as soon as you enter town. 700m on LHS.

6 in the Circle

Nikki and Paul Baker
6 Scottsville Circle, Hout Bay
Tel: 021-790-7962
Email: nikki@6inthecircle.co.za Web: www.6inthecircle.co.za

England was their launch pad, but the travel instinct propelled Nikki and Paul to various parts of the globe before they finally landed in South Africa; "when my feet touched the tarmac, I just knew this is where I wanted to stay." And so they did, cutting themselves a generous slice of tranquility cake at 6 in the Circle. There are two luxurious rooms available here and comfort is king: big beds, gigantic pillows and large bathrooms with underfloor heating and natural therapy toiletries. If you want to get nearer to nature ask for the room with the outdoor shower - some, and I am one, love an outdoor shower! Each suite also has its own fully-equipped fitted kitchen, so if you're not in the mood you don't have to slog out to a local restaurant at dinnertime. Instead wrought-iron chairs and a table placed outside on your private stoep make an ideal dining venue. There's even a herb garden so you can sprinkle on the freshest mint or thyme and the nearby harbour will provide you with the catch of the day to cook on your braai. It's only an 8-minute walk to the beach, or a short step to the solar-heated pool in the garden... but all we really wanted to do was slouch in the plump armchairs and enjoy a sundowner with our hosts.

Rooms: 2: 1 with shower, 1 with bath and shower. Both have full kitchens.
Price: R700 - R800 per suite, per night.
Meals: Self-catering. A choice of 25 restaurants in Hout Bay.
Directions: M63 to Hout Bay. L into Baviaanskloof Road. Then L into Darling Street. R into Pinedene. L into Scottsville.

Dreamhouse

Ivanka Beyer
53 Mount Rhodes Drive, Hout Bay
Tel: 021-790-1773 Fax: 021-790-4864
Email: dreamhouse@yebo.co.za Web: www.dreamhouse.de
Cell: 082-547-7328

You cannot fail to be inspired by Dreamhouse and its mountainous harbour-view setting. The staggered garden contains many intimate leafy places that envelope both you and the landscape in the foliage. This is an artist's oasis and, if the mood takes you, Ivanka will dish out brushes, watercolours, canvas and frame so you can paint your own memories and take them home. The house and rooms reflect your host's own creative flair in colour, texture and line, with sweeping-armed suede sofas (it's always handy when your other half deals in furniture), a heavy wooden-beamed fireplace and high ceilings. The rooms are all different and named after their predominant colour, my favourite being the red luxury suite at the heart of the house where I imagined star-gazing from bed or rocking in the balcony-bound hammock for two. Hand-made mirrors, draped sarongs from Pakistan and an abundance of shells adorn the daily-different table décor. "Everything has its own story," according to Ivanka. Devoted to her guests, she applies attention to detail and impeccable yet unobtrusive service at all times. Whether it's a picnic basket you need, a cocktail at the pool lounge or directions for a sunrise walk up Little Lion's Head, she'll be there. Also trained in reiki, aromatherapy, reflexology and various massages there are a multitude of blissful experiences available at her hands. As we used to say at university (for some reason), "live the dream!" *Bikes are available for guests to use.*

Rooms: 7: 6 king/twin with en-suite bath/shower, 2 with en-suite kitchenette, 1 queen with en-suite shower.
Price: R390 - R720 pp sharing. Singles on request.
Meals: Full breakfast included. Dinner and light lunches on request (preferably with 24-hours notice as only fresh produce used).
Directions: Emailed or faxed on request.

Frogg's Leap

Jôke Glauser and Stewart McLaren
15 Baviaanskloof Rd, Hout Bay
Tel: 021-790-2590 Fax: 021-790-2590
Email: info@froggsleap.co.za Web: www.froggsleap.co.za
Cell: 082-493-4403

The huge Frogg's Leap verandah, with its impressive views of the Hout Bay mountains and sea seems to be the focal point of life here. At breakfast the house springs to life with Jôke (pronounced *yokie*) and Stewart engaging in easy banter with all who emerge, and chiding guests for sitting at the long wooden table inside when the parasol-shaded tables outside are so enticing. Then, in the evening, with the sea breeze swinging the hammocks and a sundowner in your hand, it is not hard to get to grips with being lazy and on holiday. I can't remember a place where guests made themselves so at home. Jôke and Stewart used to run charter boats in the West Indies and Frogg's Leap has a breezy Caribbean feel with many open French doors and windows. Bedrooms are cool ensembles of natural materials: painted floors, seagrass matting, palms, natural stone in bathrooms, lazy wicker chairs, reed ceilings, thick cotton percale linen and old wooden furniture. Hout Bay itself is a fishing harbour enclosed by mountains and is within minutes of beaches and hiking trails. Jôke and Stewart keep a 26ft catamaran there and, when the spirit moves them and weather permits, will take guests cray-fishing, or whale-watching when whales are in town. This is a place that has been consistently recommended both before and since the first edition and it is a continued pleasure to recommend it myself. *Guest phone 021-790-6260.*

Rooms: 6: 5 doubles/twins and 1 double, all with en-suite bathrooms; 2 with shower, 4 with bath and shower. Plus extra single room.
Price: R350 - R390 pp sharing. Single supplement: +50%.
Meals: Full breakfast included and served until 10am. There are 20 restaurants nearby for other meals.
Directions: A map will be faxed to you on confirmation of booking.

Makuti Lodge

Doreen and Peter Wright

Farriers Way, Tarragona Estate, Hout Bay
Tel: 021-790-1414 Fax: 021-790-1414/1227
Email: doreen@makutilodge.co.za Web: www.makutilodge.co.za
Cell: 083-457-5231

Forget Kirstenbosch, head for Makuti Lodge! (Well, almost....) Gardeners will find plenty of common ground with Peter and Doreen who are hugely welcoming. It's not that the grounds of Makuti Lodge are especially large; but they are just so full. From the patios, the lawns, the flower beds and the 'forest' area, to the hidden bark paths that twist between the cottages, you could spend hours wandering around contemplating life (or joining in a game of pétanque, if you've the stomach for it). Even if you do manage to exhaust the riches of the garden, just minutes from the driveway you'll find yourself at the foot of Myburg Peak, with walks to waterfalls in winter and red orchids (disas) in the summer. Doreen and Peter insist on leaving 2 bottles of wine out for guests and, if you play your cards right, you may be invited to a wine-tasting session in the stone depths of the cellar! Here, among the animal carvings and hanging swords, you can sample vinous treats from all over the southern hemisphere. In the summer, because they just can't help entertaining, they put on *alfresco* dinners on invitation. Just another opportunity to sit in the garden and watch the birds as the sun goes down. The cottages themselves are quaint (Peter is responsible for construction, Doreen for the finishing touches) with local art on the walls and wood-burning fires. And I haven't even mentioned the dogs, the pool, the hot tub or the breakfasts.

Rooms: 4 cottages: 1 x 1-bed cottages; 2 x 2-bed with 2 bathrooms; 1 x 3-bed with 2 bathrooms.
Price: R250 - R400 pp sharing. Or in winter: R450 - R1,100 per cottage; summer: R600 - R2,000 per cottage.
Meals: Full or Continental breakfast an extra R60 - R75 pp.
Directions: M63 to Hout Bay. Turn R at Disa River Rd, L at end. First R into Garron Ave. Then R into Connemara Drive. Then L into Hunter's Way. R into Farrier's Way. Makuti on R.

Manor Cottage, Tranquility Base & Marmalade Sky

Christopher Grinton
50 Baviaanskloof Road, Hout Bay
Tel: 021-791-0212 Fax: 021-791-0213
Email: info@themanorcottage.co.za Web: www.themanorcottage.co.za
Cell: 072-211-7725

Christopher is one of those lucky people who just love what they do. Wonderfully friendly and ultra-efficient, his pride and joy are his three delightful self-catering cottages. Pacing around in his crocs, Christopher led me through breezy open-plan layouts, the sun pouring in across the wooden decking. I felt immediately at home and felt the urge to kick off my shoes and start moving my things in. Everything is white and fresh with blue bedding, deep creamy sofas and white-painted panelling. Tranquility Base feels the biggest with its huge white and granite kitchen, antique dining table and grandfather clock. It also houses Christopher's glass bottle collection, some of which he found himself on nearby beaches - my favourites are the decorated wooden shoes from the Greyton Arts Festival. This cottage also gets priority over the swimming pool, a real bonus in summer. Manor Cottage is the really homely one and can actually sleep more people; and Marmalade Sky (so named after a Beatles-inspired kaleidoscope from Christopher's childhood) is a cosy nest for two with great views over the valley. They all have lots of outside decking and individual gas or charcoal braai facilities. Christopher thinks of everything – an optional gate at the pool for kids, night lighting along the paths, free wireless Internet and even a computer in case you forget your own. He also knows about a leafy glade with a waterfall only 3km away, so don't forget to ask him or he might just keep it to himself!

Rooms: 3 cottages: Tranquility Base: king with en/s bath & shower, queen & twin with shared bath & shower; Manor Cottage: queen with en/s shower, queen & twin with shared bath & shower; Marmalade Sky: queen with en/s shower.
Price: Tranquility Base R1,200 - R2,350 per night, Manor Cottage R800 - R1,350, Marmalade Sky R350 - R600. All prices are for whole cottage, up to the maximum it sleeps.
Meals: Self-catering, but coffee/tea tray provided.
Directions: Please refer to the website or contact Christopher.

Paddington's

Di and Don Lilford

3 Lindevista Lane, Hout Bay
Tel: 021-790-1955 Fax: 021-790-1955
Email: dlilford@telkomsa.net Web: www.paddington.co.za
Cell: 083-259-6025

Standing in Di's garden, I sighed with relaxed satisfaction, gazing across a valley and beach bathed in late-afternoon sunshine. Well away from the hustle and bustle of Cape Town proper, Hout Bay runs at a pace of its own, and Paddington's and the Lilfords are right in step. After years on their valley-floor farm, they have moved up onto the hillside accompanied by a gaggle of visiting guinea fowl (impatiently tapping on the French doors for their tea when I arrived), Rollo the dog and their steady stream of guests. There's a relaxed feel of country living here and while the building itself may be new and square, it's full of old prints, family furniture and well-trodden rugs. Visitors have the run of the tiled ground floor, with both bedrooms just two yawns and a stagger from breakfast, tacked onto the drawing room and kitchen. One room gets the morning sun, the other the afternoon rays and both are blessed with gigantic beds. If you feel up to it, Don and Di will point you in the direction of the best golf courses and the beach, while for the lethargic loungers among you there's pétanque on the gravel patch or a book on the verandah. Oh and there's always the heated pool behind the house! Choices, choices....

Rooms: 2 king/twins, 1 with bath, 1 with shower.
Price: R700 for double room. Singles on request.
Meals: Full breakfast included.
Directions: Faxed or emailed on request.

The Hout Bay Hideaway

Sue and Martin Collins

37 Skaife Street, Hout Bay
Tel: 021-790-8040
Email: info@houtbay-hideaway.com Web: www.houtbay-hideaway.com
Cell: 082-332-7853

The Hout Bay Hideaway, painted ivy green, literally disappears into the thick foliage of its delightfully overgrown garden. Smart meranti shutters lead you out of the rooms onto the long winding verandah that wraps around the house. Making my way along the tree-lined platform, where a jacaranda tree draped its purple flowers over the rail, I ogled at mountain, beach, pool and garden. I'm sure most of the action takes place outside here, round the pool or rambling up buried garden paths to find the hammock platform. Inside, the rooms are a treat too, big, elegant and cosy with Turkish rugs decorating the floors, leather armchairs, palms in large pots, mohair blankets, giant wooden wardrobes, old trunks and original artwork, not to mention hard-working fireplaces for those less well advertised Cape Town winters. Skylight Suite is my favourite, with prime access to the outdoor Victorian bath buried in the shrubbery. Despite being rather exposed, outdoor bathing is apparently very popular. "They don't care, they're on holiday," laughed Sue and that's exactly the atmosphere she and Martin encourage – carefree and relaxed. One of the perks is breakfast in bed (or served to the room at least). "Couples love it. They're still wandering around in their dressing-gowns at midday," adds Martin. Thick fluffy gowns are provided, by the way.

Rooms: 4: 3 king/twin suites with en-suite showers and kitchenettes. 1 ground-floor apartment with king and bath and shower.
Price: R350 - R700 pp sharing (depending on season and length of stay), singles on request.
Meals: Full breakfast included, 5-10 mins walk from restaurants and the beach.
Directions: On the website and can be emailed on request, or just call.

The Tarragon

Mark and Julia Fleming
21 Hunters Way, Tarragona, Hout Bay
Tel: 021-791-4155 Fax: 021-791-4156
Email: info@thetarragon.com Web: www.thetarragon.com
Cell: 076-191-7755

These globe-trotting Brits have retired their backpacks and settled at the opposite, luxury end of the accommodation world. Seduced by South Africa's charm and sunshine, Mark and Julia permanently unpacked, kids and all, building a new life and some very stylish self-catering cottages on the wooded southern slopes of Hout Bay's leafy valley. When I arrived a fruitless effort to find a pen sent Mark dashing for a replacement and I was able to enjoy a purple moment inspired by the towering evergreens and the incredible stillness. A koi pond plinked occasionally with frogs or fish exploring the sun-freckled surface. Other visitors to the Flemings' subtly-crafted garden include peacocks, Egyptian geese, cormorants, butterflies and dragonflies. From the pool-side sun-loungers and braai area your eye will be drawn across the lawn and rocky peaks before sweeping, like the garden, into an area of dense wood. All units have private outdoor areas dappled by vine-wound frames. Marble-topped kitchens are fully kitted out with everything from top-of-the-range toasters to dishwashers, and laundering is available with the lady who does the daily servicing. Living areas, bedrooms and bathrooms are kept simple with clean-cut lines and contrasting tones; high-quality white linens gleam against dark leather headboards, fresh-cut sunflowers pose upon polished tables and square silver-tapped sinks rest against natural slate or travertine tiling. The Tarragon offers a finely-tuned mix of character and luxury.

Rooms: 5 fully-contained serviced self-catering units: 2 x 3-bedroom units, 1 x 2-bedroom unit and 2 x 1-bedroom units. All with full kitchen, living area and en-suite bathrooms.
Price: R700 - R2,200 per night.
Meals: Fully self-catering.
Directions: Faxed or emailed on request.

Ocean View House

Katrin Ludik
33 Victoria Road, Bakoven
Tel: 021-438-1982 Fax: 021-438-2287
Email: oceanv@mweb.co.za Web: www.oceanview-house.com

There's no end to Ocean View's eccentric delights with its Russian marble and award-winning gardens. Everyone has either a balcony or a terrace with fabulous views of sea, pool deck or garden. It is a hotel, but such a personal one with huge wooden giraffes hiding behind every corner and elephant print tablecloths and cushions. There's also a great pool and how many hotels run an honesty bar? To cap it all, Ocean View has its own nature reserve, a tropical garden that ushers an idyllic river from the mountains to the sea. They have placed tables and sun-loungers on the grassy river banks, a sort of exotic *Wind in the Willows* scenario with rocks, ferns, trees, tropical birds and butterflies. If you ever feel like leaving Ocean View, Camps Bay is a stroll away with its string of outdoor restaurants and zesty atmosphere. It's a good place to watch trendy Capetonians at play. Tired out long before they were, I walked back to the hotel. The nightwatchman was expecting me and escorted me to my room, which was also expecting me, tomorrow's weather report by my bed.

Rooms: 14: 7 suites (1 Presidential, 1 Milkwood, 4 Royal, 1 Garden); 5 Luxury Rooms (2 sea-facing, 3 garden views) & 2 Pool Deck rooms. 13 have showers, 1 Royal has bath & shower.
Price: R400 – R1,300 pp sharing. Single rates available all year.
Meals: Full breakfast is included and served until 10am.
Directions: On the coast road a mile out of Camps Bay towards Hout Bay.

Ambiente Guest House

Marion Baden and Peter Forsthövel
58 Hely Hutchinson Ave, Camps Bay
Tel: 021-438-4060 Fax: 021-438-4060
Email: info@ambiente-guesthouse.com
Web: www.ambiente-guesthouse.com Cell: 072-460-1953

Marion and Peter's affair with Ambiente Guest House began with a holiday. An initial joke to buy from the previous owners became a reality that ended in signatures on more than one dotted line: they not only bought the place, but also got married here. Six years later and they're still going strong. So what does Ambiente have to sustain such marital harmony? A base of sturdy functionality is hidden beneath a layer of exciting features and continual surprises. Original native masks, chairs and colour schemes are fused with a Mediterranean feel to produce an effect of African-themed modernity. Choose from beds suspended by chains or with wavy topless posts. Immerse yourself in the big luxurious bathrooms where showers are powerful, sinks are exciting (trust me, sinks can be exciting, you'll see) and baths cry out for a glass of champagne. Amidst these mirror-filled havens things aren't always what they seem. Is that an African spear disguised as a towel rail? A boulder in the shower? This place has playful passion. It has the drama of half the mountain in the breakfast room, the shock of sand beneath your feet in the loo. If that's not enough to keep you amused, the views of mountain and ocean will make you gawp, the pool and garden will refresh and the paintings, if you look long and hard enough, will make you blush.

Rooms: 4: 3 king suites, all with en-suite bath and shower; and 1 double room with en-suite bath/shower.
Price: R445 - R710 pp sharing. Airport transfers R350 per transfer, one way.
Meals: Full breakfast included. BBQs possible by arrangement.
Directions: Take the N1 or N2 to Cape Town and follow signs to Cableway/Camps Bay. Remain on M62, Camps Bay Drive, with the 12 Apostles to your left and Camps Bay down to your right. Turn Left into Ravensteyn Ave then first right into Hely Hutchinson Ave. Ambiente is number 58.

Cramond Beach

Gail Voigt
23 Strathmore Road, Camps Bay
Tel: 083-457-1947 Fax: 021-438-0457
Email: gailvoigt@mweb.co.za Web: E-brochure available via email.
Cell: 083-457-1947

Gail Voigt has reinvented self-catering as we know it. Beware to anyone naive enough to believe it just involves letting out a room with a kitchen. Gail is in town and determined to create the most perfect holiday experience a guest can dream of. When we arrived at the beautiful modern house, just minutes from the beach and restaurants of Camps Bay, she had already filled the fridge, left out an enticing-looking bottle of wine, and had her phone at the ready to book our evening meal. And that is just the beginning. If you fancy a walk on Table Mountain or Lion's head, her husband Herbert, who has been everywhere from Kilimanjaro to the Inca trail, will be a more than willing guide. And when they aren't there, her four loyal and exceptionally friendly staff (Gerald, Jan, Beauty and Miriam) are there to help you with everything. Gail even arranges caterers at the drop of a hat. All rooms have huge windows, crisp white linen, and luxurious en-suite bathrooms. This is a complete paradise for children, with its sandpit, paddling pool and gated swimming pool, not to mention a cupboard of toys. And for parents, babysitters can be arranged with trusted friends, furniture is beautiful but robust enough for a marauding toddler, and cleaning and laundry are done daily. It is a paradise for families, but that's not to say this place wouldn't be good for couples or groups: with generous-sized bedrooms, good braais for parties, incredible location and glamorous styling, it makes a great base to see the city.

Rooms: 1 self-catering villa that can be rented as a whole with 4 rooms, 2 queens and 2 twins, all en-suite; or as separate apartments, each with 1 twin and 1 queen.
Price: R250 to R500 per person or from R1,000 to R3,000 per day for the whole house. Rate includes baby cots, high chairs etc. Also airport transfers both ways for lets of a week or more.
Meals: Refrigerator filled on arrival with everything you could possibly need, but meals can be provided.
Directions: Call or email for directions.

Sundowner Guest House

Cherry Crowden and Michael Kohla
41 Geneva Drive, Camps Bay
Tel: 021-438-2622 Fax: 021-438-2633
Email: stay@sundowner-guesthouse.com
Web: www.sundowner-guesthouse.com Cell: 083-690-5683

Cherry and Michael insist on superlative quality and at Sundowner Guesthouse the freshly-ground coffee is even praised by Italians. It is Cherry's hobby to gather authentic ingredients and transform them into a specifically-tailored, innovative feast. As she spoke of locally-sourced seasonal fruits, cold meats and cheeses, home-made preserves, croissants, muesli and crispy-baked loaves, I wished I had coincided my visit with breakfast. This Anglo-Austrian duo have built up a remarkable knowledge of their locality which they enthusiastically share with guests (I also gleaned my fair share of advice). Cherry's unique flair, originating in her design background, permeates the guest-house where a wholesome base of whites, creams and dark chocolate browns are spiced up with flashes of tangy oranges and lime greens. In the Penthouse Suite strips of window frame sections of Table Mountain, which appear to hang like pictures on the wall, a peep show of the Camps Bay view. Vibrant décor, quiet reading corners and a quirky, cube-seated TV area gather to form a living space accommodating of every holiday pursuit; or you could just take it easy by the pool. I pitched up for a grapetizer at Michael's watering-hole, but there are far heftier drinks on offer for those not driving and wishing to toast the sunset. A fantastic place that will keep everyone happy. *Not suitable for children under 12.*

Rooms: 4: 3 double bedrooms with en-suite bath and shower and 1 king-size bedroom suite with en-suite bath and shower.
Price: R350 - R800 pp sharing. Singles + 50%.
Meals: Full breakfast included and light meals available on request.
Directions: Faxed or emailed on request.

Blackheath Lodge

Antony Trop and John Stewart

6 Blackheath Road, Sea Point
Tel: 021-439-2541 Fax: 021-439-9776
Email: info@blackheathlodge.co.za Web: www.blackheathlodge.co.za
Cell: 076-130-6888

Another GG accommodation inspector heard about Antony, Blackheath Lodge's owner, when her brother tried to make a booking. There was no room at the inn, but instead of turning him away, Antony located a beautiful, sea-view apartment for him and charged the same price. This sort of beyond-the-call-of-duty kindness is typical of him. When I visited on a busy morning, the patio was buzzing with the happy murmur of breakfasting guests, some sitting at tables and some lolling by the solar-heated pool. Antony, meanwhile, was helping guests with the day's 'to do' list. A short walk from Cape Town central, he and his partner John decorated the house with beautiful touches. Rooms have high, corniced ceilings, pine floors, embroidered lampshades and super-soft, super-white linen. Each has its own quirk: red pattern chaises longues, chandeliers, leopard-print armchairs, antique clocks and original cast-iron fireplaces that will warm even the coldest heart during (what can be) an icy Cape winter: "they work, let me tell you, they work!" says Antony with feeling. Most importantly guests can tuck into complimentary biscuits, and the fridge is in the bathroom so no annoying electrical hum. Lion's Head beckons for the energetic and Sea Point beach promenade, Cape Town's answer to Beverly Hills where lycra and biceps are *de rigueur*, is close by. If you're visiting at Christmas and New Year make sure you ask for the swish new apartment that the pair have lovingly renovated next door. *Children over 12 are welcome.*

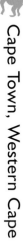

Rooms: 10: all doubles/twins with en-suite bathrooms; 9 have showers and 1 has both bath and shower.
Price: R390 - R750 pp sharing. Singles on request.
Meals: Breakfast included. Specials include quiche, French toast, cinnamon pancakes & full English. Evening meals on request from about R150.
Directions: Follow signs on N2 to Cape Town then Sea Point. At end of Table Bay Boulevard turn R at second lights onto Western Boulevard. At ocean merge L, then turn L at traffic lights into Three Anchor Bay Rd, continue over lights into Glengariff Rd, then turn R into Blackheath Rd – No. 6 is on R.

Huijs Haerlem

Johan du Preez and Kees Burgers
25 Main Drive, Sea Point
Tel: 021-434-6434 Fax: 021-439-2506
Email: haerlem@iafrica.com Web: www.huijshaerlem.co.za

Don't even try and pronounce it! Imagine, it used to be called 't Huijs Haerlem, so small thanks for small mercies! But what a great place: a secret garden, perched high on the hill above Sea Point, enclosed behind walls and gates, abloom with tropical flowers in beds and earthenware pots, with suntrap lawns, a pool (salt-water, solar-heated) and views over Table Bay. The verandah frame is snaked about with a vine and small trees provide the shade. Johan and Kees have a lovely, caring approach to their guests and look after you royally. There's no formal reception area, the bar is based on honesty, all their fine Dutch and South African antiques are not hidden away for fear of breakage. In fact both of them suffer from magpie-itis and walls and surfaces teem with eye-arresting objects: a tailor's mannequin, cabinet-making tools, old linen presses. Of course breakfast is enormous with fresh breads, rolls and croissants, fruits, cheeses, cold meats and the full cooked bonanza. This is Johan's domain, a chance for him to banter with guests and make a few suggestions. All the bedrooms are different, but all have their advantage, some with private terraces, some great views, one a four-poster. Whichever room you are in you will feel part of the whole.

Rooms: 8: 5 twins and 3 doubles; all en-suite, 2 with separate bath and shower, the rest with shower over bath.
Price: R495 – R600 pp sharing. Singles plus 25%.
Meals: Full breakfast included.
Directions: Faxed or emailed on booking.

Rosedene Lodge

Michael Ender
3 Rosedene Road, Sea Point, Cape Town
Tel: 021-439-7037 Fax: 021-433-2046
Email: info@rosedenelodge.com Web: www.rosedenelodge.com
Cell: 078-210-9886

Here's a quirky little place, hidden in Sea Point's labyrinth of quiet little streets. Once the front doors slide open – à la Star Trek – a vine-smothered cobbled path bypasses guests very much at home by the pool and heads toward a convivial community of easy chairs and a long dining table. Whenever he's in town, one screenplay writer virtually sets up shop here. The feel is immediately informal and unhurried, much like quietly-spoken owner, Michael, who divides his time between running the lodge and a restaurant in the city. However, he gets animated when he starts explaining some truly unique features of the lodge. In one of the more Spartan rooms, a huge Velaphi Mzimba portrait stares unflinchingly down from its metal frame, contrasting with more traditional comforts found elsewhere. Michael's signature room, though, is in the heart of the lodge. This shameless apartment flashes through a sheer semi-circle of windows… and while the shutters do close (and apparently the light is astonishing) it just doesn't seem right. Everything is wide open and a seamless sunken mattress is all ingenuity, like the shower with its own small arena and - get this - steam motion sensors. Even the colours are transparent and a modern kitchen is the perfect showcase for your daring cuisine. In the garden, wall-mounted speakers hint at the popular outdoor movie nights when a 3-metre projector-screen unfolds, reflecting stars of a different on the salt-water pool. Expect to stay in.

Rooms: 6: 4 twin/king, 1 queen double, 1 garden suite (all fully en-suite).
Price: R1,100 - R1,500 per room per night. Low season rates negotiable.
Meals: Full breakfast included.
Directions: Just off High Level Road, Sea Point. See website for details.

The Villa Rosa

Lynn Stacey
277 High Level Rd, Sea Point
Tel: 021-434-2768 Fax: 021-434-3526
Email: villaros@mweb.co.za Web: www.villa-rosa.com
Cell: 082-785-3238

How I managed to drive straight past the Villa Rosa I'll never know. With dramatic red- and white-tinged walls the villa is hardly a shrinking violet. But I did anyway.... I wandered up the front path through mingled scents of wild jasmine, chives and roses and was met at the stained-glass door by Lynn, who emits the same bright warmth as her villa walls. As we chatted over juice in the kitchen we were interrupted by Buttons, a newly-adopted and very vocal cat - a happy addition to the family. The villa continues its rosy persona within. Soft rose pinks are set off with hints of contrasting greens and dark wooden furniture. Most rooms are lit by enormous bay windows and intricate chandeliers, each one unique in its delicate hanging flowers, gems and metalwork. I soon discovered that Lynn had had a chandelier 'binge' at some point. And that chandeliers were just one of many such undeniable urges; the 'bathroom binge' resulted in a complete bathroom overhaul producing the fresh stone-floored en-suite beauties now in place. The metal leaf-chairs in one room (literally chairs that look like giant leaves) were "so wacky we just bought them," says Lynn. The art binge is ongoing and the walls continue to fill up with local talent. Looking at Buttons, I wondered if Lynn would ever consider an 'adoption binge'. If so I'll be volunteering myself as the next eligible stray.

Rooms: 8: all doubles, 4 with en-suite bath and shower, 4 with en-suite shower. Possibility of joining two rooms to form a family suite. 1 self-catering unit.
Price: R500 - R820. Singles R350 - R535.
Meals: Full breakfast included.
Directions: Emailed or faxed on request. Also on Villa Rosa website.

Cedric's Lodges

Jutta Frensch and Inge Niklaus
39 Dixon Street and 90 Waterkant Street, Green Point, De Waterkant
Tel: 021-425-7635
Fax: 021-425-7635
Email: info@cedricslodge.com
Web: www.cedricslodge.com
Cell: 083-327-3203
or 083-326-4438

Once Cape Muslim slave-quarters, De Waterkant's brightly-coloured, cobbled hill-side streets are amongst the most cosmopolitan in Cape Town, full of fashion labels, interior design showrooms, art galleries and trendy bars. The city's heart beats fast here and Inge and her architect sister Jutta have their fingers on the pulse. They metamorphosed a 17th-century slave-house into Cedric's, a washed-grey, contemporary town house. Downstairs is given over to an open-plan living space with steel-and-chrome kitchen, sleek dining table and grey suede sofas arranged around a concrete fireplace. There's glass, polished floorboards and colourful prints throughout and, upstairs, beds have dark headboards and chinoiserie fabrics. My room also had Indian chairs, slate bath and balcony, a blissful spot in the thrall of Table Mountain for this cold-blooded European to bake. Inge and Jutta will take you up there or up Signal Hill for champagne as the sun dissolves into the Atlantic. They'll just as likely drag you off to a concert or they might invite you to join them for lunch with friends in the Cape Flats. Inge edits the village rag and is an inspirational source of what's hot in the Mother City. Spend a lazy breakfast in one of the corner cafés and meander round this forward-looking historic area and you'll be hooked. As the Eagles (almost) said: "You can check out any time you like, but you can never (really) leave." *5 minutes' walk to Convention Center. Also now opened Cedric's Country Lodge in Greyton with 3 double rooms.*

Rooms: 10: all doubles with en-suite bath or shower.
Price: R900 – R1,400 per room. The whole house can be let from R3,600 – R5,600 per night.
Meals: Rate includes breakfast. Cape Town's most fashionable restaurant on the doorstep.
Directions: For directions see the Cedric's Lodge website.

Cheviot Place Guest House

James and Brooke Irving
18 Cheviot Place, Green Point
Tel: 021-439-3741 Fax: 021-439-9095
Email: cheviot@netactive.co.za Web: www.cheviotplace.co.za
Cell: 082-467-3660

Cheviot Place is something fresh for the Cape Town accommodation scene. This was apparent to me from the moment James opened the front door, dressed in Hawaiian shirt (sunny) and trainers (trendy), Jamie Cullum (jazzy) wafting out behind him. When he moved in a couple of years ago, this venerable, early 20th-century house, with its high ceilings, pillars and arches, was in desperate need of renovation. So, new wooden floors, natural hemp-style rugs and black metal light fittings were added to set off the original marble fireplaces. Cheviot Place has been transformed into a contemporary home while retaining the best of its Victorian heritage. And, first and foremost, a home it is. There was nothing on display to suggest that James and Brooke actually run a guest house (apart from the guest bedrooms, of course) so any visitor here would feel like an old friend come to stay. James was even sure he recognised me from somewhere. The self-catering unit below the main house is surely the ultimate in 21st-century living, reminding me of the troglodyte homes carved out of the rocks deep in the Sahara. Apart from the bed there is no free-standing furniture: everything has been sculptured from the stone. Original? Yes. Cool? In both senses of the word.

Rooms: 6: 4 queens, 2 twins (variously ensuite bath and shower, bath and shower-head, shower). Self-catering suite also available with 1 queen.
Price: R285 - R485 pp sharing. R350 - R600 for singles.
Meals: Full breakfast is included. Picnics provided on request for R35 - R150. Braai on request from R150 - R250.
Directions: Ask when booking.

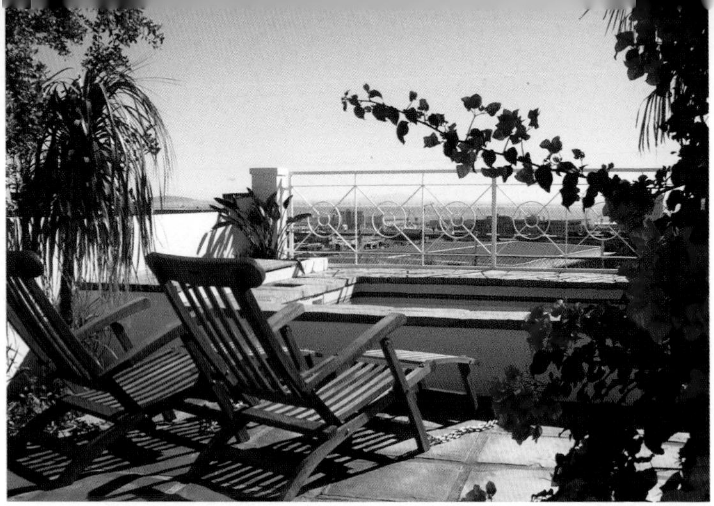

De Waterkant Cottages

Tobin Shackleford and Richard Gush

40 Napier Street, De Waterkant
Tel: 021-421-2300 Fax: 021-421-2399
Email: book@dewaterkantcottages.com
Web: www.dewaterkantcottages.com Cell: 072-457-4387

Now here is something a little bit different, the chance to have your own home (albeit only for the period of your stay), right in the centre of one of Cape Town's trendiest neighbourhoods. De Waterkant Cottages is a constantly-evolving array of brightly-painted former slave cottages (some dating from the 18th century) and more modern, but sympathetically-styled, homes in the National Preservation site that is De Waterkant Village. Each is individually owned, but all are run on a day-to-day basis by Tobin Shackleford and his team. Only the best are selected, which means you're assured of high-quality fixtures, fittings and furnishings. All have standardised luxury linen, plates, knives, forks etc, in fact everything you could ever want or need to make your stay here a pleasure. The concept is all about choice (which, trust me, will be no easy thing). First you'll have to choose between traditional and contemporary, but then you'll need to choose your exact cottage. There are too many to go through them all, but of the ones I saw I witnessed roof decks galore, exposed wooden floors, luxury leathers sofas, private gardens, roof-top jacuzzis, rain-head showers, flat-screen TVs, real fires, amazing views, total privacy, plunge pools... the list goes on. See, I said it wouldn't be an easy choice.

Rooms: 16 cottages, with one, two or three bedrooms (queen, king & twin). All main bedrooms with en-suite bathrooms, showers and air-conditioning. Online bookings and availability.
Price: R750 - R2,000 for two persons per night per cottage. Additional persons R200 - R400, under 2s stay free.
Meals: All meals can be provided on request.
Directions: See website for map and instructions.

The Village Lodge

Rodney and Robert Musielewicz
49 Napier Street, De Waterkant
Tel: 021-421-1106 Fax: 021-421-8488
Email: book@thevillagelodge.com Web: www.thevillagelodge.com

The Village Lodge is an über-stylish boutique hotel bang in the centre of De Waterkant village. Located in one of Cape Town's oldest residential areas, the lodge mixes modern design with first-class service and a warm welcome. Guests can enjoy a cappuccino while soaking up the sun on the front terrace or simply grab one of the many international papers to read over breakfast (smoked salmon and caviar anyone?). The breakfast room also doubles up as Soho, a sleek 45-seater Thai restaurant serving lunch and dinner. Black ceramic tiles, huge wall mirrors and crisp white table-cloths make it a thoroughly glamorous affair. Rooms are equally chic and come complete with all mod cons including huge flat-screen TVs, WIFI and room service, while bathrooms are effortlessly neat with white tiled flooring and spacious showers. Hidden among this warren of rooms lies a delightful spiral staircase leading out onto the roof deck. It's the perfect spot for soaking up stunning 360-degree Cape Town views while enjoying a sundowner at the Sky Bar, a refreshing dip in the pool or a delicious Thai meal. And it doesn't end there. The Village Lodge is really just the beginning when it comes to accommodation and entertainment here. For Rodney and Robert also manage the villa next door, six townhouses within the area, a Salsa restaurant and bar across the road and four suites above it. Phew!

Rooms: 15: all doubles with en-suite shower.
Price: From R750 per room.
Meals: Full breakfast included. Soho restaurant (Thai cuisine) on premises.
Directions: From airport take the N2 to the city. Follow signs to the Waterfront. At first set of traffic lights go straight on to Buitengracht Street. At third set of lights turn right into Somerset Road, then left into Napier Street. Hotel is on the left.

Dunkley House

Sharon Scudamore
3b Gordon St, Gardens
Tel: 021-462-7650 Fax: 021-462-7649
Email: reservations@dunkleyhouse.com Web: www.dunkleyhouse.com

Tucked into a quiet street in central Gardens this compact boutique hotel is a mosaic-floored, chic-Mediterranean-villa of a place. Chic maybe, but delightfully relaxed with it. Manager Sara supplied me with home-made biscuits as we chatted. This really is a place you are encouraged to feel at home in, no small feat for a hotel, however small and 'boutique'. You want to lounge under palms by the pool?… lounge; you want to help Eunice in the kitchen?… go for it. She's a fantastic cook and aside from endless breakfast delights (don't miss the fluffy omelettes), she has been known to rustle up a feast for those who want to eat in of an evening. The long dining table is neatly arranged next to a pot-bellied wood-burner for winter nights and framed by black-and-white prints of Dar es Salaam. Thankfully the bedrooms – bay-windowed, whitest linen on beds and flashes of colour in the cushions – are just a stagger away. Completed last year, Dunkley House 2 is something else. It has four ultra-modern rooms with black-and-white stucco and stained-pine flooring, an outdoor plunge pool and cubic bathrooms with angular fittings and a remote controlled, state-of-the-art lighting and air-con system. And just to add to the style, there are top-of-the-range Tivoli radios in each room. They went for the 'wow' factor... and they got it!

Rooms: 11: 6 kings, 3 queens, 1 with bath, 3 with bath and shower, all others with shower only. One apartment with 1 double and 1 twin sharing shower.
Price: From R675 – R725 pp sharing. Singles R900 – R1,100. Apartment R1,450 per night.
Meals: Full breakfast included. Other meals by arrangement.
Directions: Faxed or emailed on booking, also on website.

An African Villa

Jimmy van Tonder and Louis Nel
19 Carstens St, Tamboerskloof
Tel: 021-423-2162 Fax: 021-423-2274
Email: villa@capetowncity.co.za Web: www.capetowncity.co.za/villa
Cell: 082-920-5508

Louis ditched the interior design world to focus his full creative zeal on this magnificent house – or rather houses – and when I pitched up he was hard at work, pen in mouth, bent over plans for the next step. He and Jimmy have converted three entire houses into a den of 'African Zen'. The structure may be classically Victorian, but the décor is anything but, with bold, tribal colours offsetting black-painted floorboards and neutral carpets. Jimmy gave me the grand tour – trailed as ever by dachshunds Zip and Button – pointing out Louis' designer eye in every detail, from the lacquered ostrich eggs and porcupine quills (please don't pinch them, he pleads) to the hanging Zulu spears and African wedding hats. The bathrooms are compact but perfectly formed, the bedrooms are wonderfully roomy, and when you finally and reluctantly slide from between the percale cotton sheets, breakfast is a communal affair in the large airy kitchen or out on the terrace. This house is a haven, a cool retreat and while others may be sweating their way up Table Mountain just minutes away, you can be thumbing through a book in the shade of an orange tree or cooling off in the plunge pool. Go on… treat yourself. *Library and Internet available to all guests.*

Rooms: 12 king/twins all with a/c: 5 'Superior' with bath & shower; 5 'Classic', 3 with shower, 2 with bath & shower; 2 'Standard' (street-facing).
Price: R440 - R640 pp sharing. Singles on request.
Meals: Full breakfast included.
Directions: From central Cape Town follow signs to the Cableway. At the bottom of Kloofnek Rd double back and turn left into Carstens St. Look for the second block on the left with a yellowwood tree outside.

Bayview Guesthouse

Christine Matti
10 De Hoop Avenue,
Tamboerskloof
Tel: 021-424-2033
Fax: 021-424-2705
Email: baychris@iafrica.com
Web: www.baychris.com
Cell: 082-414-2052

Christine's partner Corinne had her arm in a sling when we met. She'd torn a tendon pulling a cork out of a bottle – an unfortunate accident, but a large tick in the 'commitment to the cause' category for GG candidates. These two are passionate about their wine and, well, passionate about just about everything. When not buzzing around the house, Swiss-born Christine is usually out cranking up Cape Town kilometres on her racing bike or working on her annoyingly low golf handicap. She arrived in South Africa a wide-eyed whippersnapper some twenty years ago, and has never quite got around to leaving. Her home is an airy haven of healthy living. White-washed walls, floor-to-ceiling tinted windows and tiled floors make this a perfect mountain-side retreat from the city centre's summer heat. Breakfasts are an Alpine feast of German breads, selected cheeses and cold meats and guests are encouraged to help themselves to a bottomless bowl of fresh fruit. Take a dip in the pool, head off for a massage at any number of nearby wellness centres, read a book on your decking balcony, and - once you've done all that - lie back on the sofa and gaze at a perfectly-framed Table Mountain through the sitting room skylight. My only disappointment? I didn't have time to stay the night. *Personal computer for guests.*

Rooms: 5: 2 queens, 1 with en-suite shower and bath, 1 with en-suite shower; 1 double with en/s shower, 1 twin with en-suite shower. 1 self-catering unit.
Price: R250 - R600 pp sharing.
Meals: Healthy breakfasts included. Cooked breakfast on request.
Directions: Follow signs from the city centre to the Cableway. From Kloofnek Rd turn R into St. Michael's Rd and then third L into Varsity St. At the T-junction turn R into De Hoop Avenue and Bayview is the second on the right.

Hillcrest Manor

Gerda and Gerhard Swanepoel
18 Brownlow Rd, Tamboerskloof
Tel: 021-423-7459
Fax: 021-426-1260
Email: hilcres@mweb.co.za
Web: www.hillcrestmanor.co.za
Cell: 082-700-5760

Step inside my fantasy world for a moment: the real state of real estate doesn't exist and you can choose anywhere in Cape Town to build your new home. You'd probably end up precisely where I am now. Sadly, you're a hundred years too late and Gerda and Gerhard already live here. Happily, however, they've opened their home to guests and you'll be assured a warm welcome. Situated at the foot of Lion's Head in a leafy hillside suburb, their Victorian townhouse looms above the street and faces the most stunning view of Cape Town. From pool, balcony or bed you can see all the detail of the city and waterfront and Table Mountain's acclaimed acclivity clearly. This elegant house, its tall windows and wooden shutters set atop an elevated blue-stone foundation, is where Gerhard grew up. Nowadays the whitewashed steps lead up past a sunny lawn, patio and pool to a sitting room with original pressed-metal ceiling and a bright breakfast room, where the local artwork is for sale. Upstairs the bedrooms are designed to give respite from the long hot summer. Floors are a mix of polished timber and seagrass, beds are pine, furniture wicker. Ceiling-fans loll lazily and curtains billow in the breeze. One bedroom is pure C.S.Lewis, though here the wardrobe leads not to Narnia, but to your own claw-foot bath.

Rooms: 6: all doubles with en-suite shower, one with bath too.
Price: R300 – R450 pp sharing. Singles R650.
Meals: Full breakfast included.
Directions: Faxed or emailed on booking.

Jardin d'Ebène

Pascale Lauber and Ulrike Bauschke
21 Warren Street, Tamboerskloof, Cape Town
Tel: 021-426-1011 Fax: 021-422-2423
Email: info@jardindebene.co.za Web: www.jardindebene.co.za

I wonder if the neighbours are aware that sandwiched between them is a tropical paradise and surely one of the most exquisite places to stay in Cape Town? Perhaps not, as this Old Cape Dutch (1900) townhouse is well sequestered behind gates, walls and giant bamboo. But on entering you will be transported by Le Jardin d'Ebène (almost pronounced day-ben). I'm not exactly sure where to, such is the eclectic nature of the decor and the originality of the design… but somewhere exotic anyway… and somewhere rather wonderful too! Every area of the house provides a powerful atmospheric 'kick'. I was served tea on the verandah, a cool place looking through billowing white drapes over a black-slate plunge pool, where gorgeous pygmy beds from central Africa are arranged on decking. Inside, much of the furniture is locally made to Pascale and Ulrike's specifications. And ALL (capitals intended) of the antiques, modern paintings and artefacts have been picked out and creatively arrayed with impeccable good taste. I loved the carved double doors from India, for example, but there are so many fascinating things to catch the eye that my tour around the house was slow and envious. Each of the five bedrooms has an African feel, but this theme is so idiosyncratic that you can put away any naff notions of zebra print or spears on the wall. On top of the gorgeous looks of this place, Pascale and Ulrike pay incredible attention to detail in caring for their guests and I have a feeling this is going to become a big favourite among GG guests. *Children over 14 are welcome.*

Rooms: 5: 1 king/twin with en-suite open-plan double shower; 1 queen with en-suite bath/shower; 1 queen with en-suite double shower; 1 luxury king with separate bath/shower; 1 luxury king with open plan bath in room.
Price: R360 pp - R550 pp. Singles on request. Airport transfer: R220 per trip for 2 people.
Meals: Full breakfast included. Freshly-squeezed orange juice and great coffee.
Directions: See website.

Navona

Elle Jahnig
Unit 25, Park Road Place, 11 Park Road, Tamboerskloof
Tel: 021-794-0945 Fax: 021-794-0945
Email: info@navona.co.za Web: www.navona.co.za
Cell: 082-882-7854

Slap bang in the middle of town, this cosy loft apartment is perfect for young couples looking for a taste of city life. Tucked away just off Kloof Street, Navona offers great privacy and calm with an enviable full-frame view of Table Mountain. Elle is passionate about interiors and this space is a showcase for her eclectic tastes. Vying for your attention are sparkling Hollywood mirrors, Louis XIV armchairs, framed photos on the wall, a giant marble chess table, modern lighting that are artworks in themselves and flower-pots of cascading palms. Upstairs, the main bedroom is a thoroughly romantic cocoon, replete with candles and a quaint and romantic roof garden to appreciate from your bed. On the landing floor there is a double bed for extra bodies and a big storage cupboard. Elle is herself the mother of an inquisitive little lady, so the apartment is safe for young children; and for the larger ones there's a 'DSTV/internet/DVD multiplex corner'. Not that there should be the need to sit indoors all day, with all Cape Town has to offer quite literally on your doorstep. Step outside into an array of chic eateries, fashionable bars and mingle with the in-crowd... though of course you do have a wonderfully-equipped modern kitchen at your disposal too! Even if you can't be bothered to cook, I'll bet you make your way through the Belgian chocolates and biscotti when you return home after hours. *The apartment is air-conditioned.*

Rooms: 2: 1 double bedroom and 1 double bed on open-plan landing.
Price: R800 - R1,500 for whole apartment dependent on season. Maximum 4 people.
Meals: Self-catering. Daily servicing can be arranged at a reasonable daily rate.
Directions: Emailed or faxed on booking. Also available on website.

Alta Bay

Ariel Glownia
12 Invermark Crescent, Cape Town
Tel: 021-487-8800 Fax: 021-487-8822
Email: info@altabay.com Web: www.altabay.com

Alta Bay is perched high up on the last bit of Table Mountain that still slopes and above me I watched the cable car disappear into the 'tablecloth', a stream of white cloud pouring off the plateau. Behind the house walls, thick purple wisteria clambers everywhere, hiding the house from view and creating any number of private corners. I stepped across what felt like a small bridge and was met by Ariel, my urbane and very friendly host, who led me onto the first-floor balcony and a wonderful branch-framed vista of the city and harbour below. Ariel's penchant is for the modern and artworks throughout the house are always gorgeous and often unexpected; one New York artist has, for example, cleverly adapted the words of various presidential inaugural speeches. Sometimes the style resonates with Ariel's Portuguese roots, but everywhere there is coolness and space. Furnishings are all of a very high 'urban chic' standard with extra-length beds with slatted, wooden headboards, percale cotton sheets, and a range of mod cons such as flat-screen TVs, phones, DVD/CD players etc. For a little more privacy, the separate apartment with its mezzanine bedroom is the obvious choice. On a lower level you'll find a breakfast room of coloured-glass tables and jaunty bulb-shaped vases. Here, too, there is a living room that opens onto a gorgeous terrace, with sun-beds and a pool. From Alta Bay you can look down on not just the city and harbour, but also on all those that have foolishly booked in elsewhere!

Rooms: 7: 4 king/twin, 3 king (3 fully en-suite, 4 shower en-suite).
Price: R1,300 - R2,700 per room per night. Prices include all beverages.
Meals: Full breakfast included. Lunch and dinner snack menu.
Directions: Near Orangezicht area. See website for details.

Acorn House

Bernd Schlieper and Beate Lietz

1 Montrose Avenue, Oranjezicht
Tel: 021-461-1782 Fax: 021-461-1768
Email: welcome@acornhouse.co.za Web: www.acornhouse.co.za

Bernd and Beate can barely contain the happiness they derive from Acorn House, and their enthusiasm rubs off quickly on all but the stoniest of their visitors. I was a pushover. The listed building, designed by busy Sir Herbert Baker in 1904, sits on the sunny, sea-facing slopes of Table Mountain with tip-top views to Table Bay. The house is typical Sir Herbert, timber colonnade, broad verandah et al, and there is an immaculate garden with black-slate swimming pool and a sun-lounging lawn, cleanly demarcated by agapanthus and lavender bushes. Breakfast, often served by the pool, is a no-holds-barred display of meats, cheeses, eggs and freshly-squeezed fruit juices; "probably the second-best breakfast in Cape Town" is Beate's carefully-worded claim! Upstairs, in your wood-floored bedroom you will find notes of welcome or farewell, chocolates and sprigs of lavender. Wine-lovers are also well served: Bernd is pazzo for the stuff, and regularly visits local vineyards to ensure that his house wines are up-to-the-moment (just for his guests' benefit, of course). Having lived in South Africa for several years now, Bernd and Beate are still awash with excitement about their surroundings; a stay in Acorn House will leave you feeling much the same.

Rooms: 9: 1 king, 3 twins and 3 doubles all with en-suite bath; 1 family suite with twin; 1 private family cottage with king.
Price: R460 - R560 pp sharing. Singles R400 - R800. Family suite and private family cottage as double R1,170 - R1,370 + R200 for up to 2 kids.
Meals: Full breakfast included.
Directions: See website or ask for fax.

Abbey Manor

Judi Buikman

3 Montrose Avenue, Oranjezicht
Tel: 021-462-2935 Fax: 021-462-3893
Email: info@abbey.co.za Web: www.abbey.co.za
Cell: 082-788-4210

If my great-grandmother, a well-known bon vivant and ex-flapper, was still alive and planning to come to Cape Town, I would send her to Abbey Manor. No new-fangled minimalist-urban-afro business here. Instead the bedrooms drip with 1920's glamour. Close your eyes and imagine men in smoking jackets drinking high-balls and pointy-toed women sucking elegantly on cigarette-holders. Judi, the welcoming manager who holds the unofficial title of hotel 'mother', will do anything and everything for her guests. This includes going on snack runs to the local deli while they lounge by the pool and organising impromptu picnics. The property is over a hundred years old and everything downstairs, from the stained-glass windows to the white-washed exterior, is original. Upstairs, each guest room has its own character. The most outrageous 'boudoir' is Harbour View with its crystal chandeliers, engraved mirrors and bedside lamps embroidered with black feathers. Not to be outdone, the balcony has views across Cape Town reaching down to the Waterfront. Elsewhere, the claret-coloured Devil's Peak View room has a Victorian slipper bath placed in front of the soaring window so that bathers can bask in bubbles while admiring the Mother City's highest peak. "Wait until you see this," Judi told me with a glint in her eye as I puffed up yet another set of stairs. On the roof terrace I found a jacuzzi frothing invitingly and, high above that, a cloud-free Table Mountain. Bliss.

Rooms: 9: 4 queens and 5 king/twins. All en-suite with bath and shower except 1 queen which has en/s shower.
Price: Grande Room: R550 - R980 pp sharing, singles R900 - R1,600. Luxury Room: R450 - R800 pp sharing, singles R720 - R1,250.
Meals: Full cooked and continental breakfast.
Directions: See website.

Lézard Bleu Guest House

Chris and Niki Neumann
30 Upper Orange St, Oranjezicht
Tel: 021-461-4601 Fax: 021-461-4657
Email: welcome@lezardbleu.co.za Web: www.lezardbleu.co.za
Cell: 072-234-4448

It's going to be hard to book the treehouse, particularly when word gets round, but you have got to try! Surely the most wonderful bedroom in Cape Town. The trunks of two giant palm trees spear through a wooden deck at vertiginous heights and a tiny balcony is in among the topmost fronds and spikes. Lézard Bleu was just about the best guest house in Cape Town anyway, so this latest extravagant addition represents one great big cherry on a mouthwatering cake. Niki is an actress and Chris is a chef, although he has hung up his hat now… no, don't even ask! They are still young and humorous and the house remains sleek and modern with solid maplewood bedframes, white pure cotton, sandy shades and tones, bright splashes of local and modern art on the walls. Breakfast is the best beanfeast in Cape Town (and that's the opinion of other guest house owners). The Blue Lizard snakes pleasingly from area to area, each room with its own doors out to a patio and to the large pool, where deck loungers take it easy on a surrounding timber deck. There are real fires in winter, an honesty bar, free ADSL Internet access - mere details, but typical. Individual, creative, very comfortable, but most importantly this is somewhere really natural and friendly.

Rooms: 7: 1 family room; 5 doubles/twins; 4 with en/s bath and shower; 1 with en/s shr; 1 tree-house double en/s bath and shower.
Price: R440 - R660 pp sharing. Single occupancy: R650 - R1,000 pp.
Meals: Full (enormous!) breakfast included and served till 10.30am.
Directions: Ask for directions when booking.

Redbourne Hilldrop

Jonny and Sharon Levin
12 Roseberry Avenue, Oranjezicht
Tel: 021-461-1394 Fax: 021-465-1006
Email: info@redbourne.co.za Web: www.redbourne.co.za

One of the happiest and most humorous guest houses in Cape Town, so it always seems to me. Many of Jonny and Sharon's guests refuse to stay elsewhere and gifts arrive daily from overseas… well almost. It's a small, intimate place and you are spoiled: free-standing baths, fluffy duvets, big white pillows, unflowery good taste in mirrors and wood floors, magazines, African artefacts, great showers. One room has a spiral staircase down to its bathroom. You eat breakfast at a diner-style bar stretched along a wall of pretty windows with incredible city views. Guests are treated as far as possible as friends and each time I visit I notice the easy rapport that Jonny and Sharon have generated with them – probably overnight. After a mere five minutes in their company I felt all the formality of my visit slipping away like a coat in hot weather. The wall-enclosed pool comes complete with a mini-waterfall spanning the length of it and Table Mountain looming above. From here you can see if the cable car is working and for the more adventurous you're not far from the start of one of several routes to the top. Otherwise it's an easy ride down to the city bustle, the Waterfront and the Atlantic beaches. Perfect location, great hosts, GSOH!

Rooms: 4: 2 doubles with en/s showers; 1 twin with en/s bath and shower and 1 twin family room with en/s bath and shower plus a sunroom (can fit 4/5 beds).
Price: R395 - R495 pp sharing. Singles on request.
Meals: Full breakfast included. Dinners by prior arrangement. Restaurants nearby.
Directions: On website.

Medindi Manor

Kyle Bowman and Lynda Bomyer
4 Thicket Road, Rosebank
Tel: 021-686-3563 Fax: 021-686-3565
Email: reservations@medindimanor.com Web: www.medindimanor.com
Cell: 082-857-9735

Medindi is a secluded Edwardian manor of grand dimensions, banded by ground and first-floor verandas with a garden and swimming pool tucked away behind tall hedges and bushes. Some of the rooms have their own doors out onto the stoep and the main building has been renovated with panache and a sensitive feel for the period. Although well-stocked with bar fridges, telephones, TVs etc, Medindi avoids like the plague any h(ot)ellish homogeneity in its décor and design. The Oregon pine floors, bay windows, intricate ceilings and marble fireplaces are original and there are unique, antique touches everywhere, such as Edwardian designs for stately marble and slate floors. Bathrooms have free-standing baths, Victorian 'plate' showerheads, brass fittings and a small antique cabinet has been found for each. There is modernity too, in bright wall colours (yellows and blues), and splashes of modern art – from the turn of one century to the turn of the next. Music is an important ingredient for Medindi's owner, and classical music and a bit of smooth jazz wafts through reception. A freewheeling, relaxed and youthful place. Kyle and Lynda share the day-to-day management of Medindi and six new rooms have been created from a converted outbuilding – the smaller rooms are cheaper.

Rooms: 13: 7 in the manor house: 6 dbles & 1 twin, 4 with en-s bath + shower, 3 with en-s shower; 3 garden rooms & 3 large garden suites in converted outbuilding, all en-s shower; 2 self-catering cottages.
Price: R395 - R745 pp sharing. Singles R695 - R1,265.
Meals: Buffet breakfast included. Full cooked breakfast extra R45. Many restaurants nearby for dinner or take-out.
Directions: See map on website or phone ahead.

3 Pear Lane

Vo Pollard
3 Pear Lane, Newlands Village
Tel: 021-689-1184 Fax: 021-689-1184
Email: pollards@iafrica.com Web: www.pearlane.co.za
Cell: 082-926-3080

At the foot of Devil's Peak mountain, deep within the lush greenery of Newlands and within one decently hooked six from the cricket ground, there lies a distinctly English garden idyll. The hugest oak I've seen marks the spot and the place in question is Vo's picture-perfect pad. A food stylist by trade, it's good to see that she employs her craft after hours too. Everything here is just as you'd like it; the huge sash windows breathe beams of light into the rooms, the king-sized bed is dressed up in the best percale linen and embroidered cotton throws and the bathroom comes with storage space aplenty, two big stone basins and a mighty-looking, pebble-floored shower. With its French wrought-iron table, silk-cushioned chairs and vase of delicate daisies, the view out to the garden could be straight from one of Vo's shoots; home-baked scones, strawberry jam and clotted cream, naturally, would be the scene's edible accompaniment. There's a nice collection of guide-books and yes, foodie mags for you to devour, perhaps whilst lounging by the salt-water pool. Lavender, moonflowers, roses and azaleas, to name but a few, adorn the patio and lawn. Manicured but never overdone, sniffable but not overwhelming, this is exactly the way gardens… well, dainty English ones anyway… should be. Should you want to stretch your legs, Newlands Forest, my favourite Cape Town walking haunt, is right next-door.

Rooms: 1 cottage with king/twin bed and en-suite shower and well-equipped kitchen.
Price: R300 - R375 pp sharing. Singles on request.
Meals: By prior arrangement, menu on request.
Directions: Take M3 from Cape Town towards Muizenberg. Take the Newlands feed-off and then turn right into Newlands Avenue. Go over one set of lights, then turn first left into Palmboom Rd. Pear Lane is half-way down on the right.

Hedge House

Judy and Graham Goble
12 Argyle Road, Newlands
Tel: 021-689-6431 Fax: 021-689-1286
Email: hedge@mweb.co.za Web: www.hedgehouse.co.za
Cell: 083-324-0888

The Gobles are an intriguing mixture of Doctor Dolittle and the Swiss Family Robinson, for Hedge House is home to all creatures - human or otherwise - great and small. It even has its own tree platform and a pirate-boat swing, not to mention prime views of Cape Town's highest mountain, Devil's Peak. Judy was once a veterinary nurse, and the family owns three dogs plus an assortment of avian oddities, including Doris the ageing parrot who insisted on calling my name throughout the whole visit - very disconcerting. She (Judy not Doris!) showed me the rambling family home whose focal point is a huge refectory table where guests eat breakfast perched on church-pew seats. Next to this a cosy seating area is just the place for tea beneath an oil painting of demure African women. Climbing the outdoor spiral stairs to a deck perforated by a camphor tree, I saw the setting sun pour into a large guestroom where the current residents, three Irish girls, were putting the storage space to good use! Elsewhere, a vast old ship's wardrobe is a family heirloom that compliments snug armchairs and gentle tones. All rooms have private entrances, so guests can stroll to the pool or wander around Judy's Wedgwood garden, which is crammed with blue and white hydrangea, lavender and agapanthus. A huge outdoor fireplace keeps everything warm and social on the new tiled verandah. Nearby Kirstenbosch Gardens are perfect for a stroll and for sports fans the Newlands Cricket Stadium is just around the corner.

Rooms: 4: 2 twin/king, 1 king & 1 queen with en-suite bath and shower. Families accommodated with single beds on request.
Price: R450 pp sharing. R670 singles.
Meals: Fruit salad and yoghurt come every day, plus a variety of home-made croissants and crumpets. Full English breakfast served daily.
Directions: From the airport travel on the N2 towards the city. Take Exit 8 – Liesbeek Parkway. At bottom of off-ramp turn left to Rondebosch. Travel 3.5km. When you see the traffic lights, one road before Keurboom Rd, turn left into Argyle Road. Hedge House is No. 12 on the RHS.

Highlands Country House

Carole Armstrong-Hooper
36 Tennant Road, Upper Kenilworth, Cape Town
Tel: 021-797-8810 Fax: 021-761-0017
Email: info@highlands.co.za Web: www.highlands.co.za

Highlands Country House, sitting splendidly on Wynberg Hill beneath Devil's Peak, is one of the Cape's most majestic homes. In front, a formal garden runs along avenues of fig trees down to trim lawns and flowerbeds - picked daily for fresh bouquets - and I went for a wander, ambling past a fountain and various Grecian urns before reaching one of two swimming pools. Here there is a spa where they will pamper you to within an inch of your life. Up at the house, meanwhile, all was efficient bustle, with smartly-dressed maids busily clearing away breakfast, leaving only the faint but delicious smell of bacon and eggs lingering on the terrace. I passed a magnificent, carved foot-throne in the foyer and a dining room all dressed up in starched white linen on my way to meet Carole in the library for a chat... and a delectable strawberry smoothie. She fell in love with the place when she once came here for tea, which is a special time of day at Highlands, honoured with freshly-baked cakes. Gourmet dinners, meanwhile, are best served by candlelight in the conservatory. Separate from the house, large European-style rooms are elegant in neutral tones, while England prevails inside a rush-carpeted warren of staircases and wings. Styles vary subtly in traditional rooms from African flourishes, to Cupid-guarded loft rooms, to Brosely-tiled bathrooms, to shades of blue in St Leger silk curtains. Part the shutters or step onto your balcony and look onto woods, sports fields, mountains and sea... and be very content with your choice.

Rooms: 14: 6 twin/king, 3 king, 4 queen and 1 honeymoon suite with king. All are fully en-suite, with the exception of one shower en-suite.
Price: R575 - R1,350 pp sharing. Singles: R925 - R2,050.
Meals: Full breakfast included. Lunch and dinner on request.
Directions: Tennant Road is a continuation of Newlands Road, reached either by the Constantia or Rondebosch exits on the M3. See website for more detailed directions.

Cape Witogie

Rosemary and Bob Child
9 Van Zyl Rd, Kreupelbosch, Constantia
Tel: 021-712-9935 Fax: 021-712-9935
Email: capewitogie@netactive.co.za Web: www.capestay.co.za/capewitogie
Cell: 082-537-6059 or 082-852-9084

Even if you're not a dog lover you'll soon find yourself falling for the charming Miss Poppy, Cape Witogie's desperately friendly Boston Terrier. In fact, such is her popularity that guests come back year after year to see her. Then again that could also be because of her equally charming owners, Rosemary and Bob. When I visited, Rosemary was frantically packing for a trip to the UK, but she happily showed me round their red-bricked home with its two guest bedrooms. Both rooms are whitewashed, tile-floored self-catering units, one with an airy conservatory/sitting room. They open on to a compact garden full of ferns and firs, lavender pots, lemon trees and citrus-smelling verbena. Hot-plates, a small oven and microwaves give ample scope for knocking up your own meals, though Rosemary enjoys making occasional breakfasts and bakes bread for those who'd rather not bake their own. I'd recommend coming with some pals and taking both rooms as a base from which to explore the Cape Town area. From the City Bowl and beaches to Table Mountain, the botanical gardens and nearby winelands there is just so much to do in the Cape that a full week with Bob and Rosemary flies by in the blink of an eye. These are great people (with a great dog) running a great-value get-away.

Rooms: 2 units: both consist of 1 twin room (1 extra single bed can be added to each if required) with en-suite showers and small kitchens.
Price: R220 - R260 pp sharing. Single supplement R50.
Meals: Breakfast on request R65.
Directions: Faxed or emailed on booking.

Constantia Stables

Lola and Rick Bartlett

8 Chantecler Lane, off Willow Rd, Constantia
Tel: 021-794-3653 Fax: 021-794-3653
Email: tstables@mweb.co.za Web: www.capestay.co.za/constantiastables
Cell: 082-569-4135

I loved The Constantia Stables and would be as happy as a pig in clover to be among Lola and Rick's regular visitors. Not only is it a stunning spot of shaded indigenous gardens and beautifully renovated stable buildings (ask for the hayloft room!), but there's a genuine family feel to the place that is immediately relaxing. The Bartlett children are actors and their photos are plastered across the drawing room and bar. This is the heart of the Stables, a congenial snug of heavy armchairs, low beams and earth-red walls where guests are encouraged to tap into a well-stocked bar. I liked the breakfast room too with its red-brick fireplace. My mouth watered as Lola reeled off her gargantuan breakfast menu: fresh fruit salad with home-grown guava, quince and peaches, hams, salamis, a giant cheese board, yoghurts, cereals and croissants and that's before you even think about cooked delights. She and Rick have done a fantastic job converting the original stables into bedrooms with old, olive-green stable doors opening onto an ivy-fringed courtyard. This year they have also added a self-catering studio accessed via an outside staircase onto a sundeck overlooking the vineyards and mountains. The garden suite overlooks the pool and, like Lily's cottage, seamlessly blends into the mass of plants that spread out beneath two enormous plane trees. And once you're suitably chilled there's a whole bunch of vineyards and restaurants to explore just next door.

Rooms: 7: all en-suite with either king, queen or twin beds with bath or shower or both; 1 self-catering cottage with 2 bedrooms, 2 showers, lounge & kitchenette; 1 self-catering studio with bath and shower.
Price: From R450 pp sharing. Singles on request.
Meals: Full breakfast included.
Directions: Follow M3 towards Muizenberg. Take Ladies Mile off-ramp. Turn L at traffic lights onto Ladies Mile and L at next lights onto Spaanschemat River Rd. Keep L at fork then turn L into Willow Rd and L into Chantecler Lane. The Stables is at the end on L.

Dendron

Shaun and Jill McMahon
21 Ou Wingerd Pad, Constantia
Tel: 021-794-6010 Fax: 021-794-2532
Email: stay@dendron.co.za Web: www.dendron.co.za
Cell: 082-4911-647 or 082-296-0691

(Quite) A few years ago, Shaun bought a Land Rover in Taunton (UK) and drove it here. Hardly odd when you see the place, now replete with relaxed family atmosphere, collie dogs and cricket pegs (or whatever they're called) on the front lawn. You get all the benefits of living the South African good life by default here. Green-fingered Jill genuinely loves having guests and her enthusiasm for life is evident in everything. The cottages are private in leafy, jasmine-scented gardens and have fully-equipped kitchens stocked with basics, a braai and stunning views to the mountains on the right and False Bay in the distance. Two cottages have terracotta-tiled or wooden floors and beds with Indian cotton throws - perfect for families. The other two are newly-renovated cottages with kilims, safari prints and plump sofas. All are fully serviced. Evening pool-side views at sunset and moonrise, helped along by wine from over-the-hedge Groot Constantia vineyard, will make you want to throw away the car keys and stay (which is exactly what Shaun did when he first clapped eyes on the place). When you are hungry, Jill will send you off there through the back gate and across the vineyards to the Simons restaurant for dinner. Return by torch- and moonlight. Dendron (GK=tree) is a small slice of heaven.

Rooms: 4: 2 cottages with 1 double and 1 twin with bath and shower; 2 cottages with twin, 1 with bath & shower, 1 with shower only. Serviced daily Mon - Sat.
Price: From R300 - R450 pp sharing. Singles on request.
Meals: Breakfast for first morning provided and afterwards if requested (R50 pp).
Directions: Fax on request.

Kaapse Draai

Annelie Posthumus
19 Glen Avenue, Constantia
Tel: 021-794-6291 Fax: 021-794-6291
Email: info@kaapsedraaibb.co.za Web: www.kaapsedraaibb.co.za
Cell: 082-923-9869

Annelie has been charming Greenwood Guide travellers since the very first edition and should be in the running for some sort of award for B&B brilliance. Relaxed, simple and beautiful seems to be the rule here. Her daughter is an interior designer and their talents combine to make the house a peaceful temple to uncluttered Cape Cod-style living. Neutral furnishings and white cottons are frisked up with pretty floral bolsters and country checks. Sunny window-seats are perfect for reading guide-books on the area and there are posies of fresh flowers in each room. I was lucky enough to stay with Annelie and once installed in my room, she invited me down for a soup later. She is a prolific gardener and you can walk (perhaps with Annelie's dogs) from the tropical greenery of Kaapse Draai, with its mountain stream, huge ferns and palms, into lovely Bel-Ombre meadow and the forest next door. From there it is a three-hour walk to the Table Mountain cable station. Porcupines come into the garden at night from the mountain (they love arum lilies apparently) and there are many birds too, including the noisy (and palindromic) hadedah. A grand old willow tree is what you'll park your car under. Delicious breakfasts are taken outside in the sunshine whenever possible. All I can say is – do. *Wine estates and Constantia shopping village nearby.*

Rooms: 3: 1 double and 2 twins with en-suite shower.
Price: R325 pp sharing. Singles R400.
Meals: Full breakfast included. Annelie sometimes cooks if the mood is upon her. But do not expect this....
Directions: Ask for fax or email when booking.

Klein Bosheuwel and Southdown

Nicki and Tim Scarborough
51a Klaassens Rd, Constantia
Tel: 021-762-2323 Fax: 021-762-2323
Email: kleinbosheuwel@iafrica.com Web: www.kleinbosheuwel.co.za

Who needs Kirstenbosch? Nicki has manipulated the paths and lawns of her own garden (which is pretty well an extension of the Botanical Gardens anyway - less than a minute's walk away) so that the views are not dished out in one vulgar dollop! Instead you are subtly led into them, with glimpses through mature trees (flowering gums, yellowwoods and camellias) and lush flower-beds. And finally your stroll leads you down to umbrellas on a ridge with Table Mountain and the Constantiaberg laid out magnificently before you and the sea distantly below. "Keep it plain" is Nicki's motto, so the upstairs bedrooms are simply white and all naturally endowed with garden views. The salt-water swimming pool is hidden deep in the garden and Klein Bosheuwel is the sort of place where you could just hang out for a few days. I was introduced to one English guest who had clearly no intention of going anywhere that day - the cat that got the cream! Or you can stay next-door at Southdown. With a small-scale Lost Gardens of Heligan on her hands, Nicki peeled back the jungle to find pathways, walls and, best of all, enormous stone-paved circles just in the right spot between the house and pool. Today the house is filled with surprises: zebra skins, porcupine-quill lamps, onyx lamp stands, a whole stuffed eagle, a wildebeest's head, a piano, two tortoises, deep carpets and couches, marble bathrooms and terraces off most rooms.

Rooms: 8: 1 twin en/s bath; 2 queens with en/s bath & sep' shower; 1 queen en/s large bath; 1 king with corner bath & separate shower; 1 twin & 1 king with en-s bath & shower. 1 self-catering cottage (2 bedrooms, 2 bathrooms, open-plan kitchen & lounge area).
Price: R565 - R630 pp sharing. Singles R830 - R930.
Meals: Full breakfast included. Other meals can be provided by prior arrangement.
Directions: Fax or website.

Lusthof Cottage

Judy Badenhorst
Rose Way, Constantia
Tel: 021-794-6598 Fax: 021-794-8602
Email: lusthof@mweb.co.za Web: www.lusthof.co.za
Cell: 083-412-3455

Everyone in the world seems to know Judy, whether through the Old Cape Farm Stall, from Buitenverwachting Wine Estate, from the Spaanschemat River Café, from her new and excellent Lucky Store restaurant in Stellenbosch... or in our case through obscure family links in Britain. You probably know her yourself. All her projects seem to be touched by magic and become social temples for the Constantia faithful. We spent our first two weeks in South Africa staying in her guest cottage in the garden and it was a terrible moment when we finally had to leave the nest and look after ourselves. The cottage, with cable TV, heaters for winter and kitchenette has doors onto its own patio where you can lie on sun-loungers or you can wallow in the pool admiring the flower garden. This can also be done from the comfort of your bed in the lovely new guest room adjoined to the main house. Judy is truly a maestro in the kitchen and literally everything that is made by her will be worth camping overnight for. You shouldn't choose Lusthof if you are after a fully-catered guest house with 24-hour service. But if you like to feel part of the furniture, and among friends, then this is the place for you. Mention must finally be made of Chebe, Judy's huge, shaggy, good-natured, lemon-loving bouvier (somewhere between a Scotty and a gorilla) - an integral part of the set-up. Chebe is a dog by the way. *Airport pick-up and car rental can be organised.*

Rooms: 1 self-catering cottage with 1 double room, kitchenette and full bathroom.
Price: R400 - R500 pp.
Meals: Breakfast and other meals on request with pleasure. Lucky Store restaurant is owned and run by Judy in Stellenbosch.
Directions: Ask for a map on booking.

Forest View

Pat Gardiner
20 Dalmore Road, Tokai, Cape Town
Tel: 021-715-1310 Fax: 021-712-6729
Email: forestview20@gmail.com
Cell: 082-745-4858

Such a pretty place that TV crews come to film here and newly-weds have their photos taken in front of the agapanthus. It's intimate too, this sweet little studio that sits just apart from the house and overlooks an abundant garden. Pat reeled out the names: hydrangeas, indigenous geraniums, drooping willows, spectacular cannas, the remains of arum lilies after the porcupines had finished with them (see her collection of quills)... and I took it all in hoping to improve my off-the-cuff horticultural knowledge. She leafs through her guest book and remembers every visitor individually, beginning with her first eight years ago. It's one of the reasons why guests tend to come back. They also love the simplicity of having just what they need. The kitchenette is well stocked, there's a writing table for postcards, wicker chairs for reading, a crisp white duvet to slink under and a sleeper-couch for any extras. We took tea on the little private balcony draped in shrub and flower, enjoying the bird-life and a splendidly trimmed lawn that dropped, by levels, past a once-in-vogue trompe l'oeil and a contemplative little pond to the garden gate below. Here, beneath a lushly-grassed and shaded arbour (shared with the neighbours), the Princess Kasteel stream trickles down from the golf and wine estates of Groot Constantia. There's no better breakfast seat this side of Table Mountain and you should choose at least one evening to braai by the large salt-water pool. Lanterns hang and the whole garden is lit by night.

Rooms: 1 studio flat with a queen double and shower en-suite.
Price: R500 - R700 for the studio per night. Self-catering: R600 for 2, R300 singles.
Meals: Full breakfast included. Health option available. Breakfast available at extra charge for self-caterers.
Directions: Take the Tokai exit (21) on the M3 heading toward Muizenberg, connecting with Tokai Road. Take the 2nd right into Lismore Avenue and then left into Dalmore Road.

Vygeboom Manor

Callie & Luli Hamman
14 Valmar Rd, Valmary Park, Durbanville
Tel: 021-975-6020 Fax: 021-976-5029
Email: info@vygeboomguesthouse.co.za Web: www.vygeboom.co.za
Cell: 083-270-4021

Vygeboom sits in the relatively sleepy suburb of Durbanville, twenty minutes from the centre of Cape Town, but there is nothing sleepy about this guesthouse. Callie, a prosthodontist and microlight pilot and Luli, an artist who has exhibited everywhere from Cape Town to the French Riviera (her silver elephants are famous), have merged their diverse talents to create a fabulous getaway. The house is awash with Luli's work, indeed there is a registered art gallery on the premises where both she and her daughter, Marie-Louise, an equally talented artist, exhibit. Each unique room has its own gigantic mural (Luli again), doffing the cap to Rubens, Matisse and Manet. Comfort, however, does not play second fiddle to artistic expression – beds are huge, bathrooms luxurious. Not to be outdone, Callie showed me his favourite part of the house. Wander outside past the braai area, follow the winding staircase down, duck and there I found myself in a dark, seductive wine-tasting room worthy of Bacchus himself. However, should you feel the need to adventure beyond the gates, any trip you desire, from boats to Cape Point, evenings at the theatre or tours of the Winelands, can be organized here. Also prisoners of the game of golf will find themselves embarrassed for choice: there are over five golf courses within driving distance. As Luli told me, "Just come, say what you want to do and it'll be done!" What more could you ask?

Rooms: 5: 1 double, 4 twins; 3 with en-suite bath, 2 with en-suite shower.
Price: R375 - R525 pp sharing. Ask about specials for families and groups.
Meals: Full breakfast included and barbeque dinners by arrangement.
Directions: Junction 23 N1, R302 north for 5km. Turn right into Valmar Rd.

Darling Lodge

Mathe Hettasch and
Suzie Venter
22 Pastorie Street,
Darling
Tel: 022-492-3062
Fax: 022-492-3665
Email: info@darlinglodge.co.za
Web: www.darlinglodge.co.za
Cell: 083-656-6670

A huge, wonderfully friendly Russian wolfhound pup going by the name of Galina is just one of Darling Lodge's many charms. Mathe, who is specifically a European (she's says she has lived in too many places to hail from just one country), came here by chance three years ago and instantly fell in love with the house. This emotion is manifest even at the front door, where a thick wired heart hangs around the knocker. The main house, whose oak floors were originally laid in 1832, is flooded with life and colour by an abundance of flowers brought down from Mathe's protea farm in nearby Hopefield. All the bedrooms are rich in light and colour too, with inviting canopies hanging over the beds and crisp white linens lying on top of them. Each room is named after a different local artist, whose work adorns the walls and is, by the bye, for sale. I would personally opt for Nicolas Maritz with its deep Victorian clawfoot bath. But it was the garden that finally stole the laurels, with its ancient pepper trees, fountain spraying water over blossoming roses and mass of lavender. Sadly I wasn't staying the night, for I could think of nothing better than sitting under a tree with a glass of wine from one of the five nearby vineyards and digging into a good book or, simply watching the industrious weaver birds, amongst others, as they built their nests. And Mathe's description of her breakfast extravaganza was also a matter of deep regret!

Rooms: 6: 2 queens, one with en-suite bath, 1 with en-suite bath and separate shower; 1 king with en-suite shower; 2 twin/doubles, one with en-suite shower and one with en-suite bath.
Price: R325 - R375 pp sharing. Singles on request.
Meals: Full breakfast included. Supper on request.
Directions: Enquire on booking.

Harbour View B&B

Marlene and Koot de Kock
8 Arum Crescent, Yzerfontein
Tel: 022-451-2615 Fax: 086-616-1363
Email: info@harbourviewbb.co.za Web: www.harbourviewbb.co.za
Cell: 082-770-3885

Protruding out on a fynbos-covered promontry, the sea seems to fill every window at Harbour View. The north-facing aspect means a continual influx of sunlight that brightens the fresh blues or oatmeal hues in each bedroom. "You can whale-watch from any bed in the house," Marlene tells me proudly and, as she is a keen birder, that's not the only watching to be had. There's an active fishing harbour alongside the property and personally I'd be content just gazing out all day at the boats as they come and go. Most mornings start with patches of mist bought up from the ocean and is the perfect time to place the day's first footprints on the 16-mile stretch of beach that runs by outside. Breakfast is a different event every day, the table decoration as changeable as the seascape it looks out on. I wondered if the ever-growing collection of wooden cats, an ongoing fad started and continued by guests, would ever make a table-top debut. "We grow crayfish in the garden," Marlene nodded and I followed her gaze. The 'lawn' at Harbour View is blue and white-crested and, if you want to pick some crayfish you just take your fishing net down to the pier. *Crayfish permits available at the local post office. The West Coast National Park is just 15 minutes away. Wind- and kite-surfing available in the area.*

Rooms: 7: 2 suites with own lounge area kitchenette and en-suite shower; 1 luxury/honeymoon suite with en-s shower and bath; 4 doubles, all with en-suite shower and shared lounge & kitchenette facility.
Price: R385 - R515 pp sharing for standard rooms. R460 - R620 pp sharing for suites. Luxury/honeymoon suite R575 - R750 pp sharing. Single supplement R290 - R400.
Meals: Full breakfast included. Kitchenette facilities in rooms for limited self-catering. Meals by prior arrangement.
Directions: On the R27 heading North from Cape Town take the left signed Yzerfontein. When arrive in village follow 'Harbour View' signs to front door.

Kersefontein

Julian Melck
between Hopefield and Velddrif
Tel: 022-783-0850 Fax: 022-783-0850
Email: info@kersefontein.co.za Web: www.kersefontein.co.za
Cell: 083-454-1025

Nothing has changed at Kersefontein since the last edition. Julian's convivial dinner parties are still a reason to book in on their own. And Julian himself remains a Renaissance man, described on his business card as 'Farmer, Pig-killer, Aviator and Advocate of the High Court of S.A.' He farms cows, sheep and horses on the surrounding fields, and wild boar appear deliciously at dinner. He also hires and pilots a six-seater plane and a flight round the Cape or along the coast is a must. He modestly leaves out his virtuosity as a pianist and organist and some of us trooped off one Sunday morning, braving a 40-minute sermon in Afrikaans, to hear him play toccatas by Bach, Giguot and Widor at the local church. When not eating, riding or flying, guests lounge on the pontoon, swim in the river or read books from Kersefontein's many libraries. Or they use the house as a base to visit the coast or the Swartland wineries, which are really taking off. The homestead is seventh generation and the rooms either Victorian or African in temperament, with antiques handed down by previous Melcks. You are fed like a king, but treated as a friend and I am always recommending people to go here.

Rooms: 5: 2 doubles, 2 twins and 1 separate 2 bedroom cottage.
Price: R410 - R530 pp sharing. No single supplements. Aircraft hire prices depend on the trip. Julian will also do fly/picnic trips out to various destinations.
Meals: Full breakfast included. Dinners by arrangement: R170 - R190 excluding wine.
Directions: From Cape Town take N7 off N1. Bypass Malmesbury, 5km later turn left towards Hopefield. After 50km bypass Hopefield, turn right signed Velddrif. After 16km farm signed on right just before grain silos. Cross bridge and gates on the left.

Farr Out B&B

Marion Lubitz and Deon van Schalkwyk

17 Seemeeusingel, Paternoster
Tel: 022-752-2222 Fax: 088-022-752-2222
Email: marion@madeinpaternoster.co.za Web:
www.madeinpaternoster.co.za Cell: 083-410-4090

The five-minute drive from Paternoster to Farr Out was not what I would exactly call far. But when you arrive in this sandy bushveld wilderness, you do feel pleasingly remote. Crunching up the glinting shell pathway came a very cheerful-looking Marion, who sat me down with an Englishman's best friend (an excellent cup of tea, of course). From the kitchen you can see across their indigenous garden and right out to sea. Earlier risers than me may catch some of the wildlife that comes by when it thinks no-one's looking. Deon showed me a picture he'd taken at five that morning of a duiker drinking right from their koi pond. After being in the air force for 26 years, Farr Out is now his playground, and the excitement has definitely not worn off. I would recommend joining him on a beach buggy excursion. I only had time for a little loop, but with a little wind in my hair, I really wished I could have packed the coolbox and gone out over the dunes. Rainy days are also covered, with a host of board games, including a much-loved thirty-year-old edition of German Monopoly. Rooms are modern, with televisions, stereos and some of the most exciting loo seats I have ever seen. Make sure you get a chance to spend a few minutes in the garden basket chair before you leave. Specially imported from Germany, it shelters brilliantly from the wind, allowing you to sit in peace, looking out over the dunes for an hour or ten. Oh yes, I'd recommend a lunch- or dinner-time braai. It's not often you'll get to eat one in a teepee, as you'll do here.... *German, English and Afrikaans spoken.*

Rooms: 3: 1 king, 1 queen and 1 family suite with 1 queen and 1 twin room. All with en-suite showers.
Price: R225 - R325 pp sharing. Singles on request.
Meals: Breakfast included. Cooked on weekends and public holidays. Otherwise full Continental. On request: 3-course braais for lunch/dinner from R140 pp. Picnic baskets from R130.
Directions: From Cape Town, take the R27 approx 125km to the R45, which passes through Vredenberg and continues 15km in the direction of Paternoster. Farr Out is situated at the far end of Pelgrimsrust - small holdings just before Paternoster on the LHS.

Hocus Pocus

Huibré Strydom
20 Kriedoring Road, Paternoster
Tel: 022-752-2660 Fax: 022-752-2660
Email: info@paternoster-villas.co.za Web: www.paternoster-villas.co.za
Cell: 083-988-4645

This neat, whitewashed, self-catering beach cottage is close to Paternoster Beach. The interior of the house is perfectly in keeping with its location: strung-together shells hang from the curtain rails, a sun-kissed kitchen table for cosy suppers and an intriguing wicker aviary, whose half-open door anticipates the return of its lodger. A sea-worn oar balustrade led me to the upstairs bedroom, where soft yellow cretestone walls and inviting linens continued the ocean feel and where French doors open onto your balcony and braai area. The real magician, however, is Huibré herself. Although this is strictly a self-catering cottage, with all the mod cons necessary for a peaceful weekend by the sea, she lives just next door and is there to help if you want her. Her excellent paintings adorn the walls and if you are VERY nice, she will be more than happy to help cook your crayfish or organize a day's fishing with the local fishermen. I certainly wouldn't blame you if you just felt like cozying up by the fire while you are here, ambling lazily up and down the beach every now and again to relieve some of the guilt. I did this and chanced upon the finest fish and chip store this side of Brighton. But should you feel a tad more energetic, there are the nearby Columbine and Groot Paternoster reserves, where you can admire the local floral and fauna. Hocus Pocus certainly does cast a few spells.

Rooms: 1 cottage: 1 double with en-suite shower and 1 twin with seperate shower room.
Price: From R850 for the cottage.
Meals: Self-catering.
Directions: Enquire on booking.

Paternoster Dunes Guest House

Gavin Sproule and Deon Van Rooyen
18 Sonkwas Street, Paternoster
Fax: 022-752-2214
Email: reservations@paternosterdunes.co.za
Web: www.paternosterdunes.co.za Cell: 083-560-5600

When I told GG guest houses in the area that I was staying at Paternoster Dunes for the night, the collective response was, "Oh, that's LOVELY." But 'lovely' simply doesn't do it justice. I was met by Gavin and escorted past the open-air courtyard with its tempting pool and daybed and shown to my room (named Vanilla). Gavin and Deon worked in interior design for ten years before swapping the big smoke for the salt breeze. If Vanilla was anything to go by – open-plan, huge bath with its own sea-facing window, equally huge stone-floored shower and king-size bed with plump pillows and Egyptian cotton - they were surely at the top of their game. But the best treat of all was my verandah, accessed through French doors. The ocean is less than ten yards away between grassy dunes and it was here that I decided to settle down and finish off my book of the moment. Clapping the covers together an hour later, I took my satisfaction up to the communal bar/lounge, with its panoramic ocean views, for a sundowner. The design throughout the house never jars and always excites. The walls are adorned with original artwork, from contemporary pastoral scenes to palette nudes, the lamp-shades are made from oryx antlers and the leather armchairs could have been found in a London gentleman's club. My egg and pastrami soufflé at breakfast was clear proof of fine cooking (dinners are also available). But by that time you would hardly expect anything less. More 'wow!' than 'lovely'! *Bikes are available for guests to use.*

Rooms: 5: 2 queen with en-suite bath/shower; 1 king/twin with en-suite shower, 2 queen with en-suite shower.
Price: R495 - R800 pp sharing. Singles on request.
Meals: Breakfast included. Light lunch on request. 3-course dinner from R150 pp.
Directions: From Cape Town take the N1 and then the R27 north following signs to Vredenburg to Paternoster (15km). At crossroads turn left then travel a full 1 km to the Columbine Reserve. Turn right into Sonkwas Street. It is No.18.

The Oystercatcher's Haven at Paternoster

Sandy and Wayne Attrill

48 Sonkwasweg, Paternoster
Tel: 022-752-2193 Fax: 022-752-2192
Email: info@oystercatchershaven.com Web: www.oystercatchershaven.com
Cell: 082-414-6705 or 083-267-7051

Sandy and Wayne, ex film and advertising people, do things in style and their guest house is a knock-out! The Cape Dutch house sits on the fringes of the Cape Columbine Nature Reserve, a spectacular, fynbos-covered, hand-shaped headland, bearing its lighthouse aloft like a nine-million-watt jewel. All along the coast and a mere 40 metres in front of the house knobbly fingers of grey and black granite merge into the sea and around the rocks there are secret white sandy coves where the dolphins come throughout the year. It is quite simply beautiful and I can assure you that the Oystercatcher is a haven by anyone's standards. Heave yourself out of that plunge-pool, off the rocks and away from the view (available from your bed) and head inside the house. The interior, with its white walls, untreated timbers and reed-and-pole ceilings, is intentionally blank-yet-rustic to showcase some exquisite pieces, such as a four-foot-high Angolan drum, some Malinese sinaba paintings (you'll have to come and see them if you don't know what they are), Persian rugs, art-deco couches, courtyards.... Just about everything is a hook for an eager eye. Beds and bedrooms too are bliss - trust me, I'm a professional. *There is now an intimate à la carte restaurant serving fresh crayfish from the bay. The chef was highly commended for the sushi and sashimi he prepared for the Japanese ambassador. Need we say more?*

Rooms: 3: 1 queen with en-suite bath and shower; 1 queen and 1 twin, both with en-suite showers. All rooms have private entrances.
Price: From R520 pp sharing.
Meals: Full breakfast included. A la carte menu in the evenings only, meals from approx. R190 pp.
Directions: From Cape Town take the N1 and then the R27 north following signs to Vredenburg. Follow signs straight through Vredenburg to Paternoster (15km). At crossroads turn left and travel a full 1km towards the Columbine Reserve. Turn right into Sonkwas Rd. It is No.48.

Villa Dauphine

David and Anne Dixon
166 Sandpiper Close, Golden Mile Bvd, Britannia Bay
Tel: 022-742-1926 Fax: 086-634-0397
Email: dadixon@mweb.co.za Web: www.villadauphine.com
Cell: 083-409-3195

The focus of Villa Dauphine is placed entirely on the bay, whose broad crescent passes not twenty yards from the stoep. Here you sit and peacefully beat out the rhythm of the waves. Two finned backs breached some 30 metres from shore, my first ever sighting of wild dolphins. David and Anne were unimpressed. The day before great schools of them had been leaping, frolicking, doing crosswords and playing chess right in front of the house. You can take boat rides out to cement the friendship and navigate the Berg River for bird-watching. The house is country cottage pretty, thatched and beamed with solid furniture, pots of fresh flowers, terracotta tiles, lots of whites and woods. Two atticky bedrooms are found up wooden steps, which lead from a flowery, sun-trapping, wind-breaking courtyard. The other is in the house itself. David is a vet and he and Anne are real bird enthusiasts. If you are too, they'll point you off to the Berg River (more than 190 bird species) but everyone must visit the beautiful West Coast National Park nearby (250,000 migratory birds and a stunning turquoise lagoon). Come here in spring and the countryside is carpeted in flowers. They appear out of nowhere and grow right down to the waterline. *Golf courses and excellent restaurants nearby.*

Rooms: 2 units: 1 suite with 2 double bedrooms with a shared bathroom (bath & shower); 1 twin with en-suite bath and shower.
Price: R300 - R350 pp sharing.
Meals: Full breakfast included. Other meals by prior arrangement.
Directions: From Cape Town take R27 to Vredenburg turn-off. Turn left to Vredenburg. At first lights, turn right to St Helena Bay. 10km to Stompneusbaai sign. Turn left. 17km turn left to Britannia Bay. After 2km, turn right at White Entrance to Golden Mile. Turn R & after 2nd speed bump turn left.

Oystercatcher Lodge

Luc and Sue Christen

1st Avenue, Shelley Point St, St Helena Bay
Tel: 022-742-1202 Fax: 022-742-1201
Email: info@oystercatcherlodge.co.za Web: www.oystercatcherlodge.co.za
Cell: 082-903-9668

You can't miss Oystercatcher Lodge. If you do, you'll end up in the sea. It's set right on the tip of Shelley Point, overlooking the full curve of Britannia Bay with its flocks of cormorants, pods of passing dolphins and wallowing whales (in season). Luc (smiley and Swiss) and Sue (home-grown, but equally smiley) are both from the hotel trade. After years doing a great job for other people deep in the Mpumalanga bushveld, they decided to work for themselves and made the move. Quite a change. Here on the West Coast the sea air has a salty freshness unlike anywhere else, the sun shines brilliantly on arcing white beaches and the crunching waves are a bottomless blue. A special spot indeed where the Christens' newly-built house juts out towards the ocean like the prow of a ship, a large pointy pool in its bows. Each of the six rooms, painted in calming sandy colours, looks across grassy dunes and beach to the sea. All have extra-large bathrooms. Breakfast feasts are served in the bar. If you're lucky Luc might summon some whales for you to view by blowing on his 'kelperoo' (a whale horn made out of seaweed!) as you munch on the Christens' 'special Swiss recipe' bread. For other meals there are restaurants nearby and, if you ask in advance, the ex-restaurateurs will do their best to cook up something scrumptious.

Rooms: 6: 4 kings, 2 with bath and shower, 2 with shower only; 2 twins with shower only.
Price: R375 - R530 pp sharing sharing.
Meals: Full breakfast included.
Directions: From R27 heading north turn L to Vredenburg. At lights turn R to St. Helena Bay. Turn L 10km on to Stompneusbaai. 17km on turn L to Britannia Bay. After 200m turn R at brown sign. Go through Shelly Point gate and continue right through to Shelley Point. Oystercatcher is at the far end.

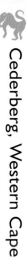

Boschkloof and Oude Boord Cottages

Mariet and Doempie Smit

Boschkloof, Citrusdal
Tel: 022-921-3533 Fax: 022-921-3533
Email: boschkloof@kingsley.co.za Web: www.boschkloof.com
Cell: 082-734-9467

We bumped along six or so sandy kilometres, past orchards of citrus trees and stumbled upon some sort of prelapsarian idyll! A private valley, cocooned in the Sneeuberg Conservancy, in the Cederberg foothills, flanked by sandstone mountains, its orange groves watered by a natural stream, the rocks and plants etched in hyper-real clarity by a setting sun. There are Bushman rock art sites, natural pools in the river to cool off in and hiking on mountain trails to be done from the house in the early morning and evening. We parked under an oak tree and were met by Mariet, her two small daughters and two large dogs. On return from a dip in the river we met Doempie and a glass of wine and were soon being treated to crayfish kebabs from the braai, seated under the oak with views up the kloof and a sensational tone to the air. Guests have a choice of staying in one of the original farmhouses (next door to the Smit's own original farmhouse) or in the newly-built, old-feel cottage hidden across the stream. Oude Boord (the new cottage) is beautifully set within the orange trees and, with only klipspringers as your early morning company, seclusion is complete. Although it is a self-catering arrangement the comparative proximity and openness of your hosts means you may as well be at a B&B, except with far more space and privacy. And the beds and baths? No time for detail - just trust me, they're spot on!

Rooms: 2 cottages each sleeping 6 with 1 double, 1 twin and double sofa-bed; all bedrooms have en/s bathrooms.
Price: R700 for the cottage for four people, per night. R100 for each person thereafter.
Meals: Fully-equipped kitchen - these are self-catering cottages. Mariet can provide breakfast materials for you by prior arrangement.
Directions: N7 to Citrusdal - turn into village, go left into Voortrekker Rd and right into Muller St (3rd turning on the right). Carry straight on. It becomes a dirt road. Follow it for 7km.

Rockwood Cottage

Brent and Nikki Mills
Rockwood Farm, Citrusdal
Tel: 022-921-3517 Fax: 086-607-5851
Email: info@rockwoodfarm.co.za Web: www.rockwoodfarm.co.za
Cell: 084-209-7150

Rockwood is an extremely beautiful protea farm in the Cederberg highlands 800 metres above sea level. Brent and his wife Nikki had just moved back from London, as I discovered over a delectable cheese lunch, to take over the farm and the cottage from Brent's parents and it was easy to see why they are happy to be back in the homeland. Both the main house and their large and lovely guest cottage have front stoeps that overlook a succession of dams, the hinterland channelled away for miles and miles by rugged sandstone mountains. The highest peaks of the Sneeuberg Conservancy are often covered with snow in winter. The guest cottage is cradled among giant rocks with the eponymous rockwood trees growing from beneath. And to the front, a story-book stream burbles past the stoep and oak trees there. A wide expanse of lawn leads to more treasure; two natural rock swimming pools are filled all year round by the river with fresh, drinkable water that cascades gently over the rocks. A sundowner in either of the pools allows you time to digest the magnificent view and feel properly smug. Behind this there is a deep gorge and waterfall, an idyllic world of water and rock (I couldn't resist a skinny-dip in the sweltering November sun!), full of wildflowers in season with many bush trails cut through natural gardens. Brent and Nikki will happily show their guests all there is to do on the property and in the region, still so unspoiled by tourism.

Rooms: 1 cottage with two bedrooms: 1 double and 1 twin sharing 1 bath/shower. Outside bedroom with 2 twin beds and ensuite shower.
Price: R550 - R750 for 2 people. R100 per additional person.
Meals: Self-catering. Restaurants are five minutes away.
Directions: From N7 into Citrusdal. At four-way intersection in centre of village straight over and up mountain for 7kms. Second white gates on the left.

Wolfkop Nature Reserve Cottages

Werner Rontgen
Wolfkop Nature Reserve, Citrusdal
Tel: 022-921-2255
Email: info@wolfkopreserve.co.za Web: www.wolfkopreserve.co.za
Cell: 083-775-0144

What better way to wind down after a long day's drive than sitting in your own jacuzzi, chilled Windhoek in hand, looking across a valley full of citrus orchards and rooibos fields, watching the sun sink behind the Cederberg mountains? And that was where I found myself on a hot spring evening while Werner, my convivial host, busied himself at the braai. I would have been just as happy, mind you, in one of the hammocks slung across the stoep, or singing happily and tunelessly to myself in the gorgeous outside shower. The two red-brick cottages are homely and simple. The main sitting room has a high, wood-beamed ceiling with deep, cushioned sofas and a big open fire, while the adjoining kitchen has all the mod cons you will need for a weekend away, including freshly-ground coffee. Both cottages even have their own small herb gardens on hand to help when you cook. Meanwhile, the two bedrooms are cool and welcoming with plump pillows, soft cotton sheets and spectacular views across the reserve. There are over 150 species of birds in the Wolfkop Nature Reserve and as Werner and I sat on the stoep, munching our perfectly-seasoned lamb chops, their various calls rang out of the dusk, eventually giving way to the sounds of the night and a sky full of stars. Waking early, I looked out across to the mountains and wished I had more time to head up and explore, but sadly the road was calling. I only hoped it would come full circle.

Rooms: 2 cottages: each with 2 twin/doubles with a shared bathroom and outside shower,
Price: R225 - R275 pp.
Meals: Breakfast is included. Lunch sandwiches or wraps R20 - R25, suppers from R50 or 6-course dinners R250 are available.
Directions: Enquire on booking.

Petersfield Farm Cottages

Hedley Peter

Petersfield Guest Farm, Citrusdal
Tel: 022-921-3316 Fax: 022-921-3316
Email: info@petersfieldfarm.co.za Web: www.petersfieldfarm.co.za
Cell: 083-626-5145

Hedley is an instantly likeable and funny host and Petersfield, his family farm (citrus and rooibos tea), ranges over the back of the mountain behind the main house, forming a huge private wilderness reserve. De Kom, an idyllic, simple-but-stylish stone cottage perched high in sandstone mountains will appeal to your inner romantic. This charming electricity-free cottage is lit by hurricane lamps and flares with gas for the stove, fridge and hot water. A private plunge pool with river stones at the bottom overlooks this secret valley with the Olifants River and purpling Cederberg peaks as a backdrop. And what a setting, guarded to the front by a citrus orchard, to the rear by craggy sandstone and looking deep and far from the stoep down the mountain. There is a secluded farm dam nearby (300 metres) to swim in or picnic by while watching nesting eagles. Or, 2km away, there is (electrified) Dassieklip Cottage, a sweet wooden mountain cabin secreted in its own kloof and reached down an avenue of oaks. It too has a plunge pool to cool off in and other mod cons such as fridge, air-conditioning, TV and CD player. This year sees the completion of a third cottage, Die Veepos. Built in the 'sandveld' style, the high bamboo-reed ceilings and cretestone walls will keep the house at perfect temperature and, along with the customary plunge pool and mod cons you can expect from Hedley's cottages, there is also an outside bath looking out across the Cederberg mountains. Bring your own food, although breakfast materials for you to cook can be provided. *Wood is supplied at no charge and pets also welcome.*

Rooms: 3 cottages: two with 2 bedrooms and one with 3.
Price: Week-nights: R450 for 2 up to R650 for 5/6. Weekends, public holidays, flower season (10 Aug - 10 Sept): R700 for up to 4 people, up to R800 for 5/6. Prices are per night for whole cottage.
Meals: Self-catering, but breakfast materials provided in the fridge by prior arrangement.
Directions: From Cape Town 4km after Citrusdal on your left on the N7 travelling towards Clanwilliam.

Oudrif

Bill and Jeanine Mitchell
Clanwilliam
Tel: 027-482-2397
Email: moondance@49er.co.za
Web: www.oudrif.co.za

Fifty kilometres of fabulous sandstone formations, dams and flower-covered passes lead you deep into the Cederberg Mountains and eventually to Oudrif, the perfect hideaway-getaway on the banks of the clear, clean, cool Doring River. I was met by my hosts Bill and Jeanine, who provided me with iced tea, before escorting me to my environmentally-friendly lodge where walls are slate and stone, roofs are straw bales and power is solar. My room was light-filled, with sofas to snooze on, but it was a hot day, so I donned my trunks and ran to the river for a dip. Plunging in, I heard the bark of the resident sheep-dog Bella, saw her jump over the rocks, dive in and swim up to me, stick in mouth, eyes pleading. So began an afternoon's game of fetch, swimming (and throwing) from bank to bank, pausing occasionally to lap up the sun on one of the many secluded beaches that line the river. All fetched out, I returned to change and headed to supper. The main house is the meeting point, library and supper room and I was quickly introduced to the other guests. Oudrif holds ten at full capacity, and evenings around the communal table can be very entertaining. After a laughter-filled evening and too much home-made bread (both Bill and Jeanine are master bakers), I headed off to bed. Well, in fact… eschewing the comforts of a lovely king-size double bed, I actually decided to sleep outside under an amazing starlit sky. This is a truly special spot.

Rooms: 5: All twin/double with en-suite shower.
Price: R600 pp sharing. Singles on request.
Meals: All meals and walks included.
Directions: Enquire on booking.

Mount Ceder

André and Jaen Marais & Thomas and Rachelle Marriott-Dodington
Grootrivier Farm, Cederberg, Koue Bokkeveld
Tel: 023-317-0848 Fax: 023-317-0543
Email: mountceder@lando.co.za Web: www.mountceder.co.za

Do not lose confidence as you rumble along the dirt roads that lead through the Koue Bokkeveld Nature Conservancy to this secluded valley - it's always a couple more turns. Finally you will arrive in the very heart of the Cederberg, dry sandstone mountains rising all around you in impressive dimensions. You will be given the key to your new home and drive off along half a kilometre of sand track to one of three fantastic rustic stone cottages. The river flows past the reeds and rock right by the cottages, clear, deep and wide all year round. You can swim and lie around drying on flat rocks. Birds love it here too. I imagine sitting out on that stoep, on those wooden chairs, looking at that view, beer or wine in hand… a piece of heaven, as they say. You can either self-cater or you can eat at André and Jaen's restaurant back at the lodge. There are a few other cottages nearer the lodge, which are fine, but you must ask for the stone cottages, which are in a league of their own. A pristine slice of unspoiled nature, cherished by a very knowledgeable Marais family who will help with Bushman rock art, horse-riding and fauna and flora. Do not reach for your red pen by the way… that is how you spell ceder (in Afrikaans) and that is how you spell Jaen! *Serious hiking is possible from here. Daughter Rachelle will happily take you horse-riding.*

Rooms: 3 river cottages with 3 bedrooms each.
Price: R1,200 – R2,200 per cottage per night self-catering (cottage sleeps 6).
Meals: Meals on request, breakfast R50, dinner R95 (extra for wine).
Directions: From Ceres follow signs to Prince Alfred's Hamlet/Op-die-Berg, up Gydo Pass past Op-die-Berg. First right signed Cederberge - follow tar for 17km then straight on on dirt road for another 34km into a green valley.

Villa Tarentaal

Graham and Brandi Hunter

Tulbagh
Tel: 023-230-0868 Fax: 023-230-0101
Email: grahamjhb@gmail.com

Graham is Mike and Christine's son and, having had an ample sufficiency of life as a highway patrolman in America (put away your Hollywood movie stereotypes, Graham is charming!), he and his wife Brandi (also charming) have returned home to take over the family business. Over a rich and spicy Cape Malay lunch, I was reassured that the feeling of the place will stay just the same, despite the change of hands. "People come here for the comfort and view," smiles Graham, "we just like to think of it as an upgrade." This being the renovation of the two original cottages and the building of a third. All the cottages now have open fireplaces, the bathrooms have been stylishly modernized with new tiling and top-of-the range showers and new ceiling fans have been installed for those hot summer nights. But fans of Mike and Christine needn't worry. Christine will still be there to offer her therapeutic massages and Mike, known locally as the 'Man of the Mountain', will still be there to enchant you with his passion for his pristine garden: wisteria and grapevines spider up the mustard-coloured house; an orgy of colour is provided by the roses; and the lawn is so well-kept it would make the green-keepers of Augusta, well… green with envy. Guests are not the only ones who flock here in numbers. You'll also witness an abundance of bird life, including Egyptian geese, fish eagles and probably a brace of mating blue crane.

Rooms: 3 cottages: 1 queen/twin, en-suite shower; 1 twin & 1 double, separate bath/shower room & fireplace; 1 double (with extra single on request) & sofa-bed in lounge, separate bath/shower room. Satellite TV in both cottages.
Price: R350 pp sharing B&B. R320 pp sharing self-catering. R375 singles.
Meals: Full breakfast included in B&B.
Directions: N1 from Cape Town to exit 47 Wellington/Franschhoek/Klapmuts turn-off, left onto R44 via Wellington. Follow for approx 1 hour to Tulbagh. Straight through town, 1.2km on left.

De Oude Herberg Guest House

Leslie and Jane Ingham

6 Church St, Tulbagh
Tel: 023-230-0260 Fax: 023-230-0260
Email: ingham@mweb.co.za Web: www.deoudeherberg.co.za
Cell: 072-241-4214

Leslie was a pilot in his former life and his last foray skywards saw him flying aid missions for the UN throughout Africa. Thankfully for a man who has lived with his head in the clouds, Jane's always been there to bring him back down to earth, and now she has brought him (luckily for us) to Tulbagh, to run a guest house. But this is not just any old Tulbagh guest house. Church Street is the town's - and indeed one of the Wineland's - most historic streets and De Oude Herberg is a jewel in the crown. Beautiful on the outside in a thatched-roofed and gable-fronted kind of way; venerably ancient on the inside in an everything-wobbles-when-you-walk-through-the-room kind of way. From the resplendent, flower-filled, basket-carrying bicycle, to the ribbon-tied towels in the rooms, and a complimentary decanter of local port by every bed, you know a lot of thought has gone into making this place special. I'd plump for the four-poster with access onto the verandah, but if you like your privacy, then go for one in the separate building out the back, which has its own access and small courtyard garden. But it will take a strong will not to be tempted back out for a drink and some lively chat at the bar. And as if that's not enough, Pielow's, an excellent gourmet restaurant, is situated on the premises.

Rooms: 4: 2 queens, 1 with additional small room attached to sleep child; and 2 twins. All have air-conditioning and baths with shower above.
Price: R350 pp sharing. Singles + R100.
Meals: Full breakfast included. Lunch and dinner available in restaurant from September to April. A la carte menu.
Directions: On reaching Tulbagh turn L at the Shell garage into Church Street and R at the church. Next door to information centre.

Old Oak Manor

Salomé and Willem Gunter
7 Church Street, Riebeek Kasteel
Tel: 022-448-1170 Fax: 022-448-1083
Email: cafe-felix@intekom.co.za Web: www.capestay.co.za/old_oak_manor

Under long shadows of a languorous summer afternoon, the unhurried tunes of French jazz and a pair of perfectly black cats were wafting through Old Oak Manor's rustic central courtyard. I sensed that, but for its Cape Dutch exterior, the place would be aptly suited to life tucked away deep in rural France. Salomé is a well-known interior designer with a passion for the country, and it shows. Nods to traditional French country design are everywhere. Iron four-posters, creaky wooden dressers, over-sized lamps, old travel cases and the odd slipper bath have all been salvaged from auctions and each room is as original as the next. Whilst Salomé has set the tone, it's the three resident cats, Felix, Julius and Misty, who set the pace. Laid-back calm is the order of the day and there's not a hint of don't-touch-me fussiness, not even in the impressive open-plan loft above the café. Once you've dragged yourself out of the deeply comfy sofa and away from the fancy TV, there's an expansive wooden table for reading (that obligingly doubles up as a cocktail bar), and a giant bathroom with wall-to-ceiling cupboards to chuck the bags into; and a free-standing bath hovered over by an inquisitive oak through the window. Out by the kitchen garden hidden by sprouting vines is another cosy nook, a little Grecian-esque whitewashed cottage. Riebeeck provides plenty of distractions: you can climb its mountain, or visit its olive farms and wineries, its antiquey shops and cosy garden cafés. Otherwise, cool off in the fresh-water pool, stretch out on a lounger and snooze.... Felix, Misty and Julius would be the first, second and third to approve.

Rooms: 6: 4 doubles in the house, 2 with en-suite shower and bath, 2 with en-suite shower; 1 double with extra single bed with en-suite shower in the separate guest cottage; 1 double and 1 twin in the open-plan loft with en-suite bath, living area & DSTV.
Price: R350 - R450 pp sharing for rooms in the main house and for the guest cottage. R1,500 per night for the loft.
Meals: Full breakfast is incl'. Restaurant serving breakfast, lunch and dinner. Closed on Mondays.
Directions: Details on website.

White Bridge Farm

Paul and Peppi Stanford

Wolseley
Tel: 023-231-0705 Fax: 023-231-1836
Email: stanford@kingsley.co.za Web: www.whitebridge.co.za
Cell: 082-578-7881

Snow on the mountains, sun blazing down on the deck, water roaring through the river below... Mother Nature could not do a better job of showing off other people's wares if she tried (I wonder what they're paying her). White Bridge Farm is a working fruit farm, and if you come at the right time of the year (Nov-Aug), you can work on it too, or at least have a tour. Guests, Peppi tells me, are always amazed when they spot the citrus, pears and plums sporting labels of the well-known supermarket brands of home. But I have to say it would take more than a succulent satsuma to tear me away from one of the two log cabins (there is a more conventional larger cottage too). They really are about as rustic as rustic can be. Bamboos have been cut down to line the walls, trees have been felled to build the tables, even old drainpipes have been used as a bright idea for lighting! Nothing has gone to waste, and you won't want to waste your time here either. With walking, fishing, swimming and bird-watching this is a nature-lover's paradise. A family of otters liked it so much, they decided to stay at White Bridge, and you cannot get a better recommendation than that. For those who like their home comforts (and breakfast with the family hand-made for them) Peppi also has a cosy room next to her house. Guarded by two wooden cheetahs, it has its own fireplace and outdoor seating area within the main garden. Just 90 minutes from Cape Town, the perfect distance for a break from the city.

Rooms: 3 units and 1 B&B bedroom: 2 log cabins with 1 double and 1 twin in loft space, shower only; 1 cottage with double and bunks, and a double futon in lounge, full bathroom; 1 double in the main house with full bathroom.

Price: R450 - R550 per unit per night for self-catering. R200 for B&B pp sharing. Singles on request.

Meals: Meals can be arranged if requested. Restaurant and coffee shop less than 1km away.

Directions: At the junction of the R43 from Worcester and the R46 between Tulbagh and Ceres.

Bartholomeus Klip Farmhouse

Lesley Gillett
Elandsberg Farm, Hermon
Tel: 022-448-1820 Fax: 022-448-1829
Email: bartholomeus@icon.co.za Web: www.bartholomeus.co.za
Cell: 082-829-4131

Heavenly scenery cossets this Victorian homestead in its lush gardens and stands of oak and olive. The wall of the Elandsberg Mountains rises up from the game reserve, reflected in the dammed lake by the house. Here guests can have breakfast on the balcony of the boathouse before heading out for an excursion onto the wheat and sheep farm. You are also taken on late-afternoon game drives to see the zebra, a variety of Cape antelope, buffalo, quaggas (a fascinating experiment to reintroduce an extinct variety of zebra), eagles, flocks of blue crane... and the largest world population of the tiny, endangered geometric tortoises. But just to be out in such nature! The spring flowers are spectacular and there are more than 850 species of plant recorded on the property. Back at the homestead you can cool down in the curious, round, raised reservoir pool, sit in chairs on the stoep; or, if you have more energy, bike off into the reserve or go on guided walks in the mountains. Staff are very friendly, food is exceptional and a reason to stay on its own (and all included in the price). I recommend splashing out on at least two nights. A great place indeed and very popular so book ahead of yourself if possible. *Closed June - July and Christmas.*

Rooms: 6: 2 doubles and 3 twins, all with bath and shower. New self-catering cottage that sleeps 8 with 3 doubles and bunk beds.
Price: R1,250 - R2,020 pp sharing. Singles + 20%. Includes meals & game drives. Self-catering cottage: R560 - R930 pp, 0 - 3 free, 4 - 15 half price.
Meals: Coffee and rusks, brunch, high tea, snacks & sundowners and 4-course dinner included.
Directions: From CT take N1 towards Paarl. Exit 47, L at stop. Continue turning L onto R44 signed Ceres. Follow for 30km, pass R46 junction signed Hermon, take next R signed Bo-Hermon. Gravel road for 2km. Bartholomeus Klip signed to L - 5km.

Bovlei Valley Retreat

Lee and Abbi Wallis
Bovlei Road, Wellington
Tel: 021-864-1504 Fax: 021-864-1504
Email: info@bvr.co.za Web: www.bvr.co.za

When I arrived at Bovlei Valley, catching a waft of baking lavender cookies and the sound of a beautiful aria drifting in from Abbi's kitchen, I was eager to get inside. It didn't disappoint. I settled onto a squishy sofa near the large fireplace, sipped my tea and tried to resist the sweet-smelling biscuits she had just pulled from the oven. Abbi did a degree in hospitality, and it shows. Her open-plan kitchen is part of the impressive-yet-cosy main room, with high ceilings, sofas and a dining area, and she does all her home-cooking there while chatting to guests. Next door is a comfy TV room with a DVD library and every board game you could possibly desire for a rainy day. But on sunny days it will be hard to leave the pool, whose depths are constantly filled with fresh water from the lips of a rather fetching bearded stone head. And if that wasn't enough to keep you there, a plump, well-stocked honesty fridge under the verandah, catering for every poolside whim, should do the trick. The whole place is a working guava, grape and lavender farm, with its own boutique winery, Dunstone. All you can see for miles are plants and mountains. The highlight of the converted stable rooms is the Lavender Suite, with a luxurious four-poster, and a view over – you've guessed it – waving fields of lavender. Guava Cottage has its own mini-vineyard and stoep, and lies in front of – wait for it – the guava plantation. A granite-topped kitchen with dishwasher and generous range mean you can really self-cater in style… that is, if you can stand a night away from Abbi's home-cooking. The cottage even has its own solar panel-heated pool, garden and braai area.

Rooms: 6: 5 in converted stables: 2 with 1 queen and 1 single bed and shower; 3 with queen beds and bath/shower. Also 1 cottage with 1 double and 1 twin. All have en-suite bathrooms.
Price: Stable suites: R400 - R600 pp sharing, singles R500 - R700. Guava Cottage: R600 - R900 pp sh.
Meals: Breakfast, freshly-baked cakes and complimentary wine included. Dinner available by prior booking.
Directions: See website for detailed directions.

Oude Wellington Estate

Rolf and Vanessa Schumacher

Bainskloof Pass Rd, Wellington
Tel: 021-873-2262 Fax: 088-021-873-4639
Email: info@kapwein.com Web: www.kapwein.com

There seems to be so much to catch the eye even as you rumble along the 800-metre paved and cobbled road to Oude Wellington: vineyards on both sides, ostentatious peacocks, geese and hadedas, pet ostriches peering over a fence. And that afternoon four pregnant alpacas that had just arrived all the way from Australia were to be added to the menagerie. Rolf and Vanessa are clearly the hospitable types (how else could ostriches find a home on a winery?). It took them two years to restore the whole estate to its former glory as a wine-grape farm. Four rustic double rooms are in the original farmhouse (built in 1790) with high, thatched ceilings, low pole beams, whitewashed walls and yet underfloor heating and air-con; the other two are in the more modern main building (well, 1836!), along with the beautiful farm kitchen with old-fashioned pots, pans and irons, billiard room and bar, and a terrace overlooking the vineyards, where breakfast is served in the summer. There is a partly-shaded pool off to the side of the main house, a brandy still in the barn, and handily on the premises is a restaurant popular with the locals (always a good sign). Guests are also invited to watch wine-making taking place at the right time of year. "We farm and dine and love company," say Rolf and Vanessa in their brochure!

Rooms: 8: all doubles with en-suite Victorian baths.
Price: R300 - R350 pp sharing. R375 singles.
Meals: Full breakfast included. Restaurant on premises, open seven days a week.
Directions: Turn into Church Street (Kerkstraat) in Wellington which becomes the Bainskloof Rd (R301/3). 2.5km out of Wellington on right-hand side follow brown signs to Oude Wellington.

Kleinfontein

Tim and Caroline Holdcroft

Wellington
Tel: 021-864-1202 Fax: 021-864-1202
Email: kleinfon@iafrica.com Web: www.kleinfontein.com
Cell: 072-108-5895

An evening leg-stretch with Tim proved the perfect antidote to a long and stressful day on the road. Guided by a German alsatian, an almost-labrador and an incredibly energetic fluffy white thing we strolled past Jersey cows, through a shaded stream and between rows of sunlit vines. Kleinfontein is just an hour from Cape Town at the foot of the Bainskloof Pass and the Holdcrofts are delightful hosts. And this truly is home hosting at its finest; they'll eat and drink with you, show you their farm and even have you out there clipping the vines or feeding the horses if you show willing (and riding them, too, if you're saddle-hardened). In fact there's enough to keep you busy here for days, from hiking in surrounding mountains and cellar tours galore, to the leisurely delights of a good book beneath magnificent oak trees, or a wallow in the pool in Caroline's fabulous garden. She is of Kenyan stock and Tim's British, but they spent years in Botswana and over a superb supper we washed down tales of Africa with home-grown cabernet sauvignon. Like me you'll stay in a roomy, restored wing of the thatched Cape Dutch farmhouse with poplar beams and reed ceilings. Like me you'll sleep like a baby. And, like me, you'll wake to breakfast on the verandah with fresh butter and milk, newly-laid eggs and honey straight from the beehive. Sound idyllic? Well, it is. *Closed June and July.*

Rooms: 2 suites, both with sitting room. 1 with en-suite bath and shower, 1 with en-suite bath with shower overhead.
Price: R1,100 - R 1,400 pp sharing. Single supplement + 20%. Includes all meals, drinks and laundry.
Meals: Breakfast, tea/coffee tray, picnic lunch and 4-course dinner included in the price.
Directions: Directions are down dirt roads so map can be emailed or faxed.

Roggeland Country House

Gordon Minkley
Roggeland Rd, Dal Josaphat Valley, Paarl
Tel: 021-868-2501 Fax: 021-868-2113
Email: rog@iafrica.com Web: www.roggeland.co.za

The highlight of a stay at Roggeland must be the food! All reports glow with praise: served different wines to taste pre-dinner, an opportunity to chat to other guests and one of the family members; then four mouth-watering courses each with a different wine specially chosen to accompany it. Vegetarians will be particularly happy and you are guaranteed that neither meals nor wines will ever be repeated during your stay, such is the quality of service here. The house is an 18th-century Cape Dutch homestead with large, thick-walled rooms - sometimes huge - with a variety of original features: beam and reed ceilings, thatch, antique furniture. The dining room, for example, is in an old kitchen with its original grate and cooking implements. Some bedrooms are in the main house and some are separate from it, all are lavender-scented and none let the side down. Character abounds: floors slope, beams curve and attractive bright-coloured walls are often uneven with age; and there are always fresh flowers and home-made soaps in the rooms. Roggeland is family-run and the atmosphere is friendly and caring as a result. Farmland and mountains surround the property and the Minkleys will happily organise evening rides on horseback into the foothills. Wonderful hospitality and very good value too. *Children by arrangement. Mountain biking.*

Rooms: 10: either twins or doubles, all with en/s bathrooms, 8 with baths and showers, 2 with baths and showers overhead.
Price: Seasonal R520 – R1,120 pp sharing. Single supplement in high season + 50%.
Meals: The highlight is a 4-course dinner with a different wine at each course and wine-tasting, all included in price. Full breakfast too. Lunches on request.
Directions: Approximately 60km from Cape Town, take exit 59 onto R301 towards Wellington. After 8km on R301 turn right at Roggeland sign. Follow sign onto gravel road for 1km.

Palmiet Valley

Frederick Uhlendorff
Palmiet Valley Estate, Sonstraal Rd, Klein Drakensberg, Paarl
Tel: 021-862-7741 Fax: 021-862-6891
Email: info@palmiet.co.za Web: www.palmiet.co.za

Frederick has scoured not just this land but several in his relentless quest for fine things. There's hardly a nut or bolt in the place that isn't antique - even the loos, showers, free-standing baths and wooden wash-stands are Victorian, not to mention the aged safes and old-school slipper bed pans (that thankfully no-one ever uses!). But this is not a museum, despite the long history of the farm - Palmiet was one of the first to be established outside Cape Town in 1692. Guests come here for the luxury and the romance of the vineyards and mountains that stretch out and up from the old farm. One four-poster bed is positioned so that you can wake up and watch the sun rise over the mountains without moving your head. The beautiful gardens are interwoven with cobbled paths and peppered with numerous dreamy spots to be peaceful in. Herbs are harvested and transformed into fresh herbal teas or added to shady lunches by the pool. In summer, candlelit dinners are held under the oaks and are as sumptuous as everything else, with top chefs employed to cook exclusively for residents. With so much character and reflection upon old-fashioned values, it's no wonder this place is a hot-spot for weddings. But you don't need to be married or coupled to enjoy it as I, a happy singleton, discovered.

Rooms: 13: 1 honeymoon suite en-suite bath/shower, 1 luxury suite, 1 presidential suite, 6 standard twins/doubles en-suite, 2 single rooms (with double beds) en-suite bath or shower. 2 self-catering cottages with bath & sep' shower.
Price: Single rooms R985 or R1,245 for a couple. Standard R925 pp sharing. Honeymoon R1,245 pp sh. Presidential R1,945 pp sh. Luxury suite/Cottages R2,095 per night. 20% off in winter.
Meals: Full breakfast included. Lunches on request. 3-course set dinner R275 pp.
Directions: Away from Cape Town on N1, take exit 62a (Sonstraal Road), turn 1st L, over cross-roads, Palmiet Valley on L. Airport Transfer R500.

Paarl Rock Suites

Udo and Carmen Mettendorf
64 Main Street, Paarl
Tel: 021-863-3192 Fax: 021-863-3192
Email: info@kapinfo.com Web: www.kapinfo.com

Based on the 'golden mile' of Paarl, ballooning-mad Udo and Carmen are pioneers in placing this "rough-diamond-of-the-Winelands-region" on the map. Golden mile basically means the 'old bit' of Paarl, a historic rush of Victorian houses, tree-lined with old oaks. The original house of Paarl Rock Suites dates back to 1860 when it featured as part of an old wine estate. Although split into various scattered sections now, you still get to look out over the Mattendorfs' rock garden and succulents and onto regiments of vines beyond. Paarl Rock sits stately in the background, a massive granite feature thrown up by volcanic activity and asking to be biked to, walked around and explored; while the swimming pool in the foreground has been craftily crafted to reflect it. Udo and Carmen themselves are an open book of local knowledge. Originally from Germany, they came and explored as tourists, gathering all the best inside information and wrapping it up with a big ballooning bow for their guests. You'll have to book fast if you want to bag a corner of the basket, however, as ballooning has seriously taken off (if you'll excuse the pun) since Udo and Carmen madly (some believed) introduced it a few years ago. I loved the luxury apartment, which caught my eye with leather sofas, spa bath and marble-topped kitchen, but all three qualify as the perfect base to negotiate all the Cape has to offer. *Bikes available for use.*

Rooms: 3 self-catering apartments: 2 with 1 double bedroom and 1 with 2 bedrooms, a double and a queen.
Price: R460 - R750 for the flat. Prefer a min of 3-night stay. ONLY OPEN OCTOBER TO MAY!
Meals: Fully self-catering, but many restaurants within easy walking distance.
Directions: On the N1 from Cape Town take exit 55 leading into Paarl Main Street. Follow until you reach no. 64 on your left, opposite number 113.

Belair

Janet Plumbly

Suid Agter-Paarl Rd,
Paarl
Tel: 021-863-1504
Fax: 021-863-1602
Email: info@belair.co.za
Web: www.belair.co.za
Cell: 082-572-7062

A straight 300-metre drive up two narrow strips of weathered red brick, past roaming gangs of guinea-fowl and rows of vines, takes you to Belair, a beautiful guest house on its own farm beneath the round dome of Paarl Mountain. The view from the doorstep (and the garden and pool) across the valley towards Franschhoek and the Groot Drakenstein is spectacular… and it is rather lovely inside too. Steps lead up from a large threshing-circle style driveway into the hallway and open sitting room, which mixes antique furniture with comfy sofas and bookshelves bursting with swashbucklers. Behind is the bright breakfast conservatory, which looks onto a rose-filled garden. Janet's light but stylish touch is in evidence everywhere at Belair, from the terraced gardens to the bedrooms themselves, each with its own distinct character. All the rooms are wonderful, but the two new luxury suites, complete with fireplaces, open-plan baths and deep Flokati rugs, are sumptuous! The honeymoon suite has a deck overhanging the rose garden with a double daybed on it, while the other suite has a patio area with a swing couch. From the house, it's a short walk up to the dam where birdlife abounds among the reeds (look out for buzzards when it all goes quiet), a great spot for a sundowner. For the more energetic, Paarl Mountain Nature Reserve is further up the hill, and there are lots of golf courses nearby. *Cape Town Waterfront is also only 35 minutes away and there are great restaurants in Paarl. Bikes for hire.*

Rooms: 6: 2 doubles & 2 double rooms with sitting rooms and air-con, all have en-suite bathrooms with bath and separate showers; 2 new luxury suites with downstairs sitting room and bedroom/bathroom upstairs.
Price: R300 - R700 pp sharing. Singles on request.
Meals: Full breakfast included.
Directions: On Suid-Agter Paarl Rd off R101 (next to Fairview Wine Estate).

Eensgevonden Vineyard Cottages

Sally and Douglas McDermott
Near Brandvlei Dam, Rawsonville/Breedekloof
Tel: 023-349-1490 Fax: 023-349-1490
Email: info@eensgevonden.co.za Web: www.eensgevonden.co.za
Cell: 082-829-8923

Bumping through vineyards of chenin blanc and merlot grapes, I came across the national monument Eensgevonden, the oldest Cape Dutch farmhouse in the Breede River Valley and home to Sally and Doug. We chatted under the shady fingers of a giant oak tree, planted nearly three centuries ago on the orders of Cape Governor Simon van der Stel, sampling a glass of the local wine cellar's finest. The sun was setting, drenching the distant mountains in pink and pouring light into the valley of creeping, curling vines. Along with four other staff, the couple hand-tend and harvest their grapes before sending them off to Daschbosch wine cellar. The farm itself is part vineyard and part natural fynbos – Sally is the scourge of all alien species! A short walk from the farmstead, the spotlessly clean self-catering cottages are surrounded by an indigenous garden. My favourite was Sunbird with its white sheets and duvets, terracotta flooring, wood fire and vases of cut herbs. In the evenings, the couple often join guests for sundowners. The property has fantastic, well-marked hiking trails across the rugged 400-hectare/1,000-acre reserve with stunning views in all directions. Keeping an eye out for klipspringer, honey-badger and the very occasional Cape leopard, the less energetic can amble up the path through sand-olives and proteas, to a natural, crystal-clear mountain rock pool. When summer temperatures reach 30 degrees, you'll be glad to plunge into its cooling waters!

Rooms: 3 self-catering units: 2 with a queen and twin room with 1 bathroom with bath and shower and 1 with a shower; 1 unit with a single room and a queen room, 1 bathroom with shower.
Price: R250 - R350 pp sharing.
Meals: Self-catering. Breakfast in basket with home-made muesli & muffins is available as extra. Cooked dinner or vacuum-packed meats provided on request. Good restaurants nearby.
Directions: Off the N1 between Rawsonville & Worcester. Full directions given on enquiry.

Fraai Uitzicht 1798

Karl and Sandra Papesch
Historic Wine and Guest Farm with Restaurant, Klaas Voogds East (Oos), Robertson/Montagu
Tel: 023-626-6156
Fax: 023-626-5265
Email: info@fraaiuitzicht.com
Web: www.fraaiuitzicht.com

'Fraai Uitzicht' means 'beautiful view' in Dutch - no idle promise as it turns out. The 17th-century wine and guest farm is four kilometres up a gravel road in a cul-de-sac valley ringed by vertiginous mountains. People come from far and wide for the well-known restaurant and the seven-course *dégustation* menu is basically irresistible. Matched with local wine, it features salmon trout, springbok carpaccio, beef fillet with a port wine jus and topped with onion marmalade and decadent Dream of Africa chocolate cake. Shall we just say I left with more than one spare tyre in the car. You could also be entertained by a Xhosa choir who give performances every other Wednesday night. Where to sleep is not an easy decision as you are spoilt for choice. A few cottages take it easy in the garden, each comfortable and pretty with impressionistic oils and views of the mountains, while others offer you masses of character with metre-thick walls and timber interiors; my favourite was the loft bedroom in the eaves. Or opt for one of the garden suites with their own entrances and balconies. Make sure you take a peek at the wine cellar - guests have first option on the (uniquely) hand-made merlot. I can't count the number of recommendations we had pointing us here. *Restaurant closed June to August. Limited menu available for guests.*

Rooms: 8: 4 cottages, 2 with 2 bedrooms (1 queen & 1 twin), 2 with 1 bedroom (queen); 4 suites, 2 with king, 2 with queen, all en/s shower.
Price: Cottages are R750 pp. Singles R1,120; Suites are R480 pp. Singles R750.
Meals: Continental breakfast included. R30 extra for English. Lunch and dinner available on premises.
Directions: On R60 between Robertson & Ashton. Approximately 5km from Ashton and 9km from Robertson, Klaas Voogds East turn-off, 4km on gravel road, turn-off to left.

Ballinderry Guest House

Luc and Hilde Uyttenhove-Van Damme

8 Le Roux Street, Robertson
Tel: 023-626-5365 Fax: 023-626-6305
Email: info@ballinderryguesthouse.com
Web: www.ballinderryguesthouse.com Cell: 073-301-6616

It's easy to forget you're in the centre of town once the black gates of Ballinderry slide shut behind you. Robertson is growing and with forty wineries in the surrounding area the villa is perfectly placed for exploring them. Luc and Hilde successfully extracted themselves from the rat race in Brussels to come and "...relax?" I suggested. "I didn't come here to retire, I came here to work," says Luc laughing. And work they do, right around the clock to keep their guests entertained. Hugely welcoming and very enthusiastic about their new venture, they are continually trying things out, moving things around and picking up designer bits from Cape Town. A favourite is the 'wooden' coffee-table, actually made of fibreglass, so strokably smooth it has become known as the 'cuddle table'. There's a tidy fusion of modern contemporary pieces; weaved, leather armchairs, coloured-glass light sculptures mixed with classic wooden antiques that have been in the family for years. This theme continues with the bedrooms: some modern with black leather chairs and smart wooden floorboards; others are classic with grand old beds and woollen blankets. Ballinderry has all the mod cons while still feeling like a cosy house centred around the dining area. The evenings buzz with guests enjoying a feast inside or a drink beneath the patio's thatched canopy. Here, before the winding garden begins, candlelight flickers across the pool and glass lanterns sway in the breeze.

Rooms: 6: 2 queens, 1 with shower, 1 with bath & shower; 1 king with shower; 1 king/twin bath & shower, 1 twin with shower, 1 Garden Suite with bedroom, living room & bathroom (king + bath + shower).
Price: R325 - R560 pp sharing. Singles on request.
Meals: Full champagne breakfast included. 3-course set menu on request.
Directions: Coming from Cape Town/Worcester, turn left at KFC into Paul Kruger Street. Go straight for 1km until you see the museum. Turn right into Le Roux Street.

Mallowdeen Gardens

Rita and Wim van de Sande
Klaasvoodgs West, Robertson
Tel: 023-626-5788 Fax: 086-509-6764
Email: info@mallowdeen.com Web: www.mallowdeen.com

Driving down a long avenue of olive trees coiled in sunshine, I could have been in the hot heart of southern Spain. Rita and Wim, emerging from their traditional Cape Dutch farmhouse, have the greenest of visions for their little bit of joy caught between the Langeberge mountains and South Africa's finest vineyards. Apparently the smell of rotting tomatoes was overpowering when they first took over, but now all that is cleared and replaced instead with herb and vegetable gardens and an apricot orchard gently fanned by swaying elephant grass. They have grand plans to install a Japanese garden and already the canna flowers are the most vivid of reds. Three rondavels, a little way from the main house, face each other across a portly figure-of-eight swimming pool. One is a breakfast room where you sit at neat tables and chairs (if not outside on the terrace) all hand-made locally or, more unusually, cupped inside giant, hand-shaped thrones. The other two cottages are simple and good. Brush aside a fly-curtain and relax into the earthiness of the floors, walls and a maze-like partition into the bathroom. Ornaments like a miniature baobab tree hint at travels around Africa, where Rita and Wim discovered they had left their hearts on return to Holland. Bird-lovers may prefer the more private flat in the main house, which is close to the dam and from its vine-strangled courtyard the views are of one tree in particular where "a lot happens" around 5 in the morning. *Carpe Diem*.

Rooms: 3 units: 2 cottages (king/twin with full en-suite bathrooms), 1 flat (twin/king with en-suite shower).
Price: R385 pp sharing.
Meals: Full breakfast included. Excellent restaurants.
Directions: 7km from Robertson toward Ashton. Take Klaasvoodgs West turning on the left onto dirt road. Mallowdeen Gardens is 1.5km on the right.

Lekkerwijn

Wendy Pickstone

Groot Drakenstein, Franschhoek Road,
Franschhoek/Groot Drakenstein
Tel: 021-874-1122 Fax: 021-874-1465
Email: lekkerwijn@new.co.za Web: www.lekkerwijn.com

Lekkerwijn (pronounced Lekkervain) is a 1790s Cape Dutch homestead with a grand Edwardian extension designed by Sir Herbert Baker. You would probably have to pay to look round if Wendy didn't live there. It positively creaks with family history. You can tell when one family have lived in a grand house for generations - all the furniture, fittings and decoration look so at home. This is not some country house hotel nor some converted annexe. You share the house fully with Wendy, whose family have lived here since the late 19th century - unless of course you would prefer the privacy of Coach House Cottage. My strongest impressions are of the central courtyard with its gallery and cloister, the yellowwood floors and beams and the towering palms planted by Wendy's grandfather, the informal taste of the nursery bedroom, a wonderful breakfast... and Wendy herself, who is full of character and together with her management team, so caring of her guests.

Rooms: 6: 5 either doubles or twins, all en-suite. 1 single. 1 self-catering cottage for couples either alone or with children.
Price: Seasonal R750 - R950 pp sharing. Quotes for singles on request. Minimum stay 2 nights. Special offers on occasion.
Meals: Full breakfast included for B&B. You can self-cater in Coach House cottage and breakfast in the courtyard is an optional extra. Other meals can be provided by prior arrangement.
Directions: On R45 at intersection with R310 from Stellenbosch (after passing Boschendal), alongside the Allée Bleue entrance walls.

Cathbert Country Inn

Ann and Robert Morley

Franschhoek Rd, Simondium, Franschhoek
Tel: 021-874-1366 Fax: 021-874-3918
Email: info@cathbert.co.za Web: www.cathbert.co.za
Cell: 082-414-0604

Ann and Robert have a complete set of correct attitudes, as far as we are concerned: they have purposefully kept Cathbert's small (only eight rooms), "so we get to know our guests"; it's smart without going over the top and yet totally relaxed; and the food is a major focus. Bedrooms have views over a reservoir, farmland, vineyards, and the Simonsberg Mountains loom behind the house. Guests can walk up Kanonkop from Cathbert, a hill from which they used to signal to ships out at sea. You sleep in chalets with open-plan bed/sitting rooms and are refreshingly simple in style (and well-equipped with towelling bathrobes and other welcome luxuries). Each chalet has its little front garden where you might be honoured with a haughty visit from one of the resident peacocks, whose home this really is. Ann spends her day between reception and the kitchen where she is *maestro* - (set) menus are based on what she finds freshest around her. Her food is truly delicious, beautifully presented (only to residents) - 'modern' without being *outré* - and a real pull for Cathbert's burgeoning fan club. Robert, meanwhile, acts as (and *is*!) the charming and knowledgeable sommelier and host.

Rooms: 8 suites: 2 standard, 4 luxury, 2 executive. All with en-suite bath and shower. All king-size/twin beds. All air-conditioned.
Price: R575 - R825 pp sharing. Singles on request supplement +50%.
Meals: Full breakfast included. Set menu 4-course dinner, R210 pp (except on Saturdays and Sundays).
Directions: From CT take N1, take exit 47, turn right at end of ramp, over 4-way stop, left at next road towards Franschhoek. Pass Backsberg Wine Estate. At the stop just before railway crossing turn right onto private tar road. Follow for 2.5km.

Les Chambres

Bill and Sandy Stemp
3 Berg Street, Franschhoek
Tel: 021-876-3136 Fax: 021-876-2798
Email: gg@leschambres.co.za Web: www.leschambres.co.za
Cell: 083-263-4926

So much to take in even as I ambled up the garden path towards the house: the palm tree, reputed to be the tallest tree in the village; the herb garden spilling over with basil, rocket and tomatoes - that stone bench would be the perfect spot to make some progress with a paperback, I noted. Venturing further, I found irises, agapanthus and roses all laid out in bloom upon bark-strewn flowerbeds. And finally the house, a verandah-fronted Victorian gem, with Bill, Sandy and Archie (a cat) and Frank (another cat) forming a reassuring welcoming committee. Refreshed with a cool drink, I was shown through to the breakfasting patio where goldfish and koi waft prettily about in a stone pond and French doors provide easy access to the continental-style buffet: fresh fruits and cereals, home-made granola and bread. Cooked options might include poached eggs on English muffins, or 'Eggs Benedict', or scrambled eggs with smoked salmon-trout. Ze bedrooms of ze title are furnished in a mix of the antique and the contemporary with mahogany dressing tables and wicker bedheads while the bathrooms have travertine tiles, roll-top Victorian baths and separate showers. All rooms have air-conditioning and underfloor heating ensuring tip-top comfort whenever it is you stay. Private courtyards are available to two rooms, red-tiled with whitewashed walls and an overhanging orange tree. There is much to enjoy cloistered behind these walls, not least the heated swimming pool.

Rooms: 4: all king-size extra-length doubles or 2 twins, and all en-suite bath and shower.
Price: R395 - R625 pp sharing. R595 - R940 singles.
Meals: Full breakfast included.
Directions: From R45 drive through village of Franschhoek and turn left into Berg Street just before monument.

Akademie Street Guesthouses

Katherine and Arthur McWilliam Smith
5 Akademie Street, Franschhoek
Tel: 021-876-3027 Fax: 021-876-3293
Email: info@aka.co.za Web: www.aka.co.za
Cell: 082-655-5308

The parade of flowers and stepping-stones through citrus trees, fig trees, rose bushes and bougainvillaea made a beautiful winter's afternoon even brighter. The airy cottages, which sit detached within the flower arrangements, open out onto private stoeps, gardens and even swimming pools. Vreugde, meaning 'joy', is a garden suite for two that has a neat kitchenette in an alcove and a sofa on the terrace. Oortuiging is a restored 1860s cottage for three that retains the old Cape style with antiques throughout. Uitsig, the newest suite, is a stylish addition to the guesthouse, with a private balcony that looks out over the Franschhoek mountains. And Gelatenheid is a luxurious villa with, again, a private swimming pool and a wide wrap-around balcony. At the end of the balcony, suitably screened by tree-tops, is an outdoor, repro Victorian bathtub in which you can soak while gazing out at the mountain views… then wrap up in a towel from the heated bath rail. Inside, an expansive open-plan studio is home for just two people (although there's space enough for a four-bed house), with high wooden ceilings, Venetian blinds and French doors… a decadent holiday home. As full as a full breakfast can be (including boerewors - a type of SA sausage if you really didn't know) is served under the vines at the homestead. Katherine and Arthur - he was formerly Mayor of Franschhoek and they are both sooo nice - are easy smilers and happy to help with any day-tripping tips.

Rooms: 4 cottages: Vreugde: king, or twin on request, en/s bath and shower; Oortuiging: 1 king and 1 single, both en/s bath and shower; Gelatenheid: 1 king and en/s bath and shower; Uitsig: 1 king, or twin on request, en/s bath and shower.
Price: R1,000 - R3,000 per cottage. Singles on request.
Meals: Full breakfast included.
Directions: From Cape Town take N1 then R45. Akademie St is parallel to main road in Franschhoek, two streets up the hill.

Auberge La Dauphine

Anne Stone and Dan McCluskey

Verdun Road, Franschhoek
Tel: 021-876-2606 Fax: 021-876-4754
Email: guests@ladauphine.co.za Web: www.ladauphine.co.za

As I drove down the long gravel driveway bordered by vines, taking in the breathtaking Franschhoek mountains, I was pretty sure I was going to enjoy Auberge la Dauphine. And the feeling was confirmed as I stepped from my car and was welcomed by a cheery and umbrella'd Anne, dogs in tow and whisked inside for a welcome pot of very good, fresh coffee. Anne and her partner Dan moved here from London three years ago and have very much made it their home. Dan takes great delight in chatting with the guests over breakfast, and his conversation is so entertaining and the breakfasts so huge, you may well be happy just sitting, eating and enjoying his company. Fortunately the rooms are also lovely: warm pastel colours, high ceilings and king-size beds. Named after various grapes, try Merlot, a suite with views over both the vineyards and an Arab stud farm (and yes, you can ride there). Or sample Shiraz, with its rich reds, four-poster bed and Victorian slipper bath. The rain subsided and I was shown the property. We headed through a flowering plum orchard, climbed twenty steps and there I found the amateur fisherman's dream; a private dam full of carp, next to which stands an elegant gazebo, ideal for the evening sundowner. Admiring the views across the valley and wishing I had my rod with me, we talked - and laughed - the afternoon away. "We're basically perfect, wonderful, gorgeous people," Dan informed me. How true!

Rooms: 6: 2 suites; 1 family suite; 2 standard rooms; 1 cottage. All rooms have en-suite bath and shower.
Price: R350 - R550 pp sharing. Singles on request.
Meals: Full breakfast included.
Directions: Will send with booking form or see website.

The Map Room

Jo Sinfield
Cabrière Street, Franschhoek
Tel: 021-876-4229
Email: bandoola@mweb.co.za Web: No website yet but please email for more comprehensive details and photos. Cell: 072-464-1240

A treasure hunt for the key led me past stands of aloe vera and a trophy mountain sheep that had wandered down from the green slopes of the Franschhoek valley. Normally Jo will meet you in person to introduce you to his very modern and uplifting self-catering cottage, on the last remaining dirt road in Franschhoek, that brings a little New York cool (even though he's English) to the pretty heart of the winelands. Left of the entrance a spiral staircase ascends through the ceiling, with the bedrooms spreading over the ground floor. The master suite with its huge bed, inventive use of milk pails, faded safari chairs, open bath of sultan-pleasing proportions and en-suite wet room. But upstairs is where it all happens as you emerge through the floor into a wonderfully sociable living and kitchen area. This is blessed by an endless dining table, backed on one side by a curving wall seat and on the other by wicker chairs. Here you can put yourself to work cooking on a smart hob, all the while bemoaning your idle companions who will be lounging about on sofas in front of the flat-screen TV or pouring over the eponymous maps or library of classic movies whilst waiting for their dinner to arrive. Better, let someone else do the cooking, fold open the glass-panelled doors, park yourself on the terrace with a glass of chardonnay and gaze out over the vineyard whence it came and the rugged mountain views. Outstanding walks include Rochelle's Peak for a dramatic picnic and some of South Africa's most renowned chefs ply their trade not five minutes away. *Book well in advance.*

Rooms: 1 self-catering cottage with 1 king with full en-suite. (Two rooms on request.)
Price: R1,300 per night for two. R1,600 for four.
Meals: Self-catering. Excellent restaurants.
Directions: Drive into Franschhoek on the R45, turning right at Reservoir St. and then at T-Junction at the end of the road, turn right onto Cabrière St, a dirt road. The Map Room is the house on the right corner at the end of the road.

The Garden House

Barry and Annette Phillips
29 De Wet St, Franschhoek
Tel: 021-876-3155 Fax: 021-876-4271
Email: info@thegardenhouse.co.za Web: www.thegardenhouse.co.za
Cell: 083-340-3439

Annette and Barry (who also run the local newspaper - *The Franschhoek Tatler*) have fully immersed themselves in village life since their impulsive holiday decision to leave London in '01 and buy their Cape Victorian house. I felt their enthusiasm from the moment I arrived. Seeing the restaurants and wineries while driving round in Barry's classic 1951 Citroen (the one with the enormous headlights), I could see why Franschhoek is known as the food and wine capital of South Africa! And the Garden House, originally called Belle Vue, just an easy walk from the main road but with views across the valley to the mountains beyond and an abundant garden (with a larger-than-usual swimming pool), well deserves both names. Guests stay in the air-conditioned and stylishly decorated cottage with its original wood-beamed bedroom and large bathroom with under-floor heating. Larger groups can overflow into a pretty guest room in the main house where the lovely double bed, being Victorian, is "only suitable for very friendly couples." Come morning, Barry took me on a rigorous ride on a mountain bike – he keeps two for guests – while Annette prepared a smoked trout breakfast for our return. Village folk talk and I had already heard about Annette's local trout treat. While many of her guests go with Annette to a nearby 'informal settlement' to feed the cats and dogs, she can also arrange fishing, horse-riding, hiking and tennis nearby and give you ideas for day trips. Internet access and a baby cot (at R50 per day) are available. Lovely, down-to-earth people.

Rooms: 2: Cottage Room: 1 queen with en-suite bath and separate shower; Main House Room: 1 standard double with en-suite bath and shower overhead.
Price: Cottage Room: R350 (winter - with a light breakfast served in the room) - R500 (October through April) pp sharing. Main House Room R350 (summer only).
Meals: Breakfast included plus complimentary drinks in room and sundowners.
Directions: N1, then R45, then, as you come into Franschhoek, turn left into de Wet St just before the canon and go up the hill. The Garden House is on R.

Plum Tree Cottage

Liz & John Atkins

Excelsior Road, Franschhoek
Tel: 021-876-2244 Fax: 021-876-2398
Email: plumtree@kleindauphine.co.za Web: www.kleindauphine.co.za

The setting could not be more perfect. A sanctum of blooming plum-blossom, vineyards and oak trees spatter dappled shadows as they rock gently in the breeze, while magnificent mountains rise steeply from the Franschhoek valley. The Plum Tree Cottage balcony is the perfect spot to soak up all this serenity. Having run B&Bs for many a year, Liz and John know exactly what people want, and with this newly-built cottage they deliver it in spades. Entirely self-contained (it even has its own separate orchard-lined driveway), it allows you the space to do your own thing. This may be in the elegantly-paved courtyard, cooling off in the invigorating plunge pool, or popping out to the restaurants and wineries in Franschhoek, itself just pip-spitting distance away. The interior is a calming refuge in blues and whites, much like the roses and lavender outside. With each room sharing the magnificent view, you won't know where to put yourself.... I'd choose the corner bath and peek through the oaks at the Arab horse stud behind. By now, Liz will be busy clothing its clotted-cream-coloured walls with wisteria, roses and any other creepers she has creeping around for when she runs out of space in the garden: "I just send the plants up the walls." Perfectly tranquil and delightfully quaint... a proper English-style country cottage.

Rooms: 1 queen with en-suite bath and shower. Mezzanine floor accessed by Swedish ladder (so sensibly made its almost impossible to fall off) can sleep two children (over the age of 12).
Price: R250 - R375 pp sharing. For additions (up to 2) R100 pp. Singles R600.
Meals: (Strictly!) self-catering.
Directions: Drive through Franschhoek and turn right at the monument. After 1.3km turn left into Klein Dauphine, then follow separate drive to the right for Plum Tree Cottage.

Nooks Pied-à-terre

Lesley and Kevin Dennis
6 Haumann Street, Franschhoek
Tel: 021-876-2338
Email: nookspied-a-terre@hotmail.com Web: www.nookspied-a-terre.co.za
Cell: 082-398-3477

After years of work, Lesley and Kevin finished their perfect home only to be called away to America. Well, their loss is our gain... and boy is it a gain! To describe this as self-catering would not do it justice – this is a personal palace. The couple left their home in the hands of old friend PJ, who was smiling when she met me at the historic church round the corner. She does everything from stocking the fridge to giving you a mobile ready-loaded with every local number you could want - even hers. Now that's what I call dedication! The second I entered the double-height doors I could see that there were no design compromises: from the turquoise glow of the chef's fridge to the cobalt blue of the mosaicked pool, it is sensational throughout. The back wall of the main room slides away to create a fully open-plan route to your garden, complete with lemon trees, brightly-coloured walls, a delicious pool and an enticing-looking outdoor shower. But it was one of the mezzanine floors that caught my eye: an entertainment area with leather armchairs and every shiny bit of machinery a gadget magpie could ask for. The master bedroom, with its air-con/heating unit, electric-blue bed-head, en-suite underfloor-heated bathroom with free-standing bath and open-plan shower is truly, well... masterful. And that's not to say that the second bedroom is plain. With Chinese black-lacquered fitted wardrobes and opulent fur bedspread they're both idyllic spots to end a wine-soaked evening in SA's gourmet capital.

Rooms: 2: 1 king with en-suite full bathroom; 1 king with own adjacent bathroom & large shower.
Price: Winter (May to October 2008) from R1,250 per night (for 2 sharing) to R1,450 per night (for 4 sharing) for the villa. Summer (Nov 2008 to April 2009) from R1,750 per night (for 2 sharing) to R2,080 per night (for 4 sharing) for the villa.
Meals: Caterers/picnic baskets available by arrangement.
Directions: From Paarl/Stellenbosch, as you enter Franschhoek, take second turn on left into Uitkyk St (signed to Chamonix). Nooks Pied-à-terre is on the left on the corner of Haumann St & Uitkyk.

L'Auberge Chanteclair

Bob and Leslie Maginley
Middagkrans Road, Franschhoek
Tel: 021-876-3685 Fax: 021-876-2709
Email: chanteclair@mweb.co.za Web: www.chanteclair.co.za
Cell: 083-376-9913

The sun had its hat firmly glued on when I stepped from my car at Auberge Chanteclair and all I could hear was birdsong. The flower garden, fruit trees, vineyards, mountains, swimming pool and the vine-shaded breakfast patio all purred in bucolic bliss. The house was built in 1910-ish, but it has since been transformed into the impressive colonial-feel country house it is now, with its thick white-washed walls, old timbers and sash windows. All the bedrooms are large and cool with vases of fresh flowers, carefully-chosen antiques and immaculate white bathrooms. One has French windows out onto the verandah and mountain views from the bed. The reed-ceilinged Studio in the garden has a curtain that separates the bedroom from the sitting room, where there is a wood fire and piles of logs. Vine Cottage also has its own sitting room and fireplace as well as a private vine-covered stoep. Both Bob and Lesley (hoteliers in a previous life) are bird-watching enthusiasts, and can tell you about all their visiting species, from the paradise fly-catcher to the hoopoe. But no specialist knowledge is needed to enjoy the cacophony of birdsong that greets you on the lake. Bob and Lesley are natural hosts and evenings are whiled away in the sitting room, talking to guests over a glass of good local wine. Or take a drink (and Bute the golden lab) to the top of the farm at sunset for the view.

Rooms: 6: 3 doubles, 1 twin, 2 cottages with double beds. All en-suite.
Price: R485 - R695 pp for the Studio and main rooms. R1,150 - R1,600 for Vine Cottage. Singles on request.
Meals: Full breakfast included. Can organise gourmet picnics.
Directions: From airport: take the N2, followed by the R300 and N1. Then take the R45 through the village and turn right at the Huguenot Memorial. Chanteclair is first on the left, 1 kilometre up a gravel road.

La Petite Providence

Ana and Andy Higgins
Middagkrans Road, Franschhoek
Tel: 021-876-4790 Fax: 021-876-4898
Email: info@laprovidence.co.za Web: www.laprovidence.com
Cell: 072-245-7607

Through gates framed by palm trees, down an immaculate fir-tree-lined drive, I rolled up to the picture-perfect cottage, La Petite Providence. I thought I'd entered a film set. A fountain was shooting silver spray into the sun from an enormous duck pond, teeming with excited birds waiting to be fed. I was greeted by Ana, who excitedly pulled back some of the reeds to reveal mother ducks sitting patiently on their eggs. Ana is wonderfully eccentric and always busy. She spends half her life in Spain running an olive oil farm (working 8 to 10 hours a day in the fields - she loves it) and half her life here working on the house and nurturing a delicious cabernet sauvignon, amongst a dozen other things I couldn't keep track of. The Cottage and The Mews Flat are stunning and it was no surprise Ana used to be in fashion. The Cottage has lots of space, filled with enormous gilt mirrors, silk throws from Pakistan, oak dressing tables, huge beds and lamps that sway in the breeze provided by fans. The Mews is furnished in bold dark and red colours and, although wacky and ambitious, it works beautifully. A brown leather chaise longue sits at the end of an enormous carved four-poster bed and both cottage and flat are full of original art, much of it by well-known artists. There's not a wall that hasn't been carefully considered and after a glass of wine in their kitchen I persuaded her and Andy to give me a tour of their own house too!

Rooms: 2: La Petite Providence has 2 kings, 1 with en-suite shower, 1 full bathroom, full kitchen and lounge area; The Mews Flat has a 4-poster king with full en-suite bathroom, lounge, open balcony and kitchen.
Price: La Petite Providence is R1,250 pp for 2 people sharing, R1,000 pp for 3-4 people sharing. The Mews Flat is R750 pp, max 2 people. Only available 1st Nov - 1st May.
Meals: Breakfast provided.
Directions: Please find directions on the website.

Clementine Cottage

Malcolm Buchanan

L'Avenir Farm, Green Valley Rd, Franschhoek
Tel: 021-876-3690 Fax: 021-876-3528
Email: lavenir@iafrica.com Web: www.clementinecottage.co.za
Cell: 082-320-2179

Running late with my mobile battery dead, I was touched to find Jef waiting expectantly for me just beyond the low-lying bridge that marks the entrance to L'Avenir Farm. He kindly guided me through the orchards of plums and clementines to meet Malcolm, who runs this 21-hectare, family-owned, working fruit farm. Jef, by the way, is a boerboel, as loyal to Malcolm as Robin is to Batman. In retrospect, my timing was perfect: the sun was setting behind the mountains that frame the Franschhoek Valley and from the stoep of Clementine Cottage, looking out over the pool and the vineyard beyond, the sky was stained a deep red. The only sounds I could hear, as I enjoyed a most welcome cold beer with Malcolm and his folks, were the frogs croaking contentedly in the dam that forms the centrepiece of the farm. If you find the pool too confining, a few lengths of this dam should satisfy any Tarzanesque impulses you may harbour. Being only 3km from the village I was able to enjoy a fine meal at the legendary Topsi's, before returning to the biggest bed I've ever had the pleasure of sleeping in. Recently refurbished in the original farm cottage style, Clementine Cottage has everything you could desire from pool, braaing area and satellite TV to large, stylish en-suite bedrooms.

Rooms: 1 cottage: 1 double with en-suite bath and shower and 1 twin with en-suite bath and shower.
Price: 1st Oct - 31st Apr: 2 people sharing R600 pp per night, 3 people R500 pp, 4 people R450 pp; 1st May - 30th September: 2 people sharing R550 pp, 3 people R450 pp, 4 people R400 pp. Minimum stay 2 nights.
Meals: Self-catering, but many restaurants nearby.
Directions: From Franschhoek Main Rd driving towards Franschhoek Monument turn R. Drive for 2km. Turn L up Green Valley Rd (Clementine Cottage signed). Turn L up 1st gravel rd (also signed) Drive over bdge onto L'Avenir, thro' orchards, pass shed on L, Cottage 150m further on R.

Natte Valleij

Charlene and Charles Milner

R44 between Stellenbosch and Paarl, Klapmuts
Tel: 021-875-5171
Email: milner@intekom.co.za Web: www.nattevalleij.co.za
Cell: 079-037-4860

Come and lose yourself in the depths of this wild and fecund garden - or do I mean jungle? Ancient trees such as the rare gingco (the oldest in South Africa, once thought extinct), several 200-year-old oaks and a wealth of growth besides keep the pool, 'moon gate' and old brandy stills secreted in their midst. Guests stay in the simple B&B room next to the main house, its verandah festooned with grandiflora, and eat a breakfast in this most lovely of Cape Dutch homesteads (pictured above), built in 1775. If the weather's fine then you eat out on the patio under its cooling roof of vine. Or you can take one of the cottages lost down garden paths. Vineyard Cottage (pictured below), with direct access to the swimming pool, is the oldest building on the property, its original 1714 reed ceilings still intact. While Cellar Cottage is the most recent addition at 'Nutty Valley', small, cute, rustic, perfect for couples. Walks are in all directions up mountains and into surrounding vineyards. Or guests are welcome to enter the park (the entrance gate is just 50m from Vineyard Cottage) where at the last count 23 wildebeest, 25 eland, 30 springbok, 4 bontebok, 3 kudu, 2 oryx and 10 zebra (among others) can be seen. Come for great charm from house and hosts alike. *Local bird-watching tours with Charles are a speciality and Charles's son is now making wine on the property. Well-positioned on the Stellenbosch and Paarl wine routes. Self-catering available in the cottages.*

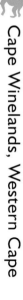

Rooms: 3: 1 B&B room, double with en/s bath; 2 cottages (self-catering): Cellar Cottage sleeps 2 (plus 2 kids' beds); Vineyard Cottage sleeps 6 (3 bedrooms and 2 bathrooms).
Price: B&B R280 pp sharing. Rates for the cottages (i.e. NOT per person) per night depending on number of people and length of stay: R400 - R950.
Meals: Full breakfast included in B&B and an optional extra in cottages.
Directions: From Cape Town take N1 Exit 47. Turn right onto R44. Farm 4km on left.

The Beautiful South Guest House

Katarina and Peter Stigsson

4 Hospital St, Stellenbosch
Tel: 021-883-8171
Email: enjoy@thebeautifulsouth.de Web: www.thebeautifulsouth.de
Cell: 072-545-3072

The genial answer-phone message informs you that Katarina and Peter are 'probably out buying lovely things for your breakfast'. They probably are too! This is a special meal at The Beautiful South, with a promise of something different every morning, always home-baked bread, muffins, scones, tomato-mozzarella toast and such specials as 'Fruity Djibuti' from the buffet bar. At weekends, not wanting to miss out on their own handiwork, the Stigssons join their guests at the feasting table. It is here that excursions into the winelands and the surrounding hills are plotted and restaurants are suggested for the evening. The house is quaintly thatched and whitewashed, with wooden windows and the surrounding garden with its mature trees and large pool is directly accessible from each of the bedrooms. While outside is all rustic cottage, inside the emphasis is on style, modernity and function: clean lines, natural materials, modern fittings in bathrooms and high-quality orthopedic beds. A waist-high wall is all that separates the oval, free-standing bath from the sleeping area in the Desert Rose room with its sandstone-tiled floor; while the Sunset Room, with its lime-washed floor and walls, boasts a private wooden terrace. Hosting comes only too naturally to Katarina and Peter.

Rooms: 9: 7 doubles, 4 with en-suite bath or shower, 1 with private shower room opposite; 2 family suites with en-suite bath or shower.
Price: R250 - R420 pp sharing.
Meals: Breakfast included with new 'special' every morning.
Directions: From N1 or N2 take turn-off marked to Stellenbosch. On entering Stellenbosch turn into Merriman Street. After white pedestrian bridge turn 2nd left into Bosman. Take 1st right into Soete Weide. Next left into Hospital Street.

Glenconner

Emma Finnemore

Jonkershoek Valley, Stellenbosch
Tel: 021-886-5120 Fax: 021-886-5120
Email: glenconner@icon.co.za Web: www.glenconner.co.za
Cell: 082-354-3510

Looking up at the imposing mountains, which rise on both sides of the property, and surrounded by lush vegetation - including all that wild strelitzia and agapanthus - it's almost impossible to believe that you're just six kilometres from Stellenbosch. Such a spectacular location. Sit with a glass of wine on whichever stoep belongs to you for the night and watch the lowering sun paint the mountains a deep pink. You don't need to do any more than this to lift the spirits by many notches. There are three simple, country-furnished sleeping locations to choose from: the homestead with its four-poster bed, Victorian bath and English country feel; Oak Cottage, with its cosy fireplace, pale blue beams and terracotta tiles, and a patio enclave that crouches beneath a looming mountain and gazes upon Emma's indigenous garden; and lastly the Studio, also a separate cottage with an open-plan bedroom, quaint stripey sitting areas, small kitchenette and second bedroom (with the best in-bed view of the lot). A round, spring-water-fed swimming pool sits directly in front of the homestead and a tan-coloured river is a little further away for paddling, picnics and otter-sighting. And horses graze peacefully on the luminous green grass in the paddocks. If all this is not enough for you, the staggering Jonkershoek Nature Reserve is just down the road with some of the best hiking in SA, from 2-hour to 2-day walks. *Trout-fishing, horse-riding and mountain-biking all available nearby.*

Rooms: 3: 2 self-catering cottages: the Studio has double, twin & private bathroom; Oak Cottage has double, twin & single room with shared bathroom & a shared shower in outside unit; 1 double room in the homestead.
Price: The homestead B&B R420 pp sharing. Self-catering cottages are from R295 pp. Under 12s half-price, under 4s free. Discounts for stays of 5 nights or longer.
Meals: Continental breakfasts included in B&B or R50 for self-caterers. 5 minutes' drive into Stellenbosch for restaurants aplenty.
Directions: From CT, N2 to Stellenbosch, follow signs to Jonkershoek Nature Reserve. 6km from Stellenbosch turn right and cross bridge on R just after entrance to Neil Ellis vineyard.

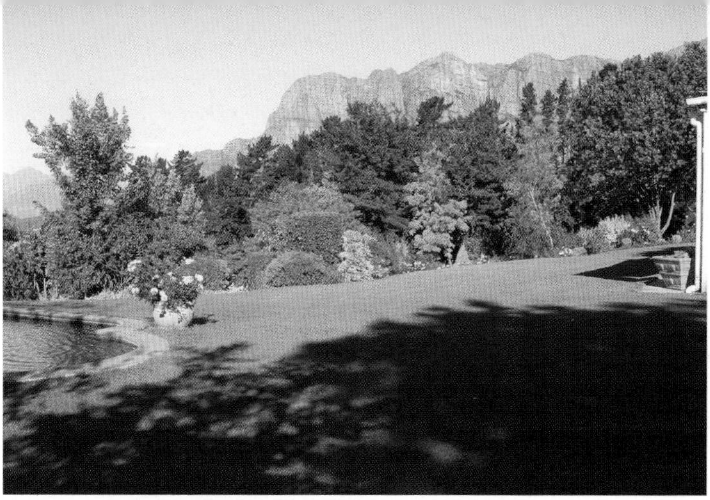

Camberley Cottage

John and Gael Nel
Camberley Wine Estate, Helshoogte Pass, Stellenbosch
Tel: 021-885-1176 Fax: 021-885-1822
Email: john@camberley.co.za Web: www.camberley.co.za
Cell: 082-690-4975

Gazing down the splendid Franschhoek Valley, all chequered with fruit farms and vineyards, Camberley occupies the kind of spot we all dream of making our own. This is exactly what Johnny and Gael did 14 years ago when they bought this former fruit farm. Heaps of pips and barrels of grape juice later, Camberley is now a small family-run vineyard producing some of the Cape's best reds and Johnny a highly-acclaimed wine-maker well-used to plum accolades (such as the Double Veritas award) being lobbed his way. An immensely likeable lot, the Nels are more than happy for you to pull up your sleeves and get busy in the picking and barrelling processes. The cottage itself sits in the thick of the vines, which screech to a halt at the rose-filled garden's edge. Although recently built, its rather sophisticated country air feels authentically matured, the floor-to-ceiling sash windows and Oregon pine floors taken from a former Cape Dutch-style bank in town. Although it has a very well-equipped kitchen and dining area, there are several top restaurants literally minutes from home, so, happily, washing-up is unlikely to feature in this holiday equation. This low-key, homely winery is the perfect point from which to explore the Winelands and Johnny helpfully has listed all his favourite places for you. Festooned with bubbles, the plunge pool makes a fantastic sunset spot for when you're well and truly corked.

Rooms: 1 king/twin, en-suite shower and bath.
Price: R400 - R450 pp B&B, R300 - R400 pp self-catering. Singles on request.
Meals: Full breakfast included in B&B prices.
Directions: From Cape Town, take N2 and turn off at Baden Powell Dr/R310 to Stellenbosch. Continue on R310 through town, about 8 mins out of S'bosch, Camberley is signed on right, opposite Le Pommier restaurant.

Allegria Guesthouse

Annemarie Marti and Jan Zevenbergen

Cairngorm Road, Stellenbosch
Tel: 021-881-3389 Fax: 021-881-3210
Email: info@allegria.co.za Web: www.allegria.co.za
Cell: 076-560-0356

Two things I noticed as I stepped into Jan and Annemarie's impressive garden: the first was an immense 20-metre pool where I pictured myself floating about looking up at a halo of mountains and vineyards; the second was a rather large statue of a cow, an old buddy from Jan's advertising days. It isn't surprising that they called this place Allegria (meaning joy); it's pretty hard to wear a frown when you wake up to that view... and everyone does. Each room has a door onto the back garden, with private patios and windows onto the Simonsberg and Helderberg mountains. Each bedroom is named after an animal and has a corresponding wall-hanging. My favourite was the Elephant Room, with a red elephant lumbering above the bed, a beautiful free-standing bath and the biggest double shower I have ever seen. The main dining and living area is a mix of grand, modern and traditional African design, with high ceilings, a friendly-looking metal rhino and earthy colour schemes. These two take hosting seriously. Jan is so dedicated to good wine that he visits all the local estates himself to double-check that he is only serving the best to guests; while Annemarie will happily give lifts into town for those who don't fancy the wobbly drive home. Breakfast is a sumptuous, healthy feast, with fresh rolls, croissants, muffins and health bread, fruit juices, cereals, muesli, fresh fruit, cheeses, meats, yoghurts, jams as well as eggs and bacon. Their motto is that everything is possible, and they really mean it.

Rooms: 6: 2 'superior' rooms with XL queen beds, en-suite bath & twin shower; 2 'deluxe' rooms with queen or twin beds, en-s bath & shower; 2 'comfort' rooms with queen or twin beds and en-s shower.
Price: R345 - R595 pp sharing. Singles on request.
Meals: Big healthy breakfast included. Light evening meals available: cheese platter and salads (order before 4pm).
Directions: From Cape Town follow N2 until R300 at Exit 22a. After 5km on R300 turn-off at Exit 21 (direction M12 - Stellenbosch Arterial). At lights turn R (direction M12 - Stellenbosch). After 10km on M12, turn L into Cairngorm Rd, driveway to Allegria.

Malans Guest House

Laetitia Malan
4 Keerom St, Stellenbosch
Tel: 021-887-8859
Fax: 086-528-2249
Email: malansgh@gmail.com
Web: www.malansgh.de
Cell: 083-664-1517

Laetitia has uniquely and beautifully decorated each of her guest rooms with antique furniture, kilims on beds, fresh flowers and even proper home-found shower caps in the bathrooms! (Ladies with long hair will know what I'm taking about.) She also collects Voortrekker wedding dresses that date back to the 1860s, while her other lace collections are displayed under glass-covered breakfast tables. And what a breakfast room: antique Chinese vases and vessels, exotic orchids, furniture inlaid with mother-of-pearl, 'grandparent' clocks, newly-painted frescoes and a flower-imprinted Chinese screen. Laetitia admitted that she may have lived in China in a previous life. She also collects porridges (!) after a fashion: try maltabela porridge (a traditional black-corn variety), maize or oatmeal at breakfast. And if you're not a porridge fan (no reason why you should be), there are plenty of mueslis, fresh fruits, bacon, eggs and all. Laetitia and her daughter treated me to their home-made chocolate cake and my first-ever rooibos tea, and sitting on the verandah in the sunshine I felt serene. A rare quote from one of our other hosts in this book: "I have stayed there myself and I often send guests on to her. Incredible value for money and an experience in its own right. A very interesting owner, with staff who know the art of hospitality and the most beautiful antiques." This all turns out to be pretty exact. *Nearby: cycling, horse-riding, golfing, fly-fishing and wine-tasting.*

Rooms: 5: 1 queen and 1 double with en-suite showers; 3 twins with en/s bath and shower.
Price: R275 - R350 pp sharing. Singles R350 - R450.
Meals: Full breakfast included. Restaurants aplenty nearby.
Directions: From Cape Town take N2, then R310 to Stellenbosch. Drive into town, at railway turn right into Dorp St. After right-hand bend turn left up The Avenue, first left to Neethling St and first left again into Keerom St.

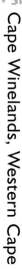

Longfield

Pieter and Nini Bairnsfather Cloete

Eikendal Rd, off R44, Somerset West/Stellenbosch
Tel: 021-855-4224 Fax: 021-855-4224
Email: ninicloete@iafrica.com Web: www.longfield.co.za

Perched on the foothills of the dramatic Helderberg mountains, Longfield occupies a truly sensational vantage that drifts across the Winelands and over to the very tip of False Bay at Cape Point. Dreamy by day and by night (when Cape Town's lights put on their glitzy show), there are three cottages from which to enjoy the view. All are fresh, breezy and decorated in a relaxed country-house style and many of the furnishings are rare, early-Cape family heirlooms. This is luxury self-catering. Comfy beds are made up with the highest-quality, hand-embroidered linen and there are spoiling lotions in the pretty bathrooms and coffee-table books on SA wine, flora and fauna etc, and African objets d'art in the cosy living areas with a wood-burner for good measure. Each has its private patio or lawn, and fridges and cupboards are re-stocked each day with breakfast materials for you to help yourself to. You'll probably want to disappear into your own world here, but Nini and Pieter, who live on the mountain with you, are the nicest people you could wish to meet. Formerly wine-farmers themselves, they can arrange exclusive garden and wine tours and will happily point you in the right direction for good restaurants and golf courses, all invariably within easy striking distance. But it's quite possible you won't want to go anywhere, what with the almond trees and olive trees and the immense pool in the rolling hills of their garden. This is a wonderfully secluded spot, serene and calm and ideally placed for many of the Cape's attractions.

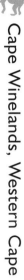

Rooms: 3 cottages: 2 with twin beds, 1 with king-size bed, all with bath and separate shower.
Price: R350 - R675 pp sharing. Single supplement by arrangement.
Meals: Breakfast included.
Directions: From CT take N2 past the airport, take exit 43 Broadway Bvd. Left at lights. From the next lights 6.3km exactly, then right into Eikendal Rd. Follow up gravel road, jink left onto tarmac and follow to top and Longfield House.

Acara

Fiona and Dave Stafford

Winery Road, Somerset West/Stellenbosch
Tel: 021-842-3161 Fax: 021-842-3159
Email: info@acara.co.za Web: www.acara.co.za
Cell: 084-958-5074

It tells you something about the view here that it only took five minutes of standing on the stoep for Fiona and Dave to decide to move in. Nestled in the valley known as 'Happy Vale', this is a truly tranquil and beautiful spot and, as I wandered through Fiona's garden, it was easy to see why she is the chairperson of the Stellenbosch Horticultural Society. The Acara garden has a huge variety of plants, from indigenous to the exotic: blossoming almond trees, fig and pepper trees, a pristine vegetable patch (help yourself to the herbs and veggies) and mounds of lavender. But the pièce de résistance is a wrought-iron pergola in a cloud of roses where people can sit and admire her handiwork. The stream that runs by it is also home to a mongoose and a couple of otters, much to the excitement of their ridgeback Bikkie. The Jacaranda Suite underneath their home has its own door out onto the garden, while two thatched cottages offer a cool retreat with their own decks and gardens. All rooms have crisp white walls, wooden beams and modern finishings, not to mention great mountain views. An excellent place for those who want to do everything: right in the mountains, near the beach and on the doorstep of several vineyards. But for lazier days, the hammock in the willow tree is perfect for digesting all that fine food and wine. David and Fiona are so friendly that one meeting wasn't enough. A week on, I caught up with them on a weekend break in Tulbagh and we shared another excellent evening of conversation... and more than one bottle of wine, if you must know!

Rooms: 3: 1 suite and 2 cottages, all with fully-equipped kitchen: Jacaranda Suite: 1 king with en-suite shower; Lavender Cottage: 1 queen and 1 twin; Willow Tree Cottage: 1 king and 1 twin, both with en-suite bathrooms.
Price: Jacaranda suite R720, Lavender Cottage R1,200 and Willow Tree R1,600. All prices per cottage per night.
Meals: Continental breakfast hamper arranged on request.
Directions: Details on website or faxed/emailed on booking.

Stellendal Guest House

Marry and Jan Willem van der Weele
169 Main Road (entrance on Stellendal Rd), Somerset West
Tel: 021-851-2599 Fax: 021-851-3224
Email: info@stellendal.co.za Web: www.stellendal.co.za
Cell: 076-101-3804

An orchestra of cicadas was playing in the leafy courtyard when I wandered into Stellendal. Marry and Jan Willem, recently arrived from Holland, were looking for a place with quick access to culture, music and good restaurants and finally settled on Somerset West. They have blended the grandeur of the old Cape Dutch style of long sweeping corridors and tinkling chandeliers with a more modern ambience of fairy-lights and jolly Picasso-style paintings. Marry is a photographer and her artistic talents are on display throughout the house. I loved the montage in the hall of individually-framed photographs of friends back home, creating a wall of happy faces in unique frames. They're strong on detail too with a red wall here, a silk throw there and a tasteful mix of African pieces (look out for the enormous white head which I walked straight past first time). Another thing I really liked about Stellendal is the variety of communal sitting rooms to choose from, such as the library at the back with its DVDs, free internet and wealth of art books; and my favourite room, the grand old lounge with gilt mirrors, a big fireplace, sofas and a piano, which "guests play if they want to." Should you feel the need to explore, chauffeured tours of both Cape Town and the Winelands can easily be organised in-house. Otherwise, there's the beautiful pool with a tempting basket of orange beach towels beside it, leaving you no excuse not to dive in. Yes it's deep enough... no puny splash pools here.

Rooms: 10: 5 kings, 2 twins all with en-suite shower except 1 with shower over bath; 1 cottage with 2 doubles with en-suite showers; 1 cottage with 2 doubles with full separate bathrooms.
Price: R300 - R500 pp sharing. Singles on request.
Meals: Full breakfast included, lunches on request. Many restaurants within walking distance.
Directions: From Cape Town take N2, then R44 direction Stellenbosch. This will take you into Somerset West, at the 1st traffic lights on R44 turn right onto Main Road.

On the Bay

Faye Townsend
Atlantica, 23 Beach Road, Strand
Tel: 021-851-1007 Fax: 021-851-1044
Email: info@on-the-bay.co.za Web: www.on-the-bay.co.za

Rarely have sun, sky and surf come together so seamlessly as to appear almost structural: to all intents and purposes they make up one whole side of this smart modern apartment. Set above the sands of the Strand promenade in a block whose left flank sweeps like a giant wave punctuated with port-hole windows, On the Bay is a perfectly-positioned self-catering apartment just ten minutes from the vineyards of Stellenbosch and halfway between the whales at Hermanus and the city lights of Cape Town. The interior is designed along blue, white and sand-coloured lines that echo the seascape. Aquamarine pillows also hint at what's a flick of the blind away in uncluttered dark-wood bedrooms, one upstairs, one down. Both are sea-facing with their own balconies, marble bathrooms, percale cotton sheets, down duvets and fluffy bath and beach towels that are also provided. Faye is happy to take grocery orders in advance, so that when you arrive the brand-new, fully-equipped kitchen – touch-glass hob, oven, microwave, fridge/freezer, dishwasher, washing-machine, tumble-dryer - is fully stocked and ready to go. A window ledge doubles as an ocean breakfast bar, so that you can eat your cereal in the salty air of False Bay. The rise and fall of the waves on the beach is a continual background soundtrack and you will probably spend quite a bit of time watching the sun pick its way across the sky or the local fishermen casting their lines on the quiet beach below. The views run 180 degrees from Gordon's Bay on your left to Cape Point to your right.

Rooms: 1 apartment with 1 queen double and 1 twin/king (1 shower en-suite and 1 full en-suite).
Price: R800 - R1,800 for apartment per night (max. 4 people).
Meals: Self-catering. Good restaurants in Gordon's Bay, Somerset West and nearby Stellenbosch.
Directions: Take N2 from Cape Town to Somerset West and then take the S'West/Strand R44 exit, turning R across the highway towards Strand and following R44. At the 3rd set of lights, turn R onto Beach Road, continue to far end of Beach Rd just before it turns inland at the Greenways Golf Course.

Manor on the Bay

Hanél and Schalk van Reenen
117 Beach Rd, Gordon's Bay
Tel: 021-856-3260
Fax: 021-856-3261
Email:
manorotb@mweb.co.za
Web:
www.manoronthebay.co.za
Cell: 082-896-5790

Hanél and Schalk van Reenen are a young couple, and their enthusiasm for the job is palpable. They have poured great vats of time and energy into restoring their property. First it was moving an impressive tonnage of earth to create a raised garden at the front below a long terrace; and now it is the addition of six new rooms and even a beauty salon. This is a great place to watch sunsets over False Bay or even whales in spring, and the view is conveniently framed by two large palms. An old English sheepdog completes the very friendly reception committee. Beach Road, you won't need telling, is just next to the sea, and a hop, skip and a dive takes you across the road and into the water. If you don't fancy the walk however, there's also a pool out the back. Of the twelve rooms, four of the new units have self-catering facilities. But if you are feeling like being spoilt, then you can still opt for the breakfast, which is either healthy (in Hanel's case eaten after an early run on the beach - you don't have to join her, but you can) or hearty, and is served in the bright dining room or on the terrace outside.

Rooms: 12: 11 doubles and 1 family room with 2 queens. All with en-suite shower and/or bath.
Price: R400 - R620 pp sharing. Singles R550 - R800.
Meals: Full breakfast included.
Directions: From Strand on the R44, take Beach Rd turning just before BP garage. From N2 take Sir Lowry's Pass to Gordon's Bay and cross over on to van der Bijl St, down to Beach Rd and L.

Acorns on Oak

Mieke Schuchard and Cecil Barrow

2 Oak Street, Greyton
Tel: 028-254-9567 Fax: 028-254-9569
Email: acornsonoak@telkomsa.net Web: www.acorns-on-oak.co.za
Cell: 082-367-2614

I was only meant to be dropping in on Mieke and Cecil but accidentally whiled away an entire afternoon with them. Drinking fresh coffee out of Wedgewood mugs we sat among a network of lily ponds which extend through their immaculate garden. The garden is a particularly peaceful place, draped in mountain scenery, scattered with oak trees and awash with white roses. I lamented the fact that I wasn't staying over… this time! The cottages bordering the garden are thatched and beautifully done out in different themes: Tuscany, Provence, and Exmoor. With slick bathrooms, outdoor showers and private sitting rooms they've created a unique brand of laid-back luxury. In the main house there's a romantic room in the eaves with its own free-standing bath. Breakfasts are a favourite here cooked up by Cecil, who together with Mieke, used to run an award-winning inn in Somerset. They moved here for some peace and quiet... and it really is quiet. Mieke is from Holland (notice the clogs on the post in the garden) and between them they seem to know everyone in the village. For hiking they'll organise you a picnic hamper from the bistro pub at the end of the road. I expect you'll be halfway here by now, but I haven't even started on the river at the end of the garden (perfect braai spot) or the generous-sized swimming pool from where you can gaze up at the mountains above.

Rooms: 5: 3 kings or twins, 2 with bath and shower, 1 with shower; 1 queen with shower; 1 queen with bath and shower.
Price: R395 pp sharing. Singles on request.
Meals: Full breakfast included, packed lunches on request and braai area available.
Directions: Take the N2 from Cape Town. Turn left 1km before Caledon onto Route 406, signposted Genadendal and Greyton. In the centre of town turn right down Oak Street. Acorns on Oak is on the left at the bottom.

Rouxwil Country House

Thys and O'nel Roux

Caledon
Tel: 028-215-8922 Fax: 028-215-8922
Email: rouxwil@intekom.co.za Web: www.rouxwil.co.za
Cell: 082-575-6612

A stony crocodile peeps out over the swimming pool. "The only real ones we have are in the river," laughs Thys as we stroll through the grounds of his vast farm. He's joking, of course, and throughout my visit his conversation is peppered with laughter... but then he has much to smile about. The farm has been in Thys' family for three generations and he has lovingly added to it; five units now overlook the open landscape complete with eland, springbok and zebra. His charming wife, and childhood sweetheart, O'nel has also been busy furnishing the rooms and giving them individual characters; chandeliers and iron furniture (inspiration from a holiday in Italy) decorate one, wooden chairs and black wattle ceilings fashion another. There's even a brightly coloured Happy Room that would lift the spirits of even the weariest traveller. "Life is too short to be unhappy and drink bad wine," she says. Quite. Back in the farmhouse lounge there's no refusing a slice of O'nel's milk tart or the comfort of their sofa. It's clear from the chat that plenty of friendships have been made sitting around the farmhouse dinner table, and out on the terrace by the braai. I only wish I'd had more time so I could have accepted Thys' invitation to hop aboard his raft, sundowner in hand, hear all about the farm and search for those elusive crocodiles.

Rooms: 5: all doubles wth en-suite bath and shower.
Price: R450 pp sharing.
Meals: Full breakfast included. Dinner R145.
Directions: From Cape Town take N2 pass Botrivier, carry on for 8km on N2 and take left turn on to the Villiersdorp R43. After 14km turn right off to Greyton and Helderstroom. Follow road for 1km, Rouxwil Country House signposted.

Beaumont Wine Estate

Jayne and Ariane Beaumont

Compagnes Drift Farm, Bot River
Tel: 028-284-9194 (office), 028-284-9370 (home) Fax: 028-284-9733
Email: info@beaumont.co.za Web: www.beaumont.co.za
Cell: 083-9906-319

Jayne's guests stay in the charming buildings of an 18th-century former mill house and wagon shed, today snug with wood-burning heaters, but left as far as comfortably possible as they were, with original fireplaces in kitchens and hand-hewn, yellowwood beamed ceilings. Outside, you can sit around an old mill stone and admire the antediluvian water wheel, while the willow-shaded jetty on the farm lake offers one of the Western Cape's prettiest settings for sundowners and wheatland views. While meandering through the flower-filled garden I realised that there is no real need to move from the farm, despite being only half an hour from Hermanus. While Jayne and her family busy themselves producing their annual 150,000-odd bottles of wine, you can swim in the informal swimming pool – being the lake - under the weeping willows where the weaver-birds make their nests; or you can roam about on their land – they own half a mountain! You can even put the idea of cooking on the backburner and instead arrange to have home-cooked meals delivered to you and wine-taste in the cellar flanked by an old wine press. The estate is a proud member of an exciting bio-diversity wine route which includes tours, tastings, hiking and mountain-bike trails (check out www.greenmountain.co.za). Also, to find horses and horse-riding you only have to trot down the road. The setting is beautiful - well worth spending several nights here.

Rooms: 2 self-catering cottages. Mill House has 2 bedrooms (plus 2 extra can sleep in living room); Pepper Tree has 1 double (again 2 extras possible).
Price: R220 - R400 pp sharing. Extra people R100 pp. Call for high season rates.
Meals: Self-catering breakfast and home-cooked meals by arrangement. All meals are self-served.
Directions: From N2 take exit 92, sign-posted to Bot River. Follow signs to Bot River and Beaumont Wine Estate is signed off to the right-hand side. Map can be faxed.

Barton Farm Villas

Peter Neill

Barton Farm (Off R43), Bot River
Tel: 028-284-9283/UK +44-1489-878-673 Fax: 028-284-9776
Email: villas@bartonfarm.co.za Web: www.bartonfarm.co.za
Cell: 084-619-4139

In the middle of the Kogel National Park, up a winding avenue of pine trees, I finally found five beautifully-designed Tuscan-style villas scattered across the raised valley of a working farm. As we climbed the track and stood under the arches the beam of my gaze shot straight out of the window, and spread across the vineyards and over the sprawling mountains beyond. The views are spectacular, a rolling canvas of working fields, rows of lavender and fynbos-clad mountains which wraps right around you. Built into and around the rocks the villas all have wide verandahs on which to conduct your feasts and to soak up the views. It's no secret Peter built them to stay in himself and consequently no expense has been spared. Notably the bedding, shipped straight in from The White Company because no other duvets would do! With huge sweeping lounges, open-plan kitchens, long tables, big fireplaces and an emphasis on natural materials, the villas are immaculately finished throughout. Peter has a soft spot for Persian carpets bringing colour and warmth to the airy rooms and I'm told a new one sneaks in on his every visit. With spa baths and swimming pools built into the rocks it's easy to forget this is a working farm abundant with wildlife. Don't miss the opportunity to get involved, especially with the wine grown on the farm. I imagined inviting everyone I knew to come for a week of long sunset dinners, lazy days of swimming, riding, tennis, golf, hiking and landscape painting....

Rooms: 5 villas: Heron, 2 doubles, indoor swimming pool & spa bath; Blue Crane, 2 doubles, 1 twin; Hammerkop, 2 doubles; Plover, 3 doubles; Lousada, 2 doubles, 1 twin & indoor swimming pool. All have en-suite bathrooms, outdoor pools, outdoor spa baths & DSTV.
Price: Seasonal R400 - R575 pp, From 15th Dec to 15th Jan, R700 pp.
Meals: Self-catering.
Directions: From Cape Town take the N2 towards Somerset West/Hermanus, exit 90. Barton Farm is situated on the R43 Bot River/Hermanus Road just past the Shell petrol Station.

Wildekrans Country House

Alison Green and Barry Gould
Houw Hoek Valley, Elgin
Tel: 028-284-9827 Fax: 028-284-9624
Email: info@wildekrans.co.za Web: www.wildekrans.co.za

From the tufts of moss poking out between the old flagstones of the front path I knew that this was my sort of place. The 1811 homestead is raised above its garden and looks down on lawns, abundant roses, pear orchards, the large swimming pool and old oak trees. The scene is magnificent with the 'wild cliffs' ('wildekrans') setting the property's limits, rising from a meadow at the back of the garden. Take a stroll beside landscaped water-courses and lily ponds that neighbour the orchards, and you will encounter wonderful, some might think surreal, sculptures that have been positioned with much thought, and I think argument, where they now stand. They add a touch of the unexpected to this magical garden. Finally a rickety bridge - where one almost expects to pay a troll a toll – crosses a stream. Home-made "Follow your Heart" sculptures (giant metal hearts on poles driven into ground) will romance you to the edge of a mystical wood, where you'll find yourself at the foot of the Groenlandberg mountain. Take a healthy hike up and the Kogelberg Biosphere Reserve will be there for you to explore. And with over 1600 species of plant life, it is no wonder they call it the 'heart of the fynbos'. The authentic homestead bedrooms, each with a four-poster bed, are originally parental gifts to Alison and her many sisters, and offer views out to the garden and beyond. And if the mountains get the better of you, Wildekrans boasts an excellent contemporary art collection and Barry's delicious wine and olive oil is available for tasting in the barn. *Wildekrans is a member of the Green Mountain Eco Route.*

Rooms: 4: 3 four-poster doubles in homestead all with en-s bath (1 has shower too, 1 has private study); and 1 s/c cottage.
Price: B&B: R400 - R490 pp sh. Singles R510. Self-catering: R275 - R425 pp sh.
Meals: Full breakfast incl'. 1-course supper R110; 3-course dinner R145; braai R65. All meals self-served.
Directions: On N2 from Cape Town for 1 hr approx, past Grabouw & 12km further turn L signed Houw Hoek Inn. Or 30 mins from Caledon on N2, at top of Houw Hoek Pass, turn R signed HH Inn. Through HH gate posts, follow rd round to L. Farm on R.

Barnacle B&B

Jenny Berrisford
573 Anne Rd, Pringle Bay
Tel: 028-273-8343 Fax: 028-273-8343
Email: barnacle@maxitec.co.za Web: www.barnacle.co.za
Cell: 082-925-7500

Come and explore Jenny's seaside idyll. Several natural environments collide right outside her cottage. From the deck at the back – with views all the way to Cape Point – you walk down to 'readers' corner', a private lawny enclave in the marsh reeds where narrow paths lead you to the river and beach. The sea is a hundred yards of the whitest, finest sand to your left; beyond the river, fynbos and milkwood 'forest' climb the mountain, a nature reserve. You don't have to be a kid to love this. There are otters in the river, baboons on the mountain, estuarine and fynbos birds aplenty… and Jenny is a horticultural expert in one of the world's most amazing natural gardens. Rooms are simple, rustic and country cosy, one with a Victorian slipper bath, another with a solid brass bed. The Cottage has a sitting area with its own fireplace which makes it cosy for winter breaks, while both the Cottage and The Sunshine Suite have fully-equipped kitchenettes for self-catering. The whole place is super relaxed… a hidden gem. Jenny has canoes to take out on the river. This area has been proclaimed a world biosphere reserve.

Rooms: 2 units both sleeping 4: 1 double with en-suite shower, kitchen/dining area and 2 singles; 1 double with en-suite 'slipper' bath, kitchenette and two single beds.
Price: R300 - R500 pp sharing. Single and family rates negotiable.
Meals: Full breakfast included. Restaurants in Pringle Bay.
Directions: From Cape Town along N2 turn towards Gordon's Bay before Sir Lowry's Pass - follow coast road for 30km to Pringle Bay turn - follow signs down dirt roads.

96 Beach Road

Annelie and Johan Posthumus

Kleinmond

Tel: 021-794-6291 Fax: 021-794-6291

Email: info@kaapsedraaibb.co.za Web: www.kaapsedraaibb.co.za

When the family bought "the beach house" in 1954, the milk was delivered by bike. Kleinmond still feels like a sleepy little town, but it's hardly surprising that more have fled here since. The house is but a kite-tail's length from the sea, the blue Atlantic stretching forth beyond a strip of fynbos. You can choose to watch the whales passing by (from August to December) from two spots, the sea-side verandah or the upstairs bedroom. The latter runs from one side of the house to the other under a vaulted ceiling and ocean-side the walls stop and the glass starts, forming a small square sitting room jutting out towards the blue. Here there is a soft couch and cushioned chairs, perfect for siestas, sunsets (and of course whale-watching). Downstairs is equally adorable. It feels a bit like a Nantucket Island house: white, light, airy and adorned with simple understated beach furnishings. Interior designers, *nota bene*! It is totally self-catering here, but walk a kilometre west and you'll find some untouristy cafés in the old harbour; a three-minute drive east will take you past a decent restaurant and miles of white, sandy, blue-flag beaches, perfect for kids, flying kites, swimming and walking. There is a rock pool about 50 yards from the house, and apart from that all the swimming takes place at the beach and lagoon which is a 15-minute walk away. Kleinmond is near the Arabella Golf Estate, the Kogelberg Biosphere with its myriad fynbos species, the wild horses of the Bot River Estuary and Hermanus, but avoids its touristy-ness.

Rooms: 1 unit with 2 rooms: 1 double with en-suite shower, 1 twin with bath. Open-plan kitchen/dining/living area. Heating. Kitchen fully equipped with dishwasher & washing-machine. Serviced once a week, more frequently on request.
Price: Max 4 persons. Minimum R600 per night or R1,000 if 4 persons. Min 2-night stay.
Meals: Self-catering. Braai areas with firewood provided.
Directions: In Kleinmond town face east. Drive thro' 3 stop signs and turn towards the sea on 6th Avenue. Keep going to the sea then turn L. No 96 is the penultimate house from the corner.

Schulphoek Seafront Guesthouse

Petro and Mannes van Zyl
44 Marine Drive, Sandbaai, Hermanus/Sandbaai
Tel: 028-316-2626 Fax: 028-316-2627
Email: schulphoek@hermanus.co.za Web: www.schulphoek.co.za
Cell: 083-346-0695

Waves roll into the bay, five foot high when I visited, and crash against rocks right in front of Schulphoek Seafront Guesthouse. The sitting room has one of the most exciting sea views you could hope for and, naturally, whales steal into Schulphoek Bay during the season for private viewings. The best room, Scallop - I don't think there is any doubt, despite the extremely high overall standard! - is upstairs, the whole seaward wall an expanse of window with a sliding glass door and parapet. The other rooms, although without sea views, have solid, hand-crafted oak or mahogany beds and spectacular bathrooms with double sinks, double showers and spa-baths. As I sunk into mine I laughed, safe in the knowledge that as far as luxury goes you will not find better anywhere. Not many places in this area feel the need to provide in-house dinners, but your hosts are not taking chances on outside eateries. Guests who want to guarantee themselves delicious food stay in (4-course *menu du jour* with herbs, salad and veg picked straight from their vegetable garden) and eat at one long table, on chairs made from vintage wine vats. Dinner is a lively affair, before which you will be led to the exhaustive cellar where you can choose from the finest South African wines. Schulphoek is an intimate, state-of-the-art seaside lodge, but still the sort of place where guests socialise with each other, drinks are on an honesty system and meals are eaten together (although you can eat separately if you prefer). *Closed in June.*

Rooms: 7 suites: superior, luxury and standard, all with luxurious en-suite bathrooms. 1 family suite.
Price: R585 - R1,348 pp sharing, includes full breakfast and 4-course dinner on first night. Singles supplement +50%. Discounted rates for longer stays all year round, plus seasonal rates. Website has more detail. Whole guest house on request.
Meals: Full b'fast incl'. Professional kitchen with chef. Dinner every night: 4-course menu du jour. Lunch on request. Wine cellar with 7,000 SA wines.
Directions: Take R43 towards Hermanus. At Engen petrol station by traffic lights (signed Sandbaai) turn R. At 2nd 'stop' turn L into 3rd Street. Continue to next stop and turn L. Entrance off Piet Retief Crescent.

Hartford Cottage

Gys and Wendy Hofmeyr

3, 3rd Ave, Voelklip, Hermanus
Tel: 028-314-0102 Fax: 028-314-0667
Email: gyswendyhof@telkomsa.net
Cell: 082-897-1773

If you were asked to paint a picture of your perfect country cottage, I suggest it might look a bit like Hartford; white walls, soaring chimney and a perfectly pitched thatched roof, all enveloped by a large, tranquil, lawned garden where I challenge you to find anything out of place. As I sat under the welcoming shade of the umbrella sipping tea and thinking how delicious it would be to live here, Wendy told me - and I didn't register much surprise - that complete strangers have knocked on the door begging to stay, even though originally they only built the cottage for the family. Hiding away from the hurlyburly of Hermanus in a seaside suburb, Hartford is enviably positioned, with mountain walks five minutes in one direction, beach, sea and whales a minute or two in the opposite. Gys is a stickler for detail and a lover of wood and thatch. Door surrounds and light switches were rescued and resurrected from a condemned house in town, while an original yellowwood door hanging on huge hinges is his pride and joy. Don't think Wendy hasn't been busy too. Her eye for interior designs led to the stunning black slate fire hearth, bathroom sink surrounds and kitchen worktops. The open-plan A-frame roof makes it cool and spacious, while the whitewashed walls and an abundance of Cape antique furniture, means it retains all of its delightfully cosy cottage charm.

Rooms: 1 cottage with 1 double room with full en-suite and 1 twin bedroom with separate bathroom. Also a large attic bed/sitter with 3 beds for children. Cottage not available 20th Dec - 15th Jan.
Price: 2 people sharing whole cottage: R900 plus R100 an extra head (May - Aug inclusive). R1,200 plus R200 a head per extra person (Sept - April inc'). Min 2-night stay. Children under 12 free.
Meals: Cottage fully self-catering, including breakfast provisions for your first morning.
Directions: 4km from Hermanus towards Stanford, take 3rd exit off r'about into 10th St (Seafront Rd), past CEM Motors & on for 300m. 3rd Ave on R, then thatched house on R. Map faxed on booking.

Hermanus Beach Villa

Charl and Riana De Kock
127, 11th Street, Voëlklip Beach, Hermanus
Tel: 028-314-1298
Email: info@hermanusbeachvilla.co.za Web: www.hermanusbeachvilla.co.za
Cell: 084-548-3844

When it comes to style and sophistication Hermanus Beach Villa has oodles. A grand piano takes centre stage in the lounge while silverware, bone china, white candles and cut-glass ashtrays are neatly placed on antique tables; inviting evening companions include a marble fireplace, chess board and decanter of sherry. I could see many a comfortable evening spent in Riana's lounge. Breakfast is an equally attractive affair with breakfast served from the marble-topped kitchen counter and enjoyed either at the dining room table with white linen and silver cutlery or, weather permitting, on the verandah with its uninterrupted sea views. Today the whales are performing and I have a front-row seat. "Sometimes it looks like Seaworld, with one whale after another jumping," Riana tells me as we ooh over the sight of another breaching southern right. Could it get more beautiful than this, I ask myself, as a guest drops his newspaper, too distracted by the performance to read? Upstairs, the suites are similarly luxurious and decorated with huge mirrors, plump feather down duvets and cream sofas. If you can tear yourself away from all this comfort, Voelklip Beach (you can feel the spray it's that close) is safe for swimming or take the famous cliff path into Hermanus. It's the perfect way to work up an appetite for lunch... although leave room for Riana's home-made scones back at the villa.

Rooms: 3 suites: each has 1 king/twin room and 1 adjoining twin room. All en/s bath + showers + kitchenette.
Price: R1,300 per suite for 2 people (extra R250 pp). Children under 12 by prior arrangement.
Meals: Full breakfast included.
Directions: From N2 take R43 to Hermanus. Go through the village and at roundabout go 3/4 way around onto 10th street. Carry on till 4-way stop. Turn right into 7th Ave. First left into 11th Street. The 3rd house on the right next to the empty plot - number 127.

Villa Blu

Riana & Tino Delle Donne
234 8th Street, Voëlklip, Hermanus
Tel: 028-314-1056 Fax: 028-314-1123
Email: info@villablu.co.za Web: www.villablu.co.za
Cell: 082-4436-340

This place does a strange thing to you. Whilst Tino was preparing my coffee (the best I've had in SA, but then he is Italian), my head began to whirl with happy memories of holidays past where faces are golden, living is easy and time passes idly by. Just another guesthouse this is certainly not. Built around an open courtyard that tinkles, trickles and crashes with the sounds of wind chimes, fountains and waves, Villa Blu inspires within you an invigorating lightness of heart. Be it the beach-time photographs, colourful paintings (some are Riana's own), antique Indonesian furnishings, shells scattered around or the blue-tinted hue, everything feels fresh, homely and so very, very relaxed. With pale-washed Oregon pine furnishings and floors, huge mirror-walls in the bathrooms and doors opening onto private patios, every room is as light and airy as the rest of the house. Head up to the roof terrace for stunning views onto the blue-flag 'Grotto' beach just ahead or the green velvet-swathed mountains which loom large behind. Regrettably, as mine was only a quick visit, I didn't get to swing carefree in the garden's hammock, doze by the pool or try Tino's wonderful breakfast (he is clearly as passionate about food as he is about the guest-house). But I didn't just want to stay here anyway... I wanted to live here. Oh, bring on those lazy, hazy days of summer.

Rooms: 8: 5 kings/twins, 2 with separate bath and shower, 2 with bath/shower, 1 with shower; 3 queens, 2 with en-suite bath/shower and 1 with en-suite shower.
Price: R380 - R650 pp sharing. Singles supplement 50%.
Meals: Full breakfast included. Culinary weekends offered in winter months.
Directions: From N2, take R43 into Hermanus. Drive through the town, staying on Main Road as you cross the roundabout. Turn right into 13th Avenue and then right into 8th Street. It's 3rd house on R.

Mosaic Farm

Breese & Kathryn Johnson (owners), Justin & Jolene Boshoff (managers)
Provincial Road, Stanford
Tel: 028-313-2814 Fax: 028-313-2811 Email: info@mosaicfarm.net
Web: www.mosaicfarm.net Cell: 082-825-3211

In 1892, visitors to Mosaic Farm would have had either to cross the lagoon or travel by horse and cart to reach it. Today the journey to this historic house is a bit more civilised. "You can arrive by helicopter if you have one," smiles Jolene as I step from my dusty car. That would be a fitting entrance, for Mosaic Farm has the feeling of a Texan ranch, but sadly I am no wealthy oil baron. This peaceful 1,000 hectare property, separated from the hurly-burly of Hermanus by an 8km lagoon (4km of which is in front of Mosaic), is rich both in history and plant and animal life. The silence here is only punctured by birdsong or the splash of a kayak paddle. The main house dates back to 1892 and, in homage to its past, new cottages have been built in the same style; high-beamed ceilings, stacked stone walls and natural finishes combine with modern-day comforts. Hidden in the bush there is far more still to be discovered. Luxury safari-style tents peek out from beneath the canopy of ancient milkwood trees, a plunge pool overlooks the lagoon, and a dining area, complete with thatched roof and canvas flaps, serves up very fine food. There are even plans to introduce game. "You get a real out-of-Africa feel here," says Jolene; this is so true despite the farm's proximity to Hermanus. I really don't think the helicopter is necessary to ensure a massive dose of luxury and romance at Mosaic Farm.

Rooms: 7: 5 luxury tents all with en-suite bathroom, outdoor shower and private deck; 2 fully-contained self-catering cottages: 1 double & 1 twin both with en-suite, loft sleeps 5 with downstairs bathroom; and 1 cottage with twin room & loft sleeps 2 children.
Price: Dinner, bed and breakfast: R695 - R990 pp sharing. Singles R990 - R1,390. Children 4 - 12 yrs R395 - R495. Self-catering cottages: R600 - R1,500 per unit per night, additional pp R100 - R220.
Meals: Dinner and b'fast are incl' with tent accom.
Directions: From Cape Town take R43 to Stanford. Take a R through the village then L at Moore Street. Go straight on until it becomes a farm road. Carry on for 10km, Mosaic Farm Reception signposted on R.

Cliff Lodge

Gill O'Sullivan and Gideon Shapiro

6 Cliff St, De Kelders
Tel: 028-384-0983 Fax: 028-384-0228
Email: stay@clifflodge.co.za Web: www.clifflodge.co.za
Cell: 082-380-1676

This is the closest land-based whale-watching you could possibly find. I could see the whites of their eyes (I was only shooting with a camera!) and the callosities on their heads. It was as though Gill and Gideon had paid them (in plankton) to put on a special show for me; blowing, breaching, spy-hopping, lob-tailing. I applauded delicately from the royal box. The viewing from my room and from the breakfast conservatory-balcony was don't-turn-your-eyes-away-for-a-minute magnetic. But the fun wasn't just in the looking. As soon as I walked through the door, Gideon, formally a dive-master, whisked me down to the ocean for a swim through the cave (bring shoes you can swim in for the rocks) and Gill kindly booked me a whale-, sea-lion- and penguin-watching boat trip for the following morning. For the 'help-danger' adrenaline rush, there is also the shark-cage diving. The guest house décor is classy and modern and there are whale-spotting terraces for those rooms on the side of the house. The luxurious penthouse suite has a huge balcony and glass-fronted living room for whale-gazing in true style. On the cliff edge is also a small swimming pool. Gill and Gideon are wonderfully hospitable hosts and really look after their guests. After the best breakfast you could possibly have - not only because of the food but also the panorama - indulge in an aromatherapy massage from Gill, nature reserve walks in front of the house and the nearby flower-farm.

Rooms: 4: 1 twin/king with bath and shower, 1 queen bed with bath & shower overhead, 1 twin/king with bath and shower overhead & 1 luxury suite with king bed, separate living room, bath & shower.
Price: R450 - R1,200 pp sharing. Single supplement +50%.
Meals: Full breakfast included.
Directions: N2, then R43 through Hermanus. Past Stanford towards Gansbaai. Turn right at first De Kelders turn-off, then right into De Villiers Rd, left into Kayser Rd and right into Cliff St.

Whalesong Lodge

Stanley and Lainy Carpenter
83 Cliff St, De Kelders
Tel: 028-384-1865 Fax: 028-384-1866
Email: stanley@whalesonglodge.co.za Web: www.whalesonglodge.co.za
Cell: 082-883-5793

I sank with delight into a candlelit bath in the midst of a raging sea storm. On a calm day I'd have been bathing before a host of whales. "There were twenty or thirty in the bay this morning," said Stanley casually. I was more than happy curled up with a book, chatting to guests in the cosy, glass-fronted living room. They had a date with some sharks in the morning and tales of these awesome creatures steered the evening's conversation. Stanley and Lainy used to run the Pontac Hotel in Paarl, but I suspect they always hankered after a nice small place where they could give their guests more love and attention, cook for manageable numbers… and be themselves. Whalesong Lodge, with just five rooms, is it. All the bedrooms have sea views, of course, either from a panoramic window or a small, private balcony, and underfloor-heated bathrooms are separated from the sleeping areas by shoulder-high walls. All is slick and modern. Many cookbooks and a well-stocked kitchen loudly trumpet Stanley's culinary expertise. "I've got a seasonal chef to do all the work for me now," he later confesses. Yet despite hanging up his chef's hat he still keeps a keen eye on the kitchen. It's clear that only the very best will pass muster with Stanley and later that night a freshly-caught fish dinner with all the trimmings proved me right. Breakfast ("from 8 till late") is fresh and all-encompassing, with home-made preserves, fresh fruit, eggs and bacon. Oh yes, and great coffee.

Rooms: 5: 2 twins, 3 doubles, all en-suite bath and shower.
Price: R500 - R800 pp sharing.
Meals: Full breakfast included.
Directions: From N2 take R43 through Hermanus and Stanford. Take first right signed to De Kelders and follow down to the sea. Turn right into Cliff Street. Third house on right.

Klein Paradijs Country House

Susanne and Michael Fuchs
Pearly Beach, Gansbaai
Tel: 028-381-9760 Fax: 028-381-9803
Email: kleinparadijs@lando.co.za Web: www.kleinparadijs.co.za

Paradise would be a proud boast, so perhaps Little Paradise is a more defensible claim. But you can see why the name stuck: nature on the one hand, man-made environment on the other, and all rounded off by delicious cooking and green fingers. I'll elaborate. The property stretches up a mountain covered in indigenous fynbos vegetation and nearer the house there is a reed-edged dam with weaver birds, an old camphor tree in the courtyard and an amazing garden whose swimming pool acts as a moat to a tiny island of plant life. Inside, high open spaces are punctuated with lovely things: bright paintings, vases of proteas and pincushions, a stinkwood grandfather clock, for example. A-shaped rooms have soaring thatched roofs, dormer windows, beams, window-seats, balconies and the curtained-off bathrooms are truly luxurious. The Fuchs are Swiss and have brought many talents with them. Susanne was a translator and speaks English, German and French, while Michael is a chef – they open a small but excellent restaurant in the evenings. *Large dam with canoe and rowboat available on the property. Whale-watching possible nearby from June – November.*

Rooms: 5: 2 twins and 3 doubles all with en-suite bathrooms; 2 with bath and shower, 3 with showers.
Price: R450 - R950 pp sharing. Single supplement +50%.
Meals: Full breakfast included. Light meals and dinner by arrangement. The restaurant is fully licensed.
Directions: From Hermanus take the R43 through Stanford and Gansbaai. Go left at Pearly Beach crossing, then 1st left again. The house is on the right.

Farm 215 Nature Retreat and Fynbos Reserve

Maarten Groos

Hartebeeskloof, Baardskeerdersbos, Overstrand Municipality
Tel: 028-388-0920
Email: book@farm215.co.za Web: www.farm215.co.za
Cell: 082-097-1655

Farm 215 perches neatly among the fynbos of this private nature reserve. It's not really that remote, yet when I visited absolute silence prevailed, so much so that you could hear the neat pitter-patter of Maarten's dogs following us along the boardwalks. The individual cottages, angled to look rosy-faced into the sunset and onto sea and mountains, squat above the 35 different species of protea that contribute to the vast and wild garden. The conservation of the reserve here is a constant priority and the cottages were very much built with sustainabilty in mind and they have won an award for their efforts. Testament to this is the yellow lichen, a sign of air purity, that paints the rock faces of this self-sufficient retreat. The log fire in the restaurant provides the under-floor heating, while solar panels heat the spectacular chlorine-free 25m-lap pool. Maarten is constantly improving his fynbos world and speaks with eager animation of plans in progress. The restaurant is capacious and contemporary with two fireplaces and folding doors that open onto a wooden deck. Here Henki (the chef) produces his incredible food, always steering clear of frivolous gourmet towers. The free-standing suites are luxurious, with cotton linen and large open-plan bathrooms of wood and black slate; or you can stay in the farmhouse rooms with their black-framed historic photographs and wide Persian rugs. With 20km of hiking trails radiating from the door of your cottage, an astonishing number of birds and horse trails on site, there is every opportunity to earn yourself a slice of heaven. *Children over 12 are welcome.*

Rooms: 6: 3 free-standing suites with kings, lounge area & en-suite bath & shower; 1 ground floor suite with private garden and 2 doubles in main house, each with en-s bath & shower.
Price: From R710 pp sharing (for rooms) and from R840 pp sharing (for the suite) in the house. Fynbos suites R940 pp sharing. Singles +50%.
Meals: Full breakfast included. On-site restaurant for lunch & 3-course dinner. Picnic baskets also available.
Directions: At Bot River take turn to Hermanus (R43). After Franskraal L into dirt rd signed to Elim. Follow for approx 10km. Gates to Farm 215 are on L after lake & vineyards.

Jan Harmsgat Country House

Brin and Judi Rebstein

Swellendam
Tel: 023-616-3407 or 023-616-3311 Fax: 023-616-3201
Email: brinreb@iafrica.com Web: www.jhghouse.com
Cell: 072-279-3138

A true country house, Jan Harmsgat is a breath of fresh air in an often-chintzy genre. Judi (a producer in the film industry) and Brin rescued it from tumbledown oblivion in 1989. They swept out the old rotted beams, mould, even pigs, and set about pouring a cellar-full of TLC into it. It is a beautiful place. The above photo does not lie but what it doesn't show is that the restaurant and its increasingly famous staff are starting to catch the food-media's eye… or that your hosts are so gracious. Past resident Hermanus Steyn proclaimed the Independent Republic of Swellendam in 1795 and farmed wine here originally, but I doubt he dined on butterfish bobotie stacks with coriander. Or perhaps he did! His 25-metre barn-cellar (now the dining room, complete with grand piano) today looks out of a glass wall. Guests are housed in old slave quarters whose large rooms and great comfort might make you forget the history of the place. However, sympathetic renovation means that windows in the clay walls have not been enlarged, and the wonky lintels, wooden shutters and vast beams all play their part in preserving the original character here. Mine was high up in the apex of the thatch, had a free-standing Victorian bath, gilded chairs and come morning I had a colour-me-happy moment when I opened my shutters and was drenched in a sweet citron-scented breeze gusting across from the orchard. Bliss.

Rooms: 5: 1 twin with en/s shower & 1 twin with en/s bath; 1 queen with Victorian bath in room & en-suite loo; 1 king with Victorian bath in room & en-suite loo; 1 king luxury room with full bathroom (bath & shower).
Price: R450 - R865 pp sharing. Luxury room R980.
Meals: Full breakfast included. Lunch by arrangement only. The restaurant is open for dinner to the public (reservations essential). Four-course set menu R225 pp.
Directions: From Cape Town on N1 to Worcester turn right into R60 (Robertson) at Worcester. Carry on thro' Robertson and Ashton. Turn R after Ashton and stay on R60. House on left after 21km. From Cape Town on N2 to Swellendam turn into R60. Carry on 24.5km after Swellendam towards Ashton, house on R.

Rothman Manor

Andreas and Franziska Gobel
268 Voortrek St, Swellendam
Tel: 028-514-2771 Fax: 028-514-3966
Email: guesthouse@rothmanmanor.co.za Web: www.rothmanmanor.co.za

With lily-littered dam, salt-water pool and cobbled courtyard Rothman Manor boasts grounds of park-like calibre. The original Cape Dutch house and venerable oak tree (whose shady canopy acts as a parasol for your breakfast table) both date back to 1834, yet fresh, clipped interiors (born of Andreas and Franziska's combined flair for design) shift matters decisively into the present. With pale-blue or cream-hued walls and cloud-white curtain-swept beds, heavenly rooms are earthed by wooden flooring and black-framed artwork, many of which are Franziska's own. Bathrooms sport chequered tiles and African-themed titbits seem to hang suspended in cubby-holes, unique reminders of the grounds and its outdoor inhabitants. Here, in wine-dominated Swellendam, I was bowled over with sightings of zebra, sprightly springbok and a couple of ostriches, all residents of the Gobel's eco-reserve. I was tempted to bag a lounger near the deck-bound jacuzzi where you can keep an eye on any animal action. Each generous room has its own view-treated patio for outdoors delight or spoil yourself indoors with a therapeutic, individually-tailored massage. With easy access to numerous nature reserves, wine farms and Bontebok National Park, Rothman Manor is its own destination and a gateway to others.

Rooms: 6: 3 kings and 3 twins, 4 with full baths, 2 with shower only.
Price: R360 - R800 pp sharing. Singles on request.
Meals: Full breakfast included.
Directions: Turn off N2 onto R60, and then turn R into Swellendam. Rothman Manor on R.

Roosje van de Kaap

Ilzebet Oosthuizen
5 Drostdy St, Swellendam
Tel: 028-514-3001 Fax: 028-514-3001
Email: roosje@dorea.co.za Web: www.roosjevandekaap.com

Where else can you get mussels for R30, a bottle of exceptional Springfield Sauvignon Blanc Special for R100 and listen to a live jazz band while you enjoy them? The candlelit restaurant at Roosje van de Kaap, that's where. Named by Eat Out magazine as one of the ten best restaurants in the Garden Route, it's charming and encourages intimacy; by the end of the evening I found myself chatting to other guests across the tables. And it doesn't just end with the food. Everything is done to make sure your stay is comfortable; during breakfast Ilzebet's wonderful book-keeper even fussed over babies and produced books and games for children so parents could eat in peace. By the end of your stay it will feel like you are part of one big family. It's not open for lunch though. Some rooms at the lodge face the pool, some are bonsai Cape Dutch cottages that face the mountain and next-door's sheep. The Honeymoon Suite is all about the view and has a huge four-poster. They vary in feel and size, but all are adorable with bunches of wild flowers everywhere you look and tidy piles of magazines. During the day guests can enjoy bike rides and hikes through the Langeberg Mountains or sneak off to the nearby ravine and swim beneath the waterfall. If all this activity leaves you out of puff why not take a leisurely stroll to the Drostdy Museum or simply soak up the Swellendam sun and bask like a reptile in the garden or by the pool.

Rooms: 10: 4 doubles, 5 twins and 1 family room, all with en-suite shower, except 1 king with bath.
Price: R280 - R340 pp sharing. Singles on request.
Meals: Full breakfast included. The restaurant is open from Tuesday till Sunday evening, but not for lunch.
Directions: From Cape Town, take the 4th exit off the N2 to Swellendam. (Count the turn-off to Swellendam industrial area as the first.) After turning off, take the first street left. From the east, after turning off the N2, it's the first street on the left.

Honeywood Farm

John and Miranda Moodie

Between Swellendam and Heidelberg
Tel: 028-722-1823 Fax: 028-722-1823
Email: john@honeywoodfarm.co.za Web: www.honeywoodfarm.co.za
Cell: 083-270-4035

Attention all botanists, ornithologists, dendrologists, zoologists and, well, pretty much any kind of "–ist", Honeywood is the place for you. Part conservation area, it's an open, free place, bang next-door to the bird-watching mountain paradise of the Grootvadersbosch Nature Reserve. John is a bee farmer and an expert on everything from olive-back shrikes to yellowwoods and tree frogs. He'll gladly take you on walks across the farm and into forest stuffed chock-a-block with rare, indigenous forest canaries, knysna woodpeckers, sunbirds and various raptors. You may not have heard of the narina trogon before you arrive, but after a stay at Honeywood you'll be able to identify it by warble alone. If mountain biking's more your thing then there are plenty of trails to explore and if you're of an artistic bent, Miranda – who exhibits in nearby Knysna – runs classes. Accommodation is in simple farm cottages stocked with well-loved books on all things African. They are close to the main house where Miranda, who also trained as a cook in Italy, whips up meals on the Aga. When I arrived the weekly Moodie get-together was in full swing, but they soon found room for me on the lengthy kitchen table. This Moodie clan hasn't moved house since 1817 and, frankly, after a few days at Honeywood, you'll understand why. *Children under 12 half price. Farm may also be hired out as a wedding venue.*

Rooms: 3: B&B units, all en-suite with a bath and shower. Self-catering option available.
Price: R400 pp sharing for bed, breakfast and a three-course evening meal including wine.
Meals: Lunch platters R55 for two sharing.
Directions: From Cape Town on N2 take the first road to Suurbraak (R324) after Swellendam and continue straight (you will pass the turn to Tradouws Pass) until you arrive at a dirt road. Carry on straight until you start seeing signs for Honeywood.

Groot Vaders Bosch Farm

Keith and Michele Moodie

Heidelberg
Tel: 028-722-2044 Fax: 028-722-2044
Email: info@grootvadersbosch.co.za Web: www.grootvadersbosch.co.za
Cell: 082-412-5991

Deep in the Overberg vales, this Jersey dairy farm was the first stop-off for the ancestral Moodie clan on their way from Orkney way back in 1818. Soon they spread far and wide (my visit coincided with that of a Kiwi Moodie for example), but a lucky few stayed on. And now, the fifth generation, Keith and Michele, want to share their very special farm with you. Exclusively yours, you'll feel right at home in the rambling country house, where guests are just as likely to be found curled up on the sofa by the blazing kitchen hearth as out checking fodder and feeding calves in the late afternoon. The rooms are delightfully rustic, my favourite being bottle-green with a yellowwood floor and ceiling and four-poster bed. Another room has its own spinning wheel (if you feel the urge, Michele will show you how) and a cavernous bathroom up in the eaves under the thatch with a free-standing Victorian slipper bath making this quite the romantic spot. Wholesome dinners are enjoyed each night with the family by candlelight taking you back to 1740 when the house was first built.

Rooms: 3: 1 queen with full en-suite bathroom; 2 twins, both with en-suite baths.
Price: R500 pp sharing, dinner B&B.
Meals: Full breakfast and 2-course evening meal with the family included in the price.
Directions: From Cape Town take N2. Turn L onto R324 & drive thro' Suurbraak (don't take turning to Barrydale). Continue along R322 towards Heidelberg onto gravel rd (only 2km). Farm signed on L. From Heidelberg, continue thro' town taking Barrydale/Suurbraak rd. Continue on R322 onto gravel rd (ignore signs to Grootvadersbosch Reserve). Farm on R, 21km from Heidelberg.

Uncle Happy's Lodge

Petro Lourens

Fordstraat 3, Heidelberg
Tel: 083-280-7814 Fax: 028-722-1400
Email: happysbb@webmail.co.za
Cell: 083-280-7814

As soon as I walked through the door I felt at home in this big old Cape Dutch house with its woody-sweet smell of hay and wild arum lilies. I explored the vast, ceiling-free rooms whose thatch soars above the rafters like a rustic cathedral. No choirs here though, just the distant hooting from outdoor water-fowl. Deep, tempting baths made from dun-coloured stone take pride of place in the open-plan room with chairs woven from natural fibres either side of the double bed. Outside, it was drizzling and the River Duivenhoks, which backs onto the property, had flooded - a couple of ducks cowered in the corner, their beaks tucked into sodden plumage. On a sunny day though, I could imagine dozing on a sun-lounger under the trellised vines with a glass of rosé to hand – heaven. Back inside, Petro pointed to a sun-bleached black-and-white photo of a grandfather with a wide, kindly smile holding his wife's hand. He was the lodge's namesake, Uncle Happy. Sipping on rooibos, I warmed my hands on the open wood fire - where guests braai in the evenings - before sitting down at the kitchen's lengthy pine table. It's a scene that would make Uncle Happy smile.

Rooms: 4: 2 queens, 1 with a bath and shower and 1 with bath only; 1 queen and single bed with bath only; 1 single with shower only.
Price: From R250 pp sharing for B&B. R300 singles. From R800 - R1,000 whole house, self-catering.
Meals: Full English or porridge for breakfast. Other meals on request.
Directions: From Cape Town on the N2 turn left into Heidelberg at the Wimpy. Turn right at the first stop sign. Carry on until you see a brown sign for 'Uncle Happy's Lodge'. Turn right into Ford St. The lodge is opposite an ochre building with a corrugated roof.

Waterkloof Guesthouse

Hannes and Christine Uys
Witsand
Tel: 028-722-1811 Fax: 028-722-1811
Email: info@waterkloofguesthouse.co.za
Web: www.waterkloofguesthouse.co.za Cell: 083-270-2348

Ever played chicken with an ostrich? Now's your chance. Admittedly I had the protection of a bull-barred pick-up truck but it was exciting stuff, rattling around the farm collecting still-warm eggs for the incubator and doing our best to avoid overly ruffling their fathers' feathers. Waterkloof is an ostrich farm through and through and there is nothing that Hannes (only the seventh generation of the Uys family to work this land!) doesn't know about these feisty fowl. They use the leather for bags, the eggs for breakfast, the eggshells for lampshades and the meat for supper. The only thing you can't do with an Uys ostrich is ride it – there are horses for that, and Hannes and Christine's daughters will happily take you out on a tour. Sunk into rolling fields of barley and wheat, this is a hard-working farm but a great place to take it easy. Cool, luxurious bedrooms open onto the garden and fountain, wild fig trees shade benches built for reading on and the pool area has its own kitchen for help-yourself Sunday lunches. And if you feel like a change of scenery (and wildlife), Witsand is the place to see migrating whales. Back at the house Hannes patiently answered my babble of questions as we sank into ostrich-leather-covered armchairs and tucked into Christine's cheesecake - no ostrich in that, I take it. Leather goods made by Italian designers in Cape Town are sold here for a third of the price too!

Rooms: 4: 2 doubles and 1 twin all with bath, 1 twin with shower.
Price: R280 - R450 pp sharing.
Meals: Full breakfast included. Dinner on request.
Directions: From the CT and the N2 turn R onto R324 after Swellendam 32 to the farm. From Mossel Bay take R322 to Witsand. At the crossroads turn R. Farm is on the L after 17 km.

River Magic

Bosky and Paul Andrew
Reservations: 35 Pear Lane, Constantia, Cape Town
Physical address: Riversdale/Vermaaklikheid Cell: 082-732-3003
Tel: 021-794-6294 or 028-713-2930 Fax: 028-713-2930 or 021-794-6294
Email: rivermagic@zsd.co.za Web: www.vermaaklikheid.co.za

"Welcome to the centre of the universe," said Paul, as our tubby little rowing boat sliced through the early morning mist, its oars stirring the clear cola-coloured water and groaning in their rollocks. We bumped gently against the jetty and then hopped out onto a dew-damp riverbank, the best and, for that matter, only way to arrive at River Magic's 'Glory Be'. Silence. I fumbled for an appropriate superlative. What a spot... what a find. Two low, stone-built, thatched cottages, buried in the folds of brush-carpeted, ancient sand dunes and, without doubt, the most enchanting place I had yet encountered. I longed to return with a gang of pals, threading our way between the banks of Spanish reed, ferrying supplies across the river, fishing for grunter from the jetty (or canoes) and sharing beers and a braai around the huge outdoor table on the even more enormous shaded verandah. Inside, the cottages are comfortably (not extravagantly) kitted-out with wooden furniture and all kitchen essentials. There are beds for as many as you can muster, some secluded, others tucked into tents or in sociable four-man rooms. On a hot tip, I wheeled mine outside to sleep under the stars where I lay heaped in a duvet, inventing constellations, listening to hadedahs in the blue gums and scribbling notes by torchlight. Sound alright?

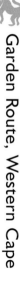

Rooms: 3 cottages: Glory Be sleeps 12 in 5 bedrooms (3 en-suite); Back Track sleeps 6 (2 twins en/s shr, 1 tented hut); Base Huis sleeps 8 -10 (3 twins, 1 double, 2 single, 1 separate bath and sh'r).
Price: From R130 - R150 pp sh. Min R400 to R500 per cottage per night. Min R500 - R800 over long weekends and R800 - R1,500 over Christmas.
Meals: Self-catering, bring towels and torches. Wood available for sale. Seafood restaurant nearby.
Directions: From Cape Town 50km after Swellendam & 3km before Heidelberg turn R at 'Port Beauford: Witsand' sign. 6km down tar rd, turn L at dirt rd signed Vermaaklikheid. 14km turn L at T-jct, cross Duivenshok River over causeway. Follow signs to Vermaaklikheid & on to River Magic.

De Doornkraal Historic Country House

Jacolette De Necker (Olivier)
8 Lang Street, Riversdale
Tel: 028-713-3838 Fax: 028-713-3050
Email: dedoornkraal@mweb.co.za Web: www.dedoornkraal.com
Cell: 082-958-0622

If the hectic pace of today's world leaves you feeling out of breath, or even slightly nauseous, I couldn't think of a more suitable antidote than a stay at De Doornkraal. Formerly a doctor's surgery (operations can still legally be performed on the premises!), this Cape Dutch beauty dates back to 1746 and is the oldest building in Riversdale. Listen very carefully and you can almost hear the history echo through the walls; at the very least you can certainly see it. After a painstaking restoration, the original yellowwood floors and ceilings, blackwood furnishings and the stunning rosewood front door are now revealed in all their former glory. Understatedly elegant rooms have simple, neutral-coloured upholstery so as not to upstage the beautiful woodwork throughout. Original paintings add splashes of colour, the work of a well-known artist who previously lived here. They also share a fine drawing room with honesty bar, the ideal place for an after-dinner nightcap. Across the road are two comfortable and airy cottages set by a large willow-shaded pond in a fruit-filled garden that rolls on into the paddocks beyond. Honeymooners can contentedly picnic under the oaks here, while children could acquaint themselves with the aquatic and farm animal neighbours. Happily, I sat listening to the fountain murmur in the tea garden, lost to the outside world; its only reminder hoots from the thrice-daily steam-train that runs through an otherwise sleepy town.

Rooms: 6: 3 rooms in Meintjes House (2 queens & 1 twin, all en-suite free-standing baths & shower, sharing lounge); Ceder Cottage (1 queen, lounge & en-suite shower); Willow Cottage (1 queen, en-s bath & shower, 1 twin en-s shower, lounge & kitchenette).
Price: R395 - R775 pp sharing. Single supplement +50%.
Meals: Full breakfast included. Restaurant, tea and wine garden on the premises open breakfast, lunch, dinner and for private functions.
Directions: N2 from Cape Town to Riversdale, L into town at the main entrance, follow signboards. Turn L just before you leave town into Lang Street. 100m on LHS.

Riversong Farm

Piers Sibson
Waterblom Avenue, Stilbaai
Tel: 082-374-8274
Email: pierss@mweb.co.za Web: www.riversongfarm.co.za

Rustic, down-to-earth and outdoorsy. If these words jump out at you, then this is a truly great find. Sheltered by reeds and milkwood trees on the banks of the Goukou River, Riversong Farm is the ideal spot to relax, get outside and experience nature's simple pleasures. In fact it would be shameful not to spend at least most of the time by, in or on the river or off exploring the farm's kloofs, dams and bushman paintings as it stretches back into the fynbos backlands beyond (also ripe for investigation). Not that the indoors is not for enjoying as well. The four wooden chalets are comfortable, unfussy and cosy affairs. Whilst 'Jordan' would be especially snug for a romantic getaway, the gargantuan 'Zambezi' could easily manage two families and then some. Each has a well-equipped kitchen, open fire and verandah from which you can follow the river as it idles its way down to the Indian Ocean. Braais in the chalets and on the lawn by the reed-lined deck provide ample opportunity to cook up the day's catch. Also living on this working farm are Simon and Manuela, both very knowledgeable about the area's wildlife, particularly the abundant bird life. Barely had I stepped out of the car before I had seen two eagles! So, with all this on hand and surfing, golf, 4x4 trails, and horse-riding nearby, I promise there won't be a dull moment. *Pets welcome!*

Rooms: 4 chalets: Zambezi sleeps 8 (2 doubles plus extra bunks, with en-s showers); Thames sleeps 4 (1 dble plus extra bunk bed, separate bathroom); Orange sleeps 4 (1 dble, 2 singles, en-s shower); Jordan sleeps 2 (1 queen, separate bathroom).
Price: R400 - R1,100 for one whole chalet depending on season. Special rates for whole farm.
Meals: Fully self-catering. Fishing and boating permits are available from the post office.
Directions: Take Stillbaai turning off N2, 12km after Riversdale. Once in town R over bridge, then immediately R into Waterblom Avenue. Farm clearly signposted about 12km upriver.

Otters Spring River Lodge

Sue Byrne
Waterblom Street, Stilbaai
Tel: 028-754-3112 Fax: 028-754-3112
Email: suebyrne@webmail.co.za Web: www.ottersspring.co.za
Cell: 082-775-5053

I heard Sue before I saw her. Her laughter is often heard echoing around the house, emblematic of a thoroughly jolly place, equally suited to family fun as to lazy, pampered getaways. Otter's Spring is plugged into the hillside above the Goukou River and surrounded by 90 hectares of paddock, riverbank and dam to let the kids loose on while you sink into a good book, the pool or both. Rooms, each with a basic but brightly-coloured bathroom, are hidden under the thatched roof or tucked into the hillside. I slept blissfully in the charming and slightly more secluded room that sits on the edge of the clumpy meadow, mowed by podgy sheep, which tumbles down to the river. Sooner or later, you'll be down there too, hurling yourself in from the bobbing pontoon, or (probably not 'and') looking out for the elusive otters. You're welcome to fish too, though to date no one has ever caught anything substantial in size. Back up at the house the chickens provide the eggs, the goose chases the dog, Sue chases the chickens and prepares the delicious evening meals (sometimes at the same time!).... And you? Your job is to lie back in a hammock or treat yourself to a massage in the village nearby (sometimes available on-site). Water-skiing and wake-boarding are available further down-river and Stilbaai has excellent surf.

Rooms: 6: 1 twin and 3 doubles, all with bath and/or shower; 1 family suite with 2 doubles, separate toilet and shared bathroom.
Price: R300 - R485 pp sharing.
Meals: Full breakfast included. Dinners on request.
Directions: From N2 take the Stilbaai turning between Riversdale and Albertinia. Arriving in town, cross the bridge and turn immediately right into Waterblom St. Otters Spring is 13km upriver on the right.

Sandpiper Cottages

Fred Orban
Strelitzia Street, Boggoms Bay, Mossel Bay District
Tel: 044-699-1204 Fax: 044-699-1204
Email: stay@sandpipersafaris.co.za Web: www.sandpiper.co.za
Cell: 082-550-4788

This secretive beachside spot is creeping shyly onto the map with Sandpiper's budding cluster of thatched white-walled fishermen's cottages. Fred, a developer by trade, started building with his children in mind but, like swallows, they have flown to Europe, leaving you to take up residence instead. My favourite was Fred's most recent project, the honeymoon cottage, christened 'Sea Mist'. Here a tender haze emanates from the affectionately planned and implemented interiors. Red clay tile floors are ornamented with yellowwood and Oregon pine furniture, while a sleeper-wood worktop and recycled timber staircase showcase Sandpiper's originality and your host's particular love of old wood. An extraordinary hearth gathers you with fire-warmed fingers into its seated inglenook and a three-roomed bathroom flaunts its own lounge. Hugely roomy yet indisputably cosy, the varied cottages combine an atmosphere of the past with luxuries of today. Fred himself is a truly lovely chap and, although the cottages are fully self-catered, he can sort you out with a 'real Boggoms breakfast' and even dinner as well. You will certainly need the energy if you want to make the most of the superb Fred-built sports centre and spa and hike the dazzling, Fred-established Oystercatcher Trail. Untamed fynbos encourages bees, buck, rabbits and birds to gather in the garden; the vegetation extends from your cottage to the beach where sand and rock scuffle with the sea, vying for attention with the distant Outeniqua Mountains.

Rooms: 5 cottages: 2 with 2 beds, and 3 with 3 beds. All have multiple bathrooms.
Price: Self-catering R290 - R550 pp sh; B&B R350 - R630 pp sh. Singles on request. Min. 2-night stay.
Meals: Meals on request. Full or continental breakfast can be delivered to self-catering cottages for R55 pp. Evening meals R110 pp (excluding wine) ordered 1-2 days in advance.
Directions: From Cape Town along N2 in direction of Mossel Bay, turn R 34km after Albertinia at Boggoms Bay junction. Continue for 11km before turning L into village. More detailed directions can be emailed on booking.

Botlierskop Private Game Reserve

The Neethling family

Little Brak River
Tel: 044-696-6055 Fax: 044-696-6272
Email: info@botlierskop.co.za Web: www.botlierskop.co.za
Cell: 082-563-8226

The Garden Route is best known for its scenery and sea life, so the last thing I expected to see as I navigated the back roads was a rhino. But there it was, chewing the cud like a contented cow. Botlierskop is a private game reserve that brings the big five south. It's not as wild as its northern counterparts (the lions are in a sanctuary) but it's a magical place to stay, set in 3,000 hectares of grassy plains and forested sandstone hills. The park is open to day visitors but it's skillfully co-ordinated to ensure your paths never cross. Two of the highlights are Sam and Totsi, orphaned elephants trained not only in giving rides, but also as actors. Did you see *Far of Place*? Or *Elephant Boy*? Trust me, they were great! Morning coffee with the rhino is also a must and personally I found nibbling on live termites pleasantly minty. Overnighters are appointed their own private guide and I had John-Lee, an animal almanac and rock art aficionado. From the cavernous hilltop restaurant, he ushered me into a dinghy and we drifted off down the wooded Moordkuil River to the guest tents. More of a marquee than a tent, each is set on its own patch of decking with steps leading to a floating jetty (a great spot to fish from). Inside it's luxury with a capital 'L'; deep armchairs, a writing desk and a room-for-two bath accompany the mosquito-netted four-poster. One tip though: zip it closed when you leave - the vervet monkeys have a penchant for coffee and cookies.

Rooms: 19 Luxury, Deluxe and Executive Tented Suites. All with en-suite bath; Deluxe and Executive have outdoor showers and Executive has its own lounge and outdoor splash pool.
Price: R1,990 - R2,490 pp sh (incl' game drive/bush walk/meals). Singles R2,986 - R3,735. 6 - 12 yr olds, half adult rate. 2-day stay incl's free helicopter ride.
Meals: Breakfast and dinner included and lunch as well if staying 2 or more nights.
Directions: From Mossel Bay and CT on N2 take Little Brak River exit (401). Heading inland turn R to Sorgfontein. Continue 4km and after causeway turn R for 4km along gravel road to Botlierskop.

Malvern Manor

Sandra and Michael Cook

Nr Fancourt, Blanco, George
Tel: 044-870-8788 Fax: 044-870-8790
Email: info@malvernmanor.co.za Web: www.malvernmanor.co.za
Cell: 084-867-6470

If you are having any difficulty understanding why the area is called the Garden Route, well, have a trundle up Michael and Sandra's drive. Much more colourful and vibrant than anything visible from the public thoroughfares. I drove past cows and dams onto a redbrick road overflowing with thick tangles of foliage that hide Malvern from view - and all this perfectly framed by the imposing Outeniqua Mountains. Here is another English couple who fell in love with South Africa, upped sticks and bought their country idyll. Both of farming stock, this 21-hectare dairy farm was perfect. But despite being just a hop, skip and a jump from George, it was no easy task converting the Manor House, the keep at the heart of the farm, into a guest house. But it's all come together so nicely. My room opened onto the garden through French doors, and lavish Greek-style pillars pick out the bath – the perfect place to unwind after a round of golf at Fancourt (recent host of the President's Cup). For non-golfers, two dams offer blue gill and big-mouth bass fishing and there's endless scope for pre-breakfast walks or watching DVDs on the newly-installed players. Play your cards right on your return and Michael might don his apron and prepare his speciality 'chocaccino'. Delightful people in an enchanting setting.

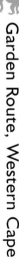

Rooms: 3: 1 queen, 1 twin or king, 1 double with single bed. All have en-suite bath and shower.
Price: R500 - R750 pp sharing. Singles on request.
Meals: Full breakfast included. Restaurants nearby and deliveries can be arranged.
Directions: From N2 take George airport exit onto R404 and follow signs to Oudtshoorn for approximately 8km. After Fancourt Golfing Estate, sign to Malvern Manor on left. Follow signs.

Fairview Historic Homestead

Philda Benkenstein
36 Stander St, George
Tel: 044-874-7781
Fax: 086-603-7840
Email:
benkenstein@mweb.co.za
Web:
www.fairviewhomestead.com
Cell: 082-226-9466

This picturesque, listed Cape Georgian house on the eastern edge of George is an intriguing place to stay. With its high ceilings and abundant Victoriana, Fairview has the feel of an old English rectory, although the vivid colours owe more to African than Anglican themes. All the bedrooms are a treat: the two on the ground floor still have their original 1880s floorboards, beams and fireplaces; the Orange Room, complete with dashing white trim, bathes in afternoon sunlight; while the Yellow Room soaks up the morning. The sitting room has the same high ceilings and wooden floors, with shuttered sash windows and enormous linen press. The whole place has a happy family atmosphere, enhanced by the original home features, which have been retained wherever possible. Philda loves to host and have people in her beautiful home. She will cook too and if you do eat here, as the GG guests visiting were, then you'll enjoy mainly South African fare. She's an intrepid hiker too and following her advice I soon found myself on a mountainside with sweeping views over George. Husband Desmond is a green-fingered doctor and the creative force in the glorious garden. There are fruit trees, an immaculate veggie patch, swathes of clivia and plans for much more.

Rooms: 3: 2 doubles with an extra bed; 1 family double and twin room. 2 have en-suite shower, 1 has en-suite bath.
Price: R300 - R360 pp sharing. Singles plus 40%.
Meals: Full breakfast included. Dinner by arrangement: R80 pp for 2 courses, R110 pp for 3 courses. Price excludes wine.
Directions: Take York Street exit off N2. Go thro' town until roundabout at top of York St. Turn R (signed Knysna) into Knysna Rd & continue down past High Sch & over railway bridge. Turn L at 1st lights after rwy bdge into First St or go over Stop St & turn R into Stander at T-jct. From Knysna turn R at 5th lights (just before bridge) into First St.

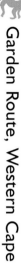

Acorn Guest House

Colin and Esther Horn

4 Kerk St, George
Tel: 044-874-0474 Fax: 086-610-7854
Email: info@acornguesthouse.co.za Web: www.acornguesthouse.co.za
Cell: 083-539-7398

With birds chirping in the tree-lined street and church bells chiming (kerk is Afrikaans for church), I approached the pink, ivy-clad walls utterly unaware of the riches hidden within. Acorn Guest House is a veritable treasure trove and Esther was quick to explain: "as some people go tc casinos, we go to auctions." Almost everything in this Edwardian house is second-hand anc antique. Persian rugs are strewn over bare floorboards; battered wooden trunks are scatterec throughout the bedrooms; mirrors and ornaments adorn the available wall space; every nook anc cranny arrests the eye. The bedrooms are equally ornate, the master room boasting a large en-suite bathroom separated from the grand sleeping area by a gold-coloured curtain. Had I stayec a little longer (and deprived the Horns of even more of Esther's delicious home-baked cake), could have joined Colin on a fishing trip… although not the leisurely pipe-and-picnic fishing I hac envisaged. "If guests are able to swim 4km in the sea with a snorkel, they're welcome to join me," he proclaimed, re-emerging with his weapon of choice, a spear gun. If all this sounds a bit toc James Bond for you, he also offers more serene tours of the Garden Route. Those with spoils tc share come evening do so on the braai, while bargain-hunters furiously jot down Esther's top tips

Rooms: 8: 3 twins with en-suite bath and shower; 1 double with en-suite shower; 1 double with en-suite bath and shower; 1 double with en-suite bath; 1 family unit with en-suite shower; 1 twin/king with full disabled provision, spa bath & shower.
Price: R275 - R650 pp sharing. Singles +50%.
Meals: Full breakfast included. Picnic basket and dinner by arrangement. Self-catering facilities available
Directions: Take York Street exit off N2 towards town. Go through town on York Street until the roundabout. Turn right (signed to Knysna) and Kerk Street is third turning on left. Second property on right.

The Waves

Liza and Iain Campbell
7 Beach Rd, Victoria Bay, George
Tel: 044-889-0166 Fax: 044-889-0166
Email: thewaves@intekom.co.za
Web: www.gardenroute.co.za/vbay/waves/index.htm

Iain and Liza have an amazing photo from 1906 when The Waves was the only house on the beach, used as a holiday home by an Oudtshoorn farmer. It is not surprising a few others have since joined the club. The hamlet is closed to vehicles – only residents hold the key to the gate, so you can park your car securely at night. I'm no surfer, but the waves here are enticing, rolling up the perfect arc of the small bay at a height that is challenging, but not scary. Iain will arrange a wetsuit and surfboard or fins and a snorkel. Or if you like your activity less damp, there is horse-riding nearby, dolphin- and whale-watching in season and walks along the bay front. The house is right on the sea (see above) to which all three bedroom suites (each with its own lounge) look out, although you may spend more time on the verandah watching the waves roll in. They are hypnotic. Breakfast is served here in the sunshine and often goes on for hours. The Outeniqua Choo-Tjoe (yes, it's a steam train) runs through Victoria Bay twice a day. Both Iain and Liza are consummate hosts, love what they do and share a great sense of fun. Bay life could be addictive. *Fully no-smoking anywhere. Children over 12 only.*

Rooms: 5: 3 B&B rooms, all doubles, 1 with en-suite shower, 2 with en-suite bath and shower; 1 cottage and 1 suite available for self-catering.
Price: R500 - R700 pp sharing. Singles R600 - R950.
Meals: Full breakfast included. Dinner can be ordered in and a table will be set for you.
Directions: From Mossel Bay on N2 past George exits where highways merge. 1km signed Victoria Bay to right - follow down hill 3km. Park and walk along beach road to collect the key for the gate.

Porcupine Pie Boutique Lodge

John and Judy McIldowie
10 Mile Lane, Wilderness Heights
Email: john@porcupinepie.co.za Web: www.porcupinepie.co.za
Cell: 083-447-6901

You really are on top of the world here - even the air smells different at this height! Porcupine Pie, nestled at the end of a winding, climbing road, has some simply breathtaking views. The Wilderness Nature Reserve and the Outeniqua Mountains unfurl before you, and a wedge of stunning blue sea looks out out between its foliage-fringed peaks. A rare commotion of birds provides possibly the best on-site birding around. You don't even need to leave the deck, just whip out a pair of bino's and watch. In the time it took me to munch just one of their biscuits, I had seen an eagle and two resident jackal buzzards. I arrived on a freakishly hot winter's day (30 degrees!), so I braved a swim before warming up in a candlelit bath. And when I looked up mid-bath, there was that view again. Each bedroom unit is a stilted wooden chalet with a patio that hovers mid-air. Judy's artwork hangs on the walls including, of course, a porcupine. During the home-made supper of chicken stuffed with feta, I had to ask, why Porcupine Pie? The morning after they laid the guesthouse path, John explained, they found a small pair of porcupine prints in the wet concrete. So really the place named itself. They do all the cooking, (don't miss Judy's breakfast bran muffins), including portered picnics in the river valley below. Dozing off that night with the French windows wide open, the bush-frogs ribbeted me to sleep. No understatement here, it was the best night's kip I'd had in months.

Rooms: 3: all kings with en-suite bath and shower.
Price: R450 - R600 pp sharing.
Meals: Full breakfast included. Two-course dinners approx R100 pp.
Directions: From George follow N2 to Wilderness. Turn L into Wilderness Village, follow road past Protea Hotel to T-junction. Turn L and travel up Heights Rd for 3.8km. Do not turn off tar until you reach T-jct marked 'Old George/Knysna Road'. Turn R onto gravel road and after 1.6km turn R onto 'Ten Mile Lane'. Follow Porcupine Signs for 3.4km.

Moontide Guest Lodge

Maureen Mansfield

Southside Rd, Wilderness
Tel: 044-877-0361 Fax: 044-877-0124
Email: moontide@intekom.co.za Web: www.moontide.co.za

It's a rare pleasure for us to stay somewhere on holiday and to experience it over a period of days. And Moontide was a palpable hit with all five of us. Its position is hard to beat, right on the banks of the lagoon, its wooden decks shaded by 400-year-old milkwood trees. Here you can sit out for bountiful breakfasts or with an evening drink from your bar fridge, and watch giant kingfishers diving for fish – well, we saw one anyway. Birdlife is profuse on the lagoon. The long, white-sanded Wilderness beach is only a two-minute walk from the house, but you can also take a canoe straight from Moontide up the lagoon into the Touw River and then walk along forest trails to waterfalls to swim in fresh-water rock pools. Whatever we did it was a pleasure to return, play cards in a relaxed sitting room, or read in the cool of a bedroom. I was delighted with 'Milkwood' because I'm a sucker for dozing on a futon, in a loft, under thatched eaves, with river views by my head. But I would like to return and try them all. Since we descended en masse, Maureen has built herself a tree-top sanctuary. The deck, day-bed, even the free-standing bath, look out across thatched roofs to the river. Sportingly, she's decided it's too nice to keep for herself!

Rooms: 8: Moonriver Luxury Suite (king, 2 twins, bath, sh'r); Treetops (qu, bath, outside sh'r); Milkwood (king/twins & queen upstairs, bath, sh'r); Stone Cottage (twins, sh'r); The Boathouse (d'ble, bath); Moonshadow 1 & 2 (kings, baths & sh'rs); Nest (king, shower).
Price: R400 - R750 pp sharing. Single +70%
Meals: Full breakfast included. Self-catering option available in the Nest.
Directions: From George on N2 ignore Wilderness turn-off. Cross Touw River bridge, first left signed Southside Rd. Moontide at the end of cul-de-sac.

Slanting Acres

Pam Ross

Bitou Road, Hoekwil, Wilderness
Tel: 044-850-1195 Fax: 044-850-1195
Email: reservations@slantingacres.com Web: www.slantingacres.com
Cell: 082-907-2404

Horses were chewing, birds were roosting, ducks were swimming, cats were purring, chickens were foraging, peacocks were displaying by the new tennis court and the guinea fowl… were just being guinea fowl. Animals are everywhere on Slanting Acres' slanting seven and a half acres, plenty of room for everyone. The immaculate lawns sweep around this white-washed, wood-decked house, hoisted high on the Hoekwil hillside, with far-reaching views over Wilderness and into the wilderness of the deep-blue Indian Ocean. Equally blue is the figure-of-eight-shaped pool, where a waterfall is a constant cooling sight and sound. If lazing by the pool is not enough to occupy your mind, there is always the 18-hole putting green and the brand-new tennis court. Personally I would prefer to sink one in the nautically-themed bar inside. Iain is a ship's captain in the merchant navy, and he'll happily tell you all about his life at sea… that is if he is not actually at sea when you visit. Pictures of the various ships he's skippered fill the walls. Pam will keep you entertained in his absence. She's the driving force behind Slanting Acres. The bedrooms are small, but perfectly formed with white cotton sheets, pine wardrobes, and plenty of light. And Pam has recently opened her new honeymoon Garden Suite with king-size bed, spa bath, TV, fridge, air-con, stunning views of mountains and sea from the private decks. Homely comforts in a very friendly house.

Rooms: 4: 2 doubles and 1 twin, all with en-suite shower rooms. New honeymoon Garden Suite, king-size bed, en suite spa bath, TV, fridge, aircon, views of mountains and sea from private decks.
Price: R350 - R550 pp sharing B&B. Singles + 25%.
Meals: Full breakfast included. Lots of restaurants nearby.
Directions: From Cape Town take the N2 past George and 2km past Wilderness turn L to Hoekwil. Pass the lake and go over railway, up hill and turn R at 1st brown B&B sign.

The Dune Guest Lodge

Gary and Melisa Grimes
31 Die Duin, Wilderness
Tel: 044-877-0298 Fax: 044-877-0298
Email: info@thedune.co.za Web: www.thedune.co.za
Cell: 083-941-1149

Gary Grimes is both consummate host and chief breakfast-maker at The Dune and when I pulled up (carefully avoiding parking in the space marked "for my girlfriend/wife") he and Melisa had just finished feeding the hordes with a man-stopping fry-up. "Anything you can do with eggs, I do it," he tells me. I made a note to arrive a little earlier next time. By most standards, he is greedily tall, but at 6'7" he insists he was pretty average among his basketball contemporaries and after years as a pro in Switzerland he dropped the ball in favour of a dishcloth, dinner plates and the wildness of Wilderness. If you're looking for a beach-house then you couldn't get much more beachy than this. As the name suggests it's smack-bang in the dunes and, to be numerically fastidious, exactly 85 wooden steps lead down to 7.5km of pristine sandy beach stretching away to both east and west. The whole place has a wonderfully soothing, seaside feel. Walls hung with seascape oils are whitewashed or sea-blue. Driftwood sculptures surround the fireplace and bedside sofas look south through wall-to-wall windows for round-the-clock whale-watching. Best of all though, wherever you are in the building, you can hear the surf heaving, sighing, thumping and crumping against the beach.

Rooms: 5: 2 doubles, 2 twins with 3/4 beds, all with en/s bath and shower. 1 self-catering cottage.
Price: R350 – R750 pp sharing B&B. Singles +R200.
Meals: Full breakfast included.
Directions: From CT pass Wilderness on N2. Cross the Touw River and turn right into Die Duin 700m later. Take the right fork and The Dune is first on the left.

Palms Wilderness

Wayne and Vicky Nel
Owen Grant Rd, Wilderness
Tel: 044-877-1420 Fax: 044-877-1422
Email: palms@pixie.co.za Web: www.palms-wilderness.com

All's well that ends well. Especially with an excellent bottle of Springfield, straight from Wayne's temperature-regulated cellar, to keep me company in my spoilingly huge room. On its label it read 'The Work of Time', as if only the best things come from with the slow passage of years. This is not always true; with remarkable alacrity, Wayne and Vicky have renovated and revitalised Palms by bringing a little piece of African bush into the heart of Wilderness. The restaurant frequently spills outside into a jungle of palm, banana and fig trees, as locals and guests alike are drawn to delicious Cape Malay cuisine. A popular lunchtime deli as well, there's a special atmosphere here in the evenings, warmed by the vibrant colours and a sense of shared enjoyment in everyone's company. Breakfast has to be taken outside in the morning sun, watching the village slowly come to life. Sunbirds hover past and an old milkwood tree shades the pool. Individual thatched rooms are dotted around, each with a private entrance. Johann, the extremely helpful and friendly manager, talked me through the rooms' rough-hewn African textures, gauzy, golden curtains, cuddlesome chairs and spa baths that warrant a few laps. There are all the natural wonders of Wilderness, such as hiking, canoeing, beach and lagoon trips all within a 500-metre radius of your bed, but if you're after a real challenge, try taking Wayne on at backgammon.

Rooms: 11: 5 queens (2 with en-suite bath, 2 with en-suite shower & 1 with bath and shower); 2 triples (both with en-suite shower); 4 twins (2 with en-suite shower, 1 with en-suite bath).
Price: R500 - R632 pp sharing B&B. Singles on request.
Meals: Breakfast included. Lunch and dinner also available.
Directions: Wilderness is signed to your left on the N2 from Cape Town. Follow the road past the Caltex Garage and Pomodoro's restaurant then sweep left to the Protea Hotel. Palms is directly opposite.

Eden B&B

Bev Campbell
370 Erica Road, Wilderness Heights, Wilderness
Tel: 044-877-0149
Email: bcampbell@telkomsa.net Web: www.edenstay.co.za
Cell: 082-627-4712

Bev is immediately herself - warm, open and completely unpretentious - and with a welcome glass of home-made lemonade in my hand and the prospect of a spicy bobotie for lunch, I didn't take long to settle into this cottage high in the foothills of the Outeniqua Mountains. Very soon we were happily talking and laughing an afternoon away, covering such diverse topics as Bev's connections with the admiralty and the building and selling of entire villages. Guests eat every morning in a very pretty and intimate breakfast room, making the short journey from their cottage across the lawns escorted by Dougal, a sprightly Jack Russel. Rustic integrity underpins this woodcutter's cottage and it is an unfussy place to unwind. "Everything's antique," says Bev, "including myself these days!" Certainly there's character a-plenty in the living area and three bedrooms: a sweet little writing desk, venerable armchairs, an old Dover stove, sturdy tankards, a meat safe and original photographs of a bygone forestry industry, above which hangs a curved saw long since decommissioned. And in the dinky kitchen too with its crockery, pots and pans. Outside a splendid wild fig tree shelters a bench and table with a BBQ and you are free to wander through a profusion of flowerbeds, wild mushrooms, a paper-bark tree and agapanthus - a favourite with the local bushbuck. The main garden is filled with indigenous plants such as aloes, proteas and fynbos. Appropriately, my last image of Bev was of her ambling blissfully through her beloved wilderness.

Rooms: 3 double/twin rooms in cottage (1 en-suite with shower, 1 family bathroom with bath).
Price: R225 - R275 pp sharing.
Meals: Choice of 'health' or cooked breakfast included.
Directions: Turn off N2 into Wilderness, turning left at Pomodoro restaurant and then driving up the hill on White's Road, passing Map of Africa turn-off and then turning left onto Erica Road, taking right fork and continuing for 100m. Eden B&B is on the right.

Lodge on the Lake

Frank Bauer
746 North Street, Wilderness
Tel: 044-877-1097 Fax: 044-877-1097
Email: info@lodgeonthelake.co.za Web: www.lodgeonthelake.co.za
Cell: 084-383-7766

Übercool has come to Wilderness. Frank used to be in film production and his eye for precision design underlies every detail in this grandly Tuscan villa, which sits resplendent on its many pillars above the lake. As I skirted the central courtyard fountain and entered beneath the portico, something magic seemed to happen. The walls suddenly disappeared, the outside was inexplicably coming inside... but most mesmerising of all was the lake that had effortlessly risen, without a ripple, to the rim of the pool and forged a seamless sheet of the deepest liquid blue, only finally interrupted by the mountains. I suppose that's what you call German engineering. There's a Zen-like tranquillity here, a faraway sound of trickling water, which recently attracted a pair of authors; no one's sure whether they wrote anything. More than likely they discovered the delights of the in-house spa where three treatment rooms employ the mineral wealth of the sea to leave you feeling as fresh as the surf. Naturally the rooms, reached by a winding staircase, are mindful of weight, colour and proportion to the enth degree. Thick carpeting softens a solemnity of dark wooden bedsteads, cupboards and ingenious concertina doors, with a sense of playfulness creeping into striking patterns, stalactite pillars, open tubs and creative positioning of mirrors. Each has its own fabulous private balcony.

Rooms: 5: 4 doubles, 1 twin; all en-suite bath and shower.
Price: R350 - R750 pp sharing.
Meals: Full or continental breakfast included.
Directions: Emailed or faxed on booking.

Serendipity

Phillip and Elsabé Kuypers
Freesia Avenue, Wilderness
Tel: 044-877-0433 Fax: 0866-717-992
Email: info@serendipitywilderness.com
Web: www.serendipitywilderness.com Cell: 082-4499-701

Where else can you dine in arguably the best restaurant on the Garden Route and then wander upstairs to snuggle into bed beneath goose-down duvets? This is a place whose name is breathed in quiet reverence all along the coast. Other Wilderness guesthouses flatly refuse to cater. "What's the point?" they say with community pride. Brushed up crisply for dinner after a three-chapter-long soak in the bath, I stepped from underfloor-heated tiles onto the shared balcony, to watch geese flighting across a sunset lagoon. Then it was an easy meander down to the guest lounge for an apéritif, where Rudolf, husband to head-chef Lizelle (her culinary accolades, which hang in the loo, are very encouraging indeed), gave a sensuous description of a South African-inspired menu combined with European haute cuisine. Agonising, I finally plumped for snoek mousse and loin of springbok, variously interspersed by an *amuse-bouche* of kudu carpaccio and delicious butternut soup. The intimate restaurant discreetly backs onto a fireplace flanked by sheer windows looking out onto the water. For dessert I cracked into an exquisitely fruity crème brûlée, even as my waiter taught me the basics of Xhosa. Following a breakfast in ebullient sunshine I found myself discussing semantics and champion deep-sea angling with owners Elsabé and Phillip, who had originally planned to run only a guesthouse… that was before they invited their daughter to cook.

Rooms: 4: all twin/king with en-suite shower bathrooms.
Price: R300 - R580 pp sharing. Singles +50%.
Meals: Full breakfast included. Dinner in restaurant by prior arrangement.
Directions: From N2 at Wilderness turn North at Caltex garage following George Road to T-junction in front of Protea Hotel. At T-junction turn right, travel along Waterside Road for 1.2km. Turn right into Freesia Avenue. Serendipity 4th house on right.

Wilderness Manor

Johan and Marianne Nicol
397 Waterside Road, Wilderness
Tel: 044-877-0264 Fax: 044-877-0163
Email: wildman@mweb.co.za Web: www.manor.co.za

Marianne has a flair for interiors. You won't need one of the hundreds of books (African art and history, its wildlife and architecture, war memoirs, children's classics and psychology texts) that rub sleeves throughout the house to find this out. Overlooking the lagoon, the glass-encased sitting room is carpeted with Afghan kilims, a low-slung ivory sofa and a pair of Morris chairs, given to the Governor of Gauteng. There's an old billiard table, too, somewhere under a pile of maps. African artefacts have been begged, borrowed or bought: Ndebele pipes and beads, bartered-for carvings and stones from the Cradle of Mankind. The bedrooms have similar horn-and-hide hues, all the luxurious trappings you could wish for, and room for Indonesian chairs and chests, chocolate leather sofas, slipper baths and dark canopied beds with reading lights. In the morning, linen tables were dressed with bone-handle cutlery and lilies in a square metal vase placed on an old country bench next to fruit and muesli. Your hosts are discreet and attentive, and after serving up a faultless (and greaseless) breakfast, will give you a map and bountiful beach-bag and set you off to explore your surrounds. Birdlife is rampant in the area and walks in the surrounding forests are a must. It is only a five-minute stroll along lagoon-side boardwalks to the beach, town and some good restaurants.

Rooms: 4: 3 lagoon suites (2 kings and 1 twin with bath and shower en-suite) and 1 garden room (king/twin with shower en-suite).
Price: R300 - R650 pp sharing. Singles on request.
Meals: Full breakfast included.
Directions: Turn into the Wilderness Village from the N2 and follow road to the T-junction. Turn right into Waterside Road and find Wilderness Manor on your left after 1km.

Kingfisher Country House

Sue Millard
1030 Dumbleton Road, Wilderness
Tel: 044-877-1955 Fax: 044-877-1955
Email: info@kingfish.co.za Web: www.kingfish.co.za
Cell: 082-808-4379

Bring your camera to breakfast as you sit on the covered verandah overlooking stunning gardens and a steam engine railway. This is the best seat in the house for catching sight of, among other startlingly beautiful birds, the Knysna loerie, whose red velvet wing feathers tease and tantalise no less than three times a day when they come to feed. Ideally situated on the edge of the Wilderness National Park, this is a paradise for birds and for those who watch them. The forest too comes right down to this family home, the sunlight dappling through the trees onto floral and feminine nuances throughout. The rooms are just like Sue: warm, gentle and immediately relaxing. Oil lamps hang low, bringing lustre to assortments of coloured bottles and pretty boudoirs. Linen arches drape over friendly beds while curtains are full of summer, complemented by fresh flowers and still-life pictures of potted trees and plants, courtesy of Sue's daughter, Alexandra. Enjoy the feel of cocoa butter soap on the skin as you rejuvenate in the shower, before wrapping yourself in soft bath robes, choosing then perhaps to lean over the stable door, hung with tiny herb garlands, to wave hello to your neighbour. Victorian christening robes float in the hallway next to African baskets and Sue loves her frills, but she has toned it down for the more 'masculine' rooms. I took tea with her in the quirky living room where she delighted in filling my diary full of canoe and hiking trips, as well as dinner reservations in a handful of excellent restaurants.

Rooms: 4: all twin/king with en-suite shower bathrooms.
Price: R250 - R370 pp sharing. Singles on request.
Meals: Full breakfast included. Plenty of good restaurants.
Directions: Take Wilderness turning from the N2 and follow Waterside Road around the far side of the lagoon. Continue for 2km until signpost to Kingfisher Country House on the right, followed by a turning immediately to the left. The house is 200m from here.

Teniqua Treetops

Robyn and Viv Patz
Sedgefield
Tel: 044-356-2868 Fax: 088-044-356-286
Email: queries@teniquatreetops.co.za Web: www.teniquatreetops.co.za

The deep, ancient forest, which surrounds Teniqua Treetops, took a bit of getting used to after bustling Knysna. Luckily, a grinning Viv was on hand to show me around the eight wooden units, which are literally built into the forest canopy. Each house, which he designed and built himself, has an outdoor braai, tented double bed – with an electric blanket – and outdoor bathroom. Showers are made from reclaimed yellowwood whose natural shape begs to be stroked if, that is, you can tear yourself from the view. Moss-strewn yellowwoods stretch above the forest canopy which plunges into the Karatara River's 160-metre-deep gorge. Karatara, apparently, is the sound that the extinct quagga zebra made when it ran uphill! This place is wild, unconfirmed spottings of the elusive (well, even perhaps mythical these days?) Knysna elephant have been made by the river, and Viv is keen to keep it that way. He stresses that the treehouses were only built in forest gaps or where he'd removed non-indigenous trees; the rainwater is harvested and the loos are dry composting. Over supper I met the couple's seven-year-old son Alex – a demon Cluedo-player, which I discovered later to my cost. This is a child's paradise, and Robyn is keen to have as many youngsters as possible tearing around the place. There's a jungle-gym, a recently-installed balancing pole across the pool and - this is the bit I loved best - a forest trail where she leaves surprise fairies for visiting toddlers. With three honeymoon treehouses too, it's a wonderful, romantic and tranquil hideout.

Rooms: 8: 4 with baths and overhead showers; 4 with showers only. Family tents available.
Price: From R540 to R1,545 per tree house. Single rates on request.
Meals: Self-catering.
Directions: Coming from Cape Town on the N2 turn off at the brown boarded 'Teniqua Treetops' sign. Follow the signposted tar road for 15 minutes until you reach the treehouses.

Forget-me-not B&B

Mary and Derek Woolmington
21 Boekenhout St, Upper Old Place, Knysna
Tel: 044-382-2916 Fax: 044-382-2916
Email: mary@forget-me-not.co.za Web: www.forget-me-not.co.za
Cell: 083-505-4225

Derek and Mary, a warm and down-to-earth English-Irish couple, embody all that we look for in hosts. Having built businesses and raised a family, they're starting out on their own again. Hence Forget-me-not (Self-catering and B&B, to give it its full title), with its sloping, slate roof, dormer windows and gravel drive. The house is edged with wisteria, primroses and forget-me-nots and other flowers Mary can't quite put a name to (and nor can I obviously) – she puts it down to "Outeniqua rust", a lethargic malaise blamed on easy living. Inside the sweep of a maranti staircase leads to two bedrooms. Iris has pine floorboards, leaning walls, blanket box and hanging space. There's a cushioned window-box from which to sit and stare. The rose room, more feminine in shades of pink with floral motifs, has Oregon pine furniture. An elongated bathroom harbours a bath tucked under the eaves. Everyone eats at the house (usually outside above the lawn and pool), even those in the self-contained flat, whose wooden deck faces the lagoon, Knysna Heads and the hills. All guests get use of the pool and the braai area and the house is within walking distance of the Waterfront and a short drive to the beaches. The long list of activities, both on water and inland, can be booked on your behalf by Derek and Mary.

Rooms: 3: 1 king B&B; 2 queen suites (either self-catering or B&B). All rooms have en-suite bath and shower.
Price: R250 - R330 pp sharing. Singles on request.
Meals: Full cooked or Continental breakfast and variety of fruit. Plenty of local restaurants.
Directions: Head east out of Knysna and turn left onto Old Toll Rd, Upper Old Place. At T-junction turn right and take first left into Boekenhout St. Forget-me-not on right.

191 Nirvana

Madi Butler

191 Rheenendal Road, Rheenendal, Knysna
Tel: 044-386-0297 Fax: 044-386-0297
Email: madibutler@cyberperk.co.za Web: www.191nirvana.co.za
Cell: 084-826-2266

Who would have thought you could make a couple of self-catering cottages out of two water reservoirs? Evidently Madi Butler did. (First you have to empty out the water of course.) Her two circular, thatched properties now stand proudly on the top of the hill. The position, at the hub of outstanding panoramic views that stretch from the end of the Outeniqua Mountains, across Knysna Lagoon and into the surrounding forest, was just too good to waste. You won't quite know where to gaze first. This is one self-catering place where you can be 100 per cent independent, yet still have the reassuring presence of a very friendly hostess just at the bottom of the hill. On top of all the added extras you require (Madi supplies beautiful white bed linen, towels, firewood and tit bits such as organic salad), a basket of home-grown herbs and veggies (depending on the season) will find its way onto your doorstep each morning. The indoor fireplace doubles up as a braai area which - and this is my favourite part - becomes virtually outdoors when you 'roll up' the walls (made of canvas blinds) at the front of the cottage. What's that? Roll up the walls? I assure you it's possible, you'll just have to come and see for yourself.

Rooms: 2 self-catering units, both sleeping two couples or two small families.
Price: Basic price for the cottage: R950 - R1,500 (for up to 4 people and children under 13). Add R150 per extra person.
Meals: Self-catering.
Directions: Heading to Knysna from George on the N2. Before you enter Knysna turn left into Rheenendal Road. Follow the road for 1.6km and the entrance to 191 Nirvana is on your right.

Blackwaters River Lodge

Pam and Colin Emmett
N2, Goukama Valley, Knysna
Tel: 044-383-0105 Fax: 044-383-0021
Email: info@blackwaters.co.za Web: www.blackwaters.co.za
Cell: 072-136-7241

The name 'Blackwaters' comes from the tannins that make for the distinctively dark waters of the Goukamma River from whose bank this rambling guesthouse emerges. It's all pure though and the water you drink comes fresh from the river. You can also jump into a canoe from here and make your way deep into this gorgeous valley, home of wild pigs and leopards and a superabundance of birdlife. There's a room for every need. Children are well accommodated, as are honeymooners in a suite that smoulders with African romance, from the delicate embroidered designs to the huge bed, fireplace and generous-sized tub. Below the balcony that looks out onto palms, Colin cooks his famous fish braai, although he is even better known for his lectures on the southern skies, which can be observed through his own telescope. Pam too is the most thoughtful and caring of managers. The self-catering rooms are furnished with attractive wicker furniture and unusual miniature elephant wall pieces; and one is made for pet-lovers with its enclosed private courtyard, with wisteria on the walls. A bright and yellow breakfast room is adorned with woven baskets; while for lunch you must take a picnic on lawns that unfold from the river rising up to a pedestal pool. All of this is beautifully floodlit by night. I could see myself reliving a 9-hole round of golf in the communal lodge, the place to gather in the evening with its honesty bar and pool table and striking statues of faces that appear to materialise from the trees.

Rooms: 10 rooms, all en-suite (2 shower only, 8 bath and shower). Two are family suites.
Price: R320 - R550 pp sharing B&B. Self-catering from R550 - R970 for whole room.
Meals: Full breakfast included. Lunch and dinner available on request.
Directions: 10 minutes outside of Knysna along the N2 toward George, opposite sign for Buffalo Bay.

Lyndos

Lynn Schaefer
Queen St, Old Belvidere, Knysna
Tel: 044-387-1241 Fax: 044-387-1241
Email: lynnschaefer@cyberperk.co.za Web: www.lyndos.co.za
Cell: 072-174-4907

Old Belvidere feels more English than England itself. With its village green and stone church (founded by the fabled George Rex, more on him later) you can almost hear the thwack of willow on leather and the polite clapping of matrons munching scones. Pull into Lyndos though, and you soon remember that this is South Africa – where the moon rises behind the lagoon, turning the water blue-purple, and emerald-crested loeries hop from branch to branch. Lynn is an artist/potter and an interior designer by trade, and it shows. She built the flat-topped house herself with its whitewashed walls that glow amber in the sun. Inside, the blue and white units boast terracotta floors, tribal-print cushions and freshly-cut flowers. Opening the door felt like coming home, after months of travelling, to a spruced-up version of my own room. And Lyndos literally is a home from home for one group of guests who are returning for their sixth summer this year! The place may be self-catering, but Lynn is completely hands-on, hosting fantastic summer braais under the pepper tree in her backyard. When cooking isn't on the cards head down to the her local, 'The Bell.' Keep your nose to the ground and you might even sniff out some juicy royal scandal. Rumour has it that George Rex, who built Old Belvidere's church, was George III's illegitimate son: "They shipped him out from the UK on the quiet." There are worse places to be exiled I thought, as the lagoon swallowed up the burning sun.

Rooms: 2: self-catering double rooms with en-suite showers.
Price: R350 - R500 pp sharing. Single rates on request.
Meals: Kitchens supplied with continental breakfasts.
Directions: From Cape Town turn left off the N2 towards Belvidere and Brenton-on-Sea (if you reach Knysna you've gone too far). Follow the road round a U-bend and take the first sign to Belvidere. Turn left past the church into Queen St. Lyndos is at the very end up a long drive.

Lindsay Castle

Shirley and Ian Berry
Noetzie, Knysna
Tel: 044-384-1849 Fax: 086-611-5111
Email: reservations@knysnacastles.co.za Web: www.knysnacastles.com

There is something peculiarly invigorating (and perhaps just peculiar) about trudging through sand and over glistening rocks, in salty sea air, crashing surf on one side, lush hillside vegetation on the other, to your own beach-marooned, stone-turreted castle. King Arthur meets Robinson Crusoe and all this just a few minutes away from the activity of Knysna and Plettenberg Bay! My enchanted eyes feasted on the view from the castle: the ocean, bordered with intensely coloured rocks, gold and orange, the gentle curve of the wide beach, the fine sand and the wild, lush coastline of Noetzie. At one end of the beach, a path leads directly to the Sinclair Nature Reserve. That night dinner was served by candlelight in a stone-walled tower around a medieval-looking table made from railway sleepers. Later, having reached my turret by a wooden ladder and cosily enveloped in crisp, white sheets, I listened for a long time to the waves breaking against the rocks below and contemplated the starlit sky through my arched window. Whales (in season) and dolphins cavort in the bay and there are otters, bushbuck and the rare oystercatcher too. You can hike, fish and swim in the estuary or sea. The castle seduces the visitor with its unique atmosphere. Romantics only need apply.

Rooms: 4 double bedrooms with en-suite bathroom (two are in turrets, one is a honeymoon suite). 1 extra room on the ground floor with an outside bathroom.
Price: R600 - R1,050 pp sh. No single supplement.
Meals: Full breakfast included. Lunch and dinner by arrangement. R225 for dinner.
Directions: From N2, 3km east of Knysna, is Noetzie turn-off. Take sand rd for 5km to public parking. On LHS is private rd with boom pole, drive down & park on L. 10m further down is beach - Lindsay Castle about 250m across it, 7th castle on far R. Call from N2 so you can be met with your bags. No cell signal down on beach.

Springtide Charters

Evelyn and Stephan Pepler
34° South Jetty, Knysna Quays, Knysna
Tel: 082-470-6022 Fax: 044-382-5852
Email: info@springtide.co.za Web: www.springtidesailing.com
Cell: 082-829-2740

As I took the helm on board the Outeniqua, 50 feet of shimmering beauty somehow suddenly under my command, and sailed her across Knysna lagoon at a leisurely six knots, I felt very special indeed. The Outeniqua is sailed daily by Greg or Stephan and their young friendly crew who clearly love what they do, and it's not hard to see why. The coastline around Knysna is spectacular, with regular sightings of marine life and pelagic birds. The vessel itself is also exceptional, and I'm not just saying that because Stephan spent four and a half years building and fitting her out! Every immaculate thing on board, excluding the hull, is his own work. Anyone who has climbed aboard will agree, from President Mbeki to baby son Alix. The day starts with a call to the harbourmaster to raise the bridge, as you head off across the lagoon to the Heads, two majestic sandstone cliffs that lead out to the open sea and a whole world of excitement. Various day trips include a 4-hour day sail with lunch, a 2.5-hour sail and the 3-hour sunset cruise where you can indulge in Knysna's famous oysters, seafood and sushi, all washed them down with a fine South African bubbly. Evenings are spent anchored in the calm lagoon where a private chef conjures up a gourmet dinner from the galley. A wonderful experience. *Advance bookings essential.*

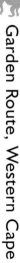

Rooms: A 50ft yacht comprising 3 double cabins, 2 heads (toilets), a galley and saloon.
Price: Overnight charter with gourmet chef & 3-course dinner: R2,200 - R3,200 pp DB&B. Day, 2-hour, dinner, sunset and champagne breakfast cruises: R350 - R700 pp.
Meals: Various packages available (see above).
Directions: Next to Deli 34° South at the Knysna Quays Waterfront.

Gallery Guest House

Lolly Hahn-Page
10 Hill St West, Knysna
Tel: 044-382-2510 Fax: 044-382-5212
Email: gallery.guesthouse@pixie.co.za Web: www.galleryguesthouse.co.za
Cell: 083-309-3920

Lolly manages the happy trick of combining her work as an artist with running a friendly, laid-back guest house in a peaceful part of Knysna. She is a strong force for the promotion of arts and crafts in the town, itself a honeypot for those that can hold a pencil steady. Thus the "Gallery". Her own and local artists' paintings and sculptures dot the walls and cover the carpets in the guest house, one of the longest-running in Knysna. The main room where breakfast etc happens is upstairs and the adjoining wooden deck has tremendous views out over the Knysna Heads, Leisure Isle and Pledge Park nature reserve. There is lots to do in town, what with sunset boat rides, the Outeniqua Choo-Tjoe, sea swimming, canoeing etc and Lolly is very knowledgeable. Best of all she has special private places – sunset spots, music venues, beaches, walks and restaurants – that you will only find with her help. She's great company too, a wonderful and eccentric raconteur who had an entire restaurant enraptured when we dined together. The bedrooms themselves are simple, showcasing more local artwork, but cater for all your needs. Choose Gallery Guest House for the irrepressible personality of both house and hostess. *Nine good restaurants within 2 mins. The recently-built perimeter fence means security is good as well.*

Rooms: 4: 2 twins and 2 doubles; 1 with private bath, 3 with en-suite bath or shower.
Price: From R300 to R490 pp sharing. Single rates on request.
Meals: Full or 'health' breakfast included and served from 8am to 10am.
Directions: From George take N2 to Knysna. At 2nd lights turn left into Grey St, then 2nd left into Hill St West, to end of cul-de-sac. Map on website.

Buffalo Hills Game Reserve and Lodges

Tony and Maria Kinahan
Plettenberg Bay
Tel: 044-535-9739 Fax: 044-535-9480
Email: buffalohills@mweb.co.za Web: www.buffalohills.co.za
Cell: 082-771-9370

Fluttering its eyelashes in my direction, an inquisitive giraffe, intently cleaning its face with its tongue, stopped me in my tracks on the road. Fresh from the beach (Plett is a mere 15km away), I was taken aback to find myself so deep in the 'real' Africa of my imagination as I drove through the bushy reserve to the camp. Although more traditional accommodation is available, for a true outdoorsy experience the tented rooms here are a must. Replete with big proper beds, plump pillows and wooden furniture, tents have certainly come on a peg or two. These ones even boast their own spa baths and the shuffling and snorting of a herd of buffalo outside mine made bubbling away all the more memorable. Tony has grand plans for a new lodge, where he'll also be training locals in traditional building methods. As the sun began to set, I discovered there's nothing more pleasurable than to kick off the walking boots, hang up the binos and re-live the events of the day watching fire-flames dance in the sheltered boma. Here, Tony cooked up a hearty feast on the braai - being a reserve, local game is his speciality - whilst regaling us wide-eyed lot with heroic tales involving rhino scuffles and marauding buffalo. After supper, it was facial contortions all round as we sampled shots from the reserve's very own distillery - its liquors are sold in Harrods. I had a great time at Buffalo Hills and, above and beyond the tents and all the animals, I think this is down to the friendly way the place is run.

Rooms: 13: 8 tents, all twin/doubles with en-suite spa baths with shower over; 1 cottage with 2 doubles and separate full bathroom; 1 lodge with 4 en-suite rooms, 3 with shower only, 1 with full bathroom.
Price: R700 - R1,100 pp sharing. Game drive and guided walk included in price.
Meals: Full breakfast and dinner included. Lunch extra.
Directions: From Cape Town take N2, turn L 4km after Plettenberg Bay onto R340. Turn L after 4km, then R after 1km onto Stofpad & follow signs.

Fynbos Ridge County House and Cottages

Liz and Brian Phillips

Plettenberg Bay
Tel: 044-532-7862 Fax: 044-532-7855
Email: fynbos.cottages@pixie.co.za Web: www.fynbosridge.co.za

Fynbos Ridge is a botanical paradise where new owners Liz and Brian have continued an eco-conscious mission to remove all invasive alien vegetation. Painstakingly, a wide variety of indigenous trees and shrubs have been reinstated to create a haven where Cape flora (fynbos) and fauna can flourish. There are birds here that you will only see in the fynbos. It is not just the environment that finds these green-fingered nature-lovers friendly… their guests kind of like them too. They will cushion your stay with super-down duvets, pure cotton sheets and a hearty breakfast in the light-filled, alfresco-esque dining room. If you're self-catering, choose from fully-equipped cottages in bright 'gazania' yellow, warm 'clivia' peach or refreshing 'aristea' blue, all inspired by indigenous flowers. But please do let Brian cook for you at least once. This private nature reserve cries out to be walked in though I, unfortunately, only made it as far as the ozone-purified swimming pool (no chemicals here - just a weird-sounding contraption). Follow the natural borders and discreet signposts to this oasis amongst the fynbos. This is the most awesome place to take a dip. Hidden within the depths of a private nature reserve and contemplating the meeting of the Outeniqua and Tsitsikamma mountains, you could easily spend the whole day here languishing with a book. Now where did I pack my swimming togs? *Children 12+ welcome.*

Rooms: 9: 6 rooms in the house: 4 luxury doubles, 1 superior luxury double and 1 self-catering studio, all with en-suite bath and shower; 3 self-catering cottages, all sleeping 4-5 with 1 bathroom & 1 shower-room.
Price: B&B R475 - R750 pp sharing. Self-catering R375 - R575 pp sharing. Singles on request.
Meals: Full breakfast included in B&B price or R85 for self-catering. Lunch and dinner on request.
Directions: 23km along N2 from Knysna heading towards Plettenberg Bay. Take L into 'Blue Hills Bird Farm'. Bear L where road forks to Fynbos Ridge.

Cornerway House

Dee and Robin Pelham-Reid
61 Longships Drive, Plettenberg Bay
Tel: 044-533-3190 Fax: 044-533-3195
Email: cornerwayhouse@mweb.co.za Web: www.cornerwayhouse.co.za

Robin and Dee moved from my Wiltshire school-town (as it happens) to start Cornerway House, and fantastic hosts they make too. Robin will ably point you off to the beach with sundowners or to the Robberg Peninsula walk, an exhilarating experience; and Dee has set up a local NGO to provide therapy for those suffering from HIV and AIDS - she can give you a different and rewarding perspective on Plett. After drinks in their English drawing room, we repaired for dinner, where wine flowed and conversation roamed. Dee uses what she can from the garden, herbs of course, but artichokes and strawberries too on the day I visited. When a professional cycling team came to stay they were so well fed they failed to win a single race (… not that professional then!). I retired to my room - wooden antiques, comfy bed and sash windows looking onto the garden – and at dawn joined Ocean Blue to spot whales, dolphins and sharks, returning to a proper breakfast, courtesy of Robin. Throughout the house there are colourful quirks, to wit the yellow-washed and lilac shutters of the house, the petunias bathing in a bath, a purple TV/sitting room with bright blue cushions and the pink and yellow mohair in the garden suite. I left Robin and Dee among the frangipani, gardenia and orange trees as I wrenched myself away.

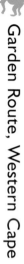

Rooms: 5: 4 twins and 1 double; 2 with en-suite shower, 3 with en-suite shower and bath.
Price: R230 - R495. Singles plus 50% in low season, per room in high season. Low season rates can be negotiated.
Meals: Full breakfast included. Lunch (salads & sandwiches); 3-course dinner from R180, includes pre-dinner drinks & bottle of wine per couple. Lunch/dinner with 24 hrs notice.
Directions: From N2 heading east, turn right into Plett. Continue to the circle and go straight over. Road descends to river and crosses it. Over circle, turn right onto Longships Dr. Continue down 0.9km to Cornerway House on right.

Bosavern

Vivienne and Gerald Dreyer
38 Cutty Sark Ave, Plettenberg Bay
Tel: 044-533-1312 Fax: 044-533-0758
Email: info@bosavern.co.za Web: www.bosavern.co.za
Cell: 082-922-4721

The striking S-shaped waves of Bosavern's timbered ceiling mimic the sea and combine with minimalist white interiors and mirrors to strike a harmonious note with the blue ocean far below. Glass doors lead off the open-plan sitting room and onto the balcony where you can treat yourself on wicker chairs to a regal cliff-top view of the Robberg Peninsula and the white beaches of Plettenberg Bay. Powerful binoculars will pick out whales and schools of dolphins which are (can be!) plentiful in the clear water. The bedrooms downstairs have the same sliding doors that disappear smoothly into the wall and the sea breeze wafts in through a square gap of sky as if from a bright blue painting. The view from your room and private balcony is no less spectacular. Comfort is a priority, with goose-down duvets on enormous beds, fine cotton sheets, a welcoming bottle of Nederberg, gowns and slippers. Vivienne and Gerald are natural hosts, who provide great breakfasts and also picnic hampers for the beach or Robberg hikes, and mountain bikes and canoes for the madly active (a pool caters for loungers). They will also point you in the right direction for golf and recommend a number of restaurants within easy walking distance.

Rooms: 5: 4 twins/doubles & 1 double; 3 with en-suite shower, 2 with en/s bath and shower. The 4 downstairs rooms and bathrooms all have heated towel rails and underfloor heating.
Price: R510 - R810 pp sharing. Singles up to 80% in season.
Meals: Full breakfast included and served from 8am - 9am.
Directions: From Knysna take N2. Right at Shell garage into Plettenberg Bay. Turn 1st right into Cutty Sark Ave. Follow road round, then turn right again into cul-de-sac. House on left.

Beacon Lodge

Al and Clo Scheffer
57 Beacon Way,
Plettenberg Bay
Tel: 044-533-2614
Fax: 044-533-2614
Email:
info@beaconlodge.co.za
Web: www.beaconlodge.co.za

This is a small (just two rooms), personal, friendly and involving B&B – and I mean B&B in the proper sense where you share the house with your hosts. Both rooms have their own separate entrances, mind you, if you want to slip about more furtively. The patio, for breakfasts, garden bird-watching or reading, has long views out to sea and it's only a short walk to the beach and the lagoon, presumably where you will want to spend at least some of your time. To this end Al and Clo have all beach necessities at the ready – umbrellas, towels and the like. The larger of the two rooms was my favourite (and also the more expensive) with sea views through a huge window and anti-glare solar blinds. There is seagrass on floors, plenty of immaculate seaside white in walls and towels and colour is added in the form of fresh flowers. The Scheffers take the greatest care of their guests. *Fridge facilities provided. Great restaurants within walking distance. Whales and dolphins in season. Closed mid-Dec to mid-Jan and either June or July. Enquire first!*

Rooms: 2: 1 twin and 1 double, both with en-suite bathrooms with showers.
Price: R200 - R350 pp sharing. Singles on request.
Meals: Full breakfast included. There are good restaurants in town for other meals.
Directions: From Knysna take the N2. Take the second turn into Plett at the Engen 1-stop garage. The house is 600 metres on your left.

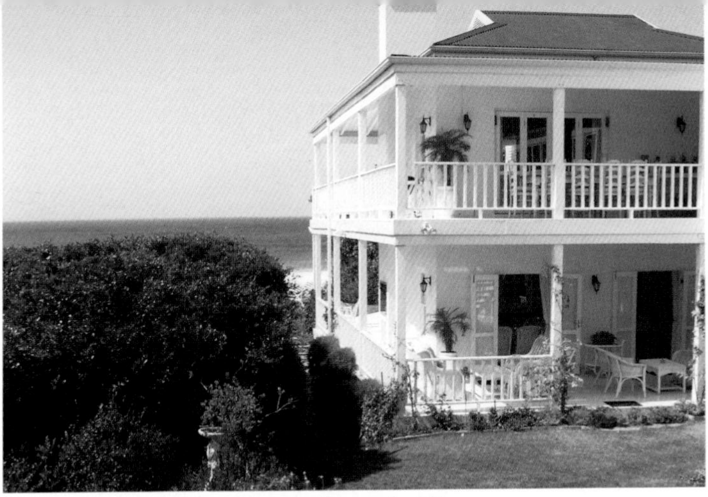

Southern Cross Beach House

Neill and Sue Ovenstone
I Capricorn Lane, Solar Beach, Plettenberg Bay
Tel: 044-533-3868 Fax: 044-533-3866
Email: info@southerncrossbeach.co.za
Web: www.southerncrossbeach.co.za Cell: 082-490-0876

... and relax. With this dreamy, whitewashed, wooden house at the quiet end of Robberg Beach's long arc, it is impossible not to. Plettenberg Bay is a lively town, with lots of restaurants and bars, but people really come here for the sea, and you would seriously struggle to get closer to it than at Southern Cross. During the Christmas holidays the beach is packed, but for the rest of the year there are more signs of life in the sea. Dolphins race by all year round, revelling in their position at the head of the food chain, with southern right whales often wallowing just in front of the house from June to November. The house itself is just up a wooden gangway from the beach. Wood predominates, with blues and white echoing the ocean. The brochure says 'plantation style', but I would plump for classic Massachussetts beach house. Wooden decking looks across the bay to the Tsitsikamma Mountains to the left and the Robberg Peninsula opposite, which is geologically identical to the Falklands, bizarrely… and a fantastic place to walk. Inside is the breakfast room and living room, and set around the garden on the ground floor (Sue and Neill live upstairs) are the five lovely rooms. Barefoot, laid-back luxury.

Rooms: 5: 1 double, 1 queen, 2 twins, 1 king. All have en-suite shower, 2 with baths as well.
Price: R375 - R750 pp sharing. 30% single supplement.
Meals: Full breakfast included. Kitchenette available for putting together salads and light meals.
Directions: From dolphin roundabout in main street descend the hill past Central Beach, over Piesang River bridge. Straight over the roundabout, past shops (kwikspar) to your left and take the first right into Longships Dr. 2km over 3 speed bumps turn left into Gris Nez Dr. Over stop street (Rothersands) turn left into Gemini St. Turn Right then left into Capricorn Lane.

Bitou River Lodge

Sue and Paul Scheepers
R340 Bitou Valley Road, Plettenberg Bay
Tel: 044-535-9577 Fax: 044-535-9577
Email: info@bitou.co.za Web: www.bitou.co.za
Cell: 082-978-6164

For well-heeled South Africans "Plett" is the place to summer and its sophisticated buzz can border on the frenetic. Which is why Bitou River Lodge is such a find. Just east of town, it's close to Plett's glass-plated beach houses, bijou shops and restaurants, yet feels a million miles away. Paul and Sue wanted to make the most of the natural environment and have created a peaceful haven for nature lovers. The drive sweeps past a citrus orchard and horse paddock to the whitewashed lodge, which sits on five hectares of neat flower-filled gardens, with pool, chipping-green and river frontage. Behind pepper trees and honeysuckle, stable-style bedrooms have river-facing patios, where dazzling sunbirds congregate. The lime-washed, painted-pine rooms have slate-floored kitchenettes and bathrooms, and sliding doors keep them light-filled. Farmhouse feasts are served in the breakfast room, which adjoins a warm lounge where you can settle into birding books (there are 134 species in the area to tick off). Outside, the liquid-smooth lawn gathers all before it – boulders, benches and flowerbeds – as it slips silently toward the lily-leafed river. While away some time out here, watching busy weaver birds build upside-down nests and lazy ones sway in the reeds, while the ripple of canoe paddles, the splash of a kingfisher and whizz of a fly-reel provide a soothing summer soundtrack. *In season the bay hosts whales, dolphins and seals.*

Rooms: 5: 3 kings and 2 twins, all with en-suite bath and shower.
Price: R295 - R525 pp sharing. Singles on request.
Meals: Full farmhouse breakfast included. Plenty of restaurants in nearby Plett.
Directions: Head east from Plettenberg Bay on N2. Immediately after bridge, turn left onto the R340. Bitou River Lodge is signed on left, 4.2km from the N2.

Emily Moon

Simon and Diane Valentine
Rietvlei Rd, Plettenberg Bay
Tel: 044-533-2982 Fax: 044-533-0687
Email: info@emilymoon.co.za Web: www.emilymoon.co.za
Cell: 083-266-2994

I stooped under Emily Moon's 400-year-old Jaipuri doors and stumbled into a far-flung bazaar in some foreign land: gold-inlaid masks on the wall, cattle skins for carpets, African bao board games and mammoth pewter candlesticks. Sipping rooibos tea, I steadied myself and worked my way along family portraits of muscle-bound men sporting over-sized fish and Blixenesque women who could pour a G&T then shoot a marauding lion without blinking an eye. And then the view... past the glass-fronted restaurant the River Bitou scrawled an 'S' through reeded wetlands before halting at the foothills of the Outeniqua Mountains. Was I hearing things? Or was the wind really carrying the low grunting of buffalo and wildebeest herds that must have grazed here centuries before? I'd clearly watched one too many repeats of 'Out of Africa', but thankfully Simon rescued me from my reverie. Apparently you're more likely to see a tortoise (60 at the last count!) than a grumpy buffalo around here, although there are plans to re-introduce springbok. He showed me the huge rooms with their fawn-coloured walls, dark wooden furniture, open fires and deep, deep leather sofas. My favourite was the split-level family room with its panoramic view. When it's free, Simon takes a cold beer down to watch the flock of sacred ibis which fly past in a 'V' at sundown. The outdoor shower in every room is also worth a mention, although it did cause a problem for one German husband who complained bitterly when his wife refused to get out! *Two golf courses 1.5km from the lodge.*

Rooms: 8: 2 twin/king, 5 king all with en-suite baths and showers. 1 family room with en-suite shower.
Price: Low Season: May - October R930 per lodge B&B sharing. High Season: November – April R930 per person B&B sharing. Single surcharge 50%.
Meals: Full English or Continental breakfast included. A table is automatically reserved for guests at the restaurant in the evening.
Directions: On N2 from Cape Town pass main Plettenberg Bay turn-off, then L at Penny Pinchers supermarket. Carry straight on. The road becomes a dirt track. Drive up a steep hill and follow signs.

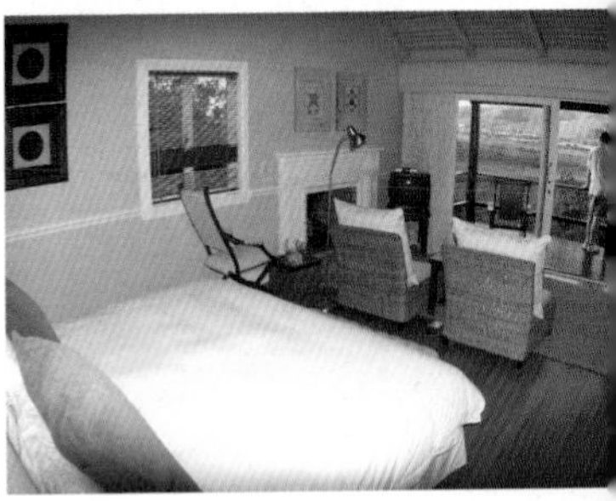

Anlin Beach House

Dermot and Fran Molloy

33 Roche Bonne Avenue, Plettenberg Bay
Tel: 044-533-3694 Fax: 044-533-3394
Email: stay@anlinbeachhouse.co.za Web: www.anlinbeachhouse.co.za

Like a moth to a lamp, the first thing I did here after dropping off my bags was head to the beach irresistibly close (100 metres away) and tantalizing from the top-floor balcony. A run along the soft sands all the way to the Robberg Peninsula was exhilarating at sunset. Beneath cobalt blue skies I passed only seals and surfers cresting the smooth ocean rollers. The beach really does seem to slow you down as both Dermot (a wine-marketer) and Fran (a trained counsellor) will attest. As we passed the quirky outdoor shower, Fran commented that she always wanted the place to be ultra up-to-date in terms of design, but comfortable at the same time, "I don't want guests to think 'I can't sit on that'". The style is therefore contemporary, with walls and furnishings in natural colours imitating the beach, the ocean and dramatic rocky outcrops. The bedrooms have tiled floors and cream-coloured furniture drenched in light from the private patios and vast windows. Dermot's an avid collector of South African art so expect to see some interesting pieces. If you can, book the upstairs room. The view, which sweeps across the ocean to the Outeniqua Mountains, finally persuaded Fran to go for the house; "when a school of dolphins swam past, I knew I had to sign!" The kitchens, with their polished-cement surfaces and hi-tech gas hobs, all come well stocked with tea, coffee, soup and other goodies. Don't forget to ask Dermot for his autograph either. He once worked as an extra on Zulu Dawn!

Rooms: 4: 1 upstairs apartment (potentially 2 units) with 3 beds and 2 bathrooms, 1 with bath/shower and 1 with shower only; 2 garden apartments, both sleep 3 with 1 shower bathroom each.
Price: R385 - R710 pp sharing valid to April 2009. Singles +25%.
Meals: Self-catering but continental breakfast can be served on the patio for R40.
Directions: From N2 heading east, R into Plett. Continue to circle & go straight over. Road descends to river and crosses it. Over circle, R onto Longships Dr then left into Roche Bonne Avenue, which has a brown B&B sign. Anlin Beach House is 50m on R.

Gulls View

Noel and Pam Mills

31 San Gonzales Street, Plettenberg Bay
Tel: 072-343-7217 Fax: 044-533-3498
Email: info@gullsview.co.za Web: www.gullsview.co.za

Gulls View is named for the feathered athletes who riot and curl in the thermals that funnel up the cliff at the sea-facing end of the garden. From the verandah, upstairs main bedroom and front rooms there are views in bands of searingly simple colour; a spread of blue sea, white beaches on the peninsula, then the green of a lawny (and wholly indigenous) garden filled with birds including the Knysna loerie. Noel and Pam (who also have a (GG) guesthouse (Rockwood) in the Cederberg) have coaxed the second oldest house in town into the 21st century and built a whole new one too. This way you can live in the new house if there are only two of you, or use both if you are more numerous. The new house has an open feel with polished timbers, nice curvy wicker chairs, soft white, cream and turquoisey-green tones and billowy ivory-coloured curtains framing the view. All of which are right and proper for the sea. The little things haven't been forgotten either; TV and DVD, stereo set, CD player and, of course, a top-notch kitchen. The house is equidistant to several beaches (down a fairly steep hill) and a five-minute walk to the vibrant and trendy town where there are excellent restaurants. Louann lives next door and will meet and greet you, and look after you, as much or as little as you wish.

Rooms: Self-catering house let as a whole, with 6 bedrooms.
Price: Low season: R800 per night for 2 sharing, + R100 per extra person; Mid: R1,000 per night as above; High (1st Dec – 20th Jan): R3,000 per night. Rates include week-day servicing.
Meals: Breakfast ingredients can be supplied on request at a cost of R30 pp.
Directions: Turn off N2 into Plett at Shell Garage. Turn right at the roundabout, then left into San Gonzales St. Gulls View is 2nd last house on the right before Signal Hill.

Orca House

Linda and David Packwood
Milkwood Glen, Keurbooms Beach, Plettenberg Bay
Tel: 044-535-9073
Fax: 044-535-9073
Email: info@orcahouse.co.za
Web: www.orcahouse.co.za
Cell: 082-890-1033

Backing onto Keurbooms Beach, Orca House is the architectural version of a well-worn quilt documenting a life spent at sea. Outside a mosaic of red, orange and yellow buoys swings on the wall; inside you'll find wooden canoes, multi-coloured model ships, sea chests, and battered copies of National Geographic. Even the house itself resembles a ship. There are north- and south-facing outdoor decks with marine-blue railings hung with lifebuoys. I half-expected to see an old sea dog, legs crossed on the sofa, puffing his tobacco pipe with a crowd of grandchildren at his slippered feet. Instead, managers Linda and David were busy putting out fresh fruit and generally sprucing the place up before rushing off to greet in-coming guests. Sunlight floods into the open-plan house with its timber beams and soaring upstairs windows where guests doze in hammocks, keeping half an eye out for passing whales. The place has a lovely atmosphere. If you can drag yourself to the bedroom downstairs, you'll find a white four-poster bed bound with sailing rope. The quirky bathroom resembles a sea officer's mess with an antique chest of drawers and blue corrugated-iron walls. In the evening, you'll tuck into piles of seafood at the outdoor table before settling down to a game of scrabble in front of the roaring fire… bliss!

Rooms: 4: 2 doubles (sea facing) and 2 rooms with a double and a single bed in each. All have bathrooms, 1 with shower/bath, 1 full bathroom en-s and 2 with en-s shower.
Price: R1,700 – R6,000 per night for the whole house.
Meals: Breakfast by arrangement. Meals can be provided at an additional cost and with prior arrangement.
Directions: Situated in the Milkwood Glen beachfront residence on Keurbooms Beach – Keurboomstrand, off the N2 just past Plettenberg Bay from Cape Town. David & Linda will make arrangements to meet you at a convenient spot and take you to the house.

Piesang Valley Lodge

John Elliott
Piesang Valley Road, Plettenberg Bay
Tel: 044-533-6283 Fax: 044-533-4477
Email: info@pvl.co.za Web: www.pvl.co.za
Cell: 072-5190-244

If ever a place resembled its owner, this is it. Unpretentious, laid-back, friendly and personal, John has bestowed these qualities on a lodge, part of which he built with his own hands using a special vertical construction technique (just nod and make understanding grunts). These are also the rooms of choice where pine and timber frame a scene of dark wood furniture, inviting beds and earthy rugs, soothed by white-washed walls and alabaster bathrooms. All open breezily onto the garden. There's a refreshing youthful energy here as well, something else you'll notice about John, who leads a tremendously healthy life. I challenge anyone to guess his correct age. When we met he had just returned from rescuing his new houseboat that had slipped its moorings. After many years in the hospitality industry, it was his dream to start his own guesthouse and where better than on family ground, whose hill-top seat looks all the way down the valley into Plett and out to the Indian Ocean. There are plenty of good restaurants in the area, but you're welcome to bring your own grub and cook lunch and dinner in the kitchen. That's if you're still hungry after a bonanza breakfast with the birds. The garden is a great place to kick back with a cold beer and enjoy a gently sloping verdant scene of lawn, bush and tree, across which playful house hounds tumble. "It's convenient and tranquil," says John. It's very good value too.

Rooms: 6 rooms: all queen doubles or twins (2 bath/shower and 4 shower en-suite).
Price: R290 - R450 pp sharing.
Meals: Full breakfast included. Guests are welcome to cook their own lunch and dinner in the kitchen.
Directions: Take Piesang Valley Road turn-off from N2 into Plettenberg Bay. 1.4km down the road the lodge is on your right-hand side.

Moleshole

Patrick and Sue Dalzell
The Tides, Plettenberg Bay
Tel: 044-535-9073 Fax: 044-535-9073
Email: marketing@plettvillas.co.za Web: www.moleshole.co.za
Cell: 082-890-1033

In five days' time it's officially National Braai (Barbeque) Day in South Africa (obviously at the time of writing) and this seaside party villa is the place where I'd choose to celebrate. An enormous verandah is its key-stone, equipped with built-in braai, long wooden dining table, easy sitting area, sun-loungers and a pretty garden that rises on staggered levels of flowers to a turquoise pool. I noticed a narrow sandy path leading off from the garden and curious to see what lay beyond I set off through the fynbos. After no more than two minutes' walk, I stumbled onto a wonderful lagoon and a deserted beach, with African spoonbills skimming the placid waters. Golfers too couldn't be happier, as you actually pass through Goose Valley Golf Course to reach this secure and hidden complex. There is a delicious sense of being removed from it all, yet town is barely five minutes away. No need to feel crowded either. There are seven large bright bedrooms, the five upstairs sporting balconies overlooking both garden and lagoon, while of the two below, one has a snug courtyard hung with creeper and the other opens through French windows onto the stoep. As your party settles in, you can easily withdraw and find quiet spaces within the house; in the sitting-room of bursting floral displays; in the separate TV room with its striking scarlet covers; or in the study. A darkly-beamed dining room verges on the stately and is served by a country kitchen - in size and character - with an oven built for medieval feasts.

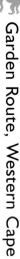

Rooms: 1 villa with 7 rooms, all variously en-suite bath/shower, shower or bath only.
Price: R4,000 – R10,500 per night for the whole villa.
Meals: Fully self-catering. Meals can be provided at an additional cost and with prior arrangement.
Directions: Shortly after Plettenberg Bay, take Goose Valley Golf Estate turning on the right, coming from Cape Town on the N2. Follow round around to the right through the golf course before coming to The Tides complex.

Hog Hollow Country Lodge

Andy and Debbie Fermor
Askop Rd, The Crags
Tel: 044-534-8879 Fax: 044-534-8879
Email: info@hog-hollow.com Web: www.hog-hollow.com
Cell: 082-578-1939

It was a little rude, but I said hello to no-one when I arrived at Hog Hollow and made a beeline for the view point, a tree-perforated deck that juts out over mile upon mile of tantalising, tumbling, Tsitsikamma forest. "Don't worry, everyone does that," said Jo, one of the bubbly team of local staff that make this place so special. Back inside, I ran out of scribbling space listing intriguing oddities: the tobacco-leaf coffee-table, the mounted outboard engine, the sewing-machine lamp. I loved the irrepressible spontaneity of it all. Returning guests suggest a pool? Andy and Debbie make it a 15-metre one. Others want a sauna? That's just been finished too, along with three new forest cottages. They're hidden among the trees down snaking brick paths and their mezzanine lay-out make the view equally good from bed or bath. There's bags of space for kids too and with buckets, spades and bed-time stories they couldn't be better catered for. That leaves you free to join other guests for a communal supper, care of Big Joe. I thumbed through a menu of crayfish thermidor, rack of lamb and pesto-crushed line fish, praying a miracle flat battery might force me to cancel my other appointments and stay the night. No such luck.

Rooms: 15: 14 king/twins and 1 queen, all with bath and shower.
Price: R1,160 - R1,276 pp B&B sharing. Singles R1,675 - R1,840 pp B&B.
Meals: Full breakfast included. 4-course dinner from R200 pp. Lunch also available.
Directions: 18km east of Plettenberg Bay, Hog Hollow is signed off to the right.

Fairview

Nicky Rattray
N2, The Crags
Tel: 034-642-1843
Email: nicky@trustnet.co.za Web: www.fugitives-drift-lodge.com
Cell: 082-832-1895

They say that scent brings back powerful memories, and to this day a whiff of jasmine takes me back to Fairview's fragrant garden. Every single bloom was chosen for its perfume alone by Gillian, authoress and doyenne of the Rattray family: the intoxicating blend of lavender, lilac, indigenous freesia, dog roses and rosemary which floods into the main bedroom is natural aromatherapy at its best. Just metres away from this English country garden, fynbos still grows wild in the Whiskey Creek Nature Reserve, home to duiker and even the occasional leopard. The Cape Dutch house's interior - with its antlers, grandfather clocks, wooden beams, and cut-glass decanters - has the stately but lived-in feel of an ageing Scottish hunting lodge. Even the distant Formosa Peak, which once served as a beacon for Portuguese sailors, could pass for the Cairngorms. It's hard to believe then that the Rattrays only built Fairview fifteen years ago. Manager, Wilhemein, showed me around with Louis, her web-footed Chesapeake Bay retriever, in tow. My favourite bedroom's cream curtains and floral wallpaper were drenched in light from the French windows exaggerating the already healthy dimensions. And joy of joys, the blue-and-white striped bathroom had a giant-sized Victorian slipper bath. Elsewhere, we passed the grand piano and an intricate frieze by Gillian herself, before stopping at the display of neolithic axes discovered whilst building the house.

Rooms: 1 cottage with 2 twin bedrooms + extra twin (1 en-suite bath/shower and 1 bath only). In main house, 1 twin (en-suite shower/bath) and 1 family suite (shared shower bathroom).
Price: R320 - R670 pp sharing. Singles +R200.
Meals: Full breakfast included. Self-catering option for all units. Catering can be organised.
Directions: Exactly 12km from Plettenberg Bay, signposted on the left-hand side of the N2 coming from Cape Town.

That Place

Jo and David Butler
The Crags
Tel: 044-534-8886
Email: info@thatplace.co.za Web: www.thatplace.co.za
Cell: 082-578-1939

This is "that place...," you know the one you talk about for years after you've been there. "Do you remember the time we went to South Africa and stayed in 'That Place' where we watched the elephants wandering through their paddock across the valley, where we hazily dreamt in the hand-crafted sauna. We braai'd and feasted for hours on the deck, the kids duck-diving and splashing in the waters of the private pool - do you remember?" Jo and David have created a memory-building, self-catering home. And that's just what it is - a home. It's not grand or pretentious, just comfortable and happy to have you. I was shown around by a very modest David who failed to mention that the great wooden table and chairs, the sauna and the three cheeky fish sculptures suspended on the wall (amongst other details) had sprung from his own gifted fingers. I met the dogs too, all six of them. Right from John Keats the Great Dane down to McGregor the feisty Jack Russell. Don't worry, these chaps live next door and won't bother you unless you want them to. But if you want them to…! "You named your dog after a poet?" I asked Jo. "David did," she replied, "he's very into his poetry." Sounds like the perfect man to me - unfortunately already taken by Jo who is equally wonderful.

Rooms: One 3-bedroom self-catering cottage let as a whole: 1 king with en-suite bath and shower, 1 king/twin and 1 twin ideal for children.
Price: From R750 - R1,500 per night for the whole house.
Meals: It's possible to pre-order dishes from a company specialising in Continental cuisine by prior arrangement.
Directions: Travelling in the direction of Port Elizabeth on the N2, 20km east of Plettenberg Bay. At the 'Curiosity African Arts' shop, turn right off the N2 and follow the signs to 'That Place.'

Lily Pond Country Lodge

Niels and Margret Hendriks

R102 Nature's Valley Road, The Crags
Tel: 044-534-8767 Fax: 044-534-8686
Email: info@lilypond.co.za Web: www.lilypond.co.za
Cell: 082-746-8782

From the moment I first saw Niels and Margret dashing out to greet me, I was confident of a great stay. Their lodge is a monument to mathematical modernity. Straight lines and strong angles prevail and sandy yellow or terracotta walls contrast strikingly with the surrounding greenery of Nature's Valley. And green it is! Lily Pond's lily ponds provide a lush home to a mesmerising array of flora and fauna, most noticeably the frogs. They serenaded me with their croaky chorus as I braved a mid-winter swim in the newly-built infinity pool, which flows almost seamlessly into the pond. Warming up in my polished concrete bath, I soaked up the garden suite's quirky design. Think African colonial (tribal paintings, gauzy curtains and kudu-skin rugs) with every bit of stuffiness surgically removed and replaced with funky exposed brickwork and a bright ochre-and-white colour scheme. Later, I strolled along the winding, wooded paths which criss-cross the property. In summer, the lilies are a carpet of colour and balmy evenings are set aside for drinks and nibbles or even a candle-lit dinner on the miniature island, followed by a many-coursed, mouth-watering meal in the (equally angular) restaurant. Margret is a supremely good cook - Niels her dashing waiter - and I was treated to springbok carpaccio and kingklip in Thai coconut and coriander sauce. For people who "never meant to run a guest house," they're doing a seriously good job. *Massage treatments on request.*

Rooms: 10: 4 en-s rooms (2 queens & 2 king/twins) & 2 luxury suites (1 queen & 1 king/twin), all en-s bath & shower; 3 luxury garden suites (all extra-length king/twin) & 1 honeymoon suite (extra-length king/double), all en-s bath & sh'r plus outdoor sh'r.
Price: R425 - R900 pp sh (single supplement 50%).
Meals: Full breakfast included. Fusion kitchen with 4-course dinner R175 (vegetarian on request). Light lunches available.
Directions: 22km east of Plettenberg Bay and close to Nature's Valley. From CT take 1st exit to Nature's Valley. From Port Elizabeth take 2nd exit Nature's Valley (14km after toll) to the L. Then follow R102 for 3km and turn R at the sign.

Tarn Country House

Guy and Erica de la Motte
N2, The Crags
Tel: 044-534-8806 Fax: 044-534-8835
Email: info@tarn.co.za Web: www.tarn.co.za

Ah, this is the life... 100 acres of bucolic bliss. Picture the scene if you will: frogs croaking contentedly, birds chirping merrily in the afternoon sun, and a smug inspector enjoying the top tea spot on the Garden Route. From the shade of a pine tree I overlooked the reservoir onto a forested valley and up to the Outeniqua Mountains stretching away into the hazy distance. My thoughts were only lightly disturbed by a lone guinea fowl clucking about in search of food and an ephemeral twinge of guilt as ruddy-faced guests returned from hikes through the foothills of the nearby Tsitsikamma Mountains in time for a fireside apéritif and a hearty dinner. But I quickly discovered that I'd also somehow earned a three-course Erica special. The restaurant enjoys the same views as my favoured tea spot, through the full-length French doors that flood the room with morning sunshine. Blissfully settled beside the ceramic wood-burning fire, I chomped my way through camembert-filled filo pastry parcels, a succulent fillet of beef with a mustard cream sauce, sorbet, rounded off with grilled plums, and all washed down with a local wine from Tarn's extensive collection. The sprawling, bungalowed building is surrounded by a brilliant moat of flowers, and as I slopped around in my over-sized tub, contemplating the king-size bed that awaited me, I realized that after only a few hours here I already felt refreshed, revitalized and raring to go.

Rooms: 8: 3 kings, 3 queens and 2 twins all with en-suite bath and shower.
Price: R380 - R890 pp sharing. + 50% single supplement. Children welcome, half price up to 12 years of age.
Meals: Full breakfast included. Light lunch on request. Dinner at our in-house restaurant from R180 for a 3-course dinner.
Directions: On N2, 15km east of Plettenberg Bay, sign to the left. Coming from PE direction, 19km from Toll Gate, sign to the right.

The Fernery Lodge and Chalets

Meg and Frans Gerber

Forest Ferns, Blueliliesbush, Tsitsikamma
Tel: 042-280-3588
Fax: 042-280-3577
Email: reservations@forestferns.co.za
Web: www.forestferns.co.za

You've heard us harping on about beautiful views before, but this time I need an even stronger superlative! As I cradled my welcome G&T, I watched an enormous waterfall plummeting 30 metres down through the river gorge before making its way to the sea. And beyond the forest you can see all the way to the ocean, where, on certain clear days, whales and dolphins complete an impossibly picturesque scene. It is not surprising, then, that The Fernery focuses on this natural visual treasure, from the lodge bedrooms, to the dining area and the jacuzzi and pool. I stayed in the main lodge, which was the perfect place to relax after another leg-achingly long drive. Here you will find yourself on the end of some serious pampering, with large inviting rooms leading to even larger bathrooms. Mine overlooked the forest and was big enough for about ten people; but I enjoyed hogging it all to myself and soothing my clutch foot. Up the hill from the lodge are the wooden chalets, which have traditional wood-burning heaters and outdoor braais to give them a back-to-nature feel... and no TVs. But don't worry, if you just fancy whipping up something quick, there is still a full modern kitchen for self-caterers. Chalet guests have their own entertainment, including a pub, a pool, and a canopied jacuzzi that juts into the waterfall valley. Meg and Frans will be happy to give you a tour of their fern farm, which sends foliage for bouquets everywhere, from Waitrose in the UK to Woolworths in South Africa.

Rooms: 14: 6 doubles en-s in lodge; 6 double/twin B&B chalets with en-s bathrooms; 2 self-catering chalets with doubles & twins with 1 bathroom.
Price: B&B chalets: R520 - R625 pp sharing; self-catering chalets (sleep 4): R1,215 - R1,460 per chalet; lodge suites: R720 - R1,070 pp sharing. Extra for singles. Includes use of row boats. Bicycles hired for small fee.
Meals: Full breakfast included for B&B chalets and lodge suites. 4-course dinner available for all guests, and a 3-course dinner braai of fish, meat or vegetables available for BBQs.
Directions: Signed off the N2 at the Bluelilies turn-off, then 7.5km down a signed track from the road.

At The Woods Guest House

Bev and Marco Coetzee

Storms River Village, Tsitsikamma
Tel: 042-2811-446 Fax: 042-2811-550
Email: info@atthewoods.co.za Web: www.atthewoods.co.za
Cell: 082-3282-371

If you go down to the woods today, you're sure of a big surprise. With its earthy colours and African background music, At The Woods has the relaxed atmosphere of a backpackers with all the grown-up mod cons of the fully-fledged guesthouse. After nine months, and seventy-five thousand bricks, Marco should give himself a pat on the back. He personally oversaw and renovated the property all the way down to its reclaimed skirting-boards, doing a great deal of the work himself. "He likes to build, this man," Bev laughed as she passed me some home-made bread. The rooms have king-size extra-length beds with Oregon pine headboards, white linen, funky lighting and colourful mohair blankets. The bathrooms, meanwhile, have bamboo ceilings and walk-in showers. My favourite room had blue painted chairs, and a patio with a view across to next-door's macadamia plantation. When staying, make sure you take full advantage of Bev's extensive Garden Route know-how. She worked at Knysna Tourism for six years. The highest bungy jump in the world is only 20km away (my answer to that is a simple no, so don't even ask), plus there's the nearby canopy tour, where you slide through the Tsitsikamma Forest's indigenous treetops. No exaggeration here... Storms River is the adventure capital of the Western Cape and Bev and Marco will help you make the most of it.

Rooms: 8: 5 kings, 3 twins, all extra-length and all with en-suite with showers.
Price: R295 - R425 pp sharing. No single supplement in winter. In summer a single is R592.50.
Meals: Breakfast includes cereals, yoghurts, fruit salad, cooked breakfast and toast & croissants. Home-cooked two-course dinner available on request.
Directions: From Cape Town turn off the N2 at Storms River. At The Woods is 600m in on your right.

Housemartin Guest Lodge

Bill & Christina Martin
16 Schoeman Street, De Rust
Tel: 044-241-2214 Fax: 044-241-2317
Email: info@housemartin.co.za Web: www.housemartin.co.za
Cell: 083-342-6456

Arriving at the gates of this Victorian homestead and lodge, though the heavens wept outside for the first time in months, inside there were nothing but smiles and laughter. Unmistakably the heart and soul of the guest lodge, the deep-red, high-beamed restaurant bustled with life. As I tucked into a hearty bobotie, jolly guests on the next table had the right idea, ordering a fresh round of Irish coffees. Bill and Christina, whose School of Food and Wine in Durban is world-renowned (my lunch was superb), bought the lodge 'on a whim' after falling for the charms of De Rust and the taste of village life it offered. And you can try a bite of it too. All rooms are similar affairs with original corrugated roofs and Klein Victoria coloured windows decorating each private verandah. Percale bed linen, mohair blankets and under-floor heating add a little luxury to the airy and tastefully decorated rooms. After a day spent exploring the dramatic Swartberg, collapse on your verandah, admire the abundant fruit garden, sample some local muscadel and then wait in anticipation for the culinary delights ahead.

Rooms: 12: all queen/twin with en-suite showers and air-conditioning.
Price: R460 - R485 pp sharing. Singles from R400 - R605.
Meals: Full breakfast included. Restaurant on site.
Directions: De Rust is just past Oudtshoorn on the N12 on route to Beaufort West, and is just 1hr from George. Guest Lodge is well sign-posted on main road through town.

De Zeekoe Guest Farm

Paula and Pottie Potgieter
R328, road to Mosselbay, Zeekoegat Farm, Oudtshoorn
Tel: 044-272-6721 Fax: 044-272-6721
Email: info@dezeekoe.co.za Web: www.dezeekoe.co.za
Cell: 082-551-3019

I'm going to come straight out and say it: I'm smitten! You'll find the house in a desert cauldron, whose dusty plains are ringed by mountains holding back the coastal cloud. I arrived on a sultry afternoon and took refuge in the cool of the tile-floored farmhouse, among soft leather chairs, vibrant oil landscapes and low Oregon pine windows. Outside, surrounding a fire, there are surprisingly comfortable seats hewn from tree-trunks, and there's an even heavier wooden table where guests congregate for breakfast. All meals here are sourced, as much as possible, from their own organic gardens. Beyond the salt-water pool is a wall of reeds where a fish eagle nests, and beyond that a river - the farm is named after the hippos once found here - where you can quietly canoe under a reliable summer sun. Paula also showed me rows of giant eggs in ostrich incubators, a still taken straight from Jurassic Park. As well as the springbok, monkeys and otters there are 1,000 ostriches that live on the farm, so borrow a bike and introduce yourself. Easily startled, your long-necked inquisitors will turn on their heels, their feathery burlesque bustle reminiscent of indignant drag queens (some might think). But I really lost my heart to my waterfront cabin. In a washed-blue dawn, the mountains now faintly outlined like mascara, bright birds busied about the reeds (there are 250 species to spot). I sat on the deck, its legs planted firmly in the dam, as my neighbour cast his line. So beautiful, so peaceful.... De Zeekoe completely relaxed me and I long to return. *Biking, hiking, canoeing & birding (162 species) opportunities abound on the farm's reserve. There is also a meerkat project in the reserve, run by TV's Meerkat Magic man Grant McIllrath.*

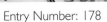

Rooms: 12: 8 in-house (king, twin and double), 6 with en/s bath and sh'r, 2 with en/s sh'r. 4 two-bedroom cabins, all with shared sh'rs and kitchenette.
Price: Rooms R395 – R680 pp sharing.
Meals: Full breakfast included. 4-course dinner available at R185 pp, excluding wine. Braais, light meals & organic salads also avail'.
Directions: Head west from Oudtshoorn (toward Calizdorp) on R62. Turn right at sign to Mossel Bay on R328. After 7km turn right on dirt road, for 2km to De Zeekoe on left.

Red Stone Hills

Petro and Hermanus Potgieter
Oudtshoorn
Tel: 044-213-3783 Fax: 044-213-3291
Email: redstone@pixie.co.za Web: www.redstone.co.za

The humbling sense of the passage of time pervades this 3,000-hectare veld, whose desert colours swirl with Van Gogh vibrancy. The current Pótgieters are the fifth generation to farm this land (ostrich, vineyards, cattle, fruit), but that lineage is put into perspective by the red stone hills. They date to the enon-conglomerate period, formed 65 million years ago when the earth twisted and a torrent of sanguine mud-stone settled and solidified; a few million years later, bushmen hid in the hills' stone pockets and painted wildlife; and in the 1790s Karoo cottages completed the picture. It's all been authenticated by erudite visitors: botanists, geologists and a chap from Roberts who identified 191 birds here, including eagles, black stork and five varieties of kingfisher. But you'll find Hermanus and Petro plenty knowledgeable themselves. We drove out along dusty tracks leading past the schoolhouse his father donated to the mixed community (which still congregates there), through babbling brooks to Chinese lanterns and blankets of fynbos and medicinal succulents. Hermanus will name them all. Petro says he lives in the past, whereas she's an artist facing the future. She's currently planning open-air opera for their natural stone auditorium. Also in the pipeline are geological, botanical and fossil tours. There are many ways to enjoy the scenery, cycling, hiking, riding, fishing… and ostrich-rich Oudtshoorn is minutes away. When you're tired out, your sleepy cottage, with original Oregon pine doors and floors and farm-made furniture, awaits.

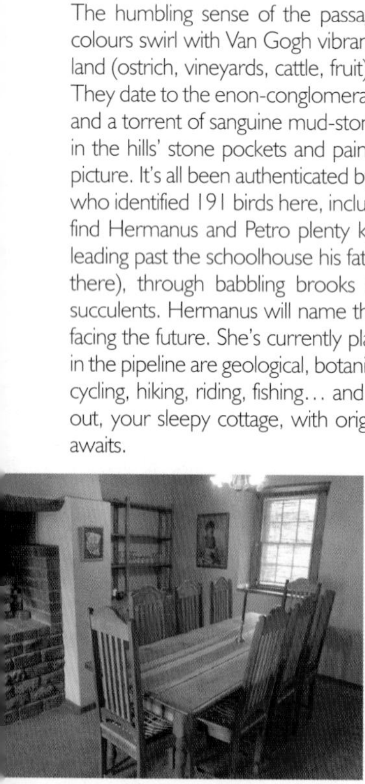

Rooms: 6 cottages: all fully self-contained with 1, 2 or 3 bedrooms and shared or en-suite bathrooms with baths and/or showers.
Price: R190 – R320 pp self-catering. Singles on request.
Meals: Full breakfast R55, Continental breakfast R45. Formal dinners or informal braai-packs on request.
Directions: Halfway between Calitzdorp & Oudtshoorn on R62. Head west from Oudtshoorn 28km, then Kruisrivier turn-off. Red Stone 6km down this road. Another entrance between foot of Swartberg mountain & Cango Caves via Matjiesrivier.

33° South

Carolyn Kent
Matjiesrivier Valley, Oudtshoorn/Matjiesrivier Valley
Tel: 044-272-4314 Fax: 044-272-4314
Email: ckent@telkomsa.net
Cell: 082-898-4179

At the foot of the daunting Swartberg Pass – still draped in snow when I arrived - lies 33° South. Apart from the silver trees gently thrilling in the breeze, the only sound to be heard was the soft bounce of small feet upon trampoline. I turned to watch Joshua leaping above the tree line. "He's the bird-watcher around here," said Carolyn pointing to her eleven-year-old now turning somersaults in the sky. "He's got all the books and the binos." I settled into the sofa on the wide verandah, the obvious centre of the action, to absorb my surroundings. Chairs around the dining table spilled over with cushions, hinting at long, lazy gatherings. I imagined guests huddled together at night, around the roaring fire, contemplating the space and the darkness beyond the edge of the stoep. At the side of the house facing the mountain, with lawns of their own, are Carolyn's two cosy guest rooms. We wandered through an old wooden door to the first. Furnished with warm orange cushions and rugs, it has an inviting black-slate walk-in shower and a smart kitchenette. The second is a bit grander with wooden floorboards, animal skin rugs, a big wooden bed and antique bits and pieces. They have braai areas outside, providing the perfect setting for a night of star-gazing, which is spectacular out here in the pollution-free semi-desert. For the ultimate star experience be sure to ask Carolyn in advance to get the man with the telescope round!

Rooms: 2: 1 queen with en-suite shower and kitchenette; 1 king or two singles with en-suite shower and kitchenette. Both rooms are separate from the house.
Price: Self-catering R225 pp sharing, singles R275. B&B rate R275 pp sharing, singles R325.
Meals: Dinners on request.
Directions: From Oudtshoorn take R328 towards Cango Caves. Just before caves turn L at the Prince Albert sign. Travel for approx 12 km and turn L at the next sign to Calitzdorp/ Matjiesrivier. Travel for 6 km, turn R at '33° South' green and white sign board, the house is 800m further. Map can be faxed.

The Retreat at Groenfontein

Marie and Grant Burton

Calitzdorp
Tel: 044-213-3880 Fax: 044-213-3880
Email: info@groenfontein.com Web: www.groenfontein.com

A tiny gravel road twists along the sides of one idyllic to another yet more secluded valley, past old Cape Dutch farm buildings which line the route and eventually arriving at the Burtons' Victorian-colonial homestead. They ran a popular wilderness lodge in Namibia before trawling southern Africa for a new Eden, and it took years to find Groenfontein. It was worth the wait. The view from the verandah, where meals are served (and where I sampled a mouthwatering smoked snoek mousse, followed by ostrich casserole with gem-squash), crosses a valley and climbs the Burtons' own mountain before joining the vast Swartberg Nature Reserve, now a UNESCO World Heritage Site. What with hiking trails to intimate rock pools and excellent mountain trails, the opportunities for merry traipsing are limitless. When it gets hot, you can swim in the river or collapse inside the gloriously cool house. The original marble fireplace and pine and yellowwood flooring remain and in similar style to the two slate-floor, reed-and-mud roof rooms (away from the house), with French-window views, two new suites have been built. Airy bedrooms benefit from simple combinations of yellow, beige and cream. It is an incredible area to explore with kloofs, mountain wilderness, half-forgotten roads, with many animals to look out for. But, best of all, you come back to award-winning hospitality: delicious dinners, welcoming hosts and a truly relaxed household. Give yourselves 2 nights!

Rooms: 8: In the main house; 1 king, 1 queen and 1 twin with sh'r and 1 twin with bath/ sh'r; also 4 luxury rooms away from house, all with views kings/twins with bath and sh'r except one with sh'r only.
Price: R360 - R780 pp sharing, includes 3 or 4-course dinner and breakfast. Singles on request.
Meals: Full b'fast & 3 or 4-course dinner (w/out wine) incl'. Fully licensed. Lunches/picnics from R35.
Directions: From Oudtshoorn take R62 towards Calitzdorp for 30km. Turn R onto dirt rd signed Kruisrivier. After 17km keep L at fork as rd gets narrower & follow for 10.7km until sign for The Retreat to your R. From Calitzdorp L at Groenfontein sign - 19km to house. Drive slowly.

Mymering Estate Guest House

Pam and Craig Miller

Dwarsrivier, Ladismith

Tel: 028-551-1548 Fax: 028-551-1548

Email: mymering@mweb.co.za Web: www.mymeringestate.co.za

Following a sinuous trail of familiar, musky scents, my nose knew I was homing in on the Mymering Estate long before my eyes confirmed it. And what a picture I saw when they did. For in its sheltered valley swaying with poplar trees, were row upon row of lavender plants, stretching ahead like tightly-knit, violet braids. Presided over by the dramatically gashed mountain, the well-known Towerkop sentinel, this estate is home to Pam and Craig, who transformed this once wild valley into the working essential-oil farm it is today. Old hands at the hospitality game, they decided to combine their new-found calling with a bit of what they do best. Nearest to the main house is an old (dates back to 1930) country-style thatched cottage, now beautifully restored. With its vaulted ceiling, wooden floors, neutral colours, Dover stove and French windows opening onto olive groves, it is wonderfully light and open, yet retains its rustic, country feel. The two suites share a pool and large deck that hovers over the valley floor. These have a more modern feel, with mirrored headboards and swing-shutters separating off their rather opulent bathrooms. With aromatherapy massage under the oaks, the Springvale hike, the vineyard "meander", sundowners, gourmet dinners, as well as eco, fynbos and small game tours, it seems they have thought of absolutely everything to make your stay a memorable one.

Rooms: 3: 2 suites with 1 king/twin, both en-suite bath & shower & kitchenettes. Optional self-catering thatched cottage: 1 double & 1 twin (both with en-suite shower), living room & kitchen.
Price: R325 - R525 pp sharing. Singles +30%.
Meals: Full breakfast included. Dinner (3 courses, fine dining) served in the manor house R190.
Directions: From Cape Town on R62, Mymering is signposted 13km before Ladismith. Continue for 10km and turn R at T-jct, after 3km look for sign on L. From Oudtshoorn, follow right thro' Ladismith, past white church, at T-jct (golf course opposite) turn L & after 9km, look for signs on R.

Rietfontein Guest Farm

Bernard and Lola Nicholls
33km from Ladismith and 45km from Barrydale on R62
Tel: 028-551-2128 or 021-875-5960
Fax: 021-875-5965 Email: info@rietfontein.co.za
Web: www.rietfontein.co.za Cell: 082-400-1092

Boldly going where no man had gone before (I wilfully imagined), mission in hand and hands on the controls, I pressed on through the otherworldly veld that stretched before me, billowing dust masking the tracks behind me. And what a magical destination I discovered… a small, blossom-filled valley in the heart of Karoo country, a gloriously green oasis, surrounded by a private nature and game reserve. Scattered within the farm are five renovated farm cottages all connected by paths or footbridges that criss-cross their way through the pepper trees and reed bushes that divide them. Comfortable and unfussy, many of the beams inside and all of the sturdy furniture have been constructed using original train-track sleepers. Each cottage has its own flame-torch-lit verandah, outdoor braai and fire area. Do make sure you bring everything you'll need as this is pretty well off-the-beaten track stuff. Speaking of tracks, a network of mountain-biking, driving and hiking routes have been specially mapped out for you in the rugged Touwsberg Mountains all around. If that sounds rather exhausting you can just as easily spend your time within the sanctuary of the valley - a spot of pétanque perhaps, or how about a G&T at the fresh-water pool's very own thatched (BYO) bar? That's the daytime covered. As for the night, there's only one place to be… stargazing from the telescope mound into the extraordinarily dark heavens above. *A wine-tasting room was being added at time of visit.*

Rooms: 5 cottages: 2 x double room, 1 twin room, 2 sofa beds & shared bathroom; 3 x double room, twin room & 1 sofa bed, both shared bathroom & 1 extra shared outdoor shower.
Price: R605 - R840 per night per cottage for 4 or more people. For 3 people or fewer R175 - R215 pp sharing.
Meals: Fully self-catering, though basics provided for first morning.
Directions: Signposted off R62, 32km from Ladismith and in the other direction 45km from Barrydale, another 10km from Main Rd.

Merwenstein Fruit and Wine Farm

Hugo and Heidi van der Merwe

8km from Bonnievale on Swellendam Road
Tel: 023-616-2806 Fax: 023-616-2806
Email: welcome@merwenstein.co.za Web: www.merwenstein.co.za
Cell: 082-377-6638 (Heidi) or 082-922-4846 (Hugo)

The van de Merwes are simply the kindest people you will ever meet. After scoffing a plate-full of Heidi's koeksisters and a glass of freshly-squeezed pomegranate juice, Hugo took me for a stroll around their beautiful fruit and wine farm. It was a stunning springtime evening, rows of peach trees were in full blossom and the air vibrated with the hum of busily pollinating bees. Rolling across the valley floor from the Breede River to the feet of the rocky Langeberg range, Merwenstein is perfectly placed to make the most of the Robertson winelands. And once the car is suitably packed with clinking bottles there's everything from guided river trips and golf to horse-riding and hot springs to enjoy. Heidi is an expert on the area and will happily take guests to a local crèche she helped set up or on a tour of nearby Bonnievale. She's also a great cook and rustled up a feast of traditional SA fare on my visit. "Here we don't decorate your plate, we fill it!" an aproned Hugo told me. Gloriously full, I slept like a log in my huge room. All three spots here have patios looking onto the garden. Come the morning I was out across the lawn for another birding walk (90 species to spot), savouring every moment at one of our most relaxing finds. They've recently started drumming workshops too which are well worth doing but do phone ahead. *Hier wird Deutsch gesprochen.*

Rooms: 3: all with en-suite shower.
Price: R450 pp sharing. Single supplement plus R50.
Meals: Full breakfast and dinner included.
Directions: Use the same turn-off as for the Merwespont Wine Cellar, 8km from Bonnievale on the road to Swellendam.

Les Hauts de Montagu Guest Lodge

Myriam and Eric Brillant

Route 62, Montagu
Tel: 023-614-2514 Fax: 023-614-3517
Email: info@leshautsdemontagu.co.za Web: www.leshautsdemontagu.co.za
Cell: 083-529-3389 (Myriam) 083-528-9250 (Eric)

If you set your sights solely on staying in Montagu itself you would completely miss this little oasis of all things fine and French nestled three kilometres further along the road. As I slunk slowly up the long driveway past the helipad (sadly the Greenwood chopper was in for a service), Les Hauts De Montagu revealed itself in all its glory. It is not difficult to see why Eric and Myriam (both Congolese by birth but with years of Parisian industry experience) instantly fell '*tête* over *talons*' with this place; its setting is sensational. Perched high on the hillside it enjoys expansive views of the valley and its ripening vines. The main Cape Dutch farmhouse dates from 1865 and it has taken two years of painstaking restoration to bring the dilapidated building back to life. Inside, under 21 huge beams that hold up the roof, I dined on food that was fabulously French - garlic snail ravioli and creamy blue cheese with green fig preserve to name just two of the five scrumptious courses. With stomach bursting at the seams I crunched more heavily than usual along the loose stone path past beds of lavender to my cottage. A soaring chimney encourages the fire beneath on cold winter nights, while the huge glass doors allow refreshing breezes on hot summer ones. The glorious outside shower the following morning meant washing in the full view of Montagu… I was thankful it was those three kilometres away!

Rooms: 6: 1 twin, 3 kings and 2 queens, all with en-suite baths with outside showers.
Price: R450 - R650 pp sharing. Self-catering option (breakfast not included, minimum 2 nights) R300 - R350 pp sharing. Single R600 - R1,200.
Meals: Full breakfast included. Restaurant on premises, 5-course set menu.
Directions: Pass Montagu, stay on R62 for 3km. Hauts de Montagu on R. Helipad and airstrip also available.

Mimosa Lodge

Fida and Bernhard Hess

Church St, Montagu
Tel: 023-614-2351 Fax: 023-614-2418
Email: info@mimosa.co.za Web: www.mimosa.co.za
Cell: 083-787-3331

Bernhard and Fida took over this two-storey Edwardian townhouse a few years ago. Being Swiss, they no doubt felt some compulsive draw to mountain-marooned Montagu. It helps that I adore Art Deco as there's a lot of it about: chandeliers, wardrobes, cabinets, revolving bookcases, chairs re-upholstered in daring colours. The bedrooms bear little resemblance one to the other. Some are in the house, others in the dazzling flower garden, with its herbs and vegetables, orchard and black marble swimming pool. Colours are used with imagination throughout, some bold, some demure, but all give a true sense of luxury and space. Each suite has a CD player and all the rooms have a host of little extras: a decanter of Muscadel, books, magazines, fresh fruit, chilled water for example. An old shop counter has become the bar where guests congregate (and salivate) before dinner. Bernhard is a chef extraordinaire who used to run restaurants in Jo'burg and is well known in his native Switzerland. Be sure to get yourself a bottle of the Mimosa Lodge Cabernet Sauvignon, which was barrel-matured and bottled in Mimosa's own cellar, the perfect accompaniment to award-winning cuisine prepared using only the freshest of ingredients, many originating from Mimosa's own lovingly-tended garden where more than 200 plant species thrive. I am very happy to be able to continue recommending Mimosa for a special treat. *Children and off-peak dinners by arrangement.*

Rooms: 16: 7 twins, 9 classic rooms, all with en/s bathrooms; 7 with bath & separate shower, 5 with shower, 4 with bath/shower.
Price: R425 - R750 pp sharing. Singles R554 - R1,022.
Meals: Full breakfast included. Four-course dinner (*table d'hôte*) in the restaurant R195.
Directions: From Ashton side on R62, Church Street is 3rd on left after entering Montagu. From Barrydale, Church Street is 5th turning on right. Mimosa Lodge is clearly sign-posted.

Collins House

Tessa Collins

63 Kerk St (Church St), Prince Albert
Tel: 023-541-1786 Fax: 023-541-1786
Email: collinsh@tiscali.co.za Web: www.collinshouse.co.za
Cell: 082-377-1340

Collins House stands out on Kerkstraat, unusual as a fine two-storey Victorian townhouse among so many Cape Dutch gable buildings. The open-plan kitchen/sitting room is the warm heart of the house - check out the beautiful tile and wood floor - and when I arrived Tessa was in her 'office', an old desk in the middle of the room, creating wire topiary and listening to the cricket on the radio. There are french doors out to the flower garden, and the very large swimming pool and air-con in all the bedrooms are a blessing during Karoo summers. The town is full of Cape Dutch national monuments and snoozes right at the foot of the spectacular Swartberg pass. You must not fail to experience this and Tessa takes guests up there with evening drinks - or you can hire your own scooter in town. Collins House is long on luxury. Bedrooms are upstairs (almost a rarity in itself in South Africa) and you are mollied and coddled with fine-quality linens and lotions. Tessa herself has been with us from the start, is refreshingly outspoken and likes grown-ups who she can have a drink with and get to know. Luxury is one thing, but character is inimitable... and Tessa and Collins House have that in spades. *No children. DSTV is available in the upstairs guest sitting room.*

Rooms: 4: 3 twins, 1 with en-suite bath, 1 with shower and 1 with bath and shower; 1 double with en-suite bath.
Price: R250 – R400 pp sharing. Single supplement R100.
Meals: Full breakfast included and served till 9.30am.
Directions: On Kerkstraat in the middle of town.

Onse Rus

Lisa and Gary Smith
47 Church St, Prince Albert
Tel: 023-541-1380 Fax: 023-541-1064
Email: info@onserus.co.za Web: www.onserus.co.za
Cell: 083-629-9196

The official pamphlet does a good job of conveying the delights of Onse Rus, but it modestly fails to bear testament to the biggest plus, the Smiths themselves. They fell in love with Prince Albert and the 150-year-old Cape Dutch Onse Rus in 1999 and their enthusiasm for both town and house has not abated since. Guests who have come down over the Swartberg Pass are given a whisky for their nerves and trips to The Hell, a famously isolated community 57km down a dirt track, are easily arranged. Back at the house, the large living room is hung with a permanent exhibition of local artists' work. The five thatched bedrooms all have private entrances, high ceilings, white walls and simple Karoo furnishings. One used to be part of the bakery, another was the printing room for a local newspaper. The house has some history! Outside there's a brand-new swimming pool (a thing of particular beauty in such a hot climate) and also a gazebo, a focal point for relaxing in the garden. Here guests are brought food and drink while leisurely hours are whiled away with good books. If the weather permits – which it usually does – you can sit out on the verandah and enjoy fig ice cream in the shade of the Cape ash and Karoo pepper trees.

Rooms: 5: 3 doubles and 2 twins (one twin sleeps 4). 4 with en-suite shower, 1 with en-suite bath and hand-shower.
Price: R295 - R350 pp sharing. Singles prices enthusiastically given on request.
Meals: Breakfast included. Light lunches and coffee shop open. Traditional dinners on request
Directions: On the corner of the main street (Kerk or Church St) and Bank Sts.

Lemoenfontein Game Lodge

Ingrid Köster
Beaufort West
Tel: 023-415-2847 Fax: 023-415-1044
Email: lemoen@mweb.co.za Web: www.lemoenfontein.co.za

Lemoenfontein, in the shadow of the Nuweveld Mountains, is one of those places where whatever your mood on arrival – and after a tiring drive down the N1 mine was ropey - a calmness envelops you like magic vapour. I was suddenly enjoying a cool drink on the vast wooden verandah, gazing over measureless miles of veld and chatting happily to Ingrid about the history of the place. It was built as a hunting lodge in 1850, then became a sanatorium for TB sufferers (the dry Karoo air was beneficial), a farm and finally (and still) a nature reserve. Everything has been done well here, no corners cut and the result is a most relaxing, hassle-free stay. Rooms are stylish and understated with top-quality fabrics and completely comfortable beds. Outside, lawns, a pool, bar and braai area and the veld are all segregated by high dry-stone walls. You *must* go on a game drive through the reserve before dinner - to look at all the buck and zebra of course, but also to be out in such scenery as the sun goes down. And one final thing: dinner when we got back was at first mouth-watering, then lip-smacking. A real South African experience. *All rooms are air-conditioned.*

Rooms: 12: 7 doubles, 5 with en-suite bath and shower 2 with just shower; 5 twins, 2 with en-suite bath and shower and 3 with just shower.
Price: From R340 pp sharing. Singles R435.
Meals: Full breakfast included. A set dinner is available every night for R125.
Directions: From the N1, 2km north of Beaufort West. Turn onto De Jagers Pass Road at the Lemoenfontein sign. Go 4km up dirt track, following signs.

Eastern Cape

Sederkloof Lodge

Thys and Alice Cilliers

PO Studtis, Baviaanskloof, Willowmore District
Tel: 049-839-1122 Fax: 049-839-1081
Email: thysbaviaans@mweb.co.za Web: www.sederkloof.co.za

Who dares, wins. The dust road that links the World Heritage Site Baviaanskloof Wilderness Area to the rest of the world also keeps it undiscovered. Old ways endure here. Warped and riven rocks line your passage through this spectacular valley, cracking open to reveal deep ravines and long forgotten roads into the earth. Do not be daunted. The lodge is as far as front-wheel drive will take you, though at times I would cut the engine anyway and step out into the awesome silence. Met by a very welcoming Thys and Alice, I was trundled up by 4x4 to the top where the air, rarified and fynbos-sweetened, blesses six mountain chalets discreetly built in glass and local stone. They are deceptively simple. I had barely stepped onto polished floors before I was burying myself in the folds of luxuriously white duvet that covered my four-poster bed... and slipping into a hot tub with moutain views and even eagles swirling beyond my toes. It was too early for a glass of port… but why not? Suddenly I was the gentleman traveller of old. Thys loves showing you his playground, for now that he has retired this is his passion, reintroducing oryx, impala and wildebeest onto the farm. A drive into the wilderness offers sightings of fabulous Knysna loeries and very rare black rhino. Let local guide, Kiewiet, walk you into the Sederkloof itself, famous for its old cedars and wild beehives. The personal attention is exceptional. Guests are treated to Alice's fine dining in the communal lodge, set to an epic vista that drops away from beyond the pool. But best of all is the 'surprise treat' to which you are led blindfold. Unforgettable.

Rooms: Six mountain chalets with king-size beds, en-suite baths and outdoor showers.
Price: R1,500 pp sharing including all meals and activities.
Meals: All meals included.
Directions: Detailed directions on request.

Oyster Bay Lodge

Hans and Liesbeth Verstrate-Griffioen

Oyster Bay
Tel: 042-297-0150 Fax: 042-297-0150
Email: info@oysterbaylodge.com Web: www.oysterbaylodge.com
Cell: 082-700-0553

Here's yet another film-set masquerading as a B&B… this one is for the beach scenes! Hans and Liesbeth have the very envy-inducing run of three and a half kilometres of pristine beach to themselves, the fine white sand of the dunes as pure as it is wind-driven (but for the odd monkey footprint). They have fifteen horses, eight of which are rideable, which roam free on the 235 hectare nature reserve, and the first time I visited there simply wasn't time for a beach ride. So I dreamt hard for two weeks and managed to dream it into reality, returning to experience for real the wind in my hair, salt air in my face and sun shining down… amazing. But there's more: Hans and Liesbeth have made hiking trails from the sand dunes through the fynbos where you'll have a chance to see some of the 140 species of bird on their land and maybe vervet monkeys. I could hear them, but didn't quite catch a glimpse. Your stay is very personable and relaxing with use of the swimming pool and self-catering facilities if you choose. Otherwise, supper could be some Oyster Bay rump steak from their cattle farm or the fresh catch of the day. Come here for the empty beach, the horses and walks along an unspoilt coastline. *Day-tours can be taken to nearby Tsitsikamma Nature Reserve and Baviaanskloof.*

Rooms: 7: all kings, 2 in the house, both with en-suite bath & shower; 4 separate chalets with open-plan, free-standing bath & shower & private verandah with sea view; 1 family room with en-suite and a separate bedroom for children or extra people. 4 also have kitchenette facilities.
Price: R440 - R700 pp sharing, all year round. Booking advisable, but walk-ins welcome.
Meals: Full breakfast included. Lunches and dune picnics available through out the day. Five-course evening dinner R150.
Directions: From Cape Town on N2 turn off at exit number 632 Palmietvlei and follow signs to Oyster Bay Lodge. From Port Elizabeth take exit to Humansdorp and then follow signs to the Lodge.

Kromme Island Lodge

Philipp & Tinie Maske and Ted & Margaret Dersley

Kromme Island Estate, Near St Francis Bay
Tel: 042-295-2380
Email: info@krommeislandlodge.co.za Web: www.krommeislandlodge.co.za
Cell: 082-365-2897

As neighbours and good friends, the Dersleys and Maskes decided to move into their holiday homes to set up a guest house. Nestled in indigenous bush on the Kromme River, the place had always been full of assorted family and friends and, since the couples' hospitality was legendary, running a guest house made a lot of sense. To make things even better, they've given us their best rooms. Both couples sacrificed amazing top-floor views over the river, with vast windows overlooking one of the most tranquil hideaways in the Eastern Cape. Decoration throughout is elegant and restful, and if you have a bigger horde the separate three-roomed cottage is the perfect place to settle the whole family for a few blissful, sunny weeks. Watch the kids paddle off to the island for some old fashioned fun, while you enjoy the abundant birdlife, fishing or simply relaxing on the river bank. On rainy days you are welcome to use the television in the main sitting room but, if the sun is beaming down (as it was on my visit), there's not much chance you'll leave the riverside. St Francis Bay is just a short drive, or an even shorter boat ride, away.

Rooms: 5 bedrooms: 2 en-suite double rooms; 1 cottage with 2 doubles, 1 twin and 1 bathroom.
Price: R300 pp sharing in cottage, or R1,500 for whole unit. R500 pp sharing in The Boathouse & Riverside.
Meals: Full breakfast included. 2-course lunch R75, 3-course dinner R175. Sundowner cruise R70 (including drinks and snacks).
Directions: Travel on the N2 (Port Elizabeth – Cape Town). Turn off to Humansdorp on the R330 and continue towards St Francis Bay. 7km from Humansdorp you will see the sign for 'Kromme Island Lodge'.

34 Lovemore Crescent

Monica Johnson

St. Francis Bay
Tel: 042-294-0825 Fax: 042-294-0825
Email: dolfinvu@intekom.co.za Web: www.b-b.co.za
Cell: 082-695-3395

34 Lovemore is an unpretentious B&B and an absolute delight. This has everything to do with Monica's warm hospitality and the character of her home, built 20 years ago, though the beachside location is an added bonus. A cuppa appears on arrival and you are then shown up to your quarters, two large rooms under a high thatched roof, with a living area between them, all looking out to sea. The aloe-filled back garden is a bird-watcher's paradise where even the neighbours pop over for the viewing. The front garden has weaver-birds' nests in the trees and possibly Africa's most southerly baobab tree, a tenacious little thing brought down from Zimbabwe by the family in the '80s. And on the other side of the garden there is another separate flat, which can be rented on a B&B basis or as a self-catering unit (but you'd be missing out on an unforgettable breakfast of delicious home-made breads, scones, jams and all...). It lacks the sea views, so Monica feels duty-bound to offer it at give-away prices. With a sweeping vista across St. Francis Bay, where southern right whales can be seen in season and dolphins year round, you cannot fail to relax here. Keen surfers will be interested to note (they will in fact salivate over the news) that Bruce's Beauties are at the end of the garden.

Rooms: 3: 1 double with en/s shower and 1 twin with private shower and bath; 1 flat sleeping up to 6 with 1 bathroom.
Price: Rooms in the house: R250 - R350 pp sharing. Flat: R200 pp self-catering (or R235 with breakfast.)
Meals: Full breakfast included for B&B in the house.
Directions: From the Humansdorp road take 1st right into Lyme Rd South, then 3rd right onto St. Francis Drive, then 5th left onto Lovemore Crescent. 34 Lovemore is sign-posted at each of these turns. 34 is the last house on the left.

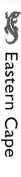

The Dunes Country House

Chantelle and Brent Cook

St. Francis Bay
Tel: 042-294-1685 Fax: 042-294-1687
Email: reservations@dunesstfrancis.com Web: www.dunesstfrancis.com
Cell: 082-324-3484

After fourteen years in the madding metropolis of LA, St. Francis Bay represents a vivid and welcome contrast for Chantelle and Brent: 600 hectares of thrumming nature on the doorstep and tranquillity in abundance. At the end of a sandy road through coastal fynbos, the guest house sits surrounded by indigenous garden with thick grass - the kind that crunches underfoot - aloe trees and strelitzias. Brent is a walking guide and takes guests through the farm on foot. He explains what they are doing for nature conservation while pointing out and expanding your knowledge of any critters spotted en route, including zebra and various species of antelope. A two-hour walk takes you to Thula Moya (the adjoining coastal reserve), via bird-watching hides and waterholes. Here, tea, scones, lunch or a well-earned sundowner will be waiting before you're whisked back to the comforts of the guest-house. Reminiscent of an old Cape farmhouse, the guest-house is part of the conservation effort with its Oregon wood floors, doors and window frames all reclaimed from an old school. The theme of comfortable splendour extends into the bedrooms, with their marble counter tops, percale linens on beds, underfloor heating, ball-and-claw baths and French doors that open onto the verandah. For even more comfort book a moonlit massage at their new outdoor bush spa... relaxation never felt so sweet. *A bush tent was being built at the time of going to print.*

Rooms: 7: 6 doubles with en-suite bath and shower, and 1 family cottage with full bathroom.
Price: Doubles: R425 - R675 pp sharing. Cottage: R450 - R595 pp sh (max 4 pp), R250 - R350 per child sh. Winter specials available on request.
Meals: Full b'fast & afternoon tea and scones incl'. Light lunches R24 - R50. Dinners by prior arrangement.
Directions: From N2, take St. Francis Bay/Humansdorp exit. Follow signs to St. Francis Bay onto R330. Go through the traffic circle, past the golf course and drive for approx. 800m. Turn right at The Dunes signboard and follow the road to the gate.

Thunzi Bush Lodge

Mark and Trenwyth Pledger
Maitland Road, Maitlands, Port Elizabeth
Tel: 041-372-2082 Fax: 041-372-1181
Email: info@thunzi.co.za Web: www.thunzibushlodge.co.za
Cell: 072-597-4810

Ex-engineer Mark has been building treehouses since he was three (well, as soon as he could co-ordinate his hands with any intricacy) and Thunzi's flawlessly planned and finished chalets are standing proof of his skill. Many personal touches are integrated within; baths wrapped in wooden decking, sinks stationed on sealed, sniffle-free sneeze-wood (strangely enough, a beautiful wood that makes you sneeze when you work with it); and a medley of wholesome games and entertainments. The completely private cabins, linked only by gravel walkways, peep timidly through indigenous forest onto the De Stades River Wetlands where an abundance of birds have been listed. Over 352 wacky-named species flock to this eco-diverse area where coastal forest, thicket and wetlands meet (try narina trogon, African rail, Knysna loerie and the often-heard buff-spotted, red-chested and striped flufftails for size). Take the night walk through the forest and you'll be greeted by a hypnotic symphony of nocturnal sounds and even a few wandering antelope. By day relaxation comes easy (the spa packages sound blissful), but should you want a little more activity simply pop down the road to Maitland's impressive duned beach, the most isolated and untouched Port Elizabeth has to offer. Here you can hike, snorkel, whale-watch, sand-board (oh yes - the dunes really *are* that big) or go power-kiting (!). Personally a lamp-lit dinner beneath the star-lined silhouette of canopy would be enough, but I suppose one really should work up an appetite first.

Rooms: 3 chalets: 2 twin/kings, both with en-suite bath & shower; 1 family unit with 1 queen & 1 twin room with en-suite bath and shower.
Price: R695 - R795 pp sharing. 40% supplement for singles.
Meals: Full breakfast included. Light lunches and 3-course dinner on request. R165 for dinner, an extra R165 for private open-air dining experience.
Directions: Thunzi Bush Lodge is signed from the N2. More detailed directions can be emailed on request.

Aquasands

Richard and Deborah Johnson
No. 7, 11th Avenue, Summerstrand, Port Elizabeth
Tel: 041-583-3159 Fax: 041-583-3187
Email: greenwood@aquasands.co.za Web: www.aquasands.co.za
Cell: 082-462-6774

Aquasands is glamorous. The welcoming, vibrant Deborah is also glamorous. By the time I left, even I felt a bit glamorous too. She is a food stylist and husband Richard is a philatelist (a stamp dealer - but glamorous too!); they excel in their acute sensitivity to each guest's needs. And their open-plan contemporary home is a repository for an ever-changing, rotating collection of fine art. The guest rooms, with their own separate entrances, are blessed with crushed velvet or silk bedspreads, percale cottons and mohair blankets, red gerberas in fish-bowls and cactus-style soap dishes, an echo of the real cactus garden out there next to the tranquil koi fishpond. Breakfast is served on the architecturally spectacular grey, slate-tiled patio under steel and wood, offset with cheerful splashes of pink, purple and cobalt paint blocks. This is surrounded by a lush garden where palm trees intermingle with indigenous plants and giant aloes... and beyond is the ocean, with safe bathing and sandy beaches a mere two minutes' walk away. If that's too far there's always the large heated saline pool, sauna and steam room within flopping distance of the breakfast table. I met Grandpa too - another asset of the house - a champion fly-fisherman with photos to prove it. Come here for a holiday and not just a stopover!

Rooms: 4: 3 king/twins and 1 queen. All with en-suite bath and shower.
Price: R500 - R650 pp sharing. Singles from R600.
Meals: Full breakfast included.
Directions: From Cape Town take N2 to Port Elizabeth. Take exit 751B at sign for Settlers Way, follow signs to Summerstrand. Keep left onto Marine Drive along the sea front until 11th Avenue.

Forest Hall

James and Hilary Bolton

84 River Road, Walmer, Port Elizabeth
Tel: 041-581-3356 Fax: 041-581-3356
Email: foresthallbb@telkomsa.net Web: www.foresthall.co.za
Cell: 072-020-9595

As I approached Forest Hall I couldn't help wondering how my car had taken such a dramatic wrong turn as to end up somewhere in the Home Counties. Built by a British architect who already owned a house in England by the same name, the building is over a hundred years old and was one of Walmer's first farms. But don't worry... no old eiderdowns or Victorian plumbing here. These rooms have all the modern comforts you could ask for: slate-floored bathrooms with frameless, open-plan showers and some seriously sumptuous bed linen. The three self-catering rooms have neat, compact kitchens and sleeper-couches in them for families, while the smaller bed and breakfast room is more old English in style, with paintings of fox hunts on the walls. Nothing is too much trouble for James, who will even happily take people to Addo Elephant Park. He may not be a qualified guide, but he has a minibus and plenty of enthusiasm and knowledge. And it's not just James who'll do anything for you. Every member of the family is involved in some way. Hilary is the gourmet cook and James's mum Ann makes the home-made rusks, which you will find in your room. Even their three kids like to get involved, especially if there are other children looking for bouncing accomplices on their ground-level trampoline. *Good hiking and mountain-biking trails are a five-minute walk away, with free use of the Forest Hall bikes.*

Rooms: 4: all doubles, 3 with en-suite bath, shower and kitchenette; 1 with en-suite shower.
Price: R350 pp sharing.
Meals: Full Continental breakfast included. Dinner served on request.
Directions: From Port Elizabeth airport turn L at 1st traffic circle into 3rd Ave Walmer. Turn left at 1st set of robots into Heugh Rd. Go up until 9th Ave robots. Turn right into 9th Ave. Go down this across the traffic lights in Main Rd until you reach the last road off 9th on left. Turn into River Road. Sign 'Forest Hall' outside gates.

Lupus Den Country House

Priscilla and Noel Walton

Addo/Sunland
Tel: 042-234-0447 Fax: 042-234-0447
Email: info@lupusden.co.za Web: www.lupusden.co.za
Cell: 072-1814-750

Priscilla and Noel have not needed to learn any tricks about how to host. They are just naturally hospitable people who make you feel instantly at home and relaxed. When I arrived, lunch was waiting on the table and, with a home-made lemon drink in hand, I already felt part of the furniture. They have been living in their farmhouse for 40 years now – although the land it stands on has been in the family's hands since 1894 – and have made some adjustments to make the rooms all the more comfortable for their guests. The latest of these – three new large rooms, each with its private entrance – are in Garden Cottage. Two have outdoor showers and all have air-con. Their citrus and cattle farm is found on the friendly dirt roads between Addo and Kirkwood. And when I say friendly, I mean locals waved hello to me all the way there! The garden, surrounded by citrus groves, blooms with bougainvillaea and an abundance of other flowers and trees. The tiled swimming pool and an enormous tipuanu tree are two of the gardens' greatest assets, while vine-shaded terraces are the perfect places of repose after a rendezvous with the elephants in Addo (only 20 minutes away). When staying at Lupus Den you can be a tourist by day out in the parks and feel a local when back in the fold. Breakfast includes freshly-baked bread (naturally). A true farm B&B with home cooking – hard to beat.

Rooms: 6: homestead: 1 twin & 2 doubles, 2 en-s bath & shr, 1 en-suite sh'r; Garden Cottage: 3 doubles/twins, all en-s bathrooms, 2 outdoor shower. All rooms own entrance, patio & air-con.
Price: Original rooms: R250 - R300 pp. Singles R325 - R390. Garden Cottage rooms: R400 - R425 pp sh. Singles R520 - R550. Ask about kid's rates.
Meals: Full breakfast included. 3-course dinners (R120) and light lunches (R40), both by arrangement. Reduced rates for children.
Directions: From PE take R335 towards Addo. Cross railway in Addo, then L onto R336 towards Kirkwood. At Sunland, R at Lupus Den B&B sign & follow signs.

Hopefield Country House & Guest Farm

Kobus Buys and Gerhard Maritz

Off the R336, between Addo and Kirkwood, Sundays River Valley, Addo
Tel: 042-234-0333
Email: info@hopefield.co.za Web: www.hopefield.co.za

Known in the Addo area as The Music Boys, Kobus and Gerhard have been upping the tempo in the Sundays River Valley. They've both done time in the fast-paced record industry in Gauteng, but now they've repaired to Kobus's family home (along with three pianos and an organ) to do what they love best: playing music, gardening and entertaining (don't miss out on dinner - the cooking is sensational!). Outside, the garden continues the musical theme. A bust of Beethoven surveys the perfect lawn and several of their 54 varieties of roses have composers' names, Edward Elgar and Benjamin Britten among them. Their palpable creative urges are certainly not confined to just music-making though. Rooms are all uniquely decorated, with one-off paintings, beautiful antique furniture and slaved-over original wood floors. Whatever happens, they don't want it to look like a catalogue: even the baths are all different, with free-standing Victorian tubs and time-warping spas. There is a fully-licensed bar with a well-stocked library next to it, as well as an open sitting and dining area, overlooking the baby grand. Guests have even commented that the affable Horatio and Ophelia, their well-loved miniature schnauzers, were more of an attraction than Addo's elephants!

Rooms: 5: 1 queen with en-suite shower, 2 queens with en-suite bath, 2 twins with full bathrooms en-suite.
Price: R350 - R500.
Meals: Full breakfast included. Set 3-course dinner available on request.
Directions: Signed from the R336 between Kirkwood and Addo. More detailed directions can be emailed.

The Elephant House

Clive and Anne Read
Addo
Tel: 042-233-2462 Fax: 042-233-0393
Email: elephanthouse@intekom.co.za Web: www.elephanthouse.co.za
Cell: 083-799-5671

The bush telegraph gave advance notice of the many charms at Elephant House. Many tourists and other guest house owners had urged us to visit with a sincerity you could not ignore. It's a stunning house, the brainchild of one night's sleepless pondering by Anne who mapped the whole thing out in her head – a small, lawned courtyard surrounded on three sides by thatched and shady verandahs. The house, is in a sense, inside out. The drawing room leads to a dining room outside on the verandah (with antiques and Persian rugs). All the bedrooms open onto the verandah too and dinner (advertised with an African gong) is served there on silver and crystal. Evening meals are lit to stunning effect with lampshades made of Tuareg bowls. Lawns, indigenous trees and the racehorse stud (Clive used to run one in Natal) surround the house and when I was there the paddocks were full of mares with their foals. The bedrooms are luxurious with antique furniture, carpets, thick duvets and deep beds; and morning tea or coffee is brought to your bed, if so desired. There are also the Stable Cottage and the Family Suite, which, separate from the main house, retain the same charm, but are just a little cosier. The Elephant House also runs open-vehicle game drives in Addo, a few minutes away, morning and afternoon. *There is now a seasonal on-site masseuse who can conduct treatments inside or outside (Mon - Fri, Oct - May).*

Rooms: 11: 9 rooms in the house; 4 twins and 4 kings, all with en-suite bath and shower. Also 2 cottages that both sleep 4.
Price: R660 - R1,450 pp sharing. Cottages R500 - R600 pp sharing.
Meals: Full breakfast included in Elephant House. Self-served continental for Stable Cottage. Lunch & dinner provided. Three-course dinners R150 – R170.
Directions: From P.E. R335 through Addo 5km on the road towards the park - you will see a sign off to your left for The Elephant House.

The Colonial on Arundel

Molly and Conor O'Hagan Ward

Arundel Farm, Rietfontein Road, Addo
Tel: 042-234-0871 Fax: 086-689-8649
Email: info@thecolonial.co.za Web: www.thecolonial.co.za
Cell: 082-558-9896

When it comes to character The Colonial on Arundel is not in short supply: from the elephant feet that proudly stand on the porch (they are authentic, Molly tells me) to the huge wooden rhino statues that grace my bedroom fireplace and the framed butterflies that decorate the wall. And then of course there is Conor, a delightful story-teller, conservationist, game driver and self-confessed lover of colonial history. Brimming with colourful anecdotes he tells me over tea and cake that the house was originally owned in the 1930s by an English gentleman from Arundel (hence, of course, the name). The couple have kept much of the original design but have also added a myriad of treasures from the game lodge that they used to run in KwaZulu Natal. Zebra, giraffe and buffalo prints decorate the bedrooms, while wildlife and history books are stacked on the table in my private lounge. There's a sense of care and attention here which extends to the garden too. Lemons and blood oranges have been planted, a herb garden packed with marjoram, thyme and parsley is bursting into life, and there are Molly's roses too, to be showcased at the Addo rose festival. For me, though, the hidden treat is The Wallow, an enchanting outdoor bath. "It's not just for honeymooners," Molly smiles. "Guests have been known to race back from the elephant park to be the first ones in there!" Guided by the light from the full moon, I later creep across the garden to enjoy my very first wallow. Ah, yes. It really is something to rush home for!

Rooms: 2: luxury suites, both with queens and en-suite shower and outdoor bath.
Price: From R425 pp sharing.
Meals: Full breakfast included. Dinner on request, three courses R130.
Directions: Detailed directions on website.

Idwala Game Lodge

Ernst and Alida Du Toit
Adjacent to Lalibela Game Reserve, Sidbury
Tel: 046-622-2163 Fax: 046-622-2163
Email: enquiries@idwalalodge.com Web: www.idwalalodge.com
Cell: 083-277-7235

I was very excited when I first discovered Idwala. This was not just because of their introductory cocktail, complete with floating pebble (in case you're wondering, it's because Idwala means 'rock'), but because this was a real family-run lodge, as luxurious as all its corporate competitors. Mother and daughter team Claudine and Alida have created their own unique take on bush lodge décor, hand-picking every detail of the rooms, right down to the rock soap dish. Taxidermy is pastiched with carefully-chosen pieces of local art and craft. Animals made from wire paper and beads are lit from beneath, wardrobe knobs are shaped like tortoises' backs, and a beautifully gnarled knobwood tree branch wound its way to the top of my thatched ceiling. The glass doors in each room slide all the way back, so you can be completely open to the unfenced wilds beyond, and the shower has a glass wall out onto the bush. But you needn't worry about privacy. Every room is surrounded by greenery and reached by its own Indiana Jones-style walkway. The only creatures sneaking a peak through the curtains will be of the distinctly wild variety. And to get really close to them, Idwala's magnificent game drives are worth every minute of the early wake-up. *Airport transfers are available as well as star-gazing with trained ranger using on-site telescope.*

Rooms: 4: all can be double or twin with en-suite showers.
Price: R1,350 - R2,750 pp sharing. 50% supplement for singles.
Meals: All meals, local drinks and game drives are included.
Directions: Take the N2 from Port Elizabeth to Grahamstown. Exit at Sidbury turn-off. The Idwala Lodge is 7km further.

The Cock House

Richard Anker-Simmons and Jean-Louis Fourie
10 Market St, Grahamstown
Tel: 046-636-1287 Fax: 046-636-1287
Email: cockhouse@imaginet.co.za Web: www.cockhouse.co.za
Cell: 082-820-5592

The Cock House offers a friendly welcome and fine dining in the setting of a historic old house in downtown Grahamstown. Nelson Mandela has stayed three times and current President Thabo Mbeki has also been a guest (their visits are recorded in photos on the walls of the bar in case you don't believe me). Former owner Belinda Tudge worked hard with her late husband Peter to build up a business to be proud of, and it is really nice to see a staff who are so obviously genuinely proud to work there. With new owner Richard, manager Jean-Louis and his team carrying on the Cock House tradition of friendly hospitality there is always an opportunity to strike up a conversation in the delightful yellowood bar. The house dates back to 1826 and was one of the first built in Grahamstown. A stone-floored verandah stretches along the front of the house (mirrored by a wooden balcony upstairs) and the interior is full of yellowwood beams and broad-planked floors. I can recommend Norden's restaurant, which offers an international cuisine with a South African flavour and has its own herb garden, using local and seasonal ingredients wherever possible. The home-made bread is a particular treat. The two large rooms in the main house have glass doors opening onto the balcony, while modern apartments and seven converted stables open onto the garden. Personal and fun.

Rooms: 13: 7 doubles, 2 twins; all with en-suite bath and shower; 4 x 2-bedroom apartments with bath and shower.
Price: R365 - R465 pp sharing. R455 - R585 singles.
Meals: Full breakfast included and served any time. Lunch and dinner available in Norden's restaurant (except Monday lunch). Dinners on request if not included.
Directions: From P.E. take 2nd exit from N2 signposted "Business District/George Street". Take off-ramp L, turn L at bridge into George St. Continue down long hill into Grahamstown. At 4-way stop with Market St turn R and you will see the Cock House on the right corner.

Rivermead

Karen and Paul Davies

Bond Street, Grahamstown
Tel: 046-636-2727 Fax: 046-636-2728
Email: helbom54@global.co.za Web: www.rivermead.co.za
Cell: 082-343-5665

Step into a Babylonian scene of orange trees, gardenias, lavender and dahlias, passing the all-weather tennis court and stone steps that descend to the swimming-pool terrace (salt-water), and up to the titanic trees that shade the entrance. A yellow black-headed oriole was singing; "it sounds like liquid," said Karen. The garden views over the trees of the Rhodes University campus and the Grahamstown Valley are nothing short of imperious. On the opposite hillside is the 1820 Settler Memorial (I'm told it resembles a ship, but you have to squint quite a bit...). Naturally the most is made of these views throughout the house, with solid, sliding glass doors and private verandahs attached to all the bedrooms with their quilted beds and private sitting rooms - not to mention the en-suite bathrooms with sit-down showers. Cool, tiled floors sweep you through the extensive farmhouse kitchen, dining and lounge area with their black granite work surfaces, kitchen dresser and whitewashed walls. The fridge is pre-stocked with bread, yoghurt and, if you're very lucky, some of Paul's home-smoked bacon from his own butchery, a tasty sideline when he's not flying helicopters over game reserves. Karen has plenty on her plate as well. When not entertaining guests, she's involved with setting up the Entambeni Township Homestays and can organize a stay if you're keen. She can also recommend the best places to eat, but for advice on where to party, then look no further than oldest son Sebastian when he's in town.

Rooms: 3: 2 suites with double beds and lounge area with sofa-beds, 1 with en-suite shower, 1 with en-suite bath and shower; 1 double with en-suite shower.
Price: R350 - R400 pp sharing. Singles R350 - R450.
Meals: Full breakfast included. Self-catering option available for other meals.
Directions: From High St, turn R into Somerset Street. Turn left into Leicester Street (immediately before St. Andrew's Prep School). Continue until Bowles Street, turn right. Rivermead is signed from here. Map can be faxed or emailed. Phone for gate code.

Dovecote

Angela Thomas
17 Worcester St, Grahamstown
Tel: 046-622-8809 Fax: 046-622-8809
Email: anthomas@imaginet.co.za Web: www.grahamstown.co.za/dovecote/
Cell: 082-695-4262

From the charming garden cottage off her quiet Grahamstown street, Angela runs a good old-fashioned B&B: very comfortable and very friendly. Even as I drove up Worcester Street, I knew I was going to like Dovecote – joggers, dog-walkers and garden potterers all offered a nod and a wave. Angela, an avid bridge player, was the most friendly of the lot, opening up her cottage to guests simply because she loves doing it. And guests quickly become devoted. Her most famous returnee, Emeritus Archbishop Desmond Tutu, often stays when he's in town – there's a photo of him and his wife standing in the Dovecote garden. Perhaps it's this small garden with pebbled paths and a stone table in the shade of the bougainvillaea; perhaps it's the quiet privacy of the studio-style cottage, with its stable door and small kitchenette; or perhaps it's Angela's delicious home baking that lures him back time after time. Big, warm, freshly-baked scones were just one small scratch on the surface of Angela's impressive breakfast repertoire. I surreptitiously held one back to savour later in the day, they were so good. All of this has certainly whetted my appetite for a return visit.

Rooms: 1 cottage with twin beds and sleeper-couch and en-suite shower.
Price: From R320 pp sharing. Singles on request.
Meals: Continental breakfast included. Selection of restaurants in Grahamstown.
Directions: On N2 from PE take first Grahamstown exit signed Beaufort Street. At lights turn left into Summerset Street. Go over three stop-streets and, as road curves left, turn left into Worcester Street.

Kichaka Luxury Game Lodge

Keith Craig
Assegaai Bush, Grahamstown
Tel: 046-622-6024 Fax: 046-622-6028
Email: info@kichaka.co.za Web: www.kichaka.co.za
Cell: 083-236-0754

The rhinos were minding their own business, but in my over-excitement at seeing them, I missed my turning. I was able to retrace my steps, though, and was received at the lodge in fine style. A cool face-towel and a fruit cocktail were followed by a glass of chilled white wine and a buffet lunch tantalizingly described by one of the waiters. After lunch, manager Keith, who is bursting with enthusiasm for Kichaka, took me on a tour. First stop was 'hippo station', a large deck that extends over a small lake in front of the trimly-thatched lodge; here an infinity pool permits the illusion of basking with the hippos as they grunt and shuffle below. Each rondavel suite is exquisite, mixing African tones with European sophistication. Neat shutters at one end partition off vast baths and showers from equally enormous beds, while at the other French windows lead out onto a private stoep inset with your own pure-blue plunge pool. Upstairs in the main lodge you are well served by a huge flat-screen TV and literary bookshelves, but it was as Keith described the gourmet dinners served each night that I really began slavering. I noticed him frowning over the (complimentary) house wine. "It's just too good," he said shaking his head. With all this you might forget that you were in the bush, but daily game drives (all the so-called big five and much much more are here) with expert guides ensure that you won't. The message was loud and clear. Kichaka is about very fine living in an exciting bush setting. *Children over 12 are welcome.*

Rooms: 10 suites, all king/twin with en-suite bath and shower and plunge-pool.
Price: R1,750 - R3,450 (single +50%) inclusive of all safari activities, meals and drinks (local beers and spirits, house wines and soft drinks).
Meals: Full board including refreshments on game drives.
Directions: Take the Assegai Bush turn-off from the N2 (30km from Grahamstown toward PE) and then drive 3.5km along gravel road to lodge entrance.

Reed Valley Bush Lodge

Rod and Tracy Weeks

Reed Valley Bush Lodge, Amakhala Game Reserve
Tel: 042-235-1287 Fax: 042-235-1263
Email: reedvalley@bulkop.co.za Web: www.amakhala.co.za
Cell: 082-783-2506

Built into the bush at the top end of an open valley, Rod and Tracy's latest venture offers their guests a large helping of unspoilt wilderness... without forgetting, of course, to accommodate fully your appetite for luxury and creature comfort at the same time. Guests are welcomed at Reed Valley Inn before being whisked away to the Bush Lodge and the Amakhala Game Reserve. Talking of creature comfort, giraffe, antelope and elephants are your neighbours here, slowly foraging their way about on the open plains under a great sweeping sky. Rooms at the lodge keep as close to nature as they can with thatched roofing, tented walls, outdoor showers and wooden flooring. Each earth-toned room - white linen, plump cushions, air-con, oval bath, fireplace - also has its own decking, complete with plunge pool, so that guests can keep an eye on the comings and goings of the animals in great comfort. Although only 15 minutes' drive from Reed Valley, the Bush Lodge is a world away. Peace and tranquillity reign, but this is also a fun, sociable place. Evening meals are served at long tables in the main building with guests and staff mingling to create a laid-back, all-in-it-together sort of atmosphere. An inviting pub with wrap-around bar is an enticing addition, and perfectly designed for late-night story-telling with its elevated wooden platform opening out onto the bush. The lodge only opened in December 2007 and is an exciting new addition to the Amakhala scene.

Rooms: 4: all doubles with en-suite bath and outdoor shower.
Price: From R2,280 - R3,180.
Meals: All meals and game drives included.
Directions: From PE take N2 for 60km towards Grahamstown and see sign to Reed Valley on the right.

Reed Valley on Amakhala

Rod and Tracy Weeks
Amakhala Game Reserve
Tel: 042-235-1287 Fax: 042-235-1263
Email: reedvalley@bulkop.co.za Web: www.amakhala.co.za
Cell: 082-783-2506 (Tracy)

Reed Valley Inn just oozes history. The 1806 homestead, complete with wattle and daub walls and wonky floors, sits on the old mail wagon route from PE to Grahamstown, where weary messengers would change horses and quench thirsts. Following in their hoofsteps (but in a car), I found Rod and Tracy had made some slight changes since the farm came into Weeks' family hands in 1898. There was no 'Big 5' game viewing in those days, and what was once the inn are now charming guest quarters, with the original roof and a gaping fireplace retained. I hear your cries of anguish: "But where do we get our booze then?" Don't despair… Rod has merely moved the pub next to the dining room, far more convenient. Before joining Rod and Tracy for supper in the colossal, chandeliered and wooden-floored dining room (unless it's being served under the stars out in the bush) you can soak up the history on display in the pub. Old farming tools dangle from the walls alongside black-and-white photos of the farm from the 1920s, and a selection of pipes and a chessboard await those of a more ruminative disposition. Days of course are spent out on the range looking at animals. The perfect stopover before I was back in the saddle and galloping on towards Grahamstown.

Rooms: 4: all doubles or twins on request, all with en-suite bath and shower.
Price: R1,408 - R2,108 per person all-inclusive with light lunch, dinner, B&B and two game activities. Single supplement 30%.
Meals: Full breakfast included. Lunch and dinner available.
Directions: From PE take N2 for 60km towards Grahamstown and see sign to Reed Valley on the right.

Leeuwenbosch

Bill and Rosemary Fowlds
Off N2 between Port Elizabeth and Grahamstown, Amakhala Game Reserve
Tel: 042-235-1252 Fax: 042-235-1252
Email: leeuwenbosch@amakhala.co.za Web: www.amakhala.co.za
Cell: 083-383-2921

Leeuwenbosch remains a real South African find offering an unbeatable colonial safari experience. Firmly established as the senior partner in the Amakhala Game Reserve, it is a place full of zest and character, which has steadily been building its portfolio. There's a whole lot more in the game reserve now, and with lion, rhino, cheetah and elephants as new additions, the 'big five' is complete. Game drives and river cruises for birding and fishing are a must and if you are staying for a few nights a bush dinner is also recommended. Meals are generally served in the Dutch settler's house and remain intimate, convivial and delicious. For their accommodation, guests can either choose the Victorian mansion with its antique furniture, antique full-sized billiard table and antique photographs of Fowlds ancestors, or the newly-converted contemporary game lodge. This now houses four luxury rooms, with a wide verandah for lounging. Bill's tiny cellar pub remains an intimate forum for story-telling and a mini-chapel rounds off the Leeuwenbosch 'village', constructed in time for William Fowlds junior's wedding. The world's first stegosaur discovery site (1845) has recently been added to the reserve. All the family chip in to make your stay personable and memorable.

Rooms: 9: 5 rooms in the manor house, 2 twins, 3 doubles all with en-suite bathrooms; 3 twins, 1 double in lodge all with en/s shower and bath.
Price: R1,780 – R 2,580 inclusive package of 2 reserve activities (game drive, river cruise, night drive, canoeing, guided walk), breakfast, lunch & dinner. Off-season & last-minute specials.
Meals: Full breakfast included and served until 10.30 am. All meals included in the package.
Directions: From P.E. take the N2 to Grahamstown (do not take Paterson) for 67km where you'll see signs for Leeuwenbosch on your right only 1.5km beyond Shamwari turn on the left.

Map Number: 6

Entry Number: 209

The Safari Lodge on Amakhala

Justine and Mike Weeks
Amakhala Game Reserve
Tel: 046-636-2750 central reservations Fax: 086-694-9454
Email: centralres@amakhala.co.za Web: www.amakhala.co.za
Cell: 082-966-5696

As I soaked in my double bath, candles lit, the late sky glowing pink with pleasure, birds twittering, bush buck barking in the surrounding hills and lions roaring from afar (or so I chose to think…), it crossed my mind that this was perhaps not the toughest assignment of my life thus far. Amakhala Safari Lodge is surely the luxurious way to experience the game parks of the Eastern Cape. Beds, equipped with mosquito nets, are super-comfortable and there's a sofa area inside each thatched hut whose canvas fronts and terraces look onto the valley brush and the waterhole below. The bedrooms and the communal hut are decorated with Cape antiques and furniture carved from the wood on Mike's farm. Mike and Justine aren't always at the camp, but their friendly rangers are sure to take good care of you. After a delicious meal – usually served round the fire outside – and a good night's sleep, an early wake-up call takes you to Amakhala Game Reserve (now a big five reserve) with its beautiful and varied scenery of bushveld, savannah, cliffs and lots and lots of animals. Back at the lodge I prefered to loll by the pool before an afternoon game drive took us back out to those magnificent animals. *Day trips to the neighbouring Born Free Foundation and Addo Elephant National Park are included in a 3-day package. Closed June. Children 9+ are welcome.*

Rooms: 11: 4 doubles with en-suite double baths with shower attachment and outside showers; 7 luxury doubles with private plunge-pools.
Price: R2,280 pp sharing - R3,180 pp sharing. Singles plus 30%. All-inclusive (meals, local beer & house wine, safari activities).
Meals: All included.
Directions: From PE take N2 for 60km towards Grahamstown. Turn left on gravel road to Paterson and follow signs.

Bushman's View

John and Karen Ling
41 Fourth Avenue, Riversbend, Bushman's River, Kenton-on-Sea
Tel: UK: (+44) 01728-861-889
Email: 3lings@eurotelbroadband.com Web: www.bushmans.co.za

'Bushman's View' offers superb bird-watching opportunities, according to John and Karen. A plethora of birds are constantly spotted, including the Knysna loerie, hadidas, spoonbills, Goliath herons... to name but a few. The house, with its white wooden slats and two good-sized verandahs, reminded me of a Nantucket holiday home. The main living area is upstairs and open-plan. On the upstairs verandah you'll find a wicker sofa and other garden furniture from which to enjoy a panoramic view; on the lower, a dining table for *alfresco* meals and a portable braai to use on the lawn alongside. There is a mature front garden and also a rear lawned garden with lime, lemon and pawpaw trees which is a fun place for children to play. The bedrooms are of a decent size with wooden floorboards, white linen and rustic lampshades. True to the house's name, the windows have fantastic views past the garden's aloes and across to the Bushman's River, with its thickly-forested banks. Brochure cliché though it is, this place really does 'have it all'. The beaches at Bushman's River Mouth and Kenton-on Sea are a mere five-minutes' drive away; and the Kariega Game Reserve is only ten in the other direction. Beach and beasts within a quarter of an hour – beat that.

Rooms: One house: 2 dbles, 2 singles, 1 twin; all share bath & 2 shrs; open-plan lounge/dining area & kitchen; garage for 1 car. One booking at a time.
Price: Whole house: May to Aug R800 per day; Feb to Apr/Sep to Nov R950; Dec, Jan & Easter week R1,500. N.B. Mini-breaks of 2-3 days can be booked outside the high season of December and January & Easter Week.
Meals: Self-catering. Well-stocked supermarket in Kenton-on-Sea.
Directions: From Kenton, R72 towards Alexandria. Over bridge, take 1st R at top of hill to Riversbend & follow signs for Sandbar Restaurant. House 1st on L at bottom bend of 4th Avenue, next to river.

Château Blanc

Ann White
32 Westbourne Road, Kenton-on-Sea
Tel: 046-648-1271 Fax: 046-648-1271
Email: annwhite@telkomsa.net Web: www.kenton.co.za
Cell: 083-980-6880

I imagine Ann standing on her balcony, drinking in the Bushman's River that opens out onto the Indian Ocean before the house, the fine, white sand, the turquoise-blue water, the dunes, an intoxicating vision that fills the senses, and thinking, "I really should share this with as many people as I can!" Ergo Château Blanc (a tongue-in-cheek play on her surname). She moved here from a farm near the Winterberg Mountains and, as she says, once a farm lass, always a farm lass. She has brought her heartfelt hospitality and baking with her (I had some yummy carrot cake) and she has even secreted a bonsai herb and vegetable garden where you wouldn't have thought one could exist. She has no lawn or vines but just three paces from her house is the beach where blue river meets blue ocean meets blue sky and gives you the best kind of garden you could wish for. In the area you can try out a variety of water-sports (water-skiing, boating, canoeing, surfing, diving), fishing, golfing, horse-riding, or simply enjoy a sunbathe and picnic on the beach. Children are especially welcome. They love playing with the pebbles in the garden. Any notions you may have that an old chateau is cold and draughty will soon be dispelled as you are assured of the warmest of welcomes in Ann's modern and comfortable home. Here you are simply a guest within unpretentious surroundings with a light-filled room and an ocean view. 100% personable B&B at its best.

Rooms: 2: 1 double with en-suite bath and shower, 1 twin with private bathroom. Single party bookings only.
Price: R275 - R350 pp sharing. Whole cottage available from R2,000 - R2,500 per day.
Meals: Full breakfast included. Dinners by arrangement. Restaurants nearby.
Directions: From PE take R72 and turn right into Kenton-on-Sea. Go down Kariega Road until 3-way stop, turn right down River Road and continue until the river. Turn left into Westbourne Road.

Wings

Marijke and Mike Kirby
21 Elliot Road, Kenton-on-Sea
Tel: 046-648-1834 Fax: 086-515-5181
Email: wings@casbusol.co.za Web: www.kenton.co.za/pop_wings.htm
Cell: 083-626-4172

Mike's parents named this homely B&B Wings because "they used to like watching the birds drifting over the sea," Marijke tells me as I stand mesmerised by the expansive sea view. "We like to think we give our guests wings too," she laughs. And it would seem they do. According to Marijke the last guest sat in front of this very same window and wrote a whole book during his stay. I waited for similar inspiration to strike me too, but was soon distracted by the large, inviting sofas in my private sitting room and the shelf-load of games, puzzles and books. There is everything here you need for a comfortable stay; a private garden overlooking the sea, a large open-plan kitchen and breakfast bar, and cosy sea-facing bedrooms. Mike and Marijke are delightful hosts and their generosity is far-reaching; they also take an active part in their community, involving themselves in a number of Outreach programmes. A Continental breakfast can be provided in the downstairs apartment, but guests are also welcome to nip upstairs and enjoy Marijke's morning cooking... which is what I did. As I lingered over another pot of coffee her friends started arriving armed with paints and brushes and I soon found myself in the midst of their weekly art group. I was urged to stay and spend the day painting the stunning view. I got my wings in the end.

Rooms: 1 unit: 2 doubles with en-suite baths and 1 twin.
Price: R230 - R250 pp.
Meals: Breakfast R45, frozen foods available in the fridge from R20.
Directions: Turn into Kenton, drive to Ocean Rd and turn R. Continue along to yellow circle, turn R into River Rd. 1st turn on L into Elliot Road, property on right.

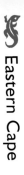

The Oyster Box Beach House

Nic and Louise Poole

19 Elliot Road, Kenton-on-Sea
Tel: 046-648-3466 Fax: 046-648-3829
Email: louise@theoysterboxbeachhouse.co.za
Web: www.theoysterboxbeachhouse.co.za Cell: 072-159-4805

It took less than a minute from the moment I walked through the doors of The Oyster Box for me to disappear out again onto the verandah. There was no time to waste. With the sun plunging ever deeper behind the horizon, the quotidian solar spectacular was well under way. And then in a flash of fiery reds and oranges, it was all over. Since we last visited, new owners Nic and Louise have spent a lot of time and effort on remodelling the house, and it certainly shows. Its crisp white and blue trim now etches the house gracefully onto the high dunes of the Kenton hillside. Such a towering position provides an unrivalled view of the Bushman's River mouth, and all the comings and goings from the Indian Ocean. Elegant rooms enjoy to the full all that the views have to offer with huge glass doors and private seating areas. The gargantuan suite upstairs even opens out onto its own balcony. Inside, all is now stylishly clean-cut: wood floors, white linen, modern bathrooms, well-stocked wine fridges and even plasma TVs mounted on the walls. After a quick supper in town, I soon found myself back out by the pool, digestif in hand and unable to resist an extra helping of those superlative moonlit views.

Rooms: 4: 2 kings with full en-suite bathrooms, and 1 queen double and 1 twin that share a full en-suite bathroom.
Price: R475 pp sharing B&B. Singles supplement plus 50%. Whole house (self-catering): R2,750 (out of season) or R4,000 (in season).
Meals: Full breakfast included. For self-catering R50 per person.
Directions: Turn into Kenton, drive to Ocean Rd and turn R. Continue along to yellow circle, turn right into River Rd. 1st turn on left into Elliot Road, property on right.

Sibuya Game Reserve

Nick Fox

39 Eastbourne Road, Kenton-on-Sea
Tel: 0861-SIBUYA (742892) or 046 648 1040 Fax: 046-648-1443
Email: reservations@sibuya.co.za Web: www.sibuya.co.za
Cell: 083-648-2020

Nick and the team greeted me quayside in Kenton, then transported me upstream on a wholly exciting journey into the wild. I felt like one of those early adventurer-pioneer chappies. You may be only half an hour from Kenton, but you'll think you're in another, pretty idyllic world of singing birds, splashing fish and rustling leaves. The flat-bottomed boat will take you to your new home, an intimate tented camp with tents on stilts protected above by a wooden roof. They are scattered among the trees, sharing the space with hammocks and hanging chairs. Beds inside are enticing with crisp, white cotton sheets and oh-so-snug green-fleece blankets for chillier nights. But Sibuya is all about being outside, even when it comes to your en-suite bathroom. A flight of stairs takes you up into a wood-decked affair where you can shower and wash your teeth while looking into the bush and wondering if anything is watching you watching them. By night the camp relaxes in the mellow glow of paraffin lamps and roaring log fires, while a fine feast of game is prepared for you. Nights will pass star-gazing and strange-sound-identifying, while days can be spent on game drives (now 2,500 hectares with rhino, elephant, leopard and buffalo) or messing about on the river. A unique reserve experience! *Children 6+ welcome.*

Rooms: 9 tents: 5 in the forest camp and 4 in the river camp. All doubles or twins.
Price: R1,500 - R2,550 pp sharing. Price includes boat transfers and cruises, game drives (unlimited), all meals and local alcoholic and non-alcoholic drinks.
Meals: Breakfast, picnic lunch and dinner included.
Directions: 120km from Port Elizabeth & 150km from East London on R72. Turn into Kenton and follow the signs.

The Bathurst Cottages

Kathy Arnold and Sue Yendall

Langholm B&B, Lyndhurst Cottage, Bathurst
Tel: 046-622-8338 Fax: 086-505-3091
Email: info@langholm.co.za or sue@lyndhurstfarm.com
Web: www.langholm.co.za/www.lyndhurstcottage.com
Cell: 083-325-4835/082-564-9399

Pineapples! If you're like me and thought that they grow on trees, then a drive through fields of them on the way to Langholm Farm will cure you of that particular misapprehension. A welcoming Kathy, whose family has been farming here for generations, helpfully explained all of this and a perfectly formed specimen sat splendidly on a little outside table to complete a relaxed pastoral scene. Partly concealed by trees, the entrance to this unassuming red-brick cottage opens through stable doors into something out of Beatrix Potter. The colours are sky-blue and fresh, the furniture neatly arranged around a kitchenette where you'll find a continental breakfast ready to eat. Two bedrooms are bright with the sun while at the end of a narrow corridor is a little gem of a bathroom. Here I knew I could be quiet and still… a hiatus before the local colour of the Pig 'n' Whistle, the oldest licensed pub in the country (and just down the road). An equally lovely place to stay is Lyndhurst Farm, run by the generous and lively Sue, whose charming cottage is made radiant by the most extravagantly red bougainvillaea I have ever seen. In fact the whole garden here is stunning with a well-manicured lawn and beds bursting with shrubs and flowers. Guests have access to a large salt-water swimming pool with a children's pool attached, and alongside there is a pool house where guests can take it easy with a sundowner and watch the antics of the many resident birds living in the greenery. Inside, demure bedrooms capture the blue of distant oceans, easily reached after a light Continental breakfast in your kitchenette, or Sue's full 'Plantation' version.

Rooms: 2 cottages: Langholm Farm (1 double, 1 twin, 1 shower bathroom) and Lyndhurst Farm (1 double, 1 triple, 1 shower bathroom).
Price: Langholm: R220 pp sharing (minimum R600 for whole cottage in season). Lyndhurst: R220 pp sharing (minimum R675 for whole cottage in season).
Meals: Full breakfast R50 pp in both properties.
Directions: Lyndhurst is 6.5km and Langholm 12km from Bathurst going toward Grahamstown. Ring for directions.

The Lookout

Louise and Alan Corrans

24 Park Rd, Port Alfred
Tel: 046-624-4564 Fax: 046-624-4564
Email: info@thelookout.co.za Web: www.thelookout.co.za
Cell: 073-273-2912

It was only after I returned to the office that I found Louise's answer-phone message inviting me to join her and Alan for lunch. Shame... I know I would have eaten well. And also as it turned out, I'd only limited time to explore everything the Corrans have done with their perfectly positioned pad. After sifting through the old photos, I can see that they've done a lot. Not for nothing is The Lookout so named, with a sight line down to the Indian Ocean over the head of a toy town Port Alfred fragmented over its harbour islands below. Each of the alluring suites downstairs opens directly onto the garden, where a royal palm and an aloe bainesii sway above the pool. While the Corrans may be up in the world (they live on the 1st floor), that doesn't mean they have forgotten about you down below. In fact they'll come knocking on your door every morning with your breakfast basket, a system Louise and Alan have now perfected. Although each guest has their own tiled verandah from which to soak up the views, I can recommend a natter around the sun-baked braai area, where patio doors lead through to the pub where I would be on 'The Lookout' for a cooling drink to match a magnificent sunset. *Each unit has a well-fitted kitchen suitable for preparing light meals.*

Rooms: 3 units: 1 king, open-plan dining/living/kitchen with en-s shower; 1 twin with private bath and shower and open-plan dining/kitchen/lounge area; 1 twin with en-s shower and open-plan dining/kitchen/lounge area. All have additional sofa-beds.
Price: R250 - R395 pp. Singles: R330 - R780. Extra guests on request.
Meals: Includes full English/Continental breakfast. Self-catering option available.
Directions: R72 from PE into Port Alfred. Turn first L after bridge into Pascoe Crescent, then immediate right into Park Road. House is signposted on the R.

Sheilan House

Joan Buckley and Mike Beaumont
27 Prince's Ave, Port Alfred
Tel: 046-624-4076 Fax: 046-624-4722
Email: mikeb@sheilanhouse.co.za Web: www.sheilanhouse.co.za
Cell: Joan 082-894-1851; Mike 082-895-9671

I may have been on a high as England emerged victorious from the World Cup, but that still didn't bias my admiration of ultra-modern Sheilan House. Instantly my eyes were drawn upwards to an intricate web of white-painted beams fanning out around the roof. The architect had done a stunning job of converting what was just a humble bungalow into this super-cool enclave and now similar designs are beginning to pop up all over Port Alfred. High vaulted ceilings dominate throughout while an abundance of glass and light heightens the sense of serenity. The bedrooms too have a Zen-like quality with their white walls, white-tiled floors, and in some, white wardrobes and white furniture - minimalist and peace-inducing without ever being Spartan. Pastel-shaded duvets add the only colour they need. Bathrooms are big, the showers enormous, while each of the four rooms benefit from their own private gardens for those times when you just want to get away from it all. Breakfast the following morning provided an ample opportunity to sample Joan's speciality, springbok carpaccio. As I munched mouth-watering morsels in the terracotta-tiled, glass-walled dining room, I looked out across the neat garden to an alluring blue swimming pool. A kingfisher sat on the decking calling a mate for a quick dip or so I understood it. If the weather had been nicer, I would have happily obliged.

Rooms: 4: 3 doubles & 1 twin. All en-suite, 2 with bath and separate shower, 2 with shower only.
Price: R325 - R500 pp sharing. Singles supplement R395 - R550.
Meals: Full breakfast included. Two-course evening meal on request from R80 pp.
Directions: On the R72 cross Port Alfred Bridge heading in Port Elizabeth direction and turn L into Wesley Hill. Then take 3rd turning to R into Prince's Ave. Pass two streets on left and property on left.

Fort D'Acre Reserve

Mel and Rory Gailey

Fish River Mouth, Port Alfred
Tel: 046-675-1091 Fax: 046-675-1095
Email: info@fortdacre.com Web: www.fortdacre.com
Cell: 082-559-8944

When the sun's gone down, you're running late and, whether you admit it or not, are ever so slightly lost, some sort of a signal is much appreciated. On cue, the Fish River Lighthouse that stands in the middle of the reserve lit up the night sky like a beacon to guide me in (or so I like to think). The lodge, where guests stay, is not actually a fort but a mammoth thatched affair, entered via heavy, sliding glass doors from a pretty redbrick garden path. It's immediately obvious that this was a lodge designed for hunters: the rustically tiled floor is strewn with animal skins and the local taxidermist has not been idle. Even the great central hearth is framed by elephant tusks. A galleried landing overlooks the communal lounge, where a cavernous leather sofa almost prevented me from making it to bed that night. The next morning I was able to see the Fort D'Acre Reserve in all its glory. Opening the curtains in the bay windows that dominated my bedroom, I looked beyond the milling herd of zebra to the Great Fish River stretching out below me towards the Indian Ocean and the reserve's private stretch of beach. I enjoyed my breakfast on the sun-drenched terrace, but the open-walled, thatched, outside bar could be equally appealing. Down on the beach is a new lapa from where whales can be watched, sundowners drunk and romantic picnics consumed. *Guided horse rides through the reserve and onto the beach now available at additional cost.*

Rooms: 4: 3 doubles and 1 twin, all with en-suite showers.
Price: R450 - R495 pp sharing. Game drives an optional extra.
Meals: Full breakfast included. Dinner by arrangement or selection of restaurants nearby.
Directions: On R72 20km from Port Alfred towards East London. First turning to right after Great Fish Point Lighthouse.

Cottage 51

Dee Simpson
50 Snipe Drive, Kaysers Beach
Tel: 043-781-8564
Email: deesimpson@telkomsa.net
Cell: 072-634-1337

Dee could see that I was feeling a little travel weary. So she sat me down with a glass of freshly-pressed lemon juice and told me to have a nap while she prepared lunch. I happily drifted off to the rhythm of the surf and the dusty miles just slipped away from me. And this is why her guests love coming here. I had barely closed my eyes for twenty minutes and already I was feeling lighter in myself. Seizing the telescope I surveyed the sea (O mirror of the soul!) finding no trace of my former lethargy and sadly on this occasion, no trace of dolphin or migrating whales either; I had to be content with landlubber buck which emerged from the bush to graze near Dee's largely indigenous garden. Lunch was an organic treat of delicious broccoli soup followed by locally-reared lamb and the meal was washed down with a good wine. I almost found myself taking a second siesta in one of two light and fresh bedrooms, the most enticing of which is sea-facing with sparkling parquet floors and its own private balcony where a table and chairs have been appealingly stripped down by the salt air. A separate bathroom is home to playful nymphs and a gentleman rabbit, an artistic quirk that continues into the en-suite bedroom. Dee has claimed as her talisman the nautilus shell that she found on the beaches here (of both geological and historical interest) and now rests on a weathered cabinet in the guest living room. Simply touch it to unwind....

Rooms: 2 rooms: 1 double (with private bathroom), 1 twin (with shower en-suite).
Price: R250 - R350 pp sharing.
Meals: Continental breakfast included. Full breakfast R40 pp. Dinner on request R100 pp.
Directions: From P.E. along the R72, take the DR 104 turn off. From East London, take the MR 500 turn off to Kaysers Beach. Either way follow the tar and gravel roads to find Cottage 51 - it is on the right at the end of the last road along the seafront.

Kob Inn Beach Resort

Daan van Zyl
Willowvale Area, Wild Coast, Qhorha Mouth
Tel: 047-499-0011 Fax: 047-499-0016
Email: info@kobinn.co.za Web: www.kobinn.co.za
Cell: 083-452-0876

This is not called the Wild Coast for nothing. Barely thirty exhilarating metres from my chalet, waves pounded the rocks in huge swells and rips that have been the demise of many a stricken vessel. Xhosa chieftains have traditionally owned this unspoilt land, which, leased to the Kob Inn, ensures a close relationship with local communities. You may even recognise in your bedroom mural one of the village scenes that you pass on the 32km drive from the highway to get here... including wandering cattle, so go slowly. Soon after arriving I was guided through a labyrinth of thatch, firstly to the earthy comfort of my room... and then to a bar whose deck juts out like a prow. Sunday night was braai night and, having heaped my plate, I joined a Durban couple that come every year because they love the lack of commercialism. Waking from the sleep equivalent of the Mariana Trench, I took breakfast to the sound of laughter from a group of elderly travellers who epitomised the prevailing informal atmosphere. The Kob Inn staff are passionately keen and were only too happy to guide me to one of their favourite places, the mouth of the Jujura River. Honeymooners will love the privacy of deserted lagoons, but with so much to do on and off the water (kayaking, boating, quad-biking, games room, etc), this is a brilliant place for families and children will be exceptionally well looked after.

Rooms: 45 rooms: 29 doubles (twin/king), 14 family and 1 honeymoon suites, 1 cottage. All en-suite bathrooms, mostly with bath and shower.
Price: R400 - R600 pp sharing. Full board. Certain activities extra.
Meals: All included. Lunch and dinner set menus. Saturday-night seafood buffet. Sunday-night braai.
Directions: Turn off N2 at Dutywa following signs to Willowvale. It's 32km from the highway along a dirt road to Kob Inn, which is signposted all the way. Make sure to branch right after 12km.

Umngazi River Bungalows & Spa

Michele and Graham Walker
Wild Coast, Port St Johns
Tel: 047-564-1115/6/7 Fax: 047-564-1210
Email: stay@umngazi.co.za Web: www.umngazi.co.za
Cell: 082-321-5841

The wild coast may be South Africa's most spectacular and yet least touristy region with its rocky coastline, indigenous forests, secluded coves and many river mouths. And all this is on your doorstep at Umngazi, a lively family holiday resort where the only time you will spend indoors will be to sleep and eat. The relaxed and informal lodge is on the banks of the Umngazi Estuary so you can choose between swimming in the pool, the river or the sea, fishing off rocks or boats, and walking in the forests. Bird-watching cruises are also organised for sunset. Ferries transport guests over to the beach from a river jetty. Meanwhile, back at home you will be missing out on tennis, snooker and table tennis. I guarantee that a week here, however lazy you are, will see the colour back in your cheeks and a bit of muscle on the arms and legs. And your sense of time will go haywire. Children are well catered for with trampoline, fort, sandpit and designated dining room. You have a choice of sea-, river- or garden-front cottages and there are four honeymoon suites with working fireplaces, sliding doors onto private patios, sea views, a big spa bath and double outside shower. Weekly fly-in packages are available Friday to Friday from Durban where you fly at 500 feet above sea level along the beautiful coastline - a wonderful experience to start a holiday. *The new spa offers (among other things) Swedish massage and a peppermint sea twist wrap while you look out on 180-degree views of the Indian Ocean.*

Rooms: 66 bungalows: twin or double on request, all have en/s bathrooms, most with baths & outdoor showers.
Price: R540 – R790 pp sharing all-inclusive. 40% single supplement charged. Fly-in package R6,680 – R7,720 pp for flight, 7 nights, all meals & transfers from Port St Johns landing strip.
Meals: All included.
Directions: From the south, Umngazi lies 90km due east of Umtata. From the north, via Flagstaff and Lusikisiki to Port St Johns on a tarred road. There is also a transfer service from Umtata and a private flight service between Durban and Port St Johns.

Leliekloof Valley of Art

Dries and Minnie De Klerk

Burgersdorp
Tel: 051-653-1240 Fax: 051-653-1240
Email: sanart@lantic.net
Cell: 083-760 7851 (please leave a message)

What a place! Magnificent Bushman art and high-altitude wilderness to nourish the soul; log fires and home-cooked meals to look after earthier parts. The river here has chiselled a tortuous gorge through the sandstone and ironstone hills and the many caves host thirteen remarkable sites of Bushman rock art, many of the paintings of indeterminable age. Dries took me for an exhilarating morning drive and we visited two of them, Eland and Dog Shelters. The quality of the paintings is superb, Dries a full reservoir of information about both the images and their artists. There is also a two-day scenic 19km hike around the valley, and two large dams for canoeing and trout/fly-fishing. Art apart, the countryside will extract from you superlatives you never knew you had. The De Klerks now live in the main house with the guests, but don't worry, they're great company and there's plenty of room for everyone! The magnificent main room is 22 metres long, with sitting area, DSTV, yellowwood bar, fireplace and huge antique Oregon pine dining table. You can self-cater, but given the stellar quality of Minnie's food (and the variety of things to do), I strongly suggest that you ask her to prepare your meals. *Two nights minimum stay recommended.*

Rooms: 1 farmhouse with 2 bedrooms (1 double with child's bed and 1 double with child's bed and 1 cot, 1 with en-suite bath, 1 en-s shower); plus a loft sleeping 4; also 1 extra bathroom with bath & shower. Only one couple/group booking at a time.
Price: Full board rates: R430 - R490 pp (for three or more). R450 - R510 pp for 2 people. Self-catering options available. Singles on request.
Meals: Breakfast, lunch and dinner included. Dinner is 3 courses including bottle of wine.
Directions: 6km south of Jamestown on N6 turn towards Burgersdorp. Turn R after 9.7km. After another 5.6km fork R again and Leliekloof is another 1km. Just follow Leliekloof signs. Map can be faxed.

The Stagger Inn

Robin & Berta Halse and Sean & Ann Bryan
Carnarvon Estate, Sterkstroom
Tel: 045-966-0408 Fax: 045-966-0408
Email: carnarvon@worldonline.co.za
Cell: 082-445-1032

So nice to arrive somewhere and instantly know that the people there will make your stay all the more enjoyable. I wasn't even asked if I'd like lunch… it was assumed and presented. Tea? That came too. Smiling, warm faces are a given at the Stagger Inn and all three generations of the family that help on the estate exude a contagious enthusiasm for it. So here you are in the great outdoors with 25,000 acres of pristine wilderness at your beck and call. You can bird-watch, fish for rainbow trout and large-mouth bass, swim in the weirs of clear spring water, go boating on the dams, do some clay-pigeon shooting and spot some of the fifteen species of antelope on game-drives (also lynx, jackal, genets, black eagles, fish eagles and vultures). Or you can just walk among the indigenous shrubs and wild flowers. Ruddy-faced and hungry from the fresh air and activities, guests cosy up by the blazing log fire before a hearty, healthy dinner of home-cooked produce fresh from the farm (cows, sheep, pigs, sawmill and a dairy). And then to bed, hunting-lodge-style in farmhouses with comfortable (rather than luxurious) rooms for a well-needed night's sleep. As I discovered in the morning, the quality of light up here is a phenomenon, and the views breathtaking. The rolling ridge-country and grassy plains reach as far as the eye can see. Make sure you stay for long enough.

Rooms: 6: 2 doubles, 2 twins with en-suite bathrooms; 2 doubles for self-catering with en-suite shower.
Price: R250 – R300 pp B&B. R175 pp self-catering.
Meals: Full breakfast included. Lunch and dinner by request.
Directions: From Queenstown, take N6 for 50km and turn right on the R344 towards Dordrecht and follow signs to Stagger Inn (gravel road for 13km).

Redcliffe Guest Farm

Johnnie and Carol Morgan
Tarkastad
Tel: 045-848-0152 Fax: 045-848-0152
Email: info@dtours.co.za Web: www.dtours.co.za

Johnnie and Carol kindly adopted me for the night when I couldn't - or rather didn't want to - leave their unspoilt country idyll in the depths of the Winterberg Mountains. Not many tourists have yet found the Winterberg, but surely it is only a matter of time. This is an escape from everything apart from cows, sheep, birds and the natural environment that supports them. The simplest way to enjoy the area is to go for a hike across the rolling grassland hills. The gorge on a neighbouring farm is, I think, the most spectacular spot I have been privy to in South Africa and it goes virtually unvisited. The plateau folds in on itself and plummets hundreds of metres down, waterfalls dropping from terrace to terrace. Or you can go swimming, trout-fishing, mountain-biking, horse-riding, bird-watching, or play tennis back at the house. Carol may cook you her speciality stuffed leg of lamb for dinner and Johnnie will happily show you around his shearing shed. He is especially proud of his Merinos whose pure white wool is used to make smart Italian suits. Guests here have all the space they could need both outside and inside the five-bedroom farmhouse, including a light-filled sun room. A real home and the area of highland farms is still to be discovered even by the more adventurous overseas traveller.

Rooms: 1 farmhouse: 5 twins, 3 en-suite and 2 with private bathrooms.
Price: R595 pp lunch, dinner, bed and breakfast or R200 pp self-catering, minimum 2 people for both options.
Meals: Breakfast, lunch and dinner on request. Self-catering also an option.
Directions: On R344 between Tarkastad and Adelaide. Directions faxed or emailed.

Cavers Country Guest House

Kenneth and Rozanne Ross

R63, Bedford
Tel: 046-685-0619 Fax: 046-685-0619
Email: ckross@intekom.co.za Web: www.cavers.co.za
Cell: 082-579-1807

I can't be the first to call Cavers an oasis, but it is irresistible. There in the distance a stand of tall oaks shimmers unconvincingly in the haze. And then suddenly you are among well-watered and mature gardens, an Eden of lawns and vivid flowers. The fine stone, ivy-encased farmhouse was built in 1840 and has been in Ken's family for four generations (now exclusively for guests). The bedrooms, with wooden floorboards, high ceilings and voluptuously draped windows, are refined and elegant. From one of the upstairs rooms I got an impression of living in the trees with an hadeda nesting at eye level and yellow orioles twittering and fluttering about. Two grand upstairs rooms with pressed-metal ceilings have balconies overlooking the profusion of flowers below. The thatched cottage also has long views over the lawns and up to the Winterberg Mountains. Rozanne is a maestro in the kitchen, cooking with fresh produce from the farm and the surrounding area and all her meals are mouth-watering feasts. The memory of that salmon cheesecake is even now a Pavlovian trigger that gets the mouth watering. There is a clay tennis court, hiking and riding or even cricket on the magnificent ground nearby. Swimming is in the pool or a big round reservoir.

Rooms: 5: 4 rooms in the manor house: all king/twins, 2 en-suite shower, 1 bath, 1 shr & bath; 1 cottage has 1 twin & 1 double sharing bath & shower.
Price: R350 – R500 pp sharing.
Meals: Full breakfast included. Dinner and light lunches on request.
Directions: 8km from Bedford on the R63 towards Adelaide, turn left at the sign and follow the dirt road for 8km.

Die Tuishuise

Sandra Antrobus
36 Market St, Cradock
Tel: 048-881-1322 Fax: 048-881-5388
Email: tuishuise@eastcape.net Web: www.tuishuise.co.za

Unique accommodation indeed! Sandra has a raptor's eye for historic detail, laced with an antique-dealer's nose and the heart of an interior designer - unparalleled in my experience of South Africa. There are 25 houses along Market Street, all antiquely furnished to reflect different styles, eras and professions. The houses were once lived in by bank managers, teachers, wagon makers etc, and you step into their 19th-century shoes when you stay - although the bathrooms, perhaps, retain a little more modernity. Each house is an antique shop in its own right, but modern comforts include fans, heaters and fireplaces. I was lucky enough to visit them all and it is no exaggeration to say I was struck dumb - reason enough for Sandra to have gone to the effort (some might feel). The hotel, a Victorian manor at the end of the street, has a further 19 rooms similarly done out in the style of the time and sherry is served in the drawing room before buffet dinners (my Karoo lamb was delicious). Sandra and her daughter Lisa are dedicated to presenting South African history in a way you can touch and feel. They do cultural performances epitomising the Xhosa and Afrikaner culture - ask in advance. *Closed 24th & 25th December.*

Rooms: 25 restored 19th-century houses, each rented out as one 'unit'. There is also a hotel.
Price: R240 - R450 pp.
Meals: Breakfast included and served 7 - 9am. Traditional dinners available.
Directions: From PE take N10. When you arrive in Cradock at 3-way stop turn left into Voortrekker St. Die Tuishuise is 4th block on left.

Wheatlands

Diana, Arthur, Kirsten and David Short
Route R75, Graaff-Reinet
Tel: 049-891-0422/4 Fax: 049-891-0422
Email: wheatlands@wam.co.za Web: www.wheatlands.co.za
Cell: 076-377-4026 or 072-251-9022

Guests at Wheatlands are thoroughly spoilt. I had read that the main house had been built on the profits of ostrich feathers in 1912 (a so-called 'feather palace'). I'm not sure why, but this led me to expect a humble farmhouse… and to get my shoes muddy finding it! But no. I found instead a gigantic manor house with a façade dominated by three extravagant gables. The house, designed by Charles Bridgeman, mingles Cape Dutch and Edwardian styles with a lovely white-pillared verandah at the back and then a green lake of lush lawn where heritage roses grow like weeds. Park your wagon (or whatever you are driving these days) in the huge sandy courtyard and enter a long, cool, wood-panelled hall, an instant pleasure as you leave the desert heat of the Karoo. It's an appropriate home for the piano, all the antique furniture and the Persian rugs. The corridors are lined with books, there is a snug for reading and guest bedrooms are not converted outhouses, but an integral, lived-in part of the house. There are wonderful wanders to be had in the revelation of a back garden. The Shorts are astoundingly nice people, brimful of the hostly arts. Diana and Kirsten cook delicious dinners, which are eaten at one large oak table. Arthur and David, meanwhile, are serious wool and mohair farmers and cricketers… they even have their own ground.

Rooms: 3: all twins, 2 with en-suite bath and shower, 1 with private bath and shower.
Price: R350 - R380 pp sharing.
Meals: Full breakfast and dinner included (Karoo lamb a speciality).
Directions: 42km on the R75 south of Graaff-Reinet, Wheatlands turn-off to the left, 8km up a gravel road.

Cypress Cottages

Hillary Palmé
76 Donkin St, Graaff-Reinet
Tel: 049-892-3965 Fax: 049-892-3965
Email: info@cypresscottage.co.za Web: www.cypresscottage.co.za
Cell: 083-456-1795

After a hot - and particularly bothersome - drive to this historic Karoo town, it came as a huge relief to wearily step through Cypress Cottage's heavy wooden doors and immerse myself in the quiet coolness lurking within. Minutes later, cold beer in hand and propped up on a stoep with a magnificent mountain view, my recent hardships evaporated into the heat-hazed sky. Both cottages are of the beautiful early 1800s Cape Dutch variety and are understatedly decorated with a (highly developed) taste for the natural and comfortable. Thus, the bedrooms display high reed ceilings, solid pine and slate floors, antique chests, fresh flowers and free-standing baths. Fresh and perfectly wholesome breakfasts are laid up on the terraces - free-range eggs from the house chickens, succulent figs, peaches, prunes and apricots straight from the orchard. You can escape the heat by splashing in the bore-hole-fed reservoir that has been converted into a swimming pool. Across the sleepy street, a familiar smell wafted over from the other cottage, where guests were merrily braaiing under the shade of its vine-covered pergola. The main garden is an extraordinary feat of will and clever engineering - desert has been transformed into an oasis of lush vegetation despite the difficulties of brackish water. Historical Graaff-Reinet is worth at least a two-day stopover in my opinion - Cypress Cottages many more.

Rooms: 6: 4 doubles and 2 twins. All with en-suite bathrooms, air-con and heating.
Price: R300 - R440 pp sharing. Singles on request.
Meals: Full breakfast included.
Directions: From south enter town and pass police academy on L and go over bridge. Two filling stations on L - take road between them (West St). Follow to very end, turn R into Donkin St, guest house first on L. From north: R at T-jct (Caledon St). 4th Left is Donkin St. House last on R.

Abbotsbury

Sue and Gordon Scott
Graaff-Reinet
Tel: 049-840-0201 Fax: 049-840-0201
Email: abbotsbury@cybertrade.co.za Web: www.abbotsbury.co.za
Cell: 072-486-8904

A three-kilometre drive on a dirt track takes you up into the land that time forgot, a small, perfectly-formed valley that the Scotts call home. Sue and Gordon are there to greet you in their improbably lush and well-tended garden, which seems immune to the Karoo sun's forbidding glare. An ingenious old water furrow running down from the dam must take some of the credit for this, although a fence has also been added to protect the garden's aloes and roses from midnight-feasting kudus… of which there are plenty, despite the privations. You can relax under the trees in the tranquil gardens, or hike up the valley in search of the ten species of antelope and other Karoo wildlife on the farm. Back at base, guests either stay in a lovely old cottage, circa 1880; or a twin-bedded suite attached to the Scotts' own, even older house; or the luxury garden suite with its sweeping views of the garden and wild valley in the distance. None lack for character, with polished yellowwood floors, restored old furniture and photographic prints and artwork on the walls. Sue takes your supper orders when you book so as to have a fresh farm supply at the ready (springbok and Karoo lamb specialities) and you are served in your own private dining room with solid silver cutlery, bone china and service bell! Breakfasts are also a royal affair. *Nearby: the sculpture garden of the Owl House, historic Graaff-Reinet, and the awe-inspiring views of the Valley of Desolation.*

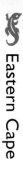

Rooms: 3 units: 1 cottage with double & en-suite twin and separate bath with shower attachment; 1 cottage with king and en-suite shower; 1 twin suite with en-suite bath and shower. All have private lounge/dining room
Price: R300 - R375 pp sharing B&B.
Meals: Full breakfast included. 3-course dinner on request: R100. Meals are served privately to each cottage.
Directions: 27km north of Graaff-Reinet on N9, turn left onto 3km farm track to Abbotsbury.

Melrose Guest Farm

Campbell Scott and Karen Koch
Graaff-Reinet
Tel: 049-891-0532 Fax: 049-891-0532/086-647-1453
Email: melroseguestfarm@telkomsa.net
Cell: 082-380-1569/083-580-2753

Melrose Guest Farm is a very welcome stop on the long R75 south. As I stepped from my overheated car, Karen and Campbell were already on hand to usher me onto their shady porch. Looking out over the vast, flat Karoo landscape and huge African sky, I felt my road weariness dissolve and my languishing spirits revive. The Scotts are a delightful young couple and, although they may be new to the business, they are natural hosts. After a restorative cool drink and an enormous plate of Bourbon biscuits, I was shown into a deliciously cool lounge; no need for air-con here as the wooden flooring and high ceilings keep everything at a perfect temperature. A lot of care and attention has gone into restoring this farmhouse to its original self. Campbell has stripped every door and window and sanded down every surface to leave a smooth polished finish. Meanwhile, Karen has been busy putting an unerring eye for design into furnishing the dining room and lounge in appropriately simple, comfortable fabrics and soothing cream and white tones. The single unit, which takes up the right wing of the house, is equally appealing with good-quality white linen and a sleep-inducing serenity that makes you want to flop straight onto the bed. Those with more energy, however, can dive into the reservoir, go in search of antelope or take the 8km walk round the farmland. As for me... that huge Karoo sky performed some sort of magic trick on me and I ended up staring hypnotically into a picture-perfect landscape.

Rooms: 1 unit: double and twin with en-suite bath and shower.
Price: R270 pp sharing.
Meals: Includes full breakfast. Dinner R70, braai on request.
Directions: Email for directions.

KwaZulu Natal

Plumbago

Mick and Libby Goodall
546 St Ives Ave, Leisure Bay
Tel: 039-319-2665
Fax: 039-319-2665
Email: info@plumbagokzn.co.za
Web: www.plumbagokzn.co.za
Cell: 082-561-6993

I think the coast of KwaZulu Natal gets better and better the further south you head, and Leisure Bay is testament to that. It's just stunning, and, buried in the banana plantations between bush and beach, is easily missed by those hammering along the N2 to more on-the-beaten-track destinations. Plumbago itself is on the crest of a hill on sandy St Ives Avenue (just off Torquay Avenue, naturally), a gentle stroll from the sea. It's an airy double-storey home, hidden from its neighbours by the thick foliage of Libby's indigenous garden, indigenous that is "except the rosemary and the lemon tree for G&Ts," she admits. The birds are amazing and hop around right under your nose, and while they chattered in the trees, we chattered (over lunch) at a long, central dining table made from an old jetty post. Downstairs, the house is open-plan with large windows, high ceilings and soft, blue walls – the perfect antidote to sizzling summer days. Upstairs a wrap-around verandah keeps the main bedroom equally cool and if you do get over-heated you can just jump in the outside shower. There are endless sea- or land-based activities to keep you busy in the area, but with a beautiful beach on hand, well, I'd be just as happy focusing on some serious R&R.

Rooms: 3: all doubles, two with bath and shower, one with bath, outside shower also available.
Price: R280 – R350 pp sharing. Singles +50%.
Meals: Full breakfast included. Dinner on request.
Directions: Follow N2 and R61 south from Durban towards Port Edward. About 5km north of town take the Torquay Ave/Leisure Bay turn off. Follow Torquay Ave to the crest of hill and turn L into St Ives Ave. Plumbago is 100 yards down on the R.

Sunbirds

643 Outlook Road
Southbroom
Tel: 039-316-8202 Fax: 086-687-1991
Email: stay@sunbirds.co.za Web: www.sunbirds.co.za
Cell: 072-993-7902

Never one to resist temptation, when Jonathan insisted that I try a Sunbirds speciality breakfast I was happy to oblige. I assumed the position on the terrace overlooking the swimming pool, then palms and bush, and finally the distant ocean horizon. Today's 'mere starter' was honeyed papaya with a swirl of fresh yoghurt on the side. My galvanised tastebuds, like baby birds, craved for more and were answered with meltingly soft scrambled eggs, enhanced with mint from the garden. Impossibly, Liz's home-made almond and cranberry slices then arrived. In sympathy perhaps, the architect has created an effortlessly light interior, which floats along white tiles into an open-plan merging of living room, dining area, terrace and bar. With the shutters thrown open, the outside floods in, the light as alabaster white as the sands which are barely 100m away. This hushed and muted elegance continues into the bedrooms, both in the house and in the cottage that overlooks a sub-tropical garden. Even the extra-large showers appear to be sound-proofed. So where does this immaculate grooming come from? Liz and Jonathan spent their lives in England as breeders and trainers of champion hounds and on closer inspection little details give this away: a dalmatian doorstop, comedy canine figures at the bar, photographs of their prize spinone (and father of one of two live pedigree specimens that can be summoned). Doggy chat aside, this is an area also dubbed the 'golf coast' with the green of the fifth hole almost within putting distance, along with two good restaurants and the beach all within a 3-minute walk.

Rooms: 4 rooms: twin/king (all en-suite 2 with bath and shower, 2 with shower only).
Price: R400 - R600 pp sharing (singles +R100).
Meals: Full breakfast included.
Directions: Driving along the R61 take the Southbroom South exit and after 400m turn right into Outlook Road. Sunbirds is 2.2km on the right-hand side.

Figtree Lodge

Paul and Barbara Reynolds

30 North Ridge Road, Southbroom
Tel: 039-316-6547 Fax: 039-316-8211
Email: sbelite@lantic.net Web: www.figtreelodge.co.za
Cell: 082-421-1172

Figtree Lodge is one of those laidback places where guests can B&B, self-cater or do both. The three self-contained lodges come with a private pool, honesty bar and a fully-equipped kitchen. Saying that, it would be an act of foolishness to miss out on Paul and Barbara's breakfast. But before being treated to a slap-up 'full English', I was first shown around. First up was 'Figtree Lodge', which is shaded by the eponymous ("yonks old") tree. Up the outdoor stairs, the wooden deck looks out across the swimming pool and covered lapa. Inside, the living and kitchen area is open-plan. The bedrooms have white linen embroidered with butterflies and wooden furniture. Over the road is the Reynolds' own house, with 'Kingfisher' attached which comes with its own kitchen and lounge. Crossing back, we passed a coral tree. "When Southbroom was divided into plots, they staked branches from these trees into the ground to mark boundaries," Barbara explained. "Now most older properties have one, and the monkeys love sucking their nectar!" Finally Barbara showed me 'Swallows Nest', the large family house next door with a double-deck and great views up the Imbezane River. After breakfast, we jumped into the car for a whirlwind tour of Southbroom. The beach is only four minutes' walk away, so bring your binoculars (whales go by from May to October) and leave your watch behind. *Within easy reach of six top golf courses.*

Rooms: 3 Units: 'Figtree Lodge': 3 bedrooms, 2 bathrooms (1 en-suite), both with showers; 'Swallows Nest': 4 bedrooms, 4 bathrooms en-suite, 3 with showers, 1 with shower and bath; 'Kingfisher': 1 bedroom with en-suite shower and bath.
Price: R280 pp sharing (self-catering) - R325 pp sharing (B&B).
Meals: Ingredients for a braai can be provided.
Directions: Faxed or emailed when you book.

Ivory Beach Lodge "The Cottage"

Massimo and Nicci Negra

379/1 Outlook Road, Southbroom
Tel: 039-316-8411 Fax: 086-615-4304
Email: masniki@venturenet.co.za Web: www.ivorybeachlodge.co.za
Cell: 082-440-9489 or 082-331-3202

Sybarites and nature-lovers will find equal delight at Ivory Beach Lodge, the Indo-African style home of Massimo and Nicci Negra. Built on a secluded beach, with vistas of pounding surf and densely-vegetated dunes, guests are accommodated in 'the cottage', a self-contained bungalow which floats in a leafy canopy of trees in the gently sloping garden. A footpath from the property leads onto seemingly endless golden miles of mostly people-less beach. Organic thatch, wood, rough walls and pigmented floors blend seamlessly with luxurious furnishings. A well-equipped kitchen and decking along the seaboard side make alfresco dining a delight, with whales and dolphins making regular appearances. The property has a salt-water rock-pool and sun deck. This stretch of coast is dubbed "the golf coast" and Ivory Beach backs onto the fifth tee of one of many excellent golf courses along the coastline. The Negras' award-winning trattoria, La Terrazza, is the obvious place to eat, a 20-minute stroll from the homestead. In July (or so!) billions of breeding sardines come to the coast, trailed by giant flocks of seabirds that dive-bomb the frothing feast. Thousands of dolphins join in too and there are tours out to watch the phenomenon. As for 'the cottage', it remains one of the best beach houses I have ever visited. *The South Coast is world-renowned for two particularly special dive sites, "Aliwal Shoal" and "Protea Banks". Ivory Beach Lodge is well connected to a dive school/shop.*

Rooms: 1 cottage: 1 king and 1 twin sharing a double shower. Open-plan with fully-equipped kitchen for self-catering and a sitting room area.
Price: R400 - R500 pp sharing. Children under 12 half price. Singles on request.
Meals: Fruit, coffee and milk provided. Full and Continental breakfasts by arrangement. For lunch and evening meals their restaurant is 800m down the road.
Directions: Take the N3 south. Exit at Southbroom South, travel 400 metres, turn first right into Outlook Rd and follow for 2km (approx). Look for number 379/1 down a driveway on your left.

Lindsay Loft

Caroline and Pepi Jankovich
26 Lindsay Avenue, Morningside, Durban
Tel: 031-207-1634 Fax: 031-208-3227
Email: caroline@lindsayloft.co.za Web: www.lindsayloft.co.za
Cell: 083-490-0963

If your loft is anything like mine it's a dark and dusty dumping ground for old junk. Caroline's loft, I can enviously assure you, is NOTHING like mine. It's enormous. Walls are whitewashed and go up forever, floors are tiled to keep it cool in summer and there's a lengthy, decked verandah, of which more later. Actually no, I can't wait. The verandah is great, accessed from both the living- and bedrooms it peaks through the trees and across the city from its hill-top look-out. Bottle-brush, mango and avocado all tickle its handrail and you're encouraged to pick the fruit to avoid it crashing down onto the neighbour's tin roof. Sadly, my visit was a little early for those fresh treats so I was duly filled up with tea and toast instead. Back inside, the bedroom is cavernous and calming with (besides a bed of course) caramel armchairs and a beautiful old writing desk. The living area too is dotted with mahogany antiques and separated from the kitchen by a breakfast bar. For the chef, there's all the cooking kit you need and Caroline will supply the essentials to get you started. This is a great base from which to explore KZN. The Drakensberg mountains are a few hours inland, the game reserves a short drive up the coast and there are excellent beaches and golf courses.

Rooms: 1 double/king with en-suite combined bath and shower with optional spare single bed for extra family member in adjoining room.
Price: R325 pp sharing. R600 single.
Meals: Starter supplies and a health breakfast provided on arrival. Otherwise, fully self-catering.
Directions: From M4 to Durban take exit 2, Moore Rd. Follow to traffic lights and turn R into Manning Rd which becomes Essenwood Rd. 100m after feeding into Montpelier Rd take Lindsay Ave up a steep hill. Lindsay Loft is just over the brow.

Westville B&B

Emma and Nic Jacobs

8a & 9 Haven Road, Westville, Durban
Tel: 031-266-5867 Fax: 031-266-4953
Email: info@westvillebandb.co.za Web: www.westvillebandb.co.za
Cell: 083-447-3520

Smart Durban chic meets wholesome family environment, where business types have to be reminded that the monkey bars in the sub-tropical garden are for U12 team-building only. Emma and Nic's own children are such favourites that one regular demands to see 'his kids' on arrival. They have gone from working in the corporate world to running a popular B&B in this desirable leafy suburb, which on cue burst into gorgeously red blossom. They have recently acquired another large home on the other side of this very neighbourly lane and transformed that too into a combination of deeply comfortable rooms and suites, relying on plenty of dark leather and custom-made mahogany furniture for that sleek finish. Each can be identified by the name of the particular artist whose framed reproductions adorn the walls, from Renoir to Vettriano. My own apartment in the original house was the one exception, named after a generous benefactor, while still maintaining a trademark sense of proportion and understated style. Indeed all is so exemplary that hospitality students come here to learn their trade under Emma's watchful eye and who, by the end of their placement, can charm even the most implacable of GG inspectors! Personal attention is key, but it all begins with Emma's own breakfasts taken in either of the two convivial dining areas. Continue conversations in lounges well stocked with sofas and erudite bookshelves, or even in one of two pools for which you'll be thankful in the summer months.

Rooms: 5: 1 twin/king, 1 king, 1 queen (all except 1 full bathroom en-suite); 1 apartment (1 double, 1 queen) with full shared bathroom, kitchen and lounge. 1 family suite (2x twin/king) with full and shower en-suite bathrooms and kitchen.
Price: From R460 pp sharing. Singles from R700.
Meals: Full breakfast included. Dinners on request.
Directions: Take Exit 13 off the N3 onto St James Avenue, which becomes Attercliffe Road, eventually turning left onto Buckingham Terrace just before the M13. Continue straight over cross-roads into Church Road, turning right at T-junction and then first left into Haven Road. B&B 50 metres on left.

Entry Number: 237

Map Number: 13 & 14

Fairlight Beach House

KwaZulu Natal

Bruce and Michele Deeb
1 Margaret Bacon Avenue,
(Corner South Beach Rd),
Umdloti Beach
Tel: 031-568-1835
Fax: 031-568-1835
Email: bdeeb@mweb.co.za
Web: www.fairlight.co.za
Cell: 082-775-9971
or 082-443-8529

I got my first taste of Bruce and Michele's laid-back hospitality as soon as I arrived. It was another hot KZN day and I was bustled off for a joyous dip in the sea just across the road – "We can talk later." And we did. This newly-refreshed 'inspector' was soon sipping a cold beer by the pool and tucking into some delicious Lebanese pastries and thoroughly South African boerewors as Bruce tended the braai. The garden behind the house is dominated by two large milkwoods, a great place to shelter from the sun, although there are also sun-loungers around the swimming pool. The front of the house has a wooden deck running all along it, from where you can watch the surfers - all the rooms open onto it. Dolphins love the surf too, and if you're lucky you can swim with them. Bruce can lend you a boogie board and flippers. Inside, it is effectively a family home and luxury guest house rolled into one – plenty of light and air as befits a beach house, family snaps on the wall and a warm, welcoming vibe to it. Rays of positive energy emanate from Michele, Bruce and their long-standing housekeeper Maria. Soak it up, then go forth and fish, surf or swim with a big smile on your face. Ten miles of heaven, a.k.a. Umdloti Beach, are but 40 paces from the house. *Durban and the airport are both within half an hour's drive.*

Rooms: 7: 5 with en-suite bath and shower, 2 with just shower (all are fully air-conditioned and have sea views).
Price: R475 – R650. Singles from R600.
Meals: Full breakfast included. Limited self-catering facilities available.
Directions: N2 exit to Umdloti. Follow down to roundabout. Keep right past Total garage and Fairlight is 500 metres along South Beach Rd.

The Dune Guest House

Michelle, Richard and Glenda de la Hey
45 Bellamont Road, Umdloti Beach
Tel: 031-568-2089 Fax: 031-568-1067
Email: enquiries@thedune.net Web: www.thedune.net
Cell: 083-407-3397

Whether it belongs to Richard, Glenda or daughter Michelle, the family-run nature of this guest house guarantees a friendly face to greet you on arrival and ease you into the view-bedazzled lounge. If you're lucky you may even catch a glimpse of son Mark, who is a yachtsman and might have the best job in the world; if not you'll just have to settle for glimpses of whales and dolphins. Both father and son are established photographers, amongst other things, and you can tell they certainly have an eye for the perfect picture, as The Dune is a panoramic paradise. Monkeys, mongooses, blue duikers and birdlife love the indigenous garden and rightly so. All the pale stone-floored rooms are softly finished in creams and browns while wicker and bamboo headboards and furniture give it that sugar cane country feel (perhaps an ode to Richard's sugar farming days). Enjoy your own private deck and ocean views or cook up some fun in the sociable braai area, kitted out with all the self-catering gizmos you could need. From the glass-captured butterflies in the lounge to the still-life marlin in the newly-licensed bar, everything seems to hold a story or fragment of de la Hey family life. I was privileged to meet the whole gang when I stayed and felt almost as if I'd been granted a family membership by the time I reluctantly left.

Rooms: 4: 2 twin/kings, 1 queen and 1 honeymoon suite; 2 with en-suite bath and shower and 2 with en-suite shower only.
Price: R350 - R450 pp sharing. Singles on request.
Meals: Full breakfast included. A shared braai facility is available for those that may wish to self-cater.
Directions: From Durban take the N2 North Coast/Stanger. Take the Umdloti/Verulam off-ramp. At the stop street turn right towards Umdloti, driving under the highway and over the M4. Turn left into Bellamont Road (you will see a dophin sign) and left again at the T-junction. The Dune is no.45 on the right.

Nalson's View

Wendy and Kelvin Nalson
10 Fairway Drive, Salt Rock
Tel: 032-525-5726 Fax: 032-525-5726
Email: nalsonsview@3i.co.za
Cell: 083-303-1533

After a long, long (long, long) day on the road I finally emerged from my car at Nalson's, wild-eyed and mud-besmattered. I couldn't have pitched up anywhere more perfect. Kelvin and Wendy welcomed me as if I had been living there for years. This was my room, these my beers and friends… I owned the place didn't I? A fantastic shower washed off the mud (don't ask) and I was invited to dinner. I couldn't tell who were guests, who were family friends, such is the open-house air of friendship here, and the meal was out of this world. Kelvin and Wendy have an oyster and mussel licence (guests can go with them and pick their own) and these were by FAR the best I've had in SA. Nalson's is one of those places where guests stop over for one night and have to be prised out of the place days later. Breakfast was sensational (both local baker and butcher are true servants of the community!) and, joy oh joy, freshly-squeezed fruit juice. Guests who make the correct decision to stay more than one night will get involved in the sea activities – dolphin- and whale-watching on boats, fishing, bird-watching and the ten kilometres of beautiful Christmas Bay Beach. There's plenty to do on dry land too, including golf galore, walking-distance restaurants and the Sibaya casino just 10 minutes away. *Ask about children.*

Rooms: 4: 2 doubles, 1 family and 1 double/twin; 3 with en-suite shower, 1 with en-suite bath and shower.
Price: From R300 pp sharing. Singles on request.
Meals: Full breakfast included and served when you want it. Dinners by prior arrangement. Price depends on what you have.
Directions: From Durban take N2 north. Take exit 214 (Salt Rock/Umhlali). Right at T-junction signed to Salt Rock, follow road round to the right past Salt Rock Hotel (on your left). Fairway Drive is next right.

Seaforth Farm

Trevor and Sharneen Thompson

Exit 214 off N2, Salt Rock, Umhlali
Tel: 032-525-5217 Fax: 032-525-4495
Email: info@seaforth.co.za Web: www.seaforth.co.za
Cell: 082-770-8376

Seaforth Farm is a full-blown treat of a guest house. Trevor and Sharneen have many interests, talents and motivations and Seaforth is a constant source of stimulation. Sharneen is a water-colourist and has also won medals for flower-arranging, so the house blooms with extravagant displays and paintings. Trevor is both an official tour guide and a skilled craftsman and much of the furniture has been made in his workshop (his latest piece, a huge lychee-wood bed) – and it is highly accomplished work. The garden is lush and wild and envelops everything at Seaforth in tropical colour. The produce from the new organic garden will always make its way to the breakfast table, in the inventive form of zucchini and feta fritters or fried mielie cakes! The cattle is now pure Nguni (the painted cattle of Africa), chickens run among the pawpaw and sweet and soursops trees and then there's the dam with its abundant bird life. Trevor is coaxing it in with a cunning plantation of pond weed, lilies and islets. The guest house provides large, well-equipped bedrooms, a pool and thatched summerhouse with dam- and sea-view for heavenly breakfasts and candle-lit curry evenings. Finally, the staff have a stake in the success of their venture. A pioneering guest house indeed.... *Zulu spoken.*

Rooms: 4: 1 family suite with 2 bedrooms, each with en/s shower; 2 doubles and 1 twin with en/s shower and bath.
Price: From R380 pp sharing. Single supplement R100. Family suite from R290 pp (min R1,020). First child free.
Meals: Full breakfast included.
Directions: From Durban take the N2 north. Exit on the 214 signed Salt Rock. Go 200m and take the 1st right into Old Fort Road, then 1st left into Seaforth Ave - the house is at the end.

The Chase

Jane and Jonathan Chennells

Eshowe
Tel: 035-474-5491 Fax: 035-474-1311
Email: thechase@netactive.co.za Web: www.thechase.co.za
Cell: 083-265-9629

Jane and Jonathan have so much to offer their guests that you hardly have to leave the premises. The weather-boarded house is gargantuan (Mrs Chennells senior had a penchant for large, open spaces) with long views of the farm's sugar cane plantations on overlapping mounds of distant hills. On clear days you can even see 90 degrees of sea. They also have ducks, chickens and (Nguni) cows like a proper farm should, of course. Also a pair of resident eagle owls. The garden is an orgy of barely controllable tropical growth, lush and colourful (check out the tulip tree and the Indian mahogany), its trees often weighed down by parasitic ferns and creepers. Birds are equally irrepressible and there are 70 species in the garden and 280 (!) in the Eshowe area. Kids will love the walled-in swimming pool (13 metres long) where you can swim by floodlight at night too. A hammock swings from a tree, a trampoline is stretched at ground level and there is a hard tennis court. Chennells Chase is an involving, very comfortable, incredibly good-value family home, with huge amounts of space inside and out. Pack a sense of humour and a pair of binoculars. *Bikes are available for use.*

Rooms: 2: 1 double with en-suite bath; 1 twin with en-suite shower. Also a self-contained farm cottage with 3 bedrooms and 2 bathrooms.
Price: R265 pp sharing. Singles R340. Self-catering cottage (sleeps 5), R550 – R600.
Meals: Full breakfast included (except in the cottage - by arrangement only) and served any time.
Directions: From Durban take N2 north for 1 hour. Turn off at Dokodweni off-ramp R66 to Eshowe. Half an hour to Eshowe. Take first left signed to Eshowe, house 1.8km signed on left.

Chennells Guest House

Graham and Richard Chennells

36 Pearson Avenue, Eshowe
Tel: 035-474-4919 Fax: 035-474-2691
Email: richard@eshowe.com Web: www.eshowe.com
Cell: 082-492-6918

The Chennells family have been an integral part of the Eshowe community for four generations, so it was no surprise that everyone waved at us as Richard and I drove through town. We were heading to the steep Signals Hill that looks across the valley to enjoy a welcome sundowner and watch the evening cane fires. As the sun bade us farewell, he told me of his and his father's passion to put Eshowe on the tourist map. After all, it was from here that the King Shaka built the Zulu empire. The family home has been elegantly converted with five light and airy bedrooms. Here the gentle morning sun will caress you from your king-size bed and the sizzling of bacon will draw you to the mahogany breakfast table. You may well spend your time back at the guest house reading on the black-and-white tiled stoep, sipping Richard's award-winning Zulu Blonde beer or diving into the pool that looks out into the hills. But I highly recommend getting out and about and taking advantage of what this wonderfully generous family have to offer. Depending on your mood, you may find yourself whisked off to the Zulu Kings Reed Dance, or strolling through the Dlinzi Forest Aerial Boardwalk… or do as I did and spend the most emotionally uplifting afternoon of your life with the children at the AIDS orphanage, learning Zulu songs. The memories I took from my stay here will undoubtedly remain with me forever.

Rooms: 5: 2 twin/double with en-suite bath/shower; 2 twin/double with en-suite shower; 1 twin/double with en-suite bath.
Price: R600 - R800 pp sharing. Singles on request.
Meals: Breakfast included. Light lunches R65 pp and 3-course suppers R100 pp on request.
Directions: Enquire on booking.

The Herb Basket Farmhouse

Melody Vorster

Empangeni
Tel: 035-792-0200
Email: herb.basket@telkomsa.net Web: www.herbbasketfarmhouse.com
Cell: 083-659-5642

The Herb Basket ignites the senses! Gently making my way through Melody's lush indigenous garden, friendly Irish terriers in tow, I suddenly felt like Grenouille (the 'hero' of *Perfume*), my nose tingling at the intoxicating scents of lavender and rosemary, taking me back to my Norfolk childhood. Soon my ears took over as the lyrical sounds of bird-song came washing over me through the trees (over 70 species of birdlife to be found here, a pair of breeding yellow bill kites and a spotted African eagle owl included). Finally my eyes came into play. Gazing skyward, my attention was drawn to the huge kapok tree that stands guard over the farm, rich in yellow fruit and pink blossom. And then there is the magnificent herb garden itself. Melody, warm and welcoming despite her jet-lag (she'd just got back from India), is an expert when it comes to putting herbs to good use, holding cooking master classes every three months and tending to her garden with a solicitousness to rival that of Florence Nightingale: rocket and tarragon, artemesia and jalapeño chilli, a whole range of indigenous herbs… even the labyrinth behind the house is laced with peppermint, bulbinella and fragrant rose geranium. The four guest rooms - with simple patterns, porcupine-needle light fixtures and soft inviting beds - have private entrances and open out onto the garden and are just as entrancing. Once Melody has bewitched your pillow with fresh lavender, you are assured of a deep and restful sleep at the The Herb Basket.

Rooms: 4:3 twin/king, 1 queen. All en-suite shower.
Price: R300 pp. Singles R375.
Meals: Dinner on request: R60 for one course, R90 for three courses.
Directions: Travelling north on the N2 towards Mtubatuba, 4kms past the Empangeni/Richards Bay turnoff, Herb Basket Farmhouse is signed on the left. Follow the farm road for 500m to the main gate.

Thula Thula

Françoise and Lawrence Anthony
D312 Heatonville, Buchanana, Ntambanana
Tel: 035-792-8322 Fax: 035-792-8324
Email: francoise@thulathula.com Web: www.thulathula.com
Cell: 082-259-9732

Pouring down the dirt roads, dust erupting behind me, I cursed myself for being late for my first-ever game drive... but I needn't have flustered. Within minutes of entering the park, I caught sight of an enormous elephant, his ears ruffling in the evening breeze. Françoise greeted me at the lodge, "I believe you've already met Big Boss? He's a bit of a delinquent teenager at the moment!" They know the elephants personally here and Lawrence, an animal conservationist, is known as the elephant-whisperer for his extraordinary ability to communicate with them. We walked over to my enormous, lavish, African-themed lodge, with its large glass coffee-table, four-poster bed, zebra rugs and sliding doors that lead out onto a terracotta stoep. Not bad for the bush! Drinks were waiting on the deck, around an inviting pool where other guests were chatting over pots of coffee. Three charming and highly informative rangers then escorted us through the bush in search of anything that moved. Thula Thula is home to elephant, rhinoceros, leopard, giraffe, zebra, nyala, hyenas, crocodile, kudu, wildebeest and no fewer than 350 bird species. On our return we found Big Boss virtually on my balcony! The boma looked magical with lanterns hanging from branches, a contented fire crackling in the centre and a four-course banquet awaiting us. I gazed out at the bush. "You know, you don't have to leave," suggested Lawrence. "I could always take your wheel off. It can easily be arranged." Temptation just made leaving harder!

Rooms: 16: 8 lodges, all twins or doubles (2 standard with en-s sh'rs, 4 luxury & 2 royal suites) with double sinks, en-s bath & sh'r; 8 luxury tents.
Price: Lodges: R1,300 - R2,500 pp sharing. Full board and inclusive of all game drives and bush walks.
Meals: Includes all meals and gourmet 4-course dinner or Zulu venison braai.
Directions: From N2 take R34 towards Empangeni. Thro Empangeni turn R towards Heatonville. Follow for 10km crossing 3 rail tracks. Turn L at next T-jct onto dirt rd for 8km. Turn R for 2km to Thula. 2 hrs from Durban. Map on website.

Thula Thula Luxury Tented Camp

Francoise and Lawrence Anthony
D312 Heatonville, Buchanana, Ntambanana
Tel: 035-792-8322 Fax: 035-792-8324
Email: francoise@thulathula.com Web: www.thulathula.com
Cell: 082-259-9731

It was the first hot day since winter as I ducked under the electric fence (elephant deterrent) and arrived at Thula Thula's glorious tented camp. Stepping out of the 4x4 a cool, damp towel was placed over my dusty face and a fresh fruit cocktail into my thirsty grasp. What a way to arrive in the bush... and boy, are you in the bush! Mischievous vervet monkeys were swinging over head as I was reliably informed by Werner, the manager, that the camp is also the home of a male wildebeest. "You see him coming to sleep," he calmly assured me as he opened up the flaps of my luxury tent. Luxury? These tents are big enough to house King Shaka and his entire family! Marvelling at my king-sized bed and slipper bath I excitedly donned my khakis for the afternoon's bush walk. It was then I discovered we'd be tracking four of the 'big five'. On foot. Gulp. First up, leopard tracks left not an hour before next to the Nseleni River, hyena tracks in pursuit. Soon after, elephant tracks. Big gulp! Stealthily heading up wind, we crept along for an hour until Werner stopped abruptly. Crouching down, we waited, breathless. There, 30 feet away a huge male bull appeared, his mate in tow. There's no finer way to watch these magnificent creatures, I promise you. Spellbound, we returned and I jumped into a cool outside shower and made my way to the boma for our braai, passing some nyala antelope en route. There, under a full-mooned African sky and gentle birdsong, a fellow guest leaned over and whispered, "This is Africa". How could I disagree?

Rooms: 8: 6 deluxe tents, all king/twin with en-suite bath/shower + outside shower; 2 family tents with en-suite bath/shower.
Price: R1,150 - R1,350 pp sh. Singles on request.
Meals: All included.
Directions: From N2 take R34 towards Empangeni. Go through Empangeni, then turn R towards Heatonville. Follow for 10km crossing three rail tracks. Turn L at next T-jct onto dirt rd for 8km. Turn R for 2km to Thula. 2 hrs from Durban. Map on website.

African Ambience

John and Laura Engelbrecht
124 Pelikaan Street, St Lucia
Tel: 035-590-1212 Fax: 035-590-1416
Email: lejon@digitalsky.co.za Web: www.africanambience.com
Cell: 082-372-1769

Having brushed through lush, rain-shiny jungle foliage, I finally banged on the enormous door to African Ambience, which opened to reveal two large wooden elephants and a beaming John ready to show me round. He and Laura built and designed the place from scratch and, after living in St Lucia for 23 years, they certainly knew what they wanted. The thatched roof is set high above the well-proportioned rooms with their cream walls and big log furniture, all built by a local carpenter. "Are you child-friendly?" I asked. "You'd hope so, I've got at least six of my own," he laughed. There was indeed a real family feel to the house with guests and kids coming and going and everyone chatting around coffee mugs waiting for the rain to stop. John's passion is boat chartering and if you're lucky he might have caught a fish or two to braai for your supper. This takes place in the garden - where John keeps an impressive collection of koi carp in a series of raised ponds - around a candlelit figure-of-eight-shaped pool. Inside, the maids were scurrying around in brightly-coloured African aprons while I was learning about the resident fruit bat that dropped off its mother and decided to stay on as a permanent guest. Whatever you get up to in St Lucia, African Ambience provides a lively base that's bound to be eventful.

Rooms: 6: 1 honeymoon suite with king, private entrance, patio and en-suite sh'r & spa bath; 3 luxury king/twin rooms with sofa-bed option and en-suite sh'r; 2 doubles with en-suite sh'r; 1 family room with 1 king and 2 singles with full bathroom.
Price: From R320 - R450 pp sharing. Family room R1,200 per night. Singles on request.
Meals: Full breakfast included. Dinners on request (speciality fish braais).
Directions: From N2 take R618 at Mtubatuba turn-off, following signs to St Lucia (approx 28km). Over bridge, turn R at T-junction into McKenzie St. At next r'about veer L into Albacore Rd & then 2nd L into Pelikaan St. African Ambience is the 1st house on L.

Lidiko Lodge

Dirk and Lyzette Kotze
95 McKenzie Street, St Lucia
Tel: 035-590-1581 Fax: 035-590-1581
Email: lidiko@wetlands.co.za Web: www.lidikolodge.co.za
Cell: 082-940-7184

At the end of the Lidiko Lodge's long lawn, I finally reached the verandah, just in time to see jugs of fruit juices disappearing to the kitchen and white wooden furniture being manoeuvred back into position. I was partly consoled for having missed out on what was clearly a sumptuous breakfast by the sight of Lyzette coming out to join me with coffee. African music wafted out with her. The last of the raindrops were dripping off the roof as we sat admiring the view across the wetlands. Once settled, I was soon quizzing Lyzette about the visit from the Zulu king. "Everyone was so nervous and excited, especially the staff!" she said proudly. Dirk and Lyzette are natural, gifted hosts and it was hard to imagine them as lawyers in Pretoria. They've turned the main house, an original 1930s colonial structure, into a gallery of local arts and crafts. A silky plum sofa occupies centre spot, surrounded by paintings, elaborate beading and hand-made jewellery – much of it so tempting I had to force myself to look away. The rooms, found by meandering through the back garden, past mango, banana and papaya trees, are decorated with contemporary African fabrics, wicker chairs and rugs, French doors from each lead out to the pool. The honeymoon suite (where the king slept) is an octagonal, thatched hut in the garden with Persian rugs and old colonial furniture. I was tempted to find a sun-lounger under a shady tree, but the nearby creatures of the wetlands needed finding and admiring first! *Bikes can be borrowed from the lodge.*

Rooms: 16: 12 twin/king with en-s bath and showers; honeymoon suite with en-s bath and shower; 2 family units sleeping 4, 1 with shared en-s bath, 1 divided with separate en-s showers.
Price: From R450 pp sh. Honeymoon suite from R950 per couple. Singles plus R100. Children on request.
Meals: Full breakfast included, dinners on request. Tea garden open for à la carte lunch and tea 'til 5pm.
Directions: Cross the bridge into St Lucia. At the first roundabout turn R into McKenzie Street. Lidiko Lodge is 800m down McKenzie Street on your L.

Makakatana Bay Lodge

Hugh and Leigh-Ann Morrison

Mtubatuba
Tel: 035-550-4189 Fax: 035-550-4198
Email: maklodge@iafrica.com Web: www.makakatana.co.za
Cell: 082-573-5641

Makakatana Bay Lodge is sensational and I can do little to improve on these photos, which do not lie. If only we had space for ten shots, to show you every aspect of the lodge: the gleaming wooden interiors; the bedrooms (including the wonderful honeymoon suite), connected by walkways through the forest, with their gargantuan slabs of glass and warm, earthy African colours; the pool encased in decking and raised above the grasses of the wetlands; the lake itself and the extraordinary St Lucia waterways. Guests are taken on drives into the wetlands to search for birds (360 species), crocodiles and hippos. You can also be taken to the beach for snorkelling and swimming or out on a game drive to a nearby reserve before returning to a sumptuous dinner with your hosts in the outdoor boma. Safari drives to Hluhluwe Game Reserve are also available if you have a hankering to see the Big 5. The family's old 'Crab House' is the only part of the lodge not raised above the tall grasses. This was once a storeroom for crabs caught in the lake, now a wine cellar with a giant tree growing out of its roof. Huge sliding doors throughout the lodge open onto wooden decks with views over the lake, and the absence of railings just adds to the feeling of openness to nature. The lodge is beautifully welded to its environment. An absolute treat.

Rooms: 6: 1 honeymoon suite with extra single bed, 2 king suites, 3 twin suites; all with en-suite bath and outside shower.
Price: R2,150 - R2,550 pp sharing, honeymoon suite R2,100 - R2,850 pp sharing. Singles R2,750 - R3,250. Children (aged 8-12) R1,395 - R1,600. All meals and in-house activities included. Drinks for own account.
Meals: Fully inclusive of all meals and safaris. DB&B option also available, enquire for rates.
Directions: Take N2 north from Durban for 250km to Charter's Creek. Follow road for 15km (14km on tar) to fork. Take right fork and follow signs to Makakatana Bay Lodge (4 more km or so).

KwaZulu Natal

Hluhluwe River Lodge and Adventures

Gavin and Bridget Dickson

Greater St Lucia Wetlands Park, Hluhluwe
Tel: 035-562-0246/7
Fax: 035-562-0248
Email: info@hluhluwe.co.za
Web: www.hluhluwe.co.za

A short drive through dense bushveld takes you to this friendly, informal, adventure-orientated lodge overlooking the shores of Lake St Lucia. Although the shallow waters of the lake have receded in recent years there is rumour that they will be back, along with the hippos, in the near future. On arrival, I dumped my kit in a wood-and-thatch chalet and headed straight for the big deck, the centrepiece of the lodge, for some orientation and to drink in the view across the Hluhluwe River flood plain. There's a plunge pool lost in the trees, but most will want to make full use of the all-seeing, all-knowing guides (including sometimes Gavin himself) who will take you exploring in this remarkable region. There are drives through the Wetland Park sand forests, or to Cape Vidal National Park, but I visited nearby Umfolozi-Hluhluwe Park. And what a trip, my first real game drive and we spotted a leopard! You can also go quad- or mountain-biking, horse-riding through False Bay Park or take botanical trips and guided walks to old fossil banks. A highlight here are the meals: breakfast, lunch and fabulous candlelit dinners were all excellent when I last visited. Whatever you choose to get up to this is an intimate, sociable place with small numbers and knowledgeable guides making the experience personal and rewarding. The focus is on the topography, the birdlife and the wetland environment as a whole, rather than just the 'Big Five'.

Rooms: 12: 8 twins & 2 family rooms, all with en/s sh'r; 2 honeymoon suites (pictured) with sh'r & bath.
Price: From R1,685 – R2,350 pp DBB + 1 game drive. From R1,390 – R1,950 pp sh for DBB. Winter Special 1 Apr - 31 Jul R1,100 to R1,540 pp sh DBB + 1 game drive. Prices from R950 - R1,330 pp sh DBB. Extra activities from R350.
Meals: Full breakfast, dinner and high tea included. Lunch on request from R65. High tea available for DBB guests for R40 pp.
Directions: From the N2 take Hluhluwe off-ramp and pass thro' Hluhluwe town. Take R22 signed towards Sodwana Bay. 3.4km after crossing the rwy line turn R onto D540. Follow 5km signs to lodge.

Bushwillow

Julian and Liz Simon

Hluhluwe
Tel: 035-562-0473 Fax: 035-562-0473
Email: info@bushwillow.com Web: www.bushwillow.com
Cell: 083-651-6777

Game reserves can be an expensive stop-over, so for visitors on a tighter budget we've uncovered some more affordable gems that still offer great access to local highlights. Bushwillow is one such, set in Weavers Nature Park. With 150 hectares to explore (on foot) you'll spot plenty of wildebeest, zebra, warthog and giraffe, setting the mood for the 'Big 5' at Hluhluwe-Umfolozi or the Greater St Lucia Wetlands Park just half an hour away. It's hidden in the sand forest and while it can be reserved for your exclusive use, here you will always find an interesting array of people with whom to spend your time. I arrived on a blisteringly hot day and, passing a greedy 'sounder' of warthogs, was only too glad when Julian shepherded me inside to the cool of the fans. The three forest-green chalets blend into the bush perfectly, cunningly positioned a stone's throw from a water-hole so you needn't go further than the deck to spot the local wildlife. The air-conditioned bedrooms are peaceful and private and just a few steps along the boardwalk from the living area, with its granite worktops for the chef, and a eucalyptus dining table that supports excellent home-cooked meals. It seems they've thought of everything.

Rooms: 3 chalets (king or twin) with bath and shower. All bedrooms now have air-con.
Price: R675 (B&B), R825 (DB&B) pp sharing. Self-catering R1,800 per night (sleeps up to 6). Single group bookings available. Long-stay discounts. Ask about all-inclusive deals, e.g. 3-nights (DB&B) + 1 game drive + 1 boat trip (R3,000 pp).
Meals: Dinner and breakfast are only available for DB&B (see above); or breakfast only for B&B guests (as above). No meals available for self-caterers.
Directions: From the N2 take the Hluhluwe off-ramp and pass through Hluhluwe town. At the bottom roundabout take the R22 towards Sodwana Bay. Continue 16km after crossing the railway line and Weavers Nature Park is on the L. Bushwillow is signed within the reserve.

Thonga Beach Lodge

Paige and Brett Gehren

Isibindi Africa Lodges, Mabibi, Greater St Lucia Wetland Park
Tel: 035-474-1473 Fax: 035-474-1490
Email: res@isibindi.co.za Web: www.isibindiafrica.co.za
Cell: 079-491-4422

I had been eagerly looking forward to my visit to Thonga Beach Lodge since before I had even left Cape Town. I knew it would be great because all the Gehrens' places are (see Isibindi Lodge, Kosi Forest Lodge and Rhino Walking Safaris) but I didn't expect it to be QUITE so beautiful! Thonga Beach is sandwiched between forested dunes and ocean, an hour's sandy drive and 4x4 trail from the nearest tar road. Huts are connected by snaking, wooden walkways and in each a huge mosquito net hangs from high rafters, separating the bed from the bathroom, a design marvel in itself. One single piece of sculpted concrete flows past glass-bowl sinks and chrome taps into an oval bath. After unpacking, I took a quick dip in the sea before being whisked out for a breath-taking sundowner on Lake Sibaya. An elegant supper followed and my perfectly light fish accompanied by a soft white wine sent me to my hut for a long, much-needed sleep. Come morning, I was raring to go for a sunrise stroll. The sky was a soft pink, the surf breaking onto footprint-free sand and, looking back to the lodge, I could just make out the thatched tops of each rounded room, twelve in all, poking out through milkwood brush. This is as luxurious and romantic a destination as you'll find anywhere, but it's super-relaxed too. All staff are hugely friendly, the birding, diving, walking and wildlife are superb and – a rare bonus – it's majority community-owned so your pennies help support the local economy.

Rooms: 12: 10 twins, 2 doubles, all with bath & sh'r, air-con, mosquito nets & sea or forest view.
Price: R1,950 - R2,300 pp sharing. Includes all meals, guided snorkelling, guided walks & kayaking. Spa treatments & scuba prices available on request.
Meals: Full board.
Directions: From Durban take the N2 north to Hluhluwe and then follow signs to Kosi Bay (Kwa-Ngwanase). 30km beyond Mbazwana follow signs right to Coastal Forest Reserve. Thonga car park (and lodge pick-up point) is now located at Coastal Cashew factory, 4.7km from tar rd. For 4x4 vehicles you will have to go 32km on along sandy road.

Kosi Forest Lodge

Paige and Brett Gehren

Isibindi Africa Lodges, Kosi Bay Nature Reserve, Kosi Bay/KwaNgwanase
Tel: 035-474-1473 Fax: 035-474-1490
Email: res@isibindi.co.za Web: www.isibindiafrica.co.za
Cell: 082-386-5483

Kosi Bay is the sort of place that novelists map out and then construct adventures in. You are picked up by a four-wheel drive, which can negotiate the sand tracks criss-crossing the region. You park up not just your car, but also the modern world you are now leaving. There is no tar and no electricity here. Instead you enter a landscape of raffia palm groves, primary sand forests, mangroves, water meadows, interconnecting lakes (yes, hippo and crocodile like it too and are regularly sighted). And then there are day trips to the sea and the mouth of the river for diving, swimming and fishing in 'perfect, white sand coves with huge overhanging trees' (says the lodge brochure). The reed-thatched camp itself perfectly balances the wild (your chalet is in the middle of a boisterous forest) with the romantic (candlelit meals and outdoor baths and showers). I loved the deep stillness of the early-morning guided canoe trip and other activities include reef snorkelling, turtle-tracking, forest walks and bird safaris. I consider Kosi Forest Lodge one of the most rewarding (and therefore best-value) places I have stayed in SA. I recommend a minimum of two or three nights.

Rooms: 8: 1 family 'bush suite'; 5 twins and 2 honeymoon doubles; all with outdoor bath and shower.
Price: R1,250 - R1,530 pp sharing. Guided canoeing on the lake and walks in raffia forest included. 1 full-day excursion included in stays of 2 nights or more.
Meals: All meals included. Dinner, bed and breakfast rates available on request.
Directions: From Durban take the N2 north to Hluhluwe and then follow signs to Kosi Bay (Kwa-Ngwanase). From JHB pass Pongola and turn R at sign Jozini. In Jozini thru' town, L over the dam and follow for 37km. Turn R at T-jct and follow for 67km to Kwangwanase. Pass through town to end, go to Total Garage for pick from lodge (9km).

Ghost Mountain Inn

Craig Rutherfoord
Mkuze
Tel: 035-573-1025 Fax: 035-573-1359
Email: gmi@ghostmountaininn.co.za Web: www.ghostmountaininn.co.za
Cell: 082-569-0596

I'd been looking forward to visiting Ghost Mountain, if only for the name, but how my excitement increased when I pulled into the car park and saw 26 pristine vintage Bentleys warming up for a day's adventure. NOT what I had expected to find deep in the heart of Zululand! This is definitely a hotel (50 rooms) and thus not a typical GG entry. But I have no doubts about its suitability for this guide. Craig, who is the very charming owner, will instantly make you feel at home. In fact, I cursed myself for not organizing to stay the night after he informed me, over a particularly rich and dark shot of coffee, that there was a boat trip to watch elephants drinking at nearby Lake Jozini or a trail in Hluhluwe-Umfolozi Park on offer if I wished to join them. I didn't even have time to sample a massage in the luxurious on-site health spa. Oh unhappy hour! I did, however, get to wander through the vast gardens that look up to Ghost Mountain (with its spooky history) and admire the fantastic double-trunked sycamore fig tree that stands next to a deep and inviting swimming pool. Naturally the rooms are also top notch: flat screen TV's for sports lovers, reed lampshades that cast gentle shadows across soft white linen and a private patio looking across to the Lebombo Mountains. I cast a green eye on those beautiful Bentleys as Craig escorted me back to my car. His phone rang and he apologetically made his excuses. A Zulu princess was expected for lunch and arrangements had to be made. *Bikes are available for guests' use.*

Rooms: 50: 23 standard twin/doubles en-suite bath/shower; 26 executive rooms en-suite bath/shower; 1 executive suite with king, 2 en-suite bath/shower + outside shower.
Price: R465 - R795 pp. Singles R575 - R1,395.
Meals: Lunch à la carte and 3-course dinner set menus at R120 pp.
Directions: Enquire on booking.

White Elephant Safari Lodge and Bush Camp

Heinz and Debbie Kohrs (owners) and Belinda Rossouw (manager)

Pongola Game Reserve South, Pongola
Tel: 034-413-2489 Fax: 034-413-2499 Email: info@whiteelephant.co.za
Web: www.whiteelephantlodge.co.za Cell: 082-945-7173

When Heinz visited the original 1920s farmstead that was to become White Elephant Lodge, he found nothing but a ruin with a giant jacaranda tree growing out of the roof and a family of warthogs scurrying beneath. A far cry indeed from the elegantly furnished lodge I found myself admiring. The lodge has been restored to recapture the colonial zeitgeist with its rattan-blinded verandah, open-plan interior, Indian-silk cushions floating over deep wooden benches, tea-sets white-pepper flowers and sprinklers nurturing the lawn. Two railway sleepers indicate the end of the colonial garden and the start of the bush, where my luxurious tent was hiding among the trees All aboard the 1970s jeep (apparently running on paraffin and local schnapps!) for an elephant- and rhino-packed game drive. At dusk we paused for drinks in the wilderness, among circling hyenas! A full moon, carving marble patterns across Lake Jozini, lit the way back to the safety of my tent where a steaming bath was waiting, evidently run by the bush elves. During our delicious dinner among fairy-lit trees, we were visited by a fruit bat, who fell with a gentle thud onto a pristine white tablecloth. Heinz, who is a vet, transported it on a napkin-stretcher to the lawn. It's an animal-packed adventure where you'll feel spoilt rotten. For families the laid-back Bush Camp seven self-catering thatched chalets set among knobthorn trees with private verandahs spectacular views and swinging hammocks, is a must and includes all the activities of the lodge.

Rooms: 2 lodges: Safari Lodge: 8 king/twin luxury safari tents with bath & outdoor shower; Bush Camp: 7 thatched chalets: 1 honeymoon king, 5 twin/kings, 1 family suite (sleeps 4) all bath & sh'r or just sh'r.
Price: Safari Lodge: R1,900 - R2,520 pp sharing. Singles R2,300 - R3,045. Full board & 2 activities. Bush Camp: From R3,200 for the whole camp. Full board & 1 activity.
Meals: All meals included.
Directions: From Durban (3-4 hrs) follow N2 towards Pongola. At sign on L reading Pongola Game Reserve South, turn R into main gate.

Tamboti Ridge

Denise and Brian Blevin
Between Pongola and Mkuze, Golela T-junction, Pongola
Tel: 034-435-1110 Fax: 034-435-1008
Email: shayalodge@saol.com Web: www.shayamoya.co.za/tamboti
Cell: 083-269-9596

What a relief! After days of inland dryness I'd made it to the Pongola Valley, a lush expanse of well-watered sugar cane farms, dripping with bougainvillaea. And at its heart, Tamboti Ridge, smiling Blevins and a restorative glass of iced juice. Phew. These two are super-relaxed and this shows in a wholesome B&B. Here, there are plenty of farm-based activities for the children and also access to next-door Shayamoya (also owned by the Blevins) for top nosh, fishing and game drives on the Pongola Nature Reserve. Brian runs his farm as holistically and organically as possible, producing everything from vegetables to sugar and yoghurt for the guests. You can watch the cows being milked, ramble across the farm or fish for bass at the dam. Otherwise, the jacaranda-shaded lawn and pool are ideal for lazing. In the heat of the day I fancied nothing more than a good book on the room-side deck, gazing through a sub-tropical garden to the river far below. But time was not on my side. I had a date at Blevin project number two! This year's renovations will take Tamboti into a new league of comfort, and will make this an even more welcome place to water the horses and break long journeys between Jo-burg and the KZN reserves and resorts.

Rooms: 4: 3 twins and 1 double, all en-suite with bath and shower, plus air-conditioning and fans.
Price: R300 - R350 pp sh B&B. Singles on request. R250 pp for game drives and river safaris. Tiger fishing R500 per boat per half-day and R200 pp.
Meals: Full breakfast included. Lunch and dinners at the main lodge: 3-course meals from R125 (excluding wine). Self-catering option also available.
Directions: When travelling north on the N2, 40km past Mkuze, turn left at the signs directly at the Golela junction. When travelling south on the N2, 30km past Pongola, turn right onto the farm, almost directly opposite the turn to Golela and Swaziland border post.

Shayamoya Tiger Fishing and Game Lodge

Denise and Brian Blevin

Pongola
Tel: 034-435-1110 Fax: 034-435-1008
Email: shayalodge@saol.com Web: www.shayamoya.co.za
Cell: 083-456-8423

Sometimes, 230 words are just not enough. Shayamoya is the Blevins' fantastic game lodge, offering all the luxuries you could want, but with a family-run atmosphere. After a blissful slosh in the pool (research, you understand) I was soon sharing a beer with Brian in the bar and planning a morning fishing trip (more research). From its hilltop look-out the lodge surveys the vast Pongolapoort Lake and 10,000 hectare reserve. Alongside boat cruises, elephant monitoring, rhino walks and game drives - as if that wasn't enough – the tiger fishing is superb. But hook and line could wait. First came supper, dining under the stars on fillet steak and a shiraz from the cellar (wine tastings and food are yet more strings to the Shayamoya bow). You can see across to Swaziland from the dining-room deck, as I could from my chalet, a hexagonal affair with cobbled outdoor shower and funky, ceramic hippo plugs. Come dawn, Nandi, the resident spotted eagle owl, woke me up and I was soon driving past giraffe and wildebeest to the lake with ranger Douglas. For some reason, despite a display of great skill, I caught absolutely nothing, while fellow fishermen were hauling them in truly agricultural fashion! They were staying on the Blevins' twelve-sleeper houseboat "Shayamanzi". That's for rent too, by the way, and with any luck, I'll be chucking my line from that next year.

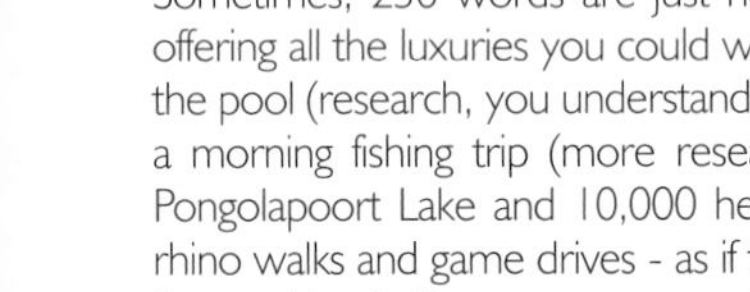

Rooms: 10 chalets: 2 premium kings, 8 standards including 2 doubles and 6 twins. All rooms have bath and outside shower.
Price: Dinner bed and breakfast rate R880 - R1,045. Singles + R250.
Meals: Dinner and full breakfast included. Lunch available on request at additional cost.
Directions: When travelling South on the N2, 27km past Pongola, take the Golela/Swaziland turning to the left. Travel for 2km until you reach the entrance on the left. From Durban, take N2 North, 40km beyond Mkuze turn right towards Golela.

Pakamisa Private Game Reserve

Isabella Stepski
Magudu District D429, Pongola
Tel: 034-413-3559 Fax: 034-413-1817
Email: pakamisa@pakamisa.co.za Web: pakamisa.co.za
Cell: 083-229-2116

At Pakamisa, I discovered that the superior game-viewing vehicle is a horse! And these divine creatures, bred and trained by Isabella herself, are more than merely a mode of transport. Many came from Spain with Isabella, where she worked with horses for 17 years, before unravelling her dream on the mountains of Pongola. There are few dangerous predators, but everything else roams in abundance and the sound closest to that of an engine was my horse's occasional neigh at a passing zebra. While I made energetic work of my mountain of salad in the Hunters Bar, Isabella told me about the good life. Hard work if you ask me! She looks after 22 horses, tends to the indigenous gardens and ensures that her guests are enjoying themselves and their red-roofed villas. These overlook bushland, green sugar cane plantations and uninterrupted mountain scenery. On a clear day, Swaziland is visible, peeping over the distant mountains. Views are inescapable from almost anywhere on the property, not least from the rooms, which are huge, lightly Mediterranean in style, with massive meranti wardrobes and fine granite bathrooms. There is so much to do here: archery, clay-pigeon shooting, bush walking, riding - of course - and all the more laid-back options like being gobbled up by the beautiful library or enjoying Isabella's impressive collection of rare African artefacts in the enormous, high-ceilinged entrance hall. Otherwise pull up a basket chair, drink in hand, and lap up the lovely big pool and sprawling views beyond.

Rooms: 8 villas: all king/twin with en-s bathrooms with twin basins and separate baths & showers.
Price: R1,200 - R1,800 pp sharing. Single supplement R500. Full board, includes 2 game-viewing activities, horse-riding, archery, clay-shooting (excluding ammunition).
Meals: All meals included.
Directions: From Pongola take the R66 for 7km. Turn R onto dirt road and follow brown Pakamisa signs for 7.5km. Turn L up towards the mountain until you reach the entrance gate to the reserve.

Isibindi Zulu Lodge

Paige and Brett Gehren

Isibindi Africa Lodges, Rorke's Drift/Battlefields, Dundee
Tel: 035-474-1473 Fax: 035-474-1490
Email: res@isibindi.co.za Web: www.isibindiafrica.co.za
Cell: 082-896-0332

Driving up to Isibindi in the early evening, the way ahead was intermittently illuminated by a spectacular thunderstorm. It seemed to be following me. Ignoring the portents, I pressed on Homerically to claim my prize, a night at the wonderful (the first line of my notes just reads 'Wow!') Isibindi Zulu Lodge. It's on a hill in the middle of a 2,000-hectare nature reserve on the Buffalo River, with six secluded chalets looking out over the bush, a modern spin on the traditional Zulu beehive hut. The best view is reserved for the pool, a great place for daytime dozing before an afternoon game drive with lodge managers who are extremely passionate about the bush. The game wasn't playing ball on our evening outing but we heard plenty of snuffling about in the twilight as we walked back under the stars to the lodge. For those not barmy about the bush there are Zulu dancing evenings laid on and there's even abseiling and white-water rafting on the reserve for the adventurous. Personally though, the tour of the nearby Isandlwana and Rorke's Drift battlefields are the highlight. Walking the 50 yards of Rorke's Drift, having the battle described to me as the rain fell and the local Zulu choir had their weekly rehearsal in the church on the battlefield itself, was a highlight not just of my trip, but will remain one of the most extraordinary experiences of my life. From nature, history and culture to adrenaline-pumped excitement... Isibindi has it all.

Rooms: 6: 4 twins, 1 double, 1 honeymoon beehive suite; all with en-suite bath and shower.
Price: R1,050 - R1,250 pp sharing. Singles plus 30%. Price includes 3 meals & 1 game activity per day plus a Zulu Boma Evening/Cultural Experience. Battlefield tours, Zulu homestead visits, rafting & abseiling extra.
Meals: Full board includes breakfast, lunch and dinner and all teas and coffees.
Directions: Take R33 from Dundee towards Greytown for 42km, then turn left onto dirt road at Isibindi Eco Reserve/Elandskraal sign. Follow signs to Isibindi which is 21km from main road.

Mawelawela Game and Fishing Lodge

George and Herta Mitchell-Innes

Fodo Farm, Elandslaagte
Tel: 036-421-1860 Fax: 036-421-1860
Email: mitchellinnes@mweb.co.za Web: www.mawelawela.co.za
Cell: 083-259-6394 or 082-734-3118

George and Herta are a natural, down-to-earth couple whose veins of hospitality run deep... and staying with them is to enjoy a few days awash with incidental pleasures. Herta, a bubbly Austrian, moved out to South Africa 28 years ago and married George, who is a beef farmer – his boerewors is delicious. He is also a keen historian and leads tours out to the site of the battle of Elandslaagte. His study is full of Anglo-Boer war prints and weighty tomes including a collection of the London Illustrated News. (Ask him to show you his father's beautiful collection of bird-eggs too.) If you stay in the main house the rooms are very comfortable and the bungalow across the jacaranda-filled garden is perfect for families or groups. A short drive away from the farm itself you'll find the thatched hunters' cottage on 1500 wild hectares set aside for game. There is a trout dam at the front into which George has built a waterfall, and there is a shower and a plunge pool to one side. The cane-sided shady braai area faces dam-wards and you can watch the eland and kudu come to drink in the evenings. Finally a toast to Herta's cooking which is wonderful! Many of the ingredients are home-grown and all is served on her collection of fine china and family silver. *Bookings essential.*

Rooms: 4: 2 twins (1 with en/s bath, 1 en/s bath & shower); 1 apartment with double, twins & single (self-catering or B&B); 1 self-catering game lodge sleeps 7.
Price: R300 - R350 pp sharing B&B. Singles on request.
Meals: All meals are in the main house. Full breakfast included. 3-course dinners (excluding wine) R100 (booking essential). Main and coffee R50.
Directions: On N11, 35km from Ladysmith, 70km from Newcastle. Also entrance on R602, 35km from Dundee towards Ladysmith. For B&B look for sign to Fodo Farm.

Oaklands Country Manor

Jamie Bruce and Caroline Tully
Van Reenen
Tel: 058-671-0067 Fax: 058-671-0077
Email: info@oaklands.co.za Web: www.oaklands.co.za

Oaklands has had a serious makeover and polo has come to town! Arriving a little late for what turned out to be a sumptuous lunch, Jamie and I boarded his 'Rhino' and sped off across the property so I could get a full glimpse of the new-look Oaklands Polo and Country Club. Having had a life-long passion for polo and indeed anything to do with the outdoors, this ex-British army officer has gone the whole hog to create something new and adventurous for his guests, kids and adults alike. I have only been riding once or twice (much to Jamie's astonishment!), but he assured me that anyone can play polo with just a little instruction, and if I'd have had more time he'd have got me up and playing that very afternoon. And what a place to play! The full-size polo field sits next to a wide, flowing river and looks across to the spectacular peaks of the Drakensberg mountains. A clubhouse is being erected for your aftergame drinks and paddocks for your weary horses. There is also tennis, garden chess and trampolines amongst everything else. But despite this, it is still a place where you can come and rest your legs if need be. The rooms are fun, converted from old stables and outbuildings. All are different in style, but consistent themes are colourful duvet covers, bright African art and stunning views from the patio. Here you're in the wilds among mountains, craggy cliffs and galloping horses, and I guarantee you'll love it.

Rooms: 13 units all have en-suite baths with showers over bath. Self-catering house sleeps 6: 1 queen en-suite large bath, 2 twins sharing shower, fully-equipped kitchen & outdoor braai.
Price: From R250 pp for room only to R450 pp full board. Singles on request. 'Ukhubona' self-catering lodge is R1,500 per night.
Meals: Full breakfast and dinner included. Lunch is also available. All meals can be provided for those staying in the self-catering lodge.
Directions: Take the N3 to Van Reenen, turn right at the Caltex garage. Go 7km down a dirt track - Oaklands is signed to the right.

Montusi Mountain Lodge

Anthony and Jean Carte

Off D119, Near Alpine Heath, Bergville
Tel: 036-438-6243
Fax: 036-438-6566
Email: montusi@iafrica.com
Web: www.montusi.co.za

Montusi feels a bit like a hotel, which just happens to be run by your aunt and uncle. You know… you haven't seen them for years, but no sooner have you stepped from the car than they've got your bed sorted (well, your thatched, Conran-style, country cottage complete with fireplace, selected DSTV and view!) and are fixing you a sundowner on the patio. Yes, the views are every bit as good as the photo suggests. Ant bought wattle-strangled Montusi Farm in the early 1990s. Being a man of X-ray vision, he saw through the undergrowth to a lodge perfectly positioned to catch the surrounding view, he saw fields of galloping horses and he saw lakes to fish in. So he did away with the wattles (via a community project) and a new Montusi emerged. Meals are superb… some examples: lamb with chargrilled lemon and mint, ostrich fillet with garlic and marinated peppers, malva pudding, custard cups. There are many ways to burn off the calories with limitless and fabulous Drakensberg hiking on your doorstep (we walked up stunning Tugela Gorge, but the Cartes can help with suggestions). But there's also horse-riding for all levels of experience, mountain-biking, swimming in the wonderful pool and fishing. But best of all is ex-skiing pro Chris's circus school! It is as professional as they come, with trapezes, bungies, nets, ropes and they sometimes put on shows too. Montusi impressed me because it's a happy, family-run place with plenty of style. *Relaxation massages are now being offered by local ladies as part of a community project. Picnics at waterfalls can be arranged.*

Rooms: 14 cottages: 4 are kings with en-suite bath and another twin with en-suite shower next door. 10 are kings with shower and bath.
Price: R870 pp sharing per night. Singles R1,100. Rate includes dinner and breakfast.
Meals: Full breakfast and 4-course dinner included (wine extra).
Directions: From the south head north thro' Pietermaritzburg, Estcourt and turn L signed Northern Drakensberg. Continue for 80km thro' Winterton & Bergville on R74. Follow signs (some small) to Montusi. From north use Harrismith & R74.

Vergezient Drakensberg Mountain Retreat

David George and Dolly Warburton
Northern Drakensberg, Bergville
Email: dollyandlen@drakensbergretreat.co.za Web: www.vergezient.co.za
Cell: 082-302-0406

It hadn't rained for seven months when I arrived at this serene retreat, but it was doing its damnedest to make up for lost time! Thunder bellowed, rain spat and the lightning gods put on a show to rival anywhere in Vegas. Totally over-excited about the storm, I was ushered inside by Dave, the retreat's congenial owner/builder, through the conservatory with its arum lilies and granadilla vines ripe with fruit and we plonked ourselves down in front of a roaring fire, cup of tea in hand. The first thing I noticed, apart from Baloo the Staffy jumping onto my lap, was the space. The communal living room is as long as the building itself and the windows stretch across the back of the house, giving a panoramic view of the night-time show. Dave's theory? "I have so much space, I'd feel guilty if people didn't use it." It is this generosity that makes Vergezient Drakensberg Mountain Retreat so special. There's no agenda here. So whether it's hiking to New Beginnings Cave, sinking into one of many books piled high in the library or tinkling away on the baby grand Steinway, your time is your own. Supper, however, is compulsory! Over three delectable courses (what a pork dish that was!), Dave and I exchanged old stories, wine flowed, candles flickered, songs were sung. The next morning, after a deep, soft-cottoned sleep, the storm had cleared and I awoke to a view so spectacular I nearly fell out of bed: miles of imposing Drakensberg Mountain, the Tugela Falls in full flight and mist still sleeping in the valley. Now I saw why Dave had to share this. It's too beautiful for one man.

Rooms: 8: all doubles. Four with en-suite bath/shower and four with en-suite shower.
Price: R450 - R750 pp. Singles on request.
Meals: Breakfast and 3-course dinner included. Light lunch on request.
Directions: See website or enquire on booking.

Spion Kop Lodge

Lynette and Raymond Heron

R600, Drakensberg and Battlefields Area, Ladysmith
Tel: 036-488-1404 Fax: 036-488-1404
Email: spionkop@futurenet.co.za Web: www.spionkop.co.za
Cell: 082-573-0224/5

Soon after arriving, we were off on a late-afternoon game drive in the park next door, winding our way through thick grasses towards a vast lake, then glowing pink-blue under the setting sun. We had the place to ourselves, if you don't count the animals, who seemed to be everywhere, including a nonchalant rhinoceros who munched his way uncomfortably close to our vehicle. Safely back at base, I began exploring. The lodge is now a 700-hectare eco-reserve with 278 bird species and a mass of flowering aloes in June and July. You can stay either in stone cottages, which are snug with fireplaces for winter and verandahs for summer; or in the colonial farmhouse with its polished floorboards and library full of history books. But the main heart of the lodge is the 108-year-old stone converted barn, now a massive glass-walled dining room with sinuous blonde branches creeping from floor to ceiling... and breath-taking views. After an excellent dinner with much red wine and merry-making, we embarked on a night safari in search of leopards and porcupines. Raymond is a registered guide, a raconteur par excellence and an expert on the tragic movements of the Battle of Spionkop. His battlefields tours are so riveting and brilliant that they are often reported as highlights, not just of a stay at the lodge, but of peoples' whole trips in South Africa. Both he and Lynette are wonderful hosts and will ensure you have an eventful stay. With horse-riding, boat cruises, fishing, birding and bushman art on offer as well, there's enough to keep you entertained for a week.

Rooms: 8 doubles, all en-suite with bath and shower. Plus 2 self-catering cottages: Aloe has 1 double, 1 twin and a bath; Acacia has 3 bedrooms and 2 bathrooms.
Price: R830 – R1,000 full board pp sh. Aloe R790 per cottage/night. Acacia R990 per cottage/night.
Meals: Full breakfast, lunch and 3-4 course dinner included. Meals available on request for self-caterers.
Directions: On the R600 between Ladysmith and Winterton. Signposted off the R74 and N11. Gravel road for 1.5km. (N3 from either Durban or Jo'burg). See website for map.

Map Number: 13

Entry Number: 264

Zingela

Mark and Linda Calverley

Weenen
Tel: 036-354-7005/7250 Fax: 036-354-7021 or 086 650 8950
Email: zingela@futurenet.co.za Web: www.zingelasafaris.co.za
Cell: 084-746-9694 (out of range 99% of the time)

Hiking, fishing, abseiling, rafting, swimming, game-viewing, hunting, quad-biking, horse-riding… perhaps I'd be better off listing the things you can't do at Zingela. Mark and Linda are delightful and, over twenty years or so, have built up their home/riverside bush camp to offer everything and anything, all the more astonishing given their location. This really is wild country. From a rendezvous in the wee village of Weenen it was an hour's 4x4 drive (not for the faint-hearted) past isolated Zulu villages and down to the Tugela River - worth every bump. There are five palatial double tents overlooking the river, all open to the elements. Showers are more outside than in, branches provide the towel rails and each tent has hefty, iron-framed beds and beautiful wooden furniture from Zanzibar. Those on the romance beat will love the "hitching post" with doubtless the world's largest headboard, a vast, mattress-to-canvas slab of sandstone. There's electricity and gallons of hot water but Zingela is essentially bush living ("don't-forget-the-loo-roll-or-matches kind of country," says Linda). When I visited the place was alive with families (there are zillions of kids' beds in extra dormitory tents). Some youngsters were preparing for a rafting adventure and everyone was thoroughly enjoying the endless fresh air, filling grub and lashings of good, wholesome fun. *There is also a thatched oil-lamp camp opening in 2008.*

Rooms: 5 bush tents: 3 doubles and 2 twins, all with shower. Self-catering option available.
Price: R850 pp includes all food plus game walk, abseiling and rafting. Eco-friendly quad-bike trails, horse-riding and stalking are extra. Transfers from Weenen for those without 4x4 are R75 pp.
Meals: Full board.
Directions: Faxed or emailed on booking.

Sycamore Avenue Treehouse Lodge

Bruce and Gloria Attwood

11 Hidcote Road, Hidcote,
Mooi River
Tel: 033-263-2875
Fax: 033-263-2134
Email:
sycamore@futurenet.co.za
Web:
www.sycamore-ave.com

Treehouses! Need you read any further? There are not many who can weave a whole house into the branches of a giant pin oak, but Bruce has done it not once, not twice, but four times. And when I visited he was busy stretching his imagination around yet another house in the trees, Pegasus, a wooden extravaganza of flying white horses and golden bridles, inspired by "the poets' fountain of knowledge" no less. All three of the original arboreal retreats are standing strong and are hidden from the house by foliage, each set above a magical garden below (where couples love to get married) and overlooking miles of rolling fields beyond. Bruce is a functional sculptor and his weapon of choice is wood. You'll spot his work all over the Midlands, but it's here that he's really gone to town, or rather, tree. From beds to bread bins to window hooks and hinges, everything is crafted from beautifully-grained cedar or wattle, or whatever he can lay his hands on. The third addition, Bottle-Tree House, is magnificent. Its spiral staircase winds up from a bottle-walled sitting room to the queen-sized bed, and set into the bedroom is an outdoor jacuzzi. Just picture it... enjoying a good soak to the sound of orioles, although you might have to turn the bubbles off first. A 100% unique, must-try experience. *Well placed for arts/crafts region and Giant's Castle.*

Rooms: 5 treehouses: 2 queen & 2 doubles, all with jacuzzis and showers; The Planequarium treehouse has 2 double rooms, both with en-suite toilet and basin, shared shower and jacuzzi.
Price: R475 - R600 pp sharing. Single supplement +50%. Seasonal rates for December only.
Meals: Full breakfast included. Dinner by arrangement: 3 courses from R95 (excluding wine).
Directions: Take exit 152 off N3. Between the N3 and the R103 turn right at the Sycamore Avenue sign. Phone if lost!

The Antbear

Andrew and Conny Attwood

Fernhust Farm, Moor Park – Giant's Castle Road, Estcourt
Tel: 036-352-3143 Fax: 036-352-3143
Email: info@antbear.co.za Web: www.antbear.co.za

Thank goodness Andrew and Conny gave up the corporate rat race in Germany for B&B'ing. They renovated the old farmhouse and, like all the buildings at The Antbear, it is thatched and sits on a hilltop surveying the Drakensberg peaks. Andrew is a canny chap. The lodge and rooms are home to his chairs, tables, doors, staircases, towel holders, candlesticks - the list of working wooden sculptures runs and runs. Just across from the lodge's leafy, colonnaded front patio an old tractor shed has been converted into four other bedrooms. Billowing white curtains frame the view and the rooms have intriguing fireplaces and plenty of humorous sculpture. The first room is superb with a staircase that climbs the right-hand wall, a loft bed-platform in the thatchy peak on the left and a six-foot causeway between the two. There's masses to keep you occupied in the area with birding, rock-art sites, river-rafting, battlefield tours and local arts and crafts. Each night weary guests congregate at the huge yellowwood table (Andrew-carved, naturally) to swap tales of their day's adventures. Homely and 100% organic (unless the horses, tortoises, chickens or geese have raided Connie's garden!); the food here is amazing with authentic flavours borrowed from Zulu neighbours or from around the world. All in all, you'd be a fool to stay for only one night.

Rooms: 5: 4 en/s doubles in renovated tractor shed, all with showers and jacuzzi bath; 1 separate double with en/s shower and jacuzzi bath.
Price: Dinner, bed and breakfast from R540 - R760 pp sharing. No single supplements.
Meals: Lunch on request from R40 pp. Dinner usually 3 courses (excluding wine).
Directions: Take exit 152 on the N3 signed Hidcote for 7km. At T-junction turn right towards Giant's Castle. After 14km turn right towards Moor Park onto dirt road. After 5.5km you will see The Antbear sign to the right. The thatched cottages are 2km up the farm road.

Engeleni Lodge & Mayfly Cottage

Graham and Sue Armstrong

Nottingham Road
Tel: 033-267-7218 Fax: 033-267-7103
Email: engeleni@futurenet.co.za Web: www.engeleni-lodge.co.za
Cell: 082-854-2338

To experience fully all that the KZN Midlands has to offer, this place should be high on your 'must-do' list. For not only is Sue a delightful host, but she is also an experienced, home-grown tour-guide who is dying to share her local knowledge with you. So whatever sparks your fancy, from private gardens, horse-studs, San rock paintings, air-ballooning (take-off point, the lawn) or Zulu spiritual healing... Sue will sort it out. There are also superb birding and fishing opportunities right here on the farm. And the accommodation is tip-top too. After years spent outcast and overgrown, the lodge has been welcomed back, and wonderfully restored and now radiates country warmth from each room. Full of beautiful original artworks and with fishing rods and binos dotted around, Engeleni is one of those places where I immediately felt right at home. From the huge wood-panelled kitchen with wagon-wheel light-fittings hanging from the rafters, to the flower-filled dining room, cosy pub, cheery bedrooms, book-filled corridors and snug living room (with traditional Gallic fishing-boat above the log-fire!), this deceptively large house, dwarfed by its magnificent setting, is a knock-out. I absolutely loved the smaller, slightly more 'African' Mayfly too; so cosy that Sue sometimes uses it as her own secret R&R retreat. Romantic couples, keen beans and lazy idlers all... I'd recommend you stay at least two nights.

Rooms: Engeleni Lodge: 5 king/twins, 1 with en-suite shower, 2 with en-suite shower & bath, 2 rooms share bath (Engeleni can only be taken by one group at a time); Mayfly Cottage: 1 king/twin with en-s double shower.
Price: Dinner, bed and breakfast R540 pp. B&B R425. Singles R600. Self-catering rate R365 pp. Engeleni Lodge minimum rate for less than 5 people R1,500. Mayfly Cottage sleeps 2.
Meals: Meals by arrangement at time of booking.
Directions: From Durban/Jo'burg, take Mooi River Toll Plaza off N3. L onto R103 to Rosetta, then R into Kamburg Rd for 18km. R into D314, then 3.7km on dirt road following signs to lodge.

Bramleigh Manor

Bettina and Roger Kauerauf
D544, Natal Midlands, Nottingham Road
Tel: 033-266-6903 Fax: 033-266-6903
Email: bramleigh@bundunet.com Web: www.bramleigh-manor.com
Cell: 083-996-0000

Bettina at first found it difficult to believe that she had her very own forest in her back garden. "I felt like I didn't deserve it," she says, recalling those early days after the move from Jo'burg with husband Roger. After a fullsome breakfast (including home-made muffins), I struck off on an exploratory mission into the trees with three bounding hounds in tow. Here I discovered a giant Outeniqua yellowwood not far from where guests are sometimes treated to a forest breakfast among a romantic tangle of bush and branch... where it has been known on more than one occasion for marriage proposals to be made. As I re-emerged onto a rolling lawn, the manor rambled on in front of me, its thatched roof curving over my suite on the left wing; the family apartment is tucked beneath a vast braai-feasting platform, while two more private rondavels climb the hill behind. It was greatly restoring to spend a few quiet moments in my own snug sitting room by a fireplace well stocked with cuts of wattle, part of Roger's attempt to be free of the Ozzie invader. He also builds traditional wattle and daub houses for his staff, now a published solution for housing shortages and one of many subjects of conversation during dinner (do allow Bettina to cook for you) that ranged from Zulu culture to rugby conspiracy theories. Their daughter's watercolours and impressions of the Nguni cattle that Roger brought in as nature's lawnmowers may tempt those looking for local artwork. Bring your hiking boots.

Rooms: 5 rooms: 1 double with en-suite shower; 2 twin/kings with full en-suite bathroom; 2 apartment suites (1 with two bedrooms) with lounge, kitchen and full bathroom.
Price: B&B: R250 - R380, singles R350 - R480. Self-catering: R260/R330, singles R360/R430. Children R60 (under 12) or R120 (12 - 16 yrs).
Meals: Full breakfast included in B&B rate. Option of forest breakfast at extra cost. Lunch (or picnic) and dinner on request. Self-catering available.
Directions: See website for map and directions.

Rockwood Forest Lodge

Tom Hancock
Karkloof Nature Reserve, Howick
Tel: 031-303-5162 Fax: 031-312-4872
Email: info@rockwood.co.za Web: www.rockwood.co.za

I half-expected a trail of breadcrumbs to lead me up to Rockwood Forest Lodge One, a wooden 'gingerbread' house snuggled among green stinkwood, Cape quince and moss-covered blackwood. Creeping up the Oregon pine stairs and ducking under the low slanting roof, I could have sworn that seven dwarfs were snoozing in the four-poster bed, their heads propped up on feather pillows. On second inspection, Dopey and co were nowhere to be seen, or heard. All was silent except the gurgling River Godwini. Passing cupboards and door frames painted in reds and greens, I retraced my steps to the large outdoor braai deck. Propped up on stilts, there's enough space here to host a Grimm's fairytale reunion. Inside, an open fire, spotted cow rugs and slouching sofas beckon when the sun sets. If you prefer open spaces, though, the solar-powered Lodge Four is in a natural clearing with views across to Howick. Karkloof Nature Reserve is on your doorstep here, a mere 2,800 hectares of endemic flora and fauna, which is open to lodge guests alone. Grab your binos and look out for samango monkeys, bushbuck (I saw three on my drive up there), blue duiker, Cape parrots and crowned eagles. If you want a closer encounter, take the Karkloof Canopy Tour, where you swing through the forest on a zip slide. Elsewhere, there are mountain-biking trails aplenty, plus fishing dams and swimming weirs. Enough to put a smile on the face of the grumpiest of dwarves!

Rooms: 2 units: Lodge One: 1 king and 2 twins, with 2 bathrooms (bath and shower); Lodge Four: 1 king and 2 twins with 2 bathrooms (bath and shower).
Price: From R320 pp per night.
Meals: Self-catering.
Directions: Check website for directions.

Stocklands Farm

Eve Mazery
4 Shafton Rd, Howick
Tel: 033-330-5160 Fax: 086-685-5657
Email: edulink@iafrica.com Web: www.stocklandsfarm.co.za
Cell: 082-975-2298

The warm welcome that I received as I tumbled out of my car, late and weary, is undoubtedl typical of Stocklands. Eve and Roland are natural hosts, thoughtful and funny, and they have put lot of love and plenty of style into the wonderful old house. The argument goes that half-measure are not really in keeping with Stocklands, and you can see their point. The walls of the origin 1850s Voortrekker Cottage, for example, are over 50 centimetres thick and the belhambra tre at the front of the house is no-less-than enormous. Birds come in droves – they love Roland indigenous trees, "a small forest", and bank upon bank of stunning flowers. I loved the fuchsia tre myself (it flowers in January). Down near the tennis court there is a koi pond and many guests lik to savour a slow, hot afternoon in the thick shade on a blanket here after a picnic. The four rooms like the cottages, are meticulously decorated in individual themes, all with a cosy, English-cottag feel about them. Eve has found hand-embroidered linen and original works by local artists t decorate and nothing is left out including teddy bears in all rooms and a generous helping c liquorice allsorts. Oh, and if you want to know more about local history, ask Eve – she's writing book on the subject. Choose from a range of breakfasts including grilled maraschino grapefruit an the Stocklands Smoothie. *Game can be viewed right next door, by the way. French spoken.*

Rooms: 7: 2 suites & 2 bedrooms, 2 with en-s bath 2 with en-s shr. Also 3 cottages: 1 with 3 bedrooms & 2 bathrooms; 2 with 1 bedroom & 2 shrs.
Price: R260 - R300 pp sharing. Singles on request. Self-catering R210 - R250 pp.
Meals: Full breakfast included or you can self-cater ir cottages. An excellent café next door & more in area
Directions: From Jo'burg take N3 to Durban. Take 1st exit to Howick signed Howick/Tweedie. At Stop sign turn L to Howick. Through lights to bottom of hill, turn L to Karkloof. 100m turn R into Shafton Rd. Stocklands is 1km. From Durban take N3 to Jo'burg. Take 3rd Howick turn-off as above.

Waterfall Cottage

Lizzie Purbrick
D51, Dargle
Tel: 033-234-4606 Fax: 033-234-4606
Email: cortaflexsa@gmail.com
Cell: 082-342-8217

A hell-raiser with a heart of gold, Lizzie Purbrick, former England eventing champion and army wife, scandalized the riding world and beat a retreat to South Africa, where she now trains sons and horses in a gorgeous slice of the Natal midlands. From the verandah of the main house an undulating panorama converges on the tip of a sumptuous hill known in Zulu as the maiden's breast (scaled yearly by the famous Michaelhouse boys' school). It was here that I also witnessed a massive fire-breaking exercise; a livid red swathe across a darkening landscape. Youngest son George put his famous chocolate pudding on to simmer and before I knew it my fifteen year-old chauffeur was driving me towards a wall of flame. (Of course this will have greened up again by the time you get there.) Normal rules don't apply here, but you can escape the furore of parrots, dogs, marauding eagles, horses of course, chickens (who provide breakfast eggs) and boys by retiring to the haven of calm and uncluttered beauty that is the old 1860 original granite farmhouse. Light the fire and sink into a book before tripping along stone floors, ducking under low doorways, into a simple kitchen on your way to a good lather in the bath, courtesy of Lizzie's own hand-made lavender soap that leaves the skin feeling butterly soft. There are walks aplenty from your doorstep that take you up through pristine indigenous bush onto high ground where herds of blesbok run free, endangered blue and wattled cranes lumber skywards. Rumour has it that the first miserly owner buried his wealth somewhere on the property - bring provisions to stay longer than you planned.

Rooms: 1 cottage with 1 double and 1 twin bedrooms, kitchen, sitting room and bathroom (bath only).
Price: R295 pp sharing.
Meals: Fully self-catering.
Directions: Contact Lizzie for directions.

Inversanda

Tom and Lucinda Bate

Howick
Tel: 033-234-4321 Fax: 033-234-4751
Email: bate@nitrosoft.co.za Web: www.inversanda.co.za
Cell: 082-781-3875

It's true that GG owners are a welcoming bunch, but the Bates go far beyond the call of duty. Actually, I don't think they see it as a duty at all. In fact, I know they don't! Hemmed in by mountains and a meander of the Mgeni River, the farm is in a world of its own, but in easy reach of the major routes. All four Bates (plus assorted hounds) are utterly charming and you're encouraged to participate in their farm and life as much or as little as you like. Talk about a welcome! We were hardly out of the car before we had a greedy calf and a bottle of milk in hand. Half an hour later we were bringing the horses in for feeding. Then just time for a bobble over the fields looking at pregnant cows before a delicious and greatly entertaining dinner with the family. Tom and Lucinda are serious horse-lovers, breeding and schooling polo ponies. Polo players are more than welcome for a weekend knock-about on the makeshift riverside pitch. Otherwise you can fish, walk or swim pretty much anywhere you want. The farmhouse itself (1800s) goes on forever and guests have the choice of their own wing, a pot-planted patio with stunning views across the valley, two enormous twin rooms and a basic kitchen; or a brand-new cottage which also has a large verandah with a commanding view over the valley and two large bedrooms. But even if you had to lie on a bed of spikes, I'd still recommend Inversanda! This is a place that allows you to unburden yourself of the tourist mantle and truly feel part of what's going on.

Rooms: 1 self-catering wing of the house with two twin rooms and shared bath and shower; 1 cottage with 2 rooms, 1 double and 1 twin. Both have en-suite bathrooms, 1 with shower and 1 with bath and shower.
Price: R240 pp self-catering.
Meals: Meals available on request.
Directions: Faxed or emailed on booking.

Leadwood Lodge

Stuart Hilcove, Tina Roche (Owners) and Catherine Garden (Manager)

Tala Private Game Reserve, Cascades, Pietermaritzburg
Tel: 031-781-8000 Fax: 031-781-8022
Email: info@tala.co.za Web: www.tala.co.za/leadwood

'Tala' means 'Land of Plenty' in Zulu and surely an apter name could not have been found. Merrily skidding my way down the dirt tracks of this 7,000-acre reserve, I encountered a 'journey' of fifteen giraffe, a herd of temporarily docile buffalo and a male greater kudu so majestic Hemingway himself would've gasped in awe (... before shooting it). On arrival I was greeted by Catherine, Leadwood's charming manageress, and escorted to the lodge. From this point on, I too was gasping in awe. It began with the waterfall cascading into the pond at the entrance which flows underneath the house and out to the watering-hole below. Inside I was immediately drawn to the perfect blossoming orchids that adorned the George IV dining table and, hiding in the corner at the entrance to a cavernous wine cellar, a rare 1900 timekeeper softly ticking away. Leadwood brings great opulence to the bush; that much was already clear. But if further proof was required, my sleeping quarters provided it. A five-minute stroll took me to my very own palatial bush-marooned lodge. Trying not to laugh at my good fortune, I disrobed, ignored a bath big enough for three and headed straight for the outside shower. This shower is indeed so 'outside' that both the head and taps are built into a tree! From there to supper - rare blue wildebeest and a rich '01 shiraz - before returning to the lodge and slipping under the covers of my king-size four-poster bed. I fell into a deep slumber, with nothing but the rustly, chirrupy night sounds of the bush for company.

Rooms: 6 lodges. All en-suite bath/shower and outside shower.
Price: R3,000 pp. Single supplement +50%. Includes game drive/walk.
Meals: All included, including 5-course gourmet supper.
Directions: See website.

Valemount Country Lodge

Dalene and Lance Bailey
Underberg
Tel: 033-701-1686 Fax: 033-701-1686 & 033-701-1653
Email: info@valemountafrica.com Web: www.valemountafrica.com
Cell: 082-828-8921

The Sani Pass is as thrilling/hair-raising a drive as you'll enjoy/undergo in SA, so thank goodness Lance and Dalene are on hand to put a stiff drink in your hand at the bottom. The Baileys came here from Johannesburg just a year or two ago and they couldn't look more at home in their new surroundings. Their home is a thatched, sunny-yellow slice of tranquillity that spreads out across a regimented English country garden, between pine and English oaks and stunning copper beeches. The rooms all have bags of space, working fireplaces and patios facing the garden or surrounding woodland. You can wander wherever you like, ambling along winding, wooded footpaths, fishing for trout in the lake or bobbing about in the heated pool. That's the latest addition and Lance proudly showed me the three separate 'Martini seats' and jacuzzi jets. He and Dalene have a real eye for detail (they even cut the grass in the forest for you!) and have all sorts of plans for paths here and gazebos there, while quietly harbouring romantic visions of a mini-cheese-factory, although "we've got to learn to make cheese first," he acknowledges. If you've spent the day clattering around the dirt roads, I can't think of anywhere better to rub the dust from your eyes and relax. *No children.*

Rooms: 6: 4 luxury kings and 2 standard twins, all with en-suite bath and shower and fireplaces.
Price: From R350 pp sharing. Singles on request.
Meals: Full breakfast included.
Directions: From N3 off-ramp 99 take R617 110km to Underberg. Continue for 8km towards Swartberg and Valemount is signed on the left.

Penwarn Country Lodge

Peta Parker
Southern Drakensberg, Underberg
Tel: 033-701-1777 or 1341 or 1342 Fax: 033-701-1341
Email: info@penwarn.com Web: www.penwarn.com
Cell: 083-305-3009

Late was the hour when I rumbled into the estate, negotiating my way past an inquisitive eland who blocked the path. From humble beginnings as an old dairy and fertilizer shed, the lodge was converted into darkly-beamed sitting rooms, a bar and bedrooms so large they make you want to run amok, before slumping into four-poster comfort. Reclining on a deep leather divan in 'Nimrod' (dedicated to a much-loved otter that previous guests may remember), I watched through vast windows the day's colours slowly fade from a lake caressed by willows and supervised by cranes. Only then did I notice my spaniel companion, Whisky, who lay outside my garden door waiting for stick-games to commence. Dinner was a buffet extravaganza, but it was a wrench having to leave the uplifting company of the Parker family and their staff (it is not easy to distinguish which is which). Peta herself is an entrepreneur with a deep sense of compassion, and she also runs an orphanage and teaches Sunday School. A fellow English couple confessed to being GG devotees and insisted that I visit them at the separate Mthini Lodge with its stellar position above the dam, looking out to foothills grazed by the naturally occuring 'rietbuck' and eland, springbok, wildebeest, zebra... and to the mountains beyond. The sense of space is liberating, with full-throttle activities rubbing shoulders with the gentler pursuits of fishing, horse-riding and excellent bird-watching at the 'Vulture Restaurant'. Trace too the bushman cave figures painted a millennium ago. A magical place.

Rooms: 11: 7 suites at Indabushe Lodge, 4 suites at Mthini lodge. All have en-suite bath and/or shower. (No cave dwelling anymore – sorry!).
Price: Full board R1,000 pp sharing. Singles +50%. Certain activities extra (from R100 - R150 pp). Enquire about reduced winter rates for locals.
Meals: Full breakfast, lunch, 4-course dinner and all snacks are included. Wine is not. Canoeing is free.
Directions: Directions on website or faxed/emailed on booking.

Free State & Lesotho

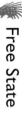

Die Ou Stal

Piet and Zenobia Labuchagné

38 George Street, Zastron
Tel: 051-673-1268 Fax: 051-673-1268
Email: dieoustal@tiscali.co.za
Cell: 082-416-7832

In a place like Zastron, it's vital to find yourself a guide to show you the unknown gems that lurk around every corner and to recount the astonishing tales of yesteryear. Look no further than Piet. His enthusiasm for the geology and pre-history of Africa is infectious. After the whistle-stop tour of intriguing local rock formations, spiced up with ancient bushman legends, I'll never look at a cliff face in the same way again. Had I stayed longer, I'd have been begging him to take me on a day trip to nearby Lesotho, but alas I had to leave even before one of Zen's delicious suppers of bobotie or chicken pie. At least I had time to sit on the stoep outside the converted stables that are now the guest rooms and watch a lightning storm hammer away at the Lesotho mountains – a majestic sight indeed. The bedrooms are simple, cosy affairs with whitewashed walls and doors that open into a small kitchen. Breakfast, however, is served at the large dining table in the main house, atop wooden floorboards and next to a fridge surely dating from before fridges were invented (also wood): this intriguing feature is now a drinks cabinet. In a town that's won awards for its friendliness (driving around with Piet, the whole town and his uncle Joe came out to give us a wave), Zen is champion of champions.

Rooms: 2: 1 double with en-suite bath and shower; 1 twin with en-suite shower.
Price: R275 - R385 pp sharing.
Meals: Full breakfast included. Dinner on request: R65 pp.
Directions: From N6 turn onto R26 and follow signs to Zastron. In town, turn right opposite the corner of the church into Mathee Street, then take third left into Berg Strat and see signs.

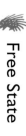

Springfontein House

Graeme Wedgwood
32 van Riebeeck Street, Springfontein
Tel: 051-783-0076 Fax: 051-783-0425
Email: wedgie@icon.co.za Web: www.springfontein-guest-house.com
Cell: 082-450-6779

Graeme used to run Smithfield House, which he brought to life with cultivated, Epicurean zeal Well, the same applies here at his new home. Those with a taste for fine living will find a kindrec spirit in Graeme, a man whose love of house and garden, countryside, good company, food anc wine now sets the tone at Springfontein House. He was once a gallery owner in Johannesbur – a far cry from his first, 26-year career as a London stockbroker – and his personal art collectior includes a rather racy Battiss, an inky Sekoto and other originals by South African artists, botl established and emerging. African rugs, powdery sofas, bowls of dried rose petals and side table proffering porcelain complete the sandy-coloured sitting room. Through glass doors is a slate floored, frond-filled sunroom and an incarnadine dining room, with Georgian tables and silve candelabras. In the bedrooms the curtains are silk, the towels soft and the comfy beds have crisp linen, plump pillows and mohair throws. Outside, white walls dazzle and creepers climb abov the stoep; there's a bricked patio and colourful flower-beds, a pool and a series of fishponds. Bu the reason you come here is to be looked after, and arriving from the biscuity veld, you'll feel luck indeed. *Graeme will explain about biking, hunting, rare bird-watching, and hiking. He regrets that th house is not suitable for children under 12.*

Rooms: 5: 3 queens, 1 with en-s bath/sh'r, 1 with en-s sh'r and 1 with full bathroom en-s; 2 twins, 1 with en-suite bath/sh'r and 1 with full bathroom en-s.
Price: R275 - R325 pp sharing. Singles on request. Booking advised.
Meals: Full breakfast included. 3-course dinner available on request from R100, excluding wine.
Directions: Heading north on the N1 turn off at Springfontein South sign. Follow road, becoming Settler St. Van Riebeeck St is on your left, and Springfontein House is at the end on right. For those travelling south on the N1 come off at Springfontein North exit and follow the signs.

Franshoek Mountain Lodge

Roz Evans

Franshoek Farm, Ficksburg
Tel: 051-933-2828 Fax: 051-933-2828
Email: lodge@franshoek.co.za Web: www.franshoek.co.za
Cell: 072-128-7356

Franshoek is a magical place where mad things happen. As I arrived, Roz emerged, beaming and welly-clad, having located her missing keys among the flowerbeds. Meanwhile the goose was trying to eat the laundry. The old, stonewalled exterior resembles a hobbit house, but through the wooden gates it's more like Aladdin's cave. Gilt mirrors, glass bowls of floating flowers, a gramophone and a tiny pet tortoise wiggling across the bar all came into view. Music played while guests, thoroughly enjoying themselves, reclined on elephant sofas. "It's a bit like one long house party," Roz reflected, loading up a roaring log fire. A storm was descending outside, but after the sky had ceased groaning and a yellow haze had descended over the mountains, we nipped out for a look around. The original farmhouse rooms are cosy and varied, many with adjoining kids rooms. There's much to do with the polo farm next door, a home-made African steam hut, horses, a beautiful round pool and nearby rock art sites (if someone can remember exactly where they are). The new self-catering cottage looks out onto a marvellous mountain view and Roz is considering naming it after Orna, the wonderful, multi-tasking, green-fingered, pig-loving Thai woman for whom no job was too much. She has sadly returned to her native land. When I stayed, one couple went horse-riding to the top of the mountain and came back engaged! It's that kind of place and after champagne in the garden and much excitement, I reluctantly bid my farewells.

Rooms: 11: the family units all sleep 4 with en-s sh'rs; Honeymoon suite with bath and adjoining room with bunk beds & separate en-s sh'r; doubles come with en-s sh'rs. New self-catering cottage.
Price: R450 pp sharing. Singles on request. Includes full breakfast and 3-course Thai or European dinner.
Meals: Breakfast and dinner included. Light lunches on request.
Directions: Signed off R26 betw' Fouriesburg & Ficksburg. 23km south of Fouriesburg on R26, take S385 on R (10km of dirt rd) or 8km north of Ficksburg on R26 take S384 on L (12km on dirt rd).

The View

Ryk and Bea and Sasha Becker

20 Bell Street, Harrismith
Tel: 058-623-0961 Fax: 058-623-0961 Email: rmbecker@internext.co.za
Web: www.harrismithaccommodation.co.za
Cell: 082-775-7381 (Bea); 082-921-3624 (Ryk)

How better to while away a sticky afternoon than by nesting in a rocking chair behind teak pillars on a shady verandah, overlooking a lush garden, slowly draining a pot of tea? Bea and Ryk have found a magic formula simply by being themselves at home! The actual view of the title is now interrupted by an abundance of verdure, but I for one was glad of the green shade and the peaceful sounds of twittering birds hidden among the branches. Inside, a portrait of Bea's big-bearded great-grandfather, President of the Free State (deceased, of course), overlooks the social epicentre of this family home. The lounge, complete with creaking wooden floorboards, vibrant rugs and daringly bright sofas, sweeps through folded-back doors into the dining room where the heavy table awaits those staying in for dinner. And I thoroughly recommend you are among them. You would travel a long way to find a better meal and you'll miss out on Ryk spilling the beans on what to do in this area where he grew up. Before heading up to my goose-feathered bed for my best night's sleep in years, no visit to The View would be complete without being introduced to the rest of the family: four springer and two cocker spaniels. *Son-in-law Simon can arrange star-gazing visits to his farm and other local activities.*

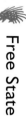

Rooms: 2: both doubles with en-suite bath and shower.
Price: R300 pp sharing. Singles R360.
Meals: Full breakfast included. Dinners on request from R165 pp.
Directions: From Jo'burg side into Warden Street (main street) go around church. 7 blocks from church turn R into Bell Street. From Durban & Bloem, on entering Harrismith turn away from Spur/Engen garage into King Street. Turn L into Warden Street at 1st stop-street. Bell Street is about 10 blocks from here on L.

Wild Horses Lodge

Jon & Trish Hawkins (Owners) and Gerrit Potgieter (Mgr)
Sterkfontein Dam, Harrismith
Tel: 058-622-7000 Fax: 058-622-7000
Email: info@wildhorses.co.za Web: www.wildhorses.co.za
Cell: 083-640-0024

On a sun-kissed spring day, I drove 20 kilometres into the Sterkfontein Nature Reserve, passing a herd of Appaloosas en route, and finally arrived at Wild Horses. Which was, in a word, majestic! The house is built entirely of hand-cut sandstone and sits on the edge of the Sterkfontein Dam, looking onto Platberg Mountain and surrounded by the Drakensberg Mountains. It's the kind of building Kerk Kerkorian might boast about. The lodge is run by Gerrit and François (a quite brilliant chef) and you couldn't ask for finer hosts. I was greeted at the foot of the sandstone steps and led past the koi pond and the infinity pool to the guest wing. My room, the Sunrise Room, looked far across the dam and the following morning I was to discover what an African sunrise truly looks like. But for now, I let my feet dig into the Persian rugs, my fingers run across the silk curtains and sat with owners Jon and Trish to watch, to everyone's surprise, England beat Australia at rugby! A victorious afternoon called for a long spa-bath, a chilled glass of white and the atmosphere was heightened by a huge electrical storm ripping through the late-evening sky in terrific flashes. Supper is a decadent affair here and François, who trained in New York, will not let you down. On my night: hunks of succulent, slow-roasted lamb shank, followed by a devilish chocolate coulant. Beckoned by my king-size bed with its Egyptian cotton sheets I slept deeply, looking forward to sunrise and - please don't think badly of me - the thought of breakfast!

Rooms: 4: 2 kings, 2 queens all with en-suite bath/shower.
Price: R1,500 pp. Singles on request. Enquire about packages.
Meals: Breakfast and supper included. Light lunch on request.
Directions: See website or enquire on booking.

Malealea Lodge and Pony Trek Centre

Mick and Di Jones
Malealea, Lesotho
Tel: 082-552-4215 Fax: 0866-481-815
Email: malealea@mweb.co.za Web: www.malealea.com
Cell: 082-552-4215

"Where are you heading?" asked the border official. "Malealea," I replied nervously. She smiled, "You'll enjoy it there." Here in the heartland of mountainous Lesotho where blanket-clad shepherds watch over their flocks, the Jones family have created a fascinating environment through a combination of their own personal warmth, native knowledge and a wealth of natural and cultural attractions. Malealea thrives on its genuine interaction with the neighbouring village and I arrived just as the choir was starting up, followed by a band playing home-made instruments with wonderful exuberance. The pony trekking centre is run entirely by the locals, who will take you on treks for up to six days (you stay in the villages you visit), and children lead you to waterfalls and rock art. Communal suppers are served canteen style - backpackers and ambassadors rub comradely shoulders – before the pub and Glen's singing around the fire lure you away. When the generator stops, your torch guides you back to thatched rondavel or farmhouse-style accommodation. I woke to the unmistakable cries of peacocks ringing out of the early-morning mist lying low in the valleys. I loved this place. For the adventurous, the family have recently opened chalets in the south of the country dramatically positioned beneath the sheer flanks of Mt Mooroosi, the scene of a fierce siege of the Maphuti by the British. As you make your way up the mountain, still strewn everywhere are cartridges, mortar and graffiti from 1879. Suddenly your trip just got longer.

Rooms: 39 Basotho rondavels and farmhouse rooms: 8 doubles and 31 twins all with en-suite shower.
Price: Rondavels R200 - R220 pp sharing, farmhouses R150 - R170 pp sharing. Single supplement 50%. Overnight horse treks R260 - R285 pp per day. Village accommodation R50 - R55 pp. Day rides from R120 pp.
Meals: Breakfast R45 - R50 pp. Lunch R50 - R60 pp. Dinner R75 - R80 pp. Four communal kitchens available.
Directions: Faxed or emailed on booking.

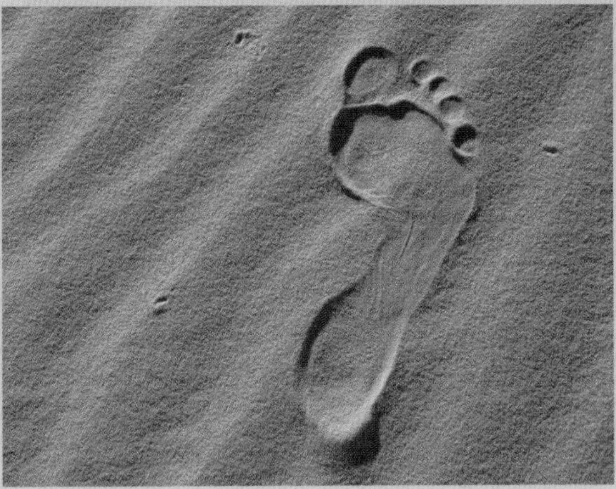

Northern Cape

Papkuilsfontein Farmhouse

Willem and Mariëtte van Wyk
Nieuwoudtville
Tel: 027-218-1246 Fax: 027-218-1246
Email: info@papkuilsfontein.com Web: www.papkuilsfontein.com

I'm going to stick my neck out and say that this is my favourite place to stay in South Africa! Anc here are my reasons.... You stay in an old stone cottage, surrounded by rock, gum tree anc wildlife, not another human in sight. The quality of peace and stillness defeats description. Gas-fired plumbing for baths, hurricane lamps for light - many guests have refused to come back i Willem installs electricity. Then there's the small matter of the gorge and waterfall, which I wouldc have kept secret if I wasn't insistent on your visiting the farm. Your jaw will drop 180 metres intc the canyon. Take a picnic to the deep rock pools for swimming (all year round) above the waterfal (which runs in winter only) and you can climb down into the gorge in an hour and a half. There is also swimming in a pool next to the cottages. The wild flowers in season are sensational ever by Namaqualand standards; the plantlife, divided between Cape fynbos and Karoo succulent, a botanist's dream; steenbok, klipspringer, porcupine and dassie love the terrain and have NOT been specially introduced. Alrie is an excellent cook (breakfast a string of surprises). It's a magica place that not many know about and the van Wyks are all lovely, friendly people who seem unable to put a proper price on what they have to offer! You should stay at least two nights. There's alsc a restored corrugated-iron cottage for those who need their electricity. *Bikes are available fo guests to use.*

Rooms: 3 stone cottages sleeping 4 and 6: two with bath and outdoor shower, and the other with shower. 1 cottage with one twin and one double, one with en/s bath and one with en/s shower.
Price: R250 - R300 pp sharing. Single rates + 50%. Minimum cost per cottage per night in flower season (without meals): Gert Boom R900, De Hoop and Rondekraal R610.
Meals: Full b'fast included. 3-course dinners R135.
Directions: From CT take N1 then N7 to Vanrhynsdorp. Turn off onto R27 to Nieuwoudtville. Turn right into town, and straight through onto dirt road for 22km. The farm is signed to the right.

Naries Namakwa Retreat

Julene Hamman
27km from Springbok (N7) on the way to Kleinzee (on R355), Namakwaland
Tel: 027-712-2462 or 021-930-4564 Fax: 021-882-9493
Email: reservations@naries.co.za Web: www.naries.co.za

Naries has several nice surprises in store for its regulars. Firstly, the road from Springbok, 27km away, has been tarred, making for quick access to the Goegap Nature Reserve, its beautiful plains scenery, its arid mountains and kopies, and its magical seasonal flower display – 600 species. Then there are the three fabulous cottages, the Namakwa Mountain Suites, which have been constructed on the edge of a high escarpment with an extraordinary eagle's eye view of the dramatic and barren mountains that march off to the sea 70km away at Kleinzee. The architecture is in the form of a domed cottage, which echoes the style of local Nama dwellings, and is perfectly integrated with the round granite kopies of the area. Their exterior simplicity, however, is deceptive, for the interiors are vast and luxurious, while retaining some very natural features: the almost woven texture of the walls of the cottage, for example, and the bare rocks which erupt into the space as bed-heads or in the sublime bathrooms. The old Cape Dutch manor, where dinners are served, also houses some fine bedrooms. The house has recently been refurnished and redecorated and the walls, painted in plain colours, offset the 1930s furniture perfectly. *Naries recommends various day excursions to explore the beauty of Namakwaland: De Beers Diamond Mines, 4x4 Shipwreck Experience, Goegap Nature Reserve, Namakwa and Richtersveld National Parks. Also, make sure you book well in advance for the desert flower season!*

Rooms: 11: 3 N'kwa Mountain Suites with en-suite bathrooms; 5 Manor House rooms with en-s bathrooms; 2 Power House economy rooms; 1 family s/c unit with en-s bath & sh'r, sleeps max 4.
Price: N'kwa Suites: From R1,005 pp sh/R1,060 single; Manor Hse: R820 pp sh/R905 single. Econ. rooms: R430 pp sh/single. Self-cat unit: R250 pp sh/single & kids (4-12) R125 pp. Low-season rates.
Meals: B'fast & dinner incl' in non s/c rates. Meals for self-cat optional for adults and kids 12 yrs plus.
Directions: 27km from Springbok (N7), on your way to Kleinzee on tarred road (R355).

La Boheme Guest House

Evelyne Meier

172 Groenpunt Rd, Upington
Tel: 054-338-0660 Fax: 054-338-0661
Email: laboheme@mweb.co.za Web: www.laboheme.co.za
Cell: 083-383-8288

La Boheme claims its rightful place in this book on many counts: its fantastic view from a green, green lawn over the Orange River flood plain; its cool-blue pool; its palm trees that rustle in the hot breeze; and the delightful breakfasts served on the verandah at a communal table or near the cosy fireplace in winter. But all of these things play second fiddle to Evelyne herself, who is hugely friendly and energetic and a wholly exceptional host. A cultural blend herself, half-Hungarian and half-Swiss, her guest house also melds various ethnic styles that mix elegant finishes with artistic touches. There are only four rooms here, guaranteeing the personal touch and each offering something different. I had a trendy-Africa room with a huge bed of sculpted 'decocrete' and its own patch of outside with iron chairs. Next door has a private verandah, but more of a tropical island feel and for those wanting a little more space and a touch of Asia, or a taste of African bush lodge there are two cottages, each with its own kitchenette and private patio or garden surrounded by lush plants and mature trees. I highly recommend you find your way to Upington, which is an Orange River oasis in the middle of the Kalahari Desert. Not many do. The Kgalagadi Transfrontier Park (Kalahari-Gemsbok Park) is just a couple of hours away, Augrabies Falls less than that, and local vineyards and river cruises closer still. *Languages spoken: French, German, Italian, English and Hungarian. Restaurants within 3 to 10 minute drive.*

Rooms: 4: 1 king with en/s bath & sh'r, 1 twin single with sep' bath & sh'r, 2 cottages with kitchenettes: one with queen & en-s sh'r (main bedroom) and twin single with en/s sh'r over bath (adjacent bedroom); one with king and single, en-s sh'r & spa bath.
Price: From R350 pp sharing. Singles from R700. Off-season rates (1 May – 30 Jun) on request.
Meals: Full breakfast (brunch-style) R90 pp. B'fast picnic & other b'fast options on request. Delivery service of take-away meals available. Cottages have s/c facilities and BBQ. Doubles have microwaves and BBQ areas in garden.
Directions: Map on website.

Riviera Garden B&B

Anneke Malan

16 Budler Street, Upington
Tel: 054-332-6554 Fax: 054-332-6554
Email: ariviera@upington.co.za Web: www.upington.co.za/ariviera
Cell: 072-447-6750

Riviera is a true patch of paradise on the banks of the impressive Orange River, a patch it's taken Anneke a lifetime to find. Considering its position in Upington's city centre, it's riverside setting is particularly special. It was the garden, though, that I loved above all, a lush parade of palm trees, roses and agapanthus and racing-green grass that cools even the most overheated of travellers (as I certainly was when I visited). The lawn flows like a tributary past the pool, right to the water's edge and a secluded, white bench at the end of the garden, the perfect spot to sit and contemplate the river's flowing depths. It's from here that guests hop onto a cruise boat at six o'clock for evening river trips, bobbing downstream, washing down the sunset with a G&T before ambling into town for some dinner. The evenings can be as hot as the days in this part of the world and you'll be glad to find the two cool garden rooms hidden among the greenery with their hefty beds and bags of cupboard space for longer stays. Another major draw at Riviera are the scrumptious and beautifully-presented breakfasts. From national parks (Upington is a gateway to the Kalahari Desert and Namibia) to vineyards there's plenty to keep you busy here and it's a must-do stop on any tour of the unspoiled Northern Cape.

Rooms: 2: 1 twin with bath and shower, 1 double with extra single and bath.
Price: R325 pp sharing. Singles on request.
Meals: Full English breakfast R55. Dinner on request.
Directions: Follow main roads right into the centre of Upington. From Schröder St turn onto River St towards the river. This leads into Budler St and Riviera is number 16 on the right about halfway down the street.

A La Fugue

Jacqueline Castella
40 Janggroentjieweg, Upington
Tel: 054-338-0424 Fax: 054-338-0084
Email: a-la-fugue@mweb.co.za Web: www.lafugue-guesthouse.com
Cell: 082-789-9324

Chaud, hot, heiss! Upington was knocking on almost 40°C when I visited, so Jacqueline definitely had the right idea, meeting me at the car in a pink swimming costume and sarong. Positively melting after hours on the road I was invited to flump myself down on a plant-shaded pillow by the pool and was fed a glass of iced tea. What initially struck me about A La Fugue, as I was led along a rose-lined and plant-dotted path, was the tropical garden, absolutely dazzling in the intense sunshine. Named after great composers, each of La Fugue's bungalows has their own unique identity. Rossini and Rusticana, two quaint wooden chalets, seem to originate from the Swiss element of your host, while studio bungalow Mozart and family unit Vivaldi perhaps embody the classic French side. The two B&B rooms in the house (Chopin and Bach), soothing in golds and creams, are found along a short landing where Jacqueline's stunning model daughter beams warmly from the wall. Jacqui's gourmet dinners and breakfasts, touched with a little foreign pizazz, are served outside on one of the bright mosaic tables (your hostess has a distinct flair for mosaics and you will find examples in many unexpected places). It's a good thing that each room has its own outdoor seating area as with such a garden you won't want to sit inside. Personally I would rarely be found far from the thatched African-themed poolside lapa and loungers. *Jacqueline is fluent in French, English and German, by the way.*

Rooms: 5: 2 self-catering studios, 1 self-catering family unit and 2 B&B double rooms. All with en-suite shower and own separate entrances.
Price: R160 to R260 B&B pp sharing. Enquire about singles and self-catering prices.
Meals: Full breakfast included in B&B rate. For self-caterers breakfast-brunch additional R65 pp. Gourmet dinners on request (preferably with 24hrs notice), R220 pp inclusive of all wine and drinks.
Directions: In Upington take Schröder St towards Olifantshoek, N14, under rail bridge past Gordonia hospital. 1.7 km after hospital, turn R at Engen garage. Turn L (Groenpunt Rd). From Bi-Lo (left), count 4 streets on R till Jangtroentjieweg.

Kuilfontein Stable Cottages

Penny and Leigh Southey

Kuilfontein Farm, Route N1, Colesberg
Tel: 051-753-1364 Fax: 051-753-0200
Email: kuil@mweb.co.za Web: www.kuilfontein.co.za
Cell: 082-552-2488

A drink is always welcome in the middle of the blazing Karoo and I was gasping when Penny poured mine in the chilled-out guest lounge. Kuilfontein has been in Leigh's family for five generations and is still a busy dairy and sheep farm. Surrounded by a vast hinterland of arid fields it's hard to believe it's only 1.2 kilometres from the N1. The white-washed Stable bedrooms are all named after race-horses, the theme continuing inside with newspaper clippings and framed shots of 'Danny Boy' or 'Equilateral' (among others) in action. French doors lead from your own verandah onto gleaming screed floors sporting locally-made furniture, as well as the odd family heirloom, while brightly-coloured walls and fine-quality linen create a homely feeling. The 'Feed Room' has been appropriately converted into a dining/breakfast room where resident chef, Maryke, produces tantalising meals from the organic produce on the farm. 'Home-grown' Karoo lamb, venison and fresh cream from the dairy are used in conjunction with cactus fruit and other Karoo specialities. Pre-dinner drinks are taken in the bar with its upside-down trough counter and a great selection of wines are available in an old feed bin. A tall wicker stool is the perfect spot to park yourself for cheerful banter, beverages and hilarity. Coffee and liqueurs are served under the spectacular starry skies. For the more energetic there is a spring-water swimming pool, boules and bird-watching. A popular stop-over point, but this farmstead is worth staying a lot longer for. *Children over 6 are welcome.*

Rooms: 8: 5 standard double bedrooms, 2 luxury double rooms and 1 family suite, all with en-suite showers.
Price: R360 - R490 pp sharing. Singles R60 supplement. Children 6+ on request.
Meals: Full 'health' breakfast included. 3-course dinner R115 - R145.
Directions: 12km south or Colesberg, 60km north of Hanover on N1.

Gauteng

Melrose Place Guest Lodge

Sue Truter
12a North St, Melrose/Johannesburg
Tel: 011-442-5231 Fax: 011-880-2371
Email: melroseplace@global.co.za Web: www.melroseplace.co.za
Cell: 083-457-4021

Once ensconced behind the electric gates at Melrose you have entered an Eden-in-the-city. The verandah overlooks a large flower garden and enormous swimming pool, all shaded by trees. Eight new rooms don't crowd it at all. It is such a pleasant environment that you may find yourself shelving projected tasks for a day's lounging about. My room was a suite attached to the main house, with mounted TV, huge bed (built up with cushions and pillows), a big bathroom and double doors onto the garden. The high levels of luxury in all the rooms are not reflected in the rates. Sue is the sweetest of hostesses, quick to smiles and reacting sensitively to the mood and wishes of each guest. On the night I stayed we had a braai with an amazing array of meat dishes and salads which appeared from nowhere, and Sue's team will cook dinner for anyone who wants it every evening. Her aim is to maximise the number of happy campers staying. This is her home after all, complete with dachshund and a talking parrot in its 40s. While guest contentment is running at 100 per cent, it's difficult to see what else she can do. *Laundry provided on request and internet available. Nearby: Wanderers cricket ground, Rosebank and Sandton shopping precincts and many restaurants. Airport transfers arranged by Sue.*

Rooms: 14: all en-suite (1 bath only, 4 bath and shower, 9 shower only); includes two cottages.
Price: R700 - R800 pp sharing. Singles R950 - R1,100.
Meals: Full breakfast included. Lunches (R50 pp) or dinners (R125 pp) by arrangement.
Directions: Ask for a map when booking. Or a map is on the website.

Maison Bordeaux

Cathy and Ron Veenis

26 Main Street, Bordeaux, Johannesburg
Tel: 082-601-6419
Email: info@maisonbordeaux.co.za Web: www.maisonbordeaux.co.za
Cell: 082-601-6419

Zen in the city. I sat by the pond and fountain, required only to listen to the sound of trickling water that somehow belonged to a land on the other side of the spray. Simply talking to Cathy and Ron is a relaxing experience in its own right. And relaxed was just how I felt after I had polished off an enormous chicken pie, courtesy of the lady next door who runs a catering company, and served by the helpful Les from Malawi. Flopping into bed came close to enjoying a second dessert, where one is rolled in a sumptuous duvet of meringue and whipped cream. Soothing neutral colours and solid wood floors go easy on the digestion and little nods to French elegance appear in the *fleur de lys* motif on the doors of the four rooms that face each other across the intimate plunge pool-courtyard and stoep. In the morning, Margaret (Cathy's mum) serves a wholesome breakfast at your choice of several petite blue tables. Cathy has done a tremendous job of renovating the house since taking over, creating an ambience of effortless ease here in the city. The only hardship was deciding where to put myself: sunning beneath the huge lavender tree, idling in a private rock garden, dipping toes into the pond, or simply sitting in my room with the shutters thrown wide open, picking from the fruit basket and listening to the birds singing. Formidable!

Rooms: 4 rooms: 2 kings with full en-suite and 2 twins with shower en-suite.
Price: Double occupancy: R342 pp. Single occupancy: R398. (All prices include VAT.)
Meals: Full breakfast included. Lunch and dinner on request.
Directions: Take William Nichol Drive exit from N1, eventually turning right onto Republic Road. Drive for 0.5km and then turn left into Main Street. Maison Bordeaux is 400m on the left.

Liz at Lancaster

Liz Delmont

79 Lancaster Ave, Craighall Park, Johannesburg
Tel: 011-442-8083 Fax: 011-880-5969
Email: lizdel@megaweb.co.za Web: www.lizatlancaster.co.za
Cell: 083-229-4223

Liz's place on its own is our idea of a B&B (more on that later), but throw in Liz as well and you get something special. In my limited experience she is an anomaly among South Africans, having no great interest in rugby, football or cricket, and this despite being surrounded by a sports-mad family. Liz taught art history and post-graduate tourism development at Witwatersrand University for over 20 years, and is a fascinating person to speak to about South Africa both past and future... and about Jo'burg. She will point you in all the right directions for a genuine, heartfelt and hard-to-come-by insight into her home city. But guests at Liz's also have plenty of space in which to do their own thing. The big, comfy rooms are either side of the main house, with their own entrances and parking spaces and now come kitted-out with internet access and satellite TV. Two more have been added since our last book; that is to say, Liz has given over even more of her home to her guests. Two separate cottages have their own kitchen and sitting room. They all open up onto their own private patios, where breakfast is generally served, with potted plants climbing up the walls and plenty of shade. Between them is a rose-filled garden, while at the front of the house is yet more green space around the pool. Finally, a mention for the friendly staff, who have a stake in the venture.

Rooms: 5: 3 doubles (2 with kitchens) with en/s bath and shower, plus 2 cottages with kitchen and sitting room.
Price: R325 - R400 pp sharing. Singles R550 - R700.
Meals: Full breakfast included. Dinners on request but very close to Rosebank and Parkhurst and many restaurants.
Directions: Jan Smuts Ave runs down the middle of the city and Lancaster Ave is off it. Directions on website.

Idwala Guest House

Judith Friese
13 Garrick Road, Darrenwood, Johannesburg
Tel: 011-888-1437 Fax: 011-888-1402
Email: info@idwala.com Web: www.idwala.com
Cell: 082-865-0327

Johannesburg has one of the highest concentrations of trees of any city in the world. Certainly the fabulous purple blossom of the jacaranda blessed the drive to this miniature village in the heart of the city. The main house was built a hundred years ago when Jo'burg looked very different, but I was still astonished by views of green hills as I climbed through layers of garden, up to a tranquil lawn fringed by exuberant beds of roses, daisies, chives (for the eggs) and rosemary (for the pillows). Stepping into the first circle of the central lodge, I could see how breakfast and meals are served, drenched in sunlight when the windows disappear and serenaded by water trickling into the plunge-pool. The inner sanctum is a lounge big enough for family gatherings and backed by a fireplace inlaid with myriad cut stones. During the day the scent of fresh flowers wafts through, while at night the candles smoke and flicker in their glass bulbs. A circular passage connects all the rondavel rooms, whose proportions, beds and leather couches are universally large and luxurious. Bonus features include an elephant-framed mirror, under-floor heating, tall African lampshades, flat-screen TVs and bathrooms chiselled from the native Idwala rock itself. Judith knows what travellers want. "It's easy to make people happy if you just listen to them," she says as she shows me around the two neatly self-contained cottages, Protea and Olive, ideal for longer stays. Twenty-five percent return guests is her favourite compliment.

Rooms: 7 units: 3 rooms in the main house, 2 garden cottages, 2 garden rooms all variously king or king/twin with full en-suite or shower bathrooms. Cottages have sleeper couches too.
Price: R650 - R700 pp sharing. Singles R950 - R1,000.
Meals: Full breakfast included. Lunch and dinner on request. (3 courses from R180 pp).
Directions: Turn right off Republic Road into Blanche Road and Idwala is on the intersection with Garrick Road.

Random Harvest Country Cottages

Linda De Luca and John Chauke

College Rd, Off Beyers Naude Drive, Muldersdrift, Mogale City
Tel: 086-1476-9464 Fax: 086-644-9552
Email: khensan@telkomsa.net/cottages@rhn.co.za Web: www.rhn.co.za
Cell: 082-927-3717

"I would make an ideal dictator...," Linda worryingly confessed shortly after I had crept through the gates and into this Narnia of saplings and shoots, "...of the environment that is," she thankfully added. There's clearly no room for democracy in Linda's world when it comes to saving the nation's plants. This self-confessed nature addict set up the Random Harvest indigenous nursery, the first of its kind, 16 years ago. Back then everyone said she was mad, but now people flock from miles around to pick up their fashionable fynbos. "I think I preferred it when I was mad," chuckles Linda. This 50-odd-acre site is a world away from the city it sits in. Paths battle with plants over rights of way and, key in hand, I navigated my way through a sea of green, winding past rondavels of chickens before tasting 'Yellowwood', my cottage for the night. It's a cosy little thatched affair with everything you could possibly want (huge bed, snug living room, secluded patio) and more besides, including a bottle of the freshest farm milk - the cows that produced it munch in a field around the corner. Sitting on my lawn surrounded by plants (indigenous only, of course), staring at the stars and listening to the frogs, it was hard to believe that I was in Africa's largest city.

Rooms: 8: all 1-bed cottages with showers, some have baths. 6 have self-catering option.
Price: R350 - R380 pp sharing or singles.
Meals: Full breakfast included. Dinners and braai packs on request from R50 - R100. Many restaurants nearby.
Directions: Directions can be faxed or emailed on booking.

Kiasoma Retreat & Bush Spa

Darlene Smith
D16 De Tweedespruit Conservancy, Near Cullinan
Tel: 012-734-2650 Fax: 012-734-2650
Email: kiasoma@telkomsa.net Web: www.kiasoma.co.za

The term 'retreat' doesn't go far enough. Come and surrender yourself physically and spiritually to a course that begins with aromatherapy, manicures and pedicures, continues onto reiki treatments and sweat lodges with firestone keepers, and culminates in a 'vision quest' with only water and the spirit world for company. Of course you may wish to splurge more than purge on lunch by the pool, followed by a massage in the tower and finally dinner in the lodge or boma, courtesy of the in-house chef. There are strong Native American accents to this ranch-style setting that spreads over an area supplied by a huge vegetable garden, bristling with tightly-canopied corkbush trees and hemmed in by clay cliffs as red as the dust I drove on to get here. Accommodation ranges from the rustic comfort of the stone cottage where wood-smoke-smelling Persian rugs have been unravelled over weathered tiled floors, to the low reed ceilings of the converted horse stables, to thick canvas teepees where everyone sleeps amazingly well. Everything has been designed to blend in with nature, but my favourite were the outdoor therapy 'rounders', circular stone structures open to the sky, one with a huge Moroccan-style bath and candle alcoves chiselled into the walls. Incredibly, Darlene, creator of this alternative paradise, is also a Johannesburg businesswoman. Such conundrums I considered as I shuffled around the meditation labyrinth towards the statue of a woman dressed in moons and stars, her arms outstretched to the heavens. Come at full moon.

Rooms: 7 units: 2 cottages sleeping 2 and 3, 1 dormitory lodge in the boma, 4 stable rooms sleeping 2 each. All have en-suite showers except for the lodge which has two shared outdoor showers.
Price: Cottages: R455 pp sh; stable rooms: R315 pp sh B&B; boma: R155 pp sh. Singles on request.
Meals: Breakfast included with the stable rooms. Cottages and boma are self-catering. Lunch and dinner on request.
Directions: 20 minutes from Cullinan, east of Pretoria on the R513. Call or see website for detailed directions.

Soweto

"Lots of tourists come for the day, but more should stay the night." If you really want to get under Soweto's skin, then staying over is a must. It is still advisable to leave the car in Jo'burg and hop onto a township tour. Apart from anything, Soweto is a labyrinthine 50 square miles, crammed with an unofficial total of four million people, so getting lost is a distinct possibility. Your tour guide can drop you off at the guest-house and arrange transport to one of the funky local restaurants where extensive wine lists sit comfortably alongside samp n'beans, mutton curry and other Sowetan favourites. I went with Vhupo Tours' David Luthaga, a friendly bear of a man with a laugh that could shake Soweto's infamous power station. "You will see all of Soweto. The good, the bad and the very ugly, nothing will be hidden," was his opening gambit. And, true to his word, David showed us Diepkloof Extension, the millionaire's row also known as Diepkloof Expensive. He then handed us over to Reginald who walked with us around the squatter camp Motsoaldi, a patchwork of corrugated iron and wooden planks that he calls home. David emphasised that wherever we were, especially in the squatter camps, the inhabitants expected us to take photos so that people worldwide could witness their living conditions. This attitude stems from pre-apartheid days, when images from the Sowetan uprising of 1976 galvanised worldwide outcry, and it put paid to any concerns that I had over voyeurism.

Vhupo Tours
David Luthaga,
www.vhupo-tours.com
maavbd@myconnection.co.za
011-936-0411

For more information go to: www.sowetobedandbreakfast.co.za. Or look out for the Soweto Township Complete Guide, published by Soweto Spaza and sold in the shop outside Nelson Mandela's former house on Vilakazi St.

Vhavenda Hills B&B

Kate Luthaga

11749 Mampuru St, Soweto
Tel: 011-936-4275 Fax: 011-936-0411
Email: maavbb@myconnection.co.za
www.sowetobedandbreakfast.co.za
Cell: 082-213-1630

Soweto born and bred, Kate lives down the road from Nelson Mandela's old house. The great man himself popped round for tea after his release from Robben Island. This is very much a family home with pictures of Kate's children around the TV and friends of various offspring popping in and out. The bedrooms are comfortable with magnolia walls and multi-coloured coverlets. Ask for the palatial double room with its bath on a plinth and king-size bed where I fell asleep to the sound of cicadas and the buzz of Jo'burg traffic in the far distance, before waking to the smell of sizzling bacon.

Rooms: 4: 1 twin with en/s bath and seperate loo, 1 twin with en/s bath, 1 king size double with en/s bath and shower, 1 double with en/s shower and seperate loo.
Price: R250 pp sharing.
Meals: Cooked breakfast, plus yoghurt and cereal.
Directions: Arrange a pick-up from Jo'burg.

Dakalo B&B

Dolly Hlophe

6963 Inhlwathi St, Soweto
Tel: 011-936-9328
Web: www.sowetobedandbreakfast.co.za
Cell: 082-723-0585

The term 'township chic' was invented for Dolly's B&B. I loved the bathroom tiled with blue-spotted mosaics and the rooms with their red quilts, mini-Zulu shields, strawberry table-cloths and zebra print curtains, hand-made by Dolly. Not only is she a wizard on the sewing-machine, but she is also heavily involved with the local tourism association, setting a high standard with her own guesthouse. With opera playing in the background and freshly-cut arum lilies on the front table, the house exudes calm. Outside guests can sit under the lapa, or admire Dolly's garden, where geraniums sprout from potjie cooking pots and pink bougainvillaea crawls up the walls. You are right in the heart of where history was made in Soweto, particularly when Dolly can count Nelson Mandela and Desmond Tutu amongst her neighbours.

Rooms: 4: 3 twins, 1 double all en/s.
Price: R250 - R280 pp sh. R350 singles.
Meals: Full cooked and cold breakfast. Evening meals on request for R65.
Directions: Arrange pick-up in Jo'burg.

Entry Number: 296

Nthateng's B&B

Nthateng Motaung

6991 Inhlwathi St, Soweto
Tel: 011-936-2676
Email: dietsiso@polka.co.za
Cell: 082-335-7956

Nthateng seems far too glamorous to be an ex-driving instructor. Snappily dressed in tight jeans and gold jewellery, she showed me around her guesthouse at breakneck speed. Optical lighting illuminates the up-to-the-minute sandy-coloured rooms that boast carved wooden bedheads inlaid with red and gold mosaics. One double room also houses a vast Louis XIV-style dressing table; it's not hard to imagine Marie Antoinette perched on the ornate seat, powdering her wig and applying beauty spots.

Rooms: 4: 2 twins, 2 queens all en/s.
Price: R250 pp sharing. R350 for singles.
Meals: Full cooked breakfast in included. Evening meals available on request for R55.
Directions: Arrange a pick-up in Jo'burg.

Entry Number: 297

North West Province

Hideaway at the Farm

Mike and Sabine Manegold

Pelindaba Road 10, Broederstroom, Hartbeespoort
Tel: 083-476-0507 Fax: 012-205-1309
Email: info@hideawayatthefarm.com Web: www.hideawayatthefarm.com
Cell: 083-476-0507

I couldn't imagine a less contrived and more relaxing place. Mike is a laid-back nurturing soul (and reformed advertising executive) with a real commitment to and passion for South Africa and this spirit reigns at the farm. With views to the Hartbeespoort Dam and magical Magaliesberg - Johannesburg's playground and natural magnets for water-sport and hiking enthusiasts - the farm consists of a four-bedroom farmhouse, the best of which boasts large, sliding glass doors leading on to the pool. Across the drive are the rondavels: slate floors, fleshy walls and towering, thatched ceilings. Though the farm no longer yields any produce, it "farms people" instead. Charming Benjamin runs the place whilst Chef Michael and assistant Deliwe, renowned for culinary wizardry, cook up homely Swiss/African fare in the open-walled restaurant below. This is a truly memorable spot to dine, with its live jazz events, cavernous fireplace and billowing cloth-panelled walls. When it's not open - trust me, go once and you'll go every night - all rooms have cooking facilities and there's also the braai area marked out by Sabine's dream symbols. But for me, the real reason to come to the farm is because it is filled with the optimism of the new South Africa. Swiss-born Mike has a wealth of knowledge about his adopted country but to listen to Benjamin's balanced tales of the Apartheid years is to witness the new hope for South Africa first-hand. An enriching experience.

Rooms: 5: in farmhouse: 3 doubles, all rooms are separate with en-s showers and private terraces; 2 rondavels, each with double and en-s bath/shower.
Price: R225 - R375 pp sharing self-catering. Singles on request. Weekly and monthly rates available.
Meals: Self-catering. African-Swiss restaurant on site (traditional Swiss food) for other meals and a good number of restaurants within a ten-minute drive.
Directions: From Johannesburg follow signs to Randburg and N1 heading north-west. Take R512 past Lanseria Airport toward Hartbeespoort Dam. At T-junction turn left and the farm is signed on the left.

Jaci's Tree Lodge

Jan and Jaci van Heteren

Madikwe Game Reserve, Molatedi
Tel: 014-778-9900 Fax: 014-778-9901
Email: jaci@madikwe.com Web: www.madikwe.com
Cell: 083-447-7929, reservations 083-700-2071

What a game drive! Lions on the hunt scattered by a charging elephant right in front of our vehicle! We're still abuzz when we return to our already-run baths and chat animatedly around the boma fire at dinner. Jaci's has this effect on you. Wonderfully indulgent, this is one of Tatler's favourites. Beyond the foyer's tree-pierced, blonde-thatch roof lies an expansive restaurant overlooking riverine forest and separated from the chic bar by a four-sided open fire, which together keep you in long cocktails and gourmet food. Relax the excess off in a hammock; alternatively there's a pool and gym. Save your gasps of delight for the treehouses. Sitting six metres above ground and linked by a rosewood walkway, their glass doors concertina open onto private decks. Vibrant colours form a backdrop for a bed festooned with silk cushions, burnt-orange suede beanbag and swollen stone bath with hand-made copper pipes. But Jaci's trump card is the rangers, whose enthusiasm creates a wonderful, wild adventure. What a job they have - daily taking breath away. Further along the river bank you'll find Jaci's Safari Lodge, opulent canvas and stone suites. The Safari Lodge is ideal for romantic safaris and children of all ages are welcome and specially catered for. Jaci's is owned and managed by Jaci and Jan and all staff members share a 25% stakeholding in the company, both of which facts make for fantastically caring service from all concerned.

Rooms: 8 tree-houses, each with king-size bed and bath and outdoor 'jungle' shower.
Price: R1,995 – R3,795 pp sharing. Game drives, walking safaris, sundowner drink and meals included.
Meals: All meals and game drives included.
Directions: Only 1.5 hours' drive from Sun City or a 3.5 to 4-hour drive from Johannesburg. Daily road and air transfers from JHB and Sun City. Ask for details when booking.

Mosetlha Bush Camp

Chris, June and Caroline Lucas
Madikwe Game Reserve
Tel: 011-444-9345
Fax: 011-444-9345
Email:info@thebushcamp.com
Web: www.thebushcamp.com
Cell: 083-653-9869

Mosetlha puts the wild into wilderness; no doors or glass here as they would hinder the feel and dust of Africa permeating your very core; no worries either as you leave them at the gate. Facilities are basic but real; guests draw their own hot water from a donkey-boiler before proceeding to the shower. Recently the kitchen was extended and a new thatch and stone lapa has been added for guests to read, relax and compare sightings, but the authenticity remains untainted. The wooden cabins are comfortable, but used only for sleeping - you are here for the wilderness experience of the outdoors. Chris's passion for conservation and his environment shines through and is contagious (which reminds me to say that the area is malaria-free). His guests depart much the wiser, not only because of the game drives, but also (conditions permitting) because of the superb guided wilderness walks. Yes, the Madikwe Game Reserve (70,000 hectares) has the so-called 'Big Five', but a game lodge worth its salt (such as this) will fire your imagination about the whole food chain. Even the camp itself is an education - all sorts of birds, small mammals and antelopes venture in. Come for a genuine and memorable bush experience. *Children welcome from 8 years old up.*

Rooms: 8 twins sharing 3 shower/toilet complexes.
Price: All-inclusive from R1,250 per person. Park levies and drinks from the bar extra.
Meals: All meals and refreshments (tea, coffee, fruit juice) included.
Directions: Detailed written directions supplied on request or see website.

Makanyane Safari Lodge

Richard Robberts
Madikwe Game Reserve
Tel: 014-778-9600
Email: enquiries@makanyane.com Web: www.makanyane.com

Makanyane Lodge, built into the forest and overlooking the Marico River, offers untrammelled luxury in an exciting wilderness environment. When I arrived, Garth, the lodge manager, had been busy chasing away elephants. "They're everywhere," he sighed as if he had a mole problem on the front lawn. As I walked to my room, I could see what he meant – trees and aloes had been flattened by the free-roaming pachyderms. My pulse quickened again when I opened the door to my room... I confess I even felt myself swoon a little! This is one good-looking game lodge, with its soft white fabrics and huge floor-to-ceiling windows. I resisted the urge to pop the cork on the champagne in the mini-fridge and instead pulled up the lounger on my private decking that overlooked the watering hole. Kudu, impala and wildebeest provided lazy afternoon viewing before the sun went down and a night guard came to walk me to dinner. One sumptuous three-course dinner later and I was safely back in my glamorous room, listening to two bull elephants fighting in the water. No way were the curtains going to get drawn tonight. Daytime activities are based around exploring the Madikwe Reserve on foot or in a game vehicle (the lodge has 1,800 hectares of private land within the 75,000 of the entire reserve), but back at the lodge there is a beautiful swimming pool area and even a spa and gym. *No children under 12.*

Rooms: 8 doubles, all with en-suite bath, shower and outdoor shower.
Price: From R4,000 - R5,000 pp sharing.
Meals: Includes all drinks, meals and game drives.
Directions: Federal Air Flight from Johannesburg to Madikwe runs daily. For other detailed directions see website.

Buffalo Ridge

Kate Naughton
Madikwe Game Reserve
Tel: 011-805-9995 Fax: 011-805-0687
Email: reservations@buffaloridgesafari.com
Web: www.buffaloridgesafari.com

At the entrance I negotiated my way past a nervy-looking wildebeest and soon found myself up on the elevated lounge area at Buffalo Ridge Lodge, enjoying tea and biscuits. Whilst I got my bearings and chatted to my hosts I could hear the chuntering of a band of baboons somewhere in the near vicinity… which added a bit of tone to my arrival. Up here the peace is more peaceful and the quiet is quieter (apart from such things as baboons, of course) and guests will soon find themselves synchronising their metabolic rate to that of the surrounding bush. The lodge has been built on the Tweedepoort Ridge overlooking the plains of the Madikwe Game Reserve and is perfectly placed for game-viewing. Wooden flooring, soft sofas, stacks of wildlife books and rock figs adorn the lower deck area, while there's an infinity pool on the upper deck which looks regally out over the mountains. And it's not just the setting that is so special. Buffalo Ridge is the first lodge in Madikwe wholly owned by a local rural community and black-and-white photos of the chief (who is involved in the project) hang on bedroom walls. Each suite - in natural colours, soft textures and with huge sliding glass doors - is sunrise-facing. At night, if you don't feel like walking to the dining area or boma, you can order up a private four-course dinner on your deck with the distant lights from Botswana as backdrop. I could hear the sound of singing as I left and I swore to return whenever I could.

Rooms: 8 doubles, all with en-suite shower.
Price: From R1,995 pp sharing.
Meals: All meals and safari activities included.
Directions: Map provided on booking.

Thakadu River Lodge

Claudia Dal Bianco
Madikwe Game Reserve
Tel: 011-805-9995 Fax: 011-805-0687
Email: reservations@thakadurivercamp.com
Web: www.thakadurivercamp.com

Surrounded by forest and built on high ground in the fork between the Marico River and one of its tributaries, Thakadu has the perfect vantage from which to look down on the many animals that make use of the water below. This is a natural paradise and all effort has been made for the lodge to jar as little as possible with its surroundings. To this end: wooden floors, rattan furniture, bare stone walls, bamboo lights and lanterns decorating the boma, poles supporting lofty thatched roofs, carved wooden doors… natural fibres and construction materials at every turn. The lodge also makes much of its high position and wonderful views by leaving a huge open wall in the lounge area and by perching its pool and bar on the edge of the gully with fab views down river. Thakadu is also fenced and so particularly child-friendly. Kids can learn bush craft and take a course in 'spoor-ology'. "We show children how to identify animal droppings… and they love it!" John D explained. They even run special game drives for the under 6s. John D is not only a wildlife expert, but he can also fill you in on Madikwe's history. To digest all this new-found knowledge, head to the infinity pool and soak up the views, book a massage or simply relax under the tented canopy of your own gorgeous private suite. Each has its own deck overlooking the river below. Decision-making was never such a pleasure. The lodge, by the way, is owned by the local community, and there are framed pictures of the Molatedi people hanging everywhere.

Rooms: 12 tents: 8 doubles and 4 family units with doubles and extra sleeper couch. All with en-suite bath and shower.
Price: From R1,995 pp sharing.
Meals: Breakfast, dinner, high tea and game activities included.
Directions: See website for detailed directions.

The Bush House

Sue and Gordon Morrison

Madikwe Game Reserve
Tel: 018-365-9011
Email: camp@bushhouse.co.za Web: www.bushhouse.co.za
Cell: 083-379-6912

Sue and her husband Gordon stayed at The Bush House as guests in 2006 and decided they didn't want to leave… so they bought the place! Since then they have turned the lodge into a home-from-home – quite a rarity out in the bush these days - with many little touches creating a warm family atmosphere. There's a TV in the reading area - "for sporting events only!" Ezelle tells me - and the bedrooms come complete with birdseed, "so that guests can feed the birds from their private patios." Dining is also a relaxed affair, with everyone eating together at the long outdoor table or in the boma. Then, of course, there is the wildlife. The colourful garden and plunge pool look out over a watering-hole. When I arrived several guests had pulled up loungers under the jacaranda tree and had cameras poised. A lioness and her cub had been drinking at the hole the night before so we all hoped for more of the same. But our patience was only rewarded with the appearance of a few mischievous baboons. Guests can retreat to the cool lounge and leaf through one of the many David Attenborough books, indulge in some high tea (delicious milk tart and meringue), or head to the beauty salon. One manicure and pedicure later and I was ready for an evening game drive – I'd never felt so glamorous out in the bush before.

Rooms: 6: 2 double, 4 twins all with en-suite bath and shower.
Price: From R1,755 pp sharing.
Meals: All meals included plus two game drives a day.
Directions: From Pretoria take N4 to Zeerust, then R49 towards Madikwe. At Madikwe turn right at the Wonderboom Gate, The Bush House is signposted 1 km from entrance. Federal Air Flight also flies to the reserve daily.

Tuningi Safari Lodge

Heidi Janson

Madikwe Game Reserve
Tel: 011-315-6194 Fax: 011-805-0687
Email: res@tuningi.co.za Web: www.tuningi.co.za

I wish I was back at Tuningi now, lying by the pool beneath the protective arms of a huge fig tree with a cool fruit cocktail in hand, watching - and being watched by - a 'dazzle' of grazing zebra. "Colonial African chic" is how they describe themselves here and I won't argue with that. There are porcupine quills on lamps, deeply comfortable wicker chairs in the open-plan lounge area and the lantern-edged, fire-centred boma is found at the end of a sweep of wooden decking. The dramatic centrepiece of each bedroom is, fittingly, a huge bed, with miniature bottles of amarula lying temptingly at its foot. There are Molton Brown toiletries by the washbasin, a huge tub, ceiling fans, air-con… and an enormous outdoor rock shower that I just had to try out. (The wildebeest and impala grazing just metres from my soapy feet were also hard to ignore.) As evening fell, so too a few drops of rain, but immediately there was someone at my door proffering an umbrella to take up to dinner. This sort of thoughtful service is typical. And what a dinner!... smoked fish, boerewors, lamb chops, the selection seemed endless. Long tables make for a convivial affair and the lodge rangers join in with that day's sightings and plans for the morrow. Finally I was drawn, along with the other guests, to the adjoining wooden bar for a nightcap… until I could resist the lure of my wonderful bed no longer. Tuningi prides itself on its ability to make guests feel part of the family… and the hospitality really does feel unconditional here.

Rooms: 8: 4 double rooms with en-suite bath and outdoor shower; 2 family units each with 2 double rooms, kitchen, dining room, en-suite bath and shower. One unit has a private pool.
Price: From R3,250 pp sharing.
Meals: Includes all meals and game drives.
Directions: See website for detailed directions.

Mpumalanga

Trees Too

Sue and Martyn Steele

Komatipoort
Tel: 013-793-8262
Email: info@treestoo.com Web: www.treestoo.com
Cell: 083-654-1778

Sue and Martyn are relatively new to this B&B malarkey. Originally from old Blighty, they clearly love their new life in Komatipoort. The "wildlife mad" couple wanted to be near animals, and you'd be hard pressed to get much closer than this. A short drive from the Kruger National Park, Trees Too is ideal for less-exalted budgets that don't quite stretch to the top-end lodges in the park itself. With its kidney-shaped pool, draped with lush palms and crawling bougainvillaea, Trees Too's atmosphere is more tropical beach than arid savannah. It's unsurprising really, when you consider that Maputo - Mozambique's steaming capital - is only a couple of hours away. After a sticky day's game drive, grab a cool sundowner from the bar and submerge yourself in the pool before sitting down at the friendly poolside restaurant. It wasn't long before I found myself happily swapping stories with the other diners while tucking into a succulent fillet steak followed by delicious cheesecake pudding. With a storm brewing it was only a short skip to bed - terracotta flooring, a soaring thatched roof and comfortable, air-conditioning thankfully keep things cool in the forty degree heat of summer. The family room is my favourite with its gramophone shipped from the UK, plus piles of wildlife magazines and board games. If you manage to tear yourself from the pool and badminton court and tire of SA's biggest game park, then Sue and Martyn have plenty of ideas up their sleeves: elephant-back safaris anyone?

Rooms: 8: 3 doubles, with en/s shower; 2 triple rooms with a double plus 1 single, with en/s bath and shower; 1 twin, with en/s bath/shower; 2 family rooms (one sleeping 4 and one sleeping 6, 1 with 4-poster bed), 1 with shower and 1 with bath/shower.
Price: R240 - R300 pp sharing.
Meals: Breakfast is a cold buffet with cheeses and cereals, plus a full English. Dinner available from small but interesting menu at restaurant.
Directions: Take N4 from Jo'burg. On reaching Komatipoort, turn L at R571 into Rissik St, go 4km thro 2 stop signs then R into Gilfillan St. Take first R into Furley St. Trees Too is No. 11 on L.

Numbela Exclusive Riverside Accommodation

Paul and Tracy Nepgen
White River
Tel: 013-751-3356 Fax: 013-751-1380
Email: relax@numbela.co.za Web: www.numbela.co.za
Cell: 084-491-2708

I happened upon Numbela by chance on a day off and got lucky. Upon arrival I was met by a happy group of guests bringing the remnants of a picnic up from the river beach, and was soon joining them on the sandy bank for a drink. Just outside White River, the lodge is on a 200-acre wet-and-woodland wonderland that teems with birdlife and which you are free to explore. Two cottages are separated by a converted mill-house. One has a raised stoep with a swing-seat piled with pillows and the interior is all about flair. The main room is enlivened by earthy red and orange paint-work, the bedroom is dressed with blushing fabrics and the washed-blue bathroom comes with an outdoor shower. The smaller, thatched cottage near the river has chalky walls and claret-coloured floor with high ceilings, an Oregon pine kitchen, stable doors and an open fire. The bedroom is decorated with African artefacts, their origins explained in a thoughtful pamphlet. There's a welcome attention to detail, from the faultless design to the delicious breakfast delivered to my patio. Paul and Tracy, your hosts, are there to make you feel very welcome and are currently constructing a network of mountain-biking and forest trails on their adjacent working farm. *Close to Casterbridge Farm shops and restaurants, golf courses and the Kruger Park gates. Children are welcome, though under 12s by prior arrangement.*

Rooms: 3: 2 self-catering/B&B cottages, 1 double with en-suite shower plus mezzanine single, 1 double & twin with en-suite bath and outdoor shower; 1 self-catering cottage with 4 twin bedrooms with en-suite showers, 1 private bath.
Price: B&B: from R400 pp sharing. Self-catering: from R700 for 2 people, R1,500 - R2,000 for 4. Singles on request.
Meals: Full breakfast included in B&B rate. Kitchen stocked with essentials.
Directions: 20km north of White River on the R40 Hazyview road. The oval sign is clearly visible on the left. Turn left and follow the signs down a dirt road for approximately 1km to the gate.

Paperbark Bush Retreat

Bill and Carol Fox
Lydenburg
Tel: 079-354-8538
Email: will@wcjfox.com Web: www.paperbarkretreat.com
Cell: 079-354-8538

Bill Fox is obsessed with leopards. "They're just such fascinating creatures," he tells me as I sip tea out on the stoep. His wife Carol is also an avid wildlife conservationist and both worked on Leopard Research with the Mpumalanga Parks Board before taking over the helm at Paperbark Bush Retreat. And a royal retreat it is too. Hidden among the indigenous forest at the foothill of the Leutla Mountain, Paperbark is chic, comfortable and, best of all, eco-friendly with electricity generated by solar power and river water re-routed for irrigation. There are also free-roaming leopards on the estate plus other resident game, waterfalls, mountain streams and pools. Rooms are wonderfully fashioned with African artefacts, locally-made furniture, soft fabrics and warm tones; sweet-smelling hand-made soap is also a welcome touch in the gleaming bathrooms. All cottages face onto a neat lawn, at the centre of which stands the retreat's namesake, quietly attracting a wonderful variety of colourful birds. Bushwalks, night drives and river bathing are just some of the activities on offer, although the natural, unspoilt beauty of the place and stylish, luxurious comfort also allow for some serious R&R. Bill and Carol also ensure your comfort serving up sumptuous three-course dinners using only the freshest ingredients, and presenting them out on the lapa under the stars. Delicious.

Rooms: 4: 3 cottages, one with 1 double and 1 twin, shower and kitchenette; 2 twins with en-suite bath and shower. Main house: 2 twins with shared shower.
Price: From R850 pp sharing.
Meals: Full breakfast and 3-course dinner included.
Directions: Pick up available from Johannesburg or Nelspruit airport. Or see website for detailed directions.

Plumbago Guest House

Ilara and Robbie Robertson
R40 between White River and Hazyview
Tel: 013-737-8806 Fax: 086-607-5222
Email: plumbagoguesthouse@mweb.co.za
Web: www.plumbagoguesthouse.co.za Cell: 082-954-0467

Through wrought-iron gates at the end of a bougainvillaea-lined drive I found Plumbago, as pretty as the flower that shares its name. Set on an avocado and banana farm, it sits above the plantation watching over it and out to Kruger Park in the distance. When I arrived, 1940s jazz was swinging out from the radio, just the right aural accompaniment to the nostalgic, colonial-inspired setting. In the drawing room and bar, an eclectic collection of antiques, paintings and rugs are interspersed with vases filled with exotic flowers and extravagant palm-leaf fans that stretch up to the ceiling. The rooms have the same casual gracefulness about them with their subtle, natural tones, Jacobean print curtains, mahogany beds and abundance of vased and water-coloured flowers. With a large lived-in verandah, elegant pool and sauna in the beautifully tended garden there's plenty of opportunity to relax and mull over days gone by, particularly in Robbie's history-reading section in the tennis court's viewing lapa. But what really makes this place stand apart are the Robertsons themselves. On my visit, Ilara (who honed her culinary skills cooking for diplomats) was deciding on that evening's dinner menu while Robbie, who has his own construction company by day, was itching to go micro-lighting (you can go too) before being back for waitering duty later on. A young and active bunch, they are often busying about doing their own thing but are more than happy to share their passions with you. *20 mins to Kruger and close to Panorama Route and God's Window. Baby-sitting service available.*

Rooms: 3 garden chalets: 1 king/twin with en-s shower; 1 king with en-s shower; 1 king extra-length sleigh-bed en-s shower & bath. All rooms air-con.
Price: R580 pp sharing. Singles +R150. Extra beds for families sharing R250. Pets & kids by arrangement.
Meals: Full breakfast included. Lunch & dinner on request.
Directions: From Jo'burg, take N4 to Nelspruit and then on to White River. Go on R40 to Hazyview, Plumbago is signposted on right 34km out of White River and 10km before Hazyview. 4hrs from Jo'burg.

Rissington Inn

Chris Harvie

Hazyview
Tel: 013-737-7700 Fax: 013-737-7112
Email: info@rissington.co.za Web: www.rissington.co.za
Cell: 082-327-6842

Informality and relaxation dictate at the Rissington Inn; you feel this even as you mount the broad steps to the verandah for the first time. Sun-lounging guests dazily contemplate the flower gardens full of frangipani; the swimming pool is a rectangle of cool aquamarine; the hazy valley shimmers beyond. In the evenings, gourmet, incredibly good-value candlelit dinners are served by friendly staff. We have eaten with Chris on four separate occasions and never been disappointed, despite much creativity and daring in the dishes. High ceilings put the lid on well-designed rooms. The one I had was enormous with a Victorian bathroom and its own sitting area. But Rissington isn't the sort of place where you feel like hiding away or watching TV. Owner/mover/shaker Chris actually seems to LIKE seeing his guests doing what they want, dressed how they feel and making friends. When you arrive there is usually a gaggle of guests lined up at his wooden bar and you could easily mistake them for Chris's personal friends. They probably only arrived a few minutes before you. *Hazyview sits at the portals of the Kruger National Park.*

Rooms: 16: 2 queens, 3 with 2 queen beds, 3 queens with an extra single, 6 king/twins, all en-suite bathrooms. Garden rooms have outside showers. 2 hillside suits, both doubles with en-suite bath and shower and shared private pool.
Price: R370 - R740 pp sharing.
Meals: Full breakfast included and served till noon. Restaurant on-site for à la carte lunch and dinner.
Directions: 2km south of Hazyview on R40 White River Numbi Gate (KNP) Rd. On right coming from main Hazyview 4-way stop - see signs for Rissington and Kiaat Park.

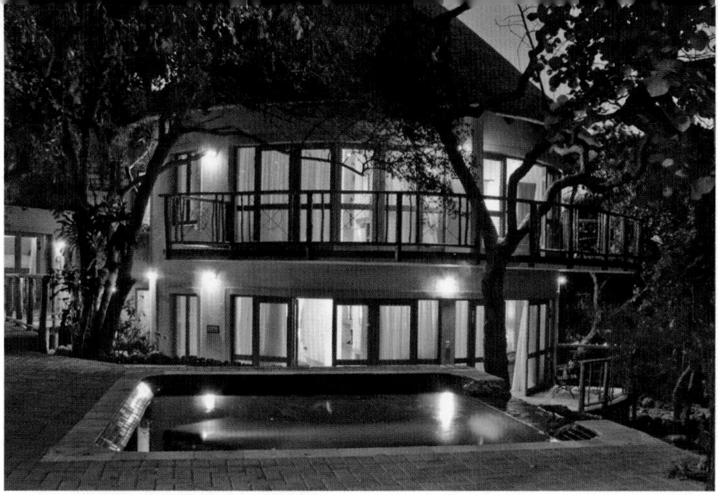

Blue Jay Lodge

Philip and Margi Nichols
645 - 647 Blue Jay Lane, Hazyview
Tel: 013-737-7546
Email: phil@bluejaylodge.co.za Web: www.bluejaylodge.co.za
Cell: 082-575-1798

I would have been happy plonked in a hippo wallow on such a hot and humid day, but Blue Jay Lodge, a cool oasis hidden among lush, indigenous forest, was so much better! I had found my very own tropical hideaway. Sensing my heat fatigue Phil showed me to my room, switched on the air-con and invited me to take a chilled drink from the mini-fridge. A new calmness prevailed and I was now able to take in the white drapes, the tiled floor, the huge bed and high thatched roof of my room. Guests can do as little or as much as they want at Blue Jay: take a 'microflight' over the Sabie River valley, enjoy the nearby quad bike trails or pop into the Kruger Park (10 minutes away). While the other guests headed off for a spot of river rafting, I took the 'little' rather than 'much' option and strolled down to the pool… where I managed to wangle myself an invite to join Phil and his family for lamb chops and boerewors on the braai. The Nichols are wonderful hosts and I slept particularly well that night. I was dragged back to consciousness by the irresistible smells of a cooked breakfast with my name on it. Sitting on the verandah, lingering over a second cup of coffee, I watched an African paradise fly-catcher ducking and diving between the leaves. With more than 80 bird species on offer you could easily forget the day's activity and just sit and bird-watch at the lodge. Like I did! *No children under 14. Blue Jay Lodge is 10 minutes from Kruger Park gates.*

Rooms: 5: 4 king/twins with en-suite bath and shower. 1 self-catering unit with king, kitchenette and en-suite bath and shower.
Price: From R395 - R595 pp sharing.
Meals: Full breakfast included.
Directions: See website for detailed directions.

Idube Private Game Reserve

Sally Kernick
Sabi Sand Game Reserve
Tel: 011-431-1120 Fax: 011-431-3597
Email: info@idube.com Web: www.idube.com

There are few establishments where the staff seem to have as much fun working together as at Idube. Be they guides, trackers, managers or chefs, the Idube crew exude a delightful sense of goodwill to each other and to all mankind. And it's not difficult to see why. Warthog roam through the camp, elephants pass nearby; there is space and greenery, beauty and beast. The land was bought in 1983 by Louis and Marilyn Marais and Louis sensibly built the swimming pool before designing and constructing the rest of the camp himself. Guests sleep in chalets dotted around the sloping grounds, while the thatched seating and dining areas look out over the Sabi Sand Game Reserve. A rope bridge over the river bed takes you to a hide where you can admire the Shadulu dam and its regulars without being admired yourself. Two game drives per day plus guided walks give you the chance to see what's happening elsewhere in the reserve and tracker Titus amazed us with his ability to read bent grasses and droppings. We took time out for sundowners by a dam, accompanied by a bull elephant and a bull hippo. There was much posturing and manliness, not least from me, before a return to camp for dinner (which was excellent!) and conviviality under the stars.

Rooms: 10: 2 kings and 8 doubles all with en/s bathrooms and outdoor shower.
Price: Winter (May to end Sept) R2,300 pp sharing. Summer (October to end April) R3,200. Single supplement +35%.
Meals: All 3 meals plus morning and evening drives and a guided walk included. Drinks and transfers extra.
Directions: 34.4km from Hazyview along R536 towards Kruger Gate. Follow signs off to the left. 19.5km along a dirt road.

Rhino Post Safari Lodge

Nikki and Gerrit Meyer (Managers)
Kruger National Park, Skukuza
Tel: 011-467-1886 Fax: 011-467-4758
Email: info@rws.co.za Web: www.isibindiafrica.co.za or www.rws.co.za
Cell: 083-631-4956

After 6 hours' drive from Jo'burg it was with a mixture of relief and anticipation that we rolled the last few kilometres through the Kruger Park to Rhino Post Safari Lodge. On arrival our bags were magically transferred to our lovely, luxurious, wood-framed chalet with its big glass windows and deck overlooking a dry river bed (or should I say animal motorway). Although the chalets have phones and electricity, it still feels as rustic and as open to nature as is safely possible. The camp is not fenced so animals are able to walk through the lodge area (you will be escorted back and forth along the boardwalks after dark). So… first an outdoor shower, then tea up at the lodge, on a deck overlooking a frequently-used waterhole; and then straight out in search of game and adventure. Our thanks to Fritz, our guide and driver, for some wonderful experiences. I don't know if we were lucky or not, but 16 rhino on our first night didn't seem bad! We also saw two prides of lion fighting over a giraffe carcass, with scores of vultures in the trees and a large pack of hyenas watching the action for scavenging opportunities. This sunlit tableau is etched on my memory and it was a sighting to brag about that evening over fireside drinks. All the meals at Rhino Post are exceptional and it does not take long to get into the new schedule of early starts, late breakfasts, siestas, late-afternoon game drives… and finally dinner. It was a proper wrench to leave when the time came.

Rooms: 16: 2 double and 6 twin chalets. All with ensuite bathrooms, deep free-standing baths, outside showers, overhead fans, mini bar, telephone, safe and hairdryer.
Price: R1,990 pp - R2,190 pp. Singles plus 30%.
Meals: All meals and safari activities included.
Directions: From the Paul Kruger Gate follow signs to Skukuza Rest Camp & Rhino Walking Safaris. Drive past Skukuza on H1-2 towards Tshokwane and Satara. Cross Sabie and Sand rivers and after second turning to Maroela Loop, turn left signed Rhino Walking Safaris.

Rhino Walking Safaris - Plains Camp

Nikki and Gerrit Meyer (Managers)
Rhino Walking Safaris, Kruger National Park, Skukuza
Tel: 011-467-1886 Fax: 011-467-4758
Email: info@rws.co.za Web: www.isibindiafrica.co.za or www.rws.co.za
Cell: 083-631-4956

This is where I fell for Africa: sitting outside my tent in the Kruger, sipping G&T (for the quinine, you understand) and watching game serenely traverse the Timbitene Plain. This is the only private lodge where you can walk in pristine wilderness - nothing short of a privilege. Here the refined, pioneer tents have dark wood furniture with brass hinges and leather straps, bathrooms with copper taps protruding from tree stumps and the largest, softest towels. During the day, you can doze on the chocolate-leather sofa or sip highball cocktails in the plunge pool. Pith helmets, surveying tools, maps and a gramophone add to the bygone feel. Walking on rhino footpaths, the trails let you soak up both the scale and detail of the bush. No mad rush to tick off half-glimpsed Big Five, this – it's all about the quality of the sightings. That said, we encountered glowering buffalo, rampant rhino, lionesses on a hunt and had a pulse-quickening showdown with a bull elephant that I'll dine out on for ages. Afterwards we sent the sun down the sky and, wrapped in rugs, headed toward gas-lamp beacons for a never-ending feast. A safari fantasy come true.

Rooms: 4: all twin-bed African-explorer style tents, each with en-suite loo, shower and overhead fan. Treehouse sleep-out option also available.
Price: R2,150 - R2,450 pp sharing. Ask about 3-, 4- or 5-night packages and single supplement.
Meals: All meals, soft drinks, house wines/beer, safari activities (primarily walking) & optional sleep-outs incl'.
Directions: From the Paul Kruger Gate follow signs to Skukuza Rest Camp & Rhino Walking Safaris. Drive past Skukuza on H1-2 towards Tshokwane and Satara. Cross Sabie and Sand rivers and after second turning to Maroela Loop, turn left signed Rhino Walking Safaris. Meet at Rhino Post Safari Lodge.

Iketla Lodge

Albert and Hennielene Botha

off R555, Ohrigstad
Tel: 013-238-0190 Fax: 013-238-0190
Email: relax@iketla.com Web: www.iketla.com

'Be relaxed… be peaceful' is Iketla's poetic English translation from the local Sotho dialect. Appropriately named, as it turns out. Surrounded on all sides by hills and rocky outcrops, Albert and Hennielene greeted me in the shebeen, where the late afternoon sun was gushing through the open sides, flooding the thatched, tiled dining area. For those that don't know, a shebeen is a drinking den and it's to this magnet that guests began to flock as they returned, brimming with exhilaration, from the day's adventures. Some had been exploring the Panorama Route, others had been walking guided trails through Iketla's 540 hectares of wilderness, inspecting all creatures great and small, and learning about the impressive range of birdlife and traditional uses of indigenous plants. They regaled us with their new-found knowledge and enthusiasm, with Albert, a bushman at heart, chipping in with many jewels of profounder expertise. A faint drumbeat interrupted the banter to signal supper, though my acute senses had already picked up the aroma of something sensational in the air… ostrich strips in a sherry sauce as it turned out. At daybreak I inspected my chalet, similar in style to the main lodge with rugged stone walls, a thatched roof and a verandah outside sliding glass doors. There I read my book and rested my bones, listening to the morning wildlife bring this African wilderness alive.

Rooms: 8 chalets: 3 doubles and 4 twins, 1 honeymoon suite, all with en-suite showers and outside showers.
Price: R785 - R865 pp sharing. Singles R1,015 - R1,120.
Meals: Full breakfast and dinner included.
Directions: From N4 turn off at Belfast and follow R540 through Dullstroom to Lydenburg. Follow R36 through Lydenburg to Ohrigstad. 4km past Ohrigstad turn left onto R555. Sign to Iketla 6km further on right.

Umlani Bushcamp

Marco Schiess

Timbavati Nature Reserve
Tel: 012-346-4028 Fax: 012-346-4023
Email: info@umlani.com Web: www.umlani.com
Cell: 083-468-2041

Rhino-tracking on foot; a rather exciting experience with a couple of bull elephants; sun-downers as the bush settles for the night... this is what safaris are supposed to be about. Umlani is set on a gentle slope above a dry river course (wet in spring) and no fence separates you from the Timbavati's more feral inhabitants. You do not, for example, leave your rondavel at night to investigate snuffling noises, and elephants regularly swing through the middle of the camp for a drink at the pool. You sleep in delightful reed-walled rondavels with thatched roofs (no bricks here), hurricane lamps (no electricity either), and you shower *au naturel*, but in complete privacy. Marco and his wife Marie ran the camp by themselves for a decade until the demands of a young family compelled them to find like-minded managers. After the evening game drive everyone sits out on the deck by the bar, or in the boma round the fire, mulling over what's just been seen, before sitting down to an excellent and often buzzy dinner at tables of 8. Thoughtful hosts and knowledgeable rangers provide the charming, human face of a full-on bush experience. I had many laughs during my stay, while another guest was in tears when she had to leave! Umlani is exceptionally personal and genuine and you live as close to nature as they dare let you. For the more adventurous a night in the treehouse 2km away is a must! Umlani Bushcamp is the 14th Establishment to receive the prestigious Fair Trade in Tourism South Africa Certification.

Rooms: 8 doubles (2 sleeping 4); all with en-suite outside showers.
Price: R2,250 pp sharing, singles R2,950, children under 12, R1,125; 3-night special: R5,750 pp sharing, R7,560 singles, R2,875 kids under 12; 7-night special & winter special also on offer.
Meals: All meals, drinks and 2 - 3 game activities included.
Directions: You will get a map when you book.

Swaziland

Phophonyane Falls Lodge

Rod and Lungile de Vletter

Pigg's Peak
Tel: +268-437-1429 Fax: +268-437-1319
Email: lungile@phophonyane.co.sz Web: www.phophonyane.co.sz
Cell: +268-604-2802

Grab your passport, pop over the border into the Kingdom of Swaziland, and immerse yourself in 500 hectares of pristine nature. Phophonyane Lodge is perched high on a valleyside in thick indigenous forest, with the constant background music of a thousand birds (230 species) and the rushing white water of the Phophonyane River cascading down the kloof below (waterfall-viewing walks are a must). You move between the main lodge and the various tents, cottages and beehives on cobbles and wooden walkways, past murals and rough wood sculptures, natural materials blending easily into the landscape. Some of the cottages have sitting rooms, private gardens, narrow wooden staircases up to bedrooms and balconies, big showers, kitchens et al. The safari tents with their private decks are simpler but more romantic. You are lost in the trees and I stayed in one of the two right down by the rushing water's edge, the best sleeping draught imaginable. The reserve is criss-crossed with hiking paths leading to natural rock pools for swimming, although there is the alternative of the recently-built saltwater pool. Phophonyane prides itself on its links with the local community, some of whom now entertain in the evenings with traditional Swazi dancing. An invigorating experience and a two-night stay is a must. *4x4 drives to mountains and bushman paintings available along with a new chalet on the Crocodile River that overlooks the Kruger Park for Phophonyane guests.*

Rooms: 11: 3 cottages (one sleeps 5, one sleeps 4 and one sleeps 2), 2 with sh'r, 1 with bath; 2 beehive huts (one sleeps 3, two sleep 2), all en-s with sh'r and king-size beds; 6 tents: five sleep 3, one sleeps 2. Two tents have en-s bathrooms: 1 with bath and sh'r and 1 with sh'r only; 4 tents have private individual bathrooms with sh's separate but close to tent.
Price: Safari tents, R420 - R460 pp sh, singles R590 - R680. Beehives, R630 pp sh, singles R890. Cottages, R550 - R590 pp sh. Singles R780 - R860.
Meals: All cottages and two tents self-cat. A la carte restaurant available & picnic lunches can be prepared.
Directions: Ask for details on when booking.

Limpopo

Pezulu Tree House Lodge

Claude and Lydia Huberty

Guernsey, Hoedspruit
Tel: 015-793-2724 Fax: 015-793-2253
Email: pezlodge@mweb.co.za Web: www.pezulu.co.za
Cell: 073-305-3520

The sorry victim of a treehouse-free childhood, I was intrigued by the concept of Pezulu - five different reed-and-thatch constructions spread among the trees surrounding the central building, which is itself entwined around a large amarula. They are all hidden from view behind branch and leaf, and many have bits of tree growing up through the floor to provide the most natural of towel rails, stools and loo paper holders. The 'houses' are named after the trees in which they sit: 'False Thorn' has a magnificent shower with views over the Thornybush Reserve – be prepared for inquisitive giraffe; while 'Huilboerboom' is a honeymoon suite set eight metres above ground (privacy even from the giraffe). Pezulu is situated in the Guernsey Conservancy on the edge of the Kruger Park. There are no predators in this area, only plains game, so you and the buck can wander around the property in perfect safety. Activities on offer include the usual two game drives a day. They can also arrange microlight flights and visits to rehabilitation centres... assuming they can persuade you down from the trees. *Children over 6 are welcome.*

Rooms: 5: 2 family units (1 double and 1 twin) and 3 doubles, variously with outside shower, and/or bath.
Price: R690 - R790 pp sharing, inclusive of all meals. Singles R800. Game drives (R250 pp), microlight flights R445 (strictly cash), visits to Kruger, an animal rehabilitiation project and other activities (including white-water rafting in season) are available.
Meals: All meals included. Drinks and game activities extra.
Directions: Ask when booking.

Gwalagwala

Dorian and Ann Harcourt-Baldwin
Guernsey Rd off the R40, Hoedspruit
Tel: 015-793-3491 Fax: 015-793-0535
Email: gwala@netactive.co.za Web: www.gwala.co.za
Cell: 083-701-2490

Kitted out in khakis and walking boots I can't imagine Dorian as a Jo'burg banker, but that's what he was until a yearning for the bush got the better of him. This is a man who clearly loves every blade of grass on his 500ha reserve and his passion is easily understandable. Stocked with plains game, Gwalagwala is a stunning spot hidden away in the greenery of the Klaserie River and the most instantaneously peaceful retreat I found in this region. Deep (deep) in the bush, just yards from the gurgling waterway, Dorian and Ann have erected six huge tents, built onto raised decks, each with natural slate bathrooms and reed walls. They're close enough to be friendly, but spaced enough for privacy, connected by shaded paths to the pool, boma and bar. And not just any old bar. Here drinks (and breakfast) are served 30 feet up in a circular treehouse wrapped around a huge jackalberry tree. Why go to the birds when they can come to you? Purple-crested loeries, the rare African finfoot... the bird list takes hours to unscroll. Canoeing and croc-spotting, antelope and acacia, this is the sort of spot that ignites in me an urge one day to own my own piece of Africa (and preferably a big, noisy Land Rover to go with it).

Rooms: 6: 3 doubles and 3 twins; 4 with shower, 1 with bath, 1 with bath and shower.
Price: R1,350 pp sharing. Full board, including 2 game activities, one of which is a 'Big 5' game drive.
Meals: All meals included.
Directions: Faxed or emailed on booking or available on website.

Mfubu Lodge & Gallery

Olga Kühnel and Jack Colenso

Balule Nature Reserve, Phalaborwa
Tel: 015-769-6252 Fax: 015-769-6252
Email: olina@telkomsa.net Web: www.mfubu.com
Cell: 073-416-0451 (bad signal at lodge)

Olga and Jack are wonderful, eccentric hosts and long-standing GG favourites! And their home, Mfubu Lodge, is also long-standing, propped up as it is on tall stilts to protect against flooding from the Oliphants River which flows past the garden. I've been deeper into the bush, but rarely has it seemed so penetrating. There are no fences here, just the guarantee of hot water, cold beer and animals that come to you. At dinner we ate the best bobotie I can remember and awaited curtain-up. Silently, hippos trotted onto centre stage, a brilliant moon silhouetting them against the white canvas of an alluvial beach. On other occasions elephants wander across the lawn and make you grateful for the tall stilts. Nowadays the river eases like oil, so in the morning we ran the gauntlet, wading through the water. Safely on the other side, we clambered aboard a Land Rover, mingled with rhino, buffalo and giraffe and watched birds from a hide. On longer drives, Jack has been known to cook eggs on a shovel. The lodge itself consists of a trio of thatched cabins with fans, electric lights and tented fronts, connected by a walkway which weaves amongst trees. Further off, there are two cottages with kitchens, game-viewing platform and art gallery. Olga collects local art and encourages guests to paint, pen or ponder. Early-morning coffee up by the gallery with Olga is a great start to the day. It's not so much "shamrackle" (one of Olga's spoonerisms) as delightfully unrushed. Our friends in the bush.

Rooms: 5: 3 twin cabins sharing two bathrooms; 1 twin timber cottage and 1 double stone cottage, both with own showers.
Price: R590 pp. Single supplement R100.
Meals: Full breakfast and 3-course dinner included. Drinks not included.
Directions: From Jo'burg N12, from Pretoria N4, through Witbank to Belfast. Left on R540 to Lydenburg, then R36 through Strijdom Tunnel following signs to Phalaborwa. Turn right onto R530 to Mica. 22km from Mica on R530 turn R on dirt road following Mfubu signs (about 9km).

Tshukudu Game Lodge

Ala Sussens
Tshukudu Reserve, Hoedspruit, R40 towards Phalaborwa
Tel: 015-793-2476 Fax: 015-793-2078
Email: tshukudugamelodge@radioactivewifi.co.za
Web: www.tshukudulodge.co.za Cell: 082-888-7199

I strolled onto the verandah on a hot dusty day at Tshukudu to find a cheetah sprawled out under one of the dining tables. After my initial panic subsided and it became clear she wasn't going to have me for lunch, I was properly introduced to Savannah. She was hand-raised here, along with other abandoned creatures, and released back into the wild… but she remains a frequent visitor. The other human guests were lounging round the pool watching the warthogs nibbling the lawn into shape and admiring the flying chillies (red-billed hornbills) dive-bombing the birdseed table. Kids will feel very at home here with animal duvets and paw-shaped soaps, while the rest of us can enjoy our private sitting areas, most of which look out onto the bush. After an animated lunch we met our rangers, Dan and Wendel, who looked after us for the duration of our stay – a great comfort with so many wild critters around! On our bush walk (and kids will LOVE this!), we were accompanied by Prince (a labrador), Smokey (a jackal), Savannah (the above-mentioned cheetah) and Chobe (a lion cub!). And after dinner altogether in the boma, we managed to persuade our ever-attentive guide to take us to see the porcupines. These secretive and extraordinary creatures stole the show for me, spinning their quills round, as if in a dance, to scare away the approaching jackals.

Rooms: 13: Doubles or twins with ensuite showers. 3 have wheelchair facilities. Family cottages available.
Price: R1,470 pp sharing. Singles R1,785. Includes all meals, 2 game drives and a bush walk. Children under 12 half price.
Meals: All-inclusive.
Directions: 4km north of Hoedspruit on R40 towards Phalaborwa, signed on the left.

Mohlabetsi Safari Lodge

Tony and Alma Williamson

Balule Nature Reserve, Hoedspruit
Tel: 015-793-2166 Fax: 015-793-9023
Email: safaris@mohlabetsi.co.za Web: www.mohlabetsi.co.za
Cell: 083-255-4956

Even the drive to the lodge was a game drive… with one hand on the wheel, and the other clutching my camera, dexterously snapping giraffe, waterbuck and warthog. Tony and Alma greeted me with a cleansing fruit cocktail before leading me to a happy table of Swedes sitting down to lunch under thatch. Ice cream topped with treacle-sweet papaya sauce stole the show. Guiltily indolent, I took up Veronica's offer of a pre-safari massage and draped myself over her forest altar, de-stressing to the click and chirrup of a thousand tiny insects. From one safe pair of hands to another, I then found myself up front in the Land Rover with Trevor, a ranger with a wit as dry as burnt bushveld. He'll do his best to get you to the 'Big 5' ("look for a break in the rhythm of the bush") but what keeps him keen are the little things. Like watching dung beetles dispose of a mountain of rhino dung, or brushing our teeth with nature's toothbrush and resin toothpaste. Swap tales later under the stars in the giant circular boma as Tony and Alma put on the dinner show, with a prelude of local women singing traditional songs, one of Mohlabetsi, a place of sweet water. Repair to your rondawel or family lodge, with cooling shade and outdoor showers, as well as tasteful authentic touches in the flagstone floors, tribal face-masks and intricate wall hangings. Outside a splendid lawn unfolds to the edge of acacia and amarula, through which the morning walk takes you back to breakfast, stopping first by the lake where the crocodile waits.

Rooms: 8 units: 6 rondawels (4 twin/king and 2 king with outdoor showers) and 2 family lodges (1 twin, 1 double with outdoor showers).
Price: R1,500 pp sharing. Children 50%. Singles +R300. Winter specials (April-September) on request. Price includes full board and 2 safari activities.
Meals: Full board.
Directions: 10km north of Hoedspruit along the R40.

Blue Cottages Country House

Pieter & Maria Van Der Merwe
Olifants River Estate, Hoedspruit
Tel: 015-795-5750 Fax: 015-795-5931
Email: info@countryhouse.co.za Web: www.countryhouse.co.za
Cell: 072-699-0291

Pieter and Maria are the proud owners of Blue Cottages, individually-wrapped rondavels and cosy-looking cottages set amidst a lush jungle of indigenous and tropical trees. Luckily they were just as enthusiastic about our book as I was about their magical little spot. Crane and Quail are small, round and thatched, whitewashed on the outside with blue doors and smothered in Virginia creeper. Inside, delphinium-blue walls, quaint cottage furniture and just enough space for a bed - sweet as pie. The private bathroom is in a separate hut just a few steps away. Crane and Garden Cottage come replete with delightful sitting rooms and kitchen(ette)s and all rooms keep their cool with air-con and overhead fans. Bedrooms, sitting rooms and the terrace are decorated with a showcase of superb African artefacts, the best pieces from the well-established Monsoon Gallery. Food is another bonus; choose from the fresh fusion-cuisine menu in their ever-popular afro-chic restaurant or perhaps enjoy a tasty home-cooked dinner served on the verandah by lamplight. Whichever you decide, a traditional or 'health' breakfast will greet you in the morning. A delightful (re-)discovery and a good base for the Blyde River Canyon (truly magnificent!) and the Kruger Park. *All rooms have air-con or overhead fans.*

Rooms: 6: 4 rondavels: 2 twins with en/s showers; 2 doubles with outside bathrooms, 1 with bath, 1 with shower; 1 family suite, sleeps up to 5, with en/s bath and shower; 1 double cottage with en/s shower and self-catering kitchen/ braai area.
Price: R210 - R420 pp sharing. Singles R270 - R480.
Meals: Breakfast included. Lunch available in Mad Dogz Café and dinner on request in the lodge.
Directions: On the Hoedspruit to Lydenberg road (R527) 28km from Hoedspruit.

Lesheba

Peter and Kathryn Straughan and John and Gill Rosmarin
Makhado
Tel: 015-593-0076
Fax: 086-689-4790
Email: lesheba@mweb.co.za
Web: www.lesheba.co.za
Cell: 083-444-0456 or 083-266-9502

Lesheba is like a lost kingdom from a novel by Ryder Haggard. Creeping up (you'll see!) to 4,400ft, I was amazed to reach not a rocky ridge but a huge plateau with its own mini-mountains, grassy plains and thick-bushed gorge. Kathy's parents own this 2,600-hectare game farm and over fourteen years the family have rebuilt an original Venda village, created a secluded bush camp, started a traditional arts and crafts school, discovered seven rock art sites… and raised four children. The village is stunning, a gaggle of clay-red rondavels regenerated with the help of Venda artist Noria Mabasa. She sculpted dozens of figures around the clustered bedrooms and a huge kitchen/dining room with views across the bushy heights. In my room - one of two fabulous suites with inter-linked bedroom, bathroom and kitchen - a curvaceous mermaid stretched seductively around the bath. In the other, the outdoor shower springs from a standing man's ear. We (Simon and Tory) spent no less than three whole wonderful, super-relaxing days up here this year, spending our days on guided walks where we jauntily passed giraffes and other plains game en route into the forested hills. We were more circumspect when it came to the rhinos! Or we just lay back at the lodge with a novel, gazing out over the valley, checking birds against a book and waiting for the next delicious dinner. This is a magical, see-it-to-believe-it kind of place and a hiker's paradise.

Rooms: Venda village (sleeps 13): all rooms with en-s showers: 2 luxury king suites with huge rock baths, indoor and outdoor showers & kitchen. Hamasha Bush Camp (also exclusive) sleeps 8; all rooms with en-s showers.
Price: R1,100 - R1,450 full board. Self-catering or semi-catering on request.
Meals: All game drives, guided rock art walks included. Horse-riding trails available. Courses in 'Centre of Indigenous Knowledge' school are extra.
Directions: Take N1 north from Jo'burg to Makhado. At 1st crossr'ds in town turn L onto R522 towards Vivo. Continue for 36km. Lesheba signed R down gravel road.

Mopane Bush Lodge

Paul and Rosemary Hatty, Andrew and Moira Rae
Mapungubwe, Off the R572, Musina
Tel: 083-633-0795 Fax: 015-534-7906 or 086-610-3410
Email: info@mopanebushlodge.co.za Web: www.mopanebushlodge.co.za
Cell: 083-679-8884

This is a fascinating, under-visited frontier of South Africa and both these facts make this a great destination. Hidden in 6,000 hectares of semi-desert mopane scrub, the lodge itself is an oasis where fine food (either taken in the huge, open-plan reception-dining area or outside in the boma round a fire), a swimming pool and intimate cottage-rooms provide all the trappings of sophistication and luxury you could wish for. The game reserve has plains game only, so walking about is safe and I recommend taking the track to a waterhole to birdwatch before dinner. But during the day I loved my two visits to the Mapungubwe National Park, five minutes' down the road. First an early-morning visit to the archeological site of South Africa's earlier version of Great Zimbabwe. This ancient civilisation took place on and around a gigantic rock in dramatic scenery interspersed with giant other-worldly baobab trees. And then a second visit took us to the lush confluence of the Limpopo and Shashi rivers and to a heavenly sundowner spot where you can look out onto Zimbabwe and Botswana. As for wildlife they have it all up here ('big five' etc), but the birdlife takes the palme d'or. You'll find some real rarities, including the broad-billed roller and the collared palm thrush. Another big draw at Mopane is the nearby wild dog breeding centre. I have been round and round South Africa, but this area was a real find and I heartily recommend both the lodge and its environment. *Mountain bikes are available for guests to use.*

Rooms: 8 rondavels: all can be double or twin, with en-suite indoor and outdoor showers.
Price: R990 pp sharing. Singles R1,230.
Meals: All meals and all activities on Mopane's own private nature reserve are included. Excursions to Mapungubwe and other attractions: R190 - R450 pp (incl. refreshments and all fees).
Directions: Take N1 from Jo'burg to Pietersberg. Follow signs thro' town for R521 to Dendron. Travel 140km to Alldays, then turn R to Pontdrif. Travel 46km & turn R onto R572 to Musina & Mapungubwe. Mopane Bush Lodge 29km along this rd, just past cell phone tower on R. Map on website.

Jembisa Safari House

Charles and Jane Whitbread

Waterberg
Tel: 014-755-4415 Fax: 014-755-4444
Email: jane@jembisa.com Web: www.jembisa.com
Cell: 082-570-8474

Jembisa is simply the perfect safari destination for families and small groups; a home from home planted in some of the most spectacular bush you'll see. Bookings are on an exclusive basis so you will have this spoiling lodge all to yourselves and you'll be beautifully looked after while you're there. This stone and thatch house could not feel more welcoming, its living and dining area providing a central attraction, strewn with well-loved sofas and complete with a honky-tonk piano and vast fireplace. Rhodesian teak staircases sweep up each side to immense and luxurious bedrooms, and whether you're flying solo (like me) or a team of ten, you'll enjoy cart-wheeling through them. You can enjoy sipping tea on the verandah or sundowners overlooking the river, swinging racquets on the floodlit tennis court or thumbing through the volumes of a snug library. At the foot of the garden, beyond salt-water pool and shaven lawns, a huge deck juts from the hillside gazing proprietarily across the Palala River, a deep, snaking watercourse sliding through the forest far below (favoured spot for wallowing hippo and catchable yellowfish). You won't see the boundaries of the reserve from the deck – particularly when face-down, enjoying a massage treatment. It covers some 3,000ha (an awful lot of acres) and is packed with trackable game from rhino to leopard and hyena. Game drives, bush walks and camp-outs can be enjoyed on the reserve and horse-riding and elephant-back safaris can be arranged nearby.

Rooms: 6: 1 king, 2 queens & 2 king/twins all en/s bath & shower; 1 twin bunk sharing bath & shower.
Price: Bookings on an exclusive use basis. R3,100 includes all meals, wine and soft drinks, game drives, guided bush walks, laundry and babysitting. Children under 12 half price. Please contact the lodge for last-minute specials.
Meals: All meals, afternoon tea and cakes freshly prepared by the 2 chefs and drinks are included.
Directions: Faxed or emailed on booking. An easy 3-hr drive from Jo'burg. Road and air transfers can also be arranged.

Namibia

Introduction

Namibia is a big country and knowing where to stay has always proved a problem for independent travellers there in the past. Until now, despite the wealth of information on accommodation available, there has never been any help in making the choice, i.e. while many brochures are distributed for free at the airport etc, there was no selective and evocative guide-book hand-picking places with charm and leaving out the rest. Which is were we come in.

I knew the accommodation gems were there somewhere... but where? What I really needed was a resident expert to show us the way...

Just when I was pondering this very issue, Lily emerged out of my email inbox like the genie from the bottle, and our wishes were granted. She has lived in Windhoek for a few years now and has spent a great deal of that time travelling to every out-of-the-way corner of the country staying at lodges and B&Bs. In fact she tells me that, with her husband at the wheel, they have driven 60,000km in just two years. Her interest was not merely that of the holiday-maker, although her enthusiasm for the wonders of nature to be found across Namibia is certainly catching. She had already written two books on accommodation in Thailand and The Phillipines. By the time we were in contact she already knew which places we wanted for the most part.

The photos (most of which were taken by Lily) and descriptions tell their own tale. It looks entirely enticing... edible almost!

This is the first countrywide guide to great places to stay in Namibia with all the information you need for independent travel freely available within the pages of this book. As always the places to stay that Lily has chosen are all run by friendly enthusiastic people. This is the sine qua non of GG selections. But beyond this you will see a huge variety in styles of accommodation, in rates, in geographical position etc. Our view is always that great places to stay are found right across the price spectrum. And that a great guide-book will offer you all sorts of different excitements while never compromising on the essence of hospitality.

If you are about to make use of this part of our guide-book, well, frankly I am jealous!

Simon.

The next part of this introduction is by Lily herself.

DRIVING IN NAMIBIA

You can drive a saloon car on many roads in Namibia: the main tarmac roads from Windhoek to Swakopmund, to Etosha or to Rundu/Katima Mulilo/Kasane; and also on the many excellent dirt roads of the country. But you will definitely feel more comfortable with a 4x4 on the dirt roads. If it rains a 4x4 is definitely the best plan. However, in some parts of Damaraland (for example), if the river is flooding (a rare occurrence), even with a 4x4 you might wait from a few hours to a few days for the water level to drop. That is Namibia for you! So it is always a good idea to check with the place you are going to visit to see if you're going to need a 4x4 and if, during the rainy season, the rivers can be crossed. (In Kaokoland you would need GPS, but the only accommodation that we have in Kaokoland, Serra Cafema, is accessible only by plane.)

All the dirt roads are very well signposted, quite amazing in the middle of nowhere! In my experience, the best map – even if it is not always perfect - is "Map Studio Tourist Atlas - Namibia" published by Struik, and this can be bought in CNA. This map is also very useful as it indicates the fuel stations.

Take care to refill your tank every time you find a fuel station, as there are not that many in some parts of the country.

CAR HIRE

If you get enough time to visit and have a tight budget, it is much cheaper to rent a car in South Africa than in Namibia…but you will have to drive a long way. For example Cape Town to Windhoek is about 1400km. You can make interesting stops on the way, of course, but the distances generally in Namibia are huge.

PRICES IN NAMIBIA.

Accommodation is Namibia is more expensive than in South Africa, despite the fact that it is generally not as sophisticated. This is a pity, but you have to consider the fact that the guest farms or small lodges are often very remote, and that makes everything more logistically difficult and therefore expensive to run. For example in some places the owners have to drive 2 hours - or sometimes even 4 hours! - to do their shopping. So be prepared to spend a little more, but I never met anyone who felt that Namibia was bad value for money.

In Namibia there is a wonderful sense of wilderness. You can drive for hours without passing another car. The average size of a farm, for example, is 8,000 hectares! As you drive through most of the country you will see amazing landscapes of red sand dunes, fascinating rock formations and many animals and plants that don't exist anywhere else. The Caprivi Strip is very different – lush and green - and it is cheaper than Botswana and Zimbabwe although you will see the same kind of wetland terrain and wildlife.

MOBILE/CELL PHONES

In Namibia, many places have no coverage for cell phone. They work in the main towns (Windhoek, Swakopmund, Rundu, Katima Mulilo) but more whimsically in other parts. A word of advice: try calling from the highest point of the road or guest farm.

ADVANCE BOOKING

This is essential across the whole country except perhaps in the cities.

TELEPHONE NUMBERS

To call Namibia from the UK dial 00264, then drop the 0 from the local code.
The numbers given in the Namibian chapter are all from within Namibia.

WILDLIFE

On the main roads you will see signboards with symbols of a kudu crossing, or a warthog crossing etc…This might seem quaint, but one day in a 100km stretch we counted 50 warthogs on the bend of the roads! Many accidents occur because of kudu or oryx crossing the road – this occurs mostly at dawn, but not only. Or on dirt roads. As they are often excellent, people forget that they are driving on a dirt road and go too fast. It is advisable to keep your maximum speed down to between 80km and100km an hour on dirt roads.

TIPPING

In restaurants you give 10%, and if you pay by credit card, you write down the tip you want to give and add it to the bill.

TIME OF YEAR

All seasons are nice in Namibia, so there is no obvious best time to visit. It depends what you are looking for.

Winter in Namibia is approximately from June to end of August. During the day it is 20 to 25 degrees, very agreeable for hiking. At night, the temperature can drop to 4 degrees, or even to around zero.
Summer is approximately from November to March. It can be pretty hot during the day, 30 degrees or more in some desert areas.
In good years, there is a small rainy season in November. The main rainy season usually starts in January and ends in April, but in some regions, such as the south the rains come only every 2 years or even less frequently, and never last long. Except in the Caprivi, you will never have whole days of rain. The rain lasts for one or two hours a day. Namibia is beautiful after the rains, all green and blooming. It is hard to imagine that it's the same country that was so dry and yellow before!
But during the rains it is more difficult to see animals.
In the Caprivi, when the rain starts, the elephants go deep into the forest, but the hippo are still there and it is a good season for birding. It is very hot and humid during the rainy season in the Caprivi.
In Swakopmund, it is cool most of the time all year round (14 to 18 degrees during the day) and misty, except during summer where the temperature is very pleasant. Namibians love to go to Swakopmund to escape the heat. The sea is generally freezing (around 12 degrees) – that's what I think, anyway, but some people don't seem to mind! - because of the Benguela current. That explains the huge seal colony in Cape Cross. In summer the water can reach the dizzy heights of 20 degrees.

Lily.

The Hilltop Guesthouse

Angela Curtis and Allen Uys

12 Lessing Street, Windhoek
Tel: 061-249-116
Fax: 061-247-818
Email: hilltop@iafrica.com.na
Web:
www.thehilltophouse.com
Cell: 081-127-4936

Hilltop is a Bavarian-style building (1958) constructed, unsurprisingly, on a hill in a quiet *cul-de-sac*. The house is surrounded by a wooden balcony and guarded by a majestic araucaria that stands in the garden. Formerly a photographic studio, it was transformed by Angela and Allen into a guest-house full of character. They have retained the old-world look of the interior with its Oregon-pine floors, wood-lined semi-circular doors and dark, colonial furniture - these contrast strikingly with the ecru walls decorated with watercolours of animals. The Honeymoon suite is charming, with an antique fireplace remodelled in earthenware tiles. Antique charm, certainly, but you have every modern convenience as well. Meals are served in your room or on the garden terrace near the swimming pool looking out at the view over Klein Windhoek. Allen adores cooking and he also takes care of the service himself. His cuisine is light and creative: I feasted on an excellent spiced leek consommé followed by a tasty chicken curry with couscous and vegetables. Angela's specialities are the raising of white shepherd dogs - to whom she'll take great pleasure in introducing you - and making gourmet desserts (in that order). Both are absolutely charming hosts and very happy and able to advise you on your travel arrangements. And guess what? At Hilltop, you have both freshly-squeezed orange juice and great coffee for breakfast... details perhaps, but indicative of the approach here.

Rooms: 7: 1 single, 3 doubles and 2 family rooms; 1 single in a separate cottage.
Price: N$1,250 double, single N$700, triple N$1,600 and family room N$1,800.
Meals: Full breakfast included. Prices vary from N$25 to N$90 for other meals.
Directions: Take Nujoma Drive from international airport. Turn R at Nelson Mandela Ave, L at Robert Mugabe Ave, L again at Lilien Crohn St and L again at Langenhoven. Then take a R into Promenaden Rd and a final R into Lessing St.

Vondelhof Guesthouse

Yvonne Schadee

2 Puccini street, Windhoek
Tel: 061-248-320 Fax: 061-240-373
Email: vondelhof@mweb.com.na Web: www.vondelhof.com

As you approach Vondelhof your eye is first captured by the green turret of the old house in the middle of the garden. The atmosphere here, informal and convivial, is down to Yvonne who so effortlessly puts her guests at their ease with attention that is at once personal and relaxed. She looks after everything, from the booking to the cooking, and she is always ready to listen to you, to help with reservations or trips into town… she will even share her recipes with her guests. There are several menus, but it is the first guest's order that determines the day's menu. So there's a tip for you! The hake in sweet and sour sauce is very good. There's another. The outdoor patio is the focal point from which emanate the reception area, low buildings harbouring the bedrooms, the restaurant and the verandah. Guests come there to have a drink, write or simply to relax in one of the hammocks displayed around the swimming pool embedded in its wooden deck. The rooms are comfortable, each slightly different from the others with original crete-stone walls the colour of sand. They are simply, but tastefully furnished with tall wooden giraffes, basketwork and African fabrics. One of the rooms in the main building has a large wooden deck overlooking the gardens. Children will be delighted to find a jungle gym and a trampoline in the garden.

Rooms: 8: 7 double rooms and 1 triple room all with en-suite bathroom.
Price: Doubles N$390 pp sharing; singles N$540; triples N$310 pp sharing.
Meals: Continental breakfast buffet included. Light lunches from N$17.50. Three-course dinner N$120.
Directions: Leaving the international airport, turn right onto the B6. When entering Windhoek after approximately 42km, turn right onto Sam Nujoma Drive and follow all the way through city centre. Go underneath the railway line, turn right onto Hosea Kutako Drive, then turn left into Puccini Street.

Olive Grove Guesthouse

Roger Fusell and Lindy van den Bosch
20 Promenade road (corner with Ngami street), Windhoek
Tel: 061-239-199 Fax: 061-234-971
Email: info@olivegrove-namibia.com Web: www.bigsky-namibia.com
Cell: 081-128-0951

Olive Grove will immediately surprise and seduce you, combining great elegance with an informal atmosphere, a classically-styled house with refined contemporary décor. The original house has been preserved with its beautiful Indonesian wooden doors and its stairway up to a stone tower. Harmony is achieved through the use of natural colours of grey and ochre, while huge bay windows in wrought iron, a material also used in the outside furniture, bring in the light. Bedrooms are minimalist in style and equipped with every possible comfort. Original hanging lights from Morocco add a warm, oriental touch and their shadows form magical, abstract patterns on the walls. Bathrooms are equally marvellous, created in this same spirit of Zen and the Orient. The guests (and they seem to love this) can enjoy a jacuzzi, found on a terrace on the first floor. A modern kitchen opens convivially onto the elegant dining room, allowing you to observe the preparation of the dishes. These are served on the terrace, warmed in winter by gas lamps. Roger and Lindy - and their pet animals - divide their time between Olive Grove and Erongo Wilderness Lodge, near Omaruru, ensuring a caring eye is kept on your well-being. When I visited, they were planning the opening in 2008 of an exclusive suite with a private pool, surrounded by olive trees. And in August they opened a Wellness Room offering massages, waxes, facials, pedicures. This whole place is wonderfully relaxing and perfect for restoring energy.

Rooms: 11 rooms (3 standard en-suite, 7 luxury en-s rooms & 1 executive suite). All rooms have en-suite bathrooms (2 with sh'rs, 3 with sh'rs and bath combined, 6 with separate sh'r and bath).
Price: Standard room: N$580 pp sh. Singles N$695; Luxury room: N$680 pp & N$790 singles; Executive suite: N$980 pp & N$1,150 singles.
Meals: Full breakfast included. Lunch à la carte, dinner N$170.
Directions: Take Nujoma Dr from airport. Turn R at Nelson Mandela Ave, L into Schanzen Rd, sharp R in Promenaden Rd, R into Ngami St & entrance of Olive Grove. Map and directions on website.

Eningu Clayhouse Lodge

Kate Dunstan
On D1471, 65km from Windhoek airport
Tel: 062-581-880 and 061-240-020 Fax: 062-581-577 and 061-304-290
Email: info@eningulodge.com and reservations@eningulodge.com
Web: www.eningulodge.com

The architecture at Eningu is unique in Namibia with its clay walls - all 120,000 clay bricks were hand-made! – built into stark geometric structures. The results meld perfectly with the red ochre colour of the Kalahari desert sand. A good network of footpaths allows you to walk out and experience the immense solitude of this desert with its infinite horizons; and to sight the special birds and animals that live here. The interior decoration of the lodge is always original and puts a high value on natural materials; walls rendered in warm colours, wooden beams, antique furniture, tree stumps, bouquets of dried flowers, lily seeds in the form of bowls that you'll see bloom after the rains. Paintings, sculptures and an interesting crafts shop complete a thoroughly artistic picture and atmosphere. In the cosy bedrooms check out the beautiful floors painted in naïve motifs. Kate administers everything with energy and kindness… and her chef is excellent. The cooking is every bit as creative as everything else at Eningu, to be feasted on first with the eyes and to be enjoyed with a South African wine from a cellar of some 1,000 bottles. I can personally vouch for the chicken breast in a peanut crust and the chilled espresso-mousse which were a delight. Candlelit meals are taken in the thatched lapa or in the welcoming restaurant, heated in winter by a cast-iron stove. At night, a hide at the waterhole is a great spot from which to observe the enchanting ballet of the porcupines that come to be fed and from which the lodge takes its name.

Rooms: 9 rooms (2 double rooms, 6 triple rooms and one family room with 4 beds) with en-suite bathroom.
Price: N$680 pp sharing. N$780 single.
Meals: Breakfast and 3-course dinner included. N$60 light lunch.
Directions: 1 hour (65km) drive from Windhoek international airport. Accessible from Windhoek or Dorbabis. From Windhoek take B6, turn R on M51 for 60km, then R on 1482 for 1km, then L on D1471 for 5km. Map on website.

Okambara Elephant Lodge

Christian and Uschi Schmitt

Off D1800, 95km from the airport of Windhoek, Windhoek/Witvlei
Tel: 062-682 070 Fax: 062-682 071
Email: okambara@iway.na Web: www.okambara.de
Cell: 081-128-0669

What a pleasure to enter this bucolic garden, where birdsong thrills among the jacarandas, eucalyptus and bougainvillaea and the orange trees and palms of its orchard. A long-haired donkey and her foal, followed by two calves and some sheep, crossed the road just in front of our car. Children will love this place, even more because they can swim in the huge, natural swimming pool hidden high up among the foliage. Christian and Uschi also took a plunge when they came to Namibia on holiday 15 years ago, fell in love with the country and decided to move here with their two little girls. Christian's pleasure was evident as he took me on a long game drive through his property to find the white rhinoceros and elephants that he himself introduced - they both gave birth this year! You have a very good chance of seeing a wide variety of animals. The accommodation is very comfortable, whether you are in the round, thatched chalets that are set to one side for a little seclusion, or in the main house. The latter, designed by Christian's father, has echoes of a stone castle with its red rough-cast turrets. However, the interior, with its high wooden beams, has a distinctly African flavour. The perfect place to enjoy a drink is ensconced in one of the comfortable leather sofas arranged near the fire where there's a library of interesting nature books to choose from. The terrace at the back of the house faces a waterhole where kudu often come to drink. Uschi herself excels in the warmth of her welcome and in her *bellissimo* (predominantly Italian) cooking. *Only an hour and a half from Windhoek airport, an excellent alternative to the capital.*

Rooms: 6: 2 cottages and 4 rooms in the main house: 2 double rooms with en-suite shower and 2 family rooms with 2 bedrooms sharing an en-suite shower (1 with living room).
Price: N$690 pp sharing. No single supplement. Game drives: N$150 pp.
Meals: Full breakfast, light lunch and 3-courses dinner included.
Directions: Take B6 (Windhoek/Gobabis), turn onto D1808, then onto D1800 direction Witvlei for 20km before turning right to Okambara (7km).

Guest Farm Kiripotib

Hans Georg and Claudia von Hase

On D1448, 160km (2 hours) from both Windhoek and international airport, Dorbabis
Tel: 062-581-419 Fax: 062-581-419
Email: hans@kiripotib.com Web: www.kiripotib.com Cell: 081-243-2628

This is one of the rare places in Namibia where you can learn how a livestock farm operates and Hans, a third-generation Namibian farmer, is an erudite teacher with a passion for his work. He also has experience as a safari operator, and can advise you in the organisation of your trip with plenty of anecdotes about his own travels to tell. Claudia manages the jewellery design studio and the karakul carpet weaving (the karakul is a sheep if you didn't know). The African Kirikara Arts & Crafts creations are displayed in the adjacent farm gallery… and they are decidedly difficult to resist! In addition to their diverse talents, Hans and Claudia are sensitive hosts with a desire to take care of their guests. The guest farm has an artistic atmosphere with a liberal sprinkling of good humour. The thatched lounge in front of the house is where everyone congregates for good home-cooked meals, which make use of home produce from the farm. The buildings and the swimming pool are surrounded by indigenous trees, such as baobabs, African olives and acacias with Madagascan periwinkles at their bases. Claudia's artistic talent - art pieces in African woods, basketwork from the north and colourful karakul carpets from the studio - is evident in the décor of the rooms and the two new chalets. These recent additions are more independent, roomy and light-filled spaces, but all face out onto the flat, golden Kalahari landscape. Wedding ceremonies are offered in the typically African and very beautiful farm church… tempted? *Two hours from Windhoek international airport and thus a perfect first or last stop on any Namibian safari.*

Rooms: 5: 3 rooms and 2 chalets (can sleep 3), all with en-suite shower.
Price: Chalets: N$575 pp sharing, singles N$689, triples N$520; Rooms: N$468 pp sharing & singles N$550. Ask for off-season rate and for wedding ceremonies. Tour of farm at sunset included.
Meals: Full-breakfast included. N$80 light lunch. N$130 dinner.
Directions: From Dorbabis take dirt road C15/MR33 direction Uhlenhorst. At Klein Nauas pass an old white tower. From there drive straight for about 12km on D1448.

Bagatelle Kalahari Game Ranch

Fred and Onie Jacobs

On D1268, Mariental
Tel: 063-240-982 or 061-224-712 Fax: 063-241-252 or 061-224-217
Email: info@bagatelle-kalahari-gameranch.com
Web: www.bagatelle-kalahari-gameranch.com

On my arrival, the raucous cries of peacocks in the midst of the red parallel-running sand dunes of the Kalahari made me wonder if I had a touch of sunstroke! But it is just that Onie has a passion for animals: 38 peacocks, 7 cats who lounge at the entry in a wicker basket (taking turns in pairs!), 9 dogs, 4 cheetahs entrusted by the Cheetah Conservation Fund and several orphaned animals that Onie feeds by bottle… a delight for children. The lodge is the former home of Fred and Onie and with all their furniture and décor still in place, the atmosphere is warm, personal and relaxed. The library, near the fireplace, is filled with books about Namibia. You serve yourself from the fridge in the kitchen or from the bar, writing down what you take. Each of the different spaces of the lodge opens onto the next until you reach a shaded verandah overlooking the pool and the open-air lapa. In the evenings, everyone gathers here to enjoy a good dinner in a convivial atmosphere, seated at candlelit tables that are arranged in a semi-circle facing the campfire. The air-conditioned chalets are all very comfortable, but it is the Dune chalets that command superb views over the Kalahari landscape of red dunes dotted with acacias. Each Dune chalet bathroom is equipped with a wonderful bathtub set in an alcove so that you can contemplate glorious sunsets whilst lying in your bath, sipping a chilled glass of wine!

Rooms: 10: 4 Dune chalets with en-suite bath and shower and 6 Strohbale chalets with en-suite shower.
Price: N$1,150 pp sharing for Dune chalet and N$1,050 pp sharing for strohbale chalet (additional adult possible in strohbale N$650). Single supplement N$350.
Meals: Full breakfast and afternoon tea included. N$95 light lunch. N$165 dinner (buffet style).
Directions: Accessible from Kalkrand and Mariental. On D1268, 25km from the intersection with the C20, and 40km from the intersection with the C21.

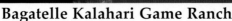

Goibib Mountain Lodge

François De Wet and
Elsje Wieringa
(Reservations -
Suzanne Bonitz)
Keetmanshoop 9000
Tel: 00264-61-224-712
Fax: 00264-61-224-217
Email:
reservations@resdes.com.na
Web:
www.goibibmountainlodge.com
Cell: 00264-812-427-375

After a five-hour drive across the blazing Namibian desert, it was a pleasure to be introduced to François and his indelible smile… and also to one of his ice-cold lagers. I was first shown to my room, then introduced to Alta, who is not only wonderful company, but also the maker of the finest kudu biltong I have ever tasted. That afternoon, I was given the keys to my own 4x4 and invited to speed around the farm and search for game! Jumping into a 1970's Range Rover, I drove through the farm gates and off-roaded towards the Karas Mountains. My search did not take long. Five minutes of skidding and bumping and a herd of young male springbok bounded out in front of me, shortly followed by a large herd of oryx, who raced alongside my jeep as if to test out their speed. I also saw kori bustards, klipspringer and steenbok before returning to the lodge, intact and hungry. You don't have to self-drive and guided drives are available in the morning or even at night. After a cooling dip in the pool, I put François' enthusiasm for his Namibian mutton to the test. After my fourth helping of the rich, spicy hunks of meat, washed down with glugs of Kalahari wine, I was most definitely convinced. I was lucky enough to stay here for two nights. I recommend you do the same.

Rooms: 8: all twin/doubles with en-suite showers.
Price: N$700 - N$800 pp sharing. Singles supplement $100.
Meals: Breakfast included. Light lunch on request N$75. 3-course dinner N$150.
Directions: From Grunau, take the B1 north to Keetmanshoop. Goibib is 50km up on the left-hand side.

White House

Kinna and Dolf de Wet

4km off B1, 11km north of Grunau
Tel: 063-262-061
Email: withuis@iway.na Web: www.withuis.iway.na
Cell: 081-285-6484

The great attraction here is to be able to stay in the old house, which dates back to 1912. From the road, you cannot miss its white façade, set proudly at the foot of a kopie in the middle of the vast plain. You first stop at Kinna and Dolf's home to collect your keys before going on to the White House, 2km away. The proprietors have lovingly renovated it, maintaining its wonderful character from the past: rooms with high ceilings, Oregon pine floors, turn-of-the-century furniture. The kitchen is welcoming, with its old-fashioned enamel stove and interesting collection of antique boxes. You share the house with other guests and meet them over meals, served individually in a pretty dining room with walls decorated with engravings. You can cook for yourself, but that would be a shame as you would miss Dolf's arrival by car, carrying plates wrapped up in blankets to keep them warm. We waited expectantly for the headlights of his car on a cold, foggy winter night and were rewarded by excellent lamb chops – you are in sheep country here and all the lamb and venison served at the White House is organic - melting pumpkin pancakes, a sauce infused with nutmeg, green vegetables and everything accompanied by a crisp salad! You can also stay in 3 small bungalows, more simple but comfortable, situated close to the house. When available, Dolf will take you on a day or night farm/game drive on the property, with a visit to his rose quartz mine.

Rooms: Main House has 4 family rooms (double bed + 2 single beds) and 1 small double room, each room with own toilet facilities; also 3 chalets with shower-rooms (2 with double bed + 2 'bunker' beds & 1 with 2 single beds), well equipped for self-catering.
Price: N$200 pp sharing.
Meals: N$70 dinner. N$60 braai. N$40 breakfast. Also self-catering.
Directions: On B1, 11km north of Grunau. Then 4km on the farm road.

Klein Aus Vista

Willem, Piet and Johan Swiegers
2km west of Aus on the B4
Tel: 063-258-021 or 063-258-116 Fax: 063-258-021
Email: ausvista@namibhorses.com Web: www.namibhorses.com and www.gondwana-desert-collection.com

Set against the Aus Mountains almost a mile above sea level, Klein Aus Vista overlooks the endless plains of the Southern Namib Desert. This is a proper family-run business managed by the three friendly Swiegers brothers, Piet, Johann and Willem. Near the reception and restaurant, the Desert Horse Inn offers tastefully-decorated rooms that are scattered on a small hillside each with a verandah facing the sunset. For those who seek solitude, the Eagles Nest chalets at the foot of an impressive chaos of granite boulders and just 7km from the lodge will be the right option. The rocks have been integrated into the buildings, hugging the chalets or emerging in the interiors in the most unexpected places. Each self-catering chalet is different: 'The Rock', my favourite, is perched on the side of a hill between two enormous boulders. The interiors are spacious, rustic and imaginative, each with a fireplace for cold winter nights. In the kitchen, the table is already set and the fridge is full of cold drinks. In the evening, the fiery rays of the setting sun touch the rocks and the chalets in dramatic fashion. The landscape around the Aus Mountains, not far from the red dunes of the Namib Desert, is spectacular and a paradise for hikers, with numerous trails on the 51,000 hectares of the private Sperrgebiet Rand Park. The flora is exceptionally rich after winter rains and boasts a stunning variety of succulent plants that paint the landscape in purples and yellows at times. You'd need a couple of days to fully explore Klein Aus Vista's own park and neighbouring Namib Naukluft Park. One of the excursions on offer gives you the opportunity to drive out to the wild horses of the Namib that gather around a waterhole 20km away on the road to Lüderitz.

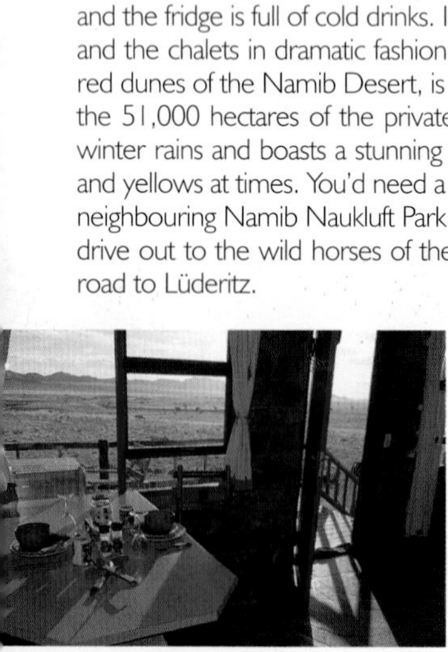

Rooms: 6 self-catering chalets in 'Eagles Nest Lodge'; 24 rooms in 'Desert Horse Inn'.
Price: Eagles Nest Chalets: N$645 pp sharing B&B, N$805 single B&B; Desert Horse Inn: N$445 pp sharing B&B, N$555 single B&B. Rates only applicable till 31 Oct 2008.
Meals: N$55 breakfast, N$75 lunch, N$140 dinner.
Directions: Accessible from Aus (2km) and from Lüderitz (115km) on B4.

NamibRand Family Hideout

Andreas and Mandy Brückner
Farm Stellerine, off C27, Namibrand Nature Reserve
Tel: 061-226-803 (office hrs) 081-127-2957 (after hrs) Fax: 061-220-634
Email: ambruck@mweb.com.na Web: www.hideout.iway.na
Cell: 081-127-2957

NamibRand Family Hideout is a simple and serene house set in the magical landscape of the Namibrand Nature Reserve and its extraordinary red dunes punctuated with acacias and boscia and inhabited by oryx, kudu, zebra, hartebeest, ostrich, springbok.... Thanks to Mandy and Andreas, the Stellerine farm - established in 1945 but later abandoned to the desert sands - has now been restored to life, renovated and equipped with essentials without disturbing its riveting feel of a bygone era. The house has a holiday-home atmosphere with its rough-cast white walls, cotton fabrics and rattan furniture. There are no doubt other more luxurious places to stay in this guide, but if you are searching for peace, sensational remoteness and a place to call home for a few days, then look no further. This is certainly a place for nature lovers, but it is also especially suited for families with children - there are board games, books... and dune boards. The guestbook brims with children's drawings and comments of approval (the outdoor shower comes in for particular praise during the hot summer months). Here you'll find deafening silence, views over the desert, oryx and springbok coming to drink at the waterhole just 20m from the terrace and superb starlit nights. You can explore the dunes behind the house either on foot or in your own vehicle – for driving on dunes you need a 4x4 and to deflate your tyres to 120 kPa. A circular track enables you to cross this incredible landscape in about 1-2 hours. In case of any problems, the management of Tok Tokkie Trails, on the neighbouring farm, will be able to help you.

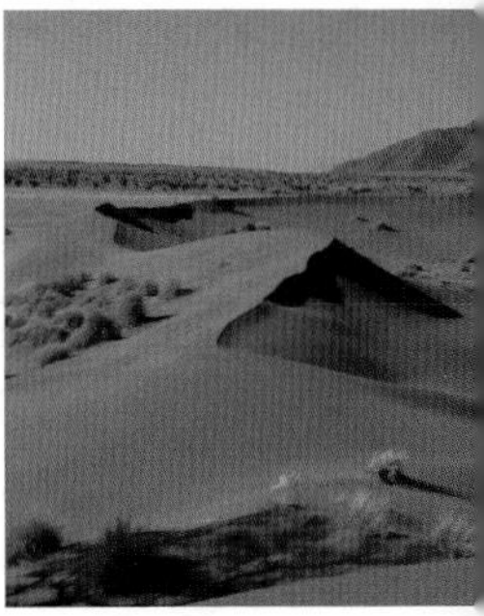

Rooms: Self-catering farmhouse sleeps 10-12: 2 doubles & 1 room sleeping 4 (can sleep 2 extra in lounge & 2 in outbuilding); 2 sh'rs & 1 outside sh'r & full kitchen (fridge, stove, solar lamps). Guests provide bedding, can be arranged at extra cost.
Price: N$560 - N$1,365 per night for the entire house, dependent on size of group, country of residence & length of stay.
Meals: Fully self-catering. Bring all your own food, beverages & firewood for braai and hot shower. 1st shop in Maltahöhe, about 100km away.
Directions: 110km south of Sesriem, accessible from Solitaire, Maltahöhe or Helmeringhausen, on C27. An information sheet and a map provided on booking. Landing strip nearby.

Sossusvlei Mountain Lodge

NamibRand Nature Reserve
Tel: +27-11-809-4300 Fax: +27-11-809-4400
Email: reservations@ccafrica.com Web: www.ccafrica.com

Perched on a promontory in splendid isolation, Sossusvlei Mountain Lodge combines extravagance, refinement, intimacy… and a perfect welcome from Brian and his staff. Its location, the immense 180,000 hectare private reserve of the NamibRand, is absolutely fantastic! The futuristic architecture of the lodge, in curves of glass and stone, resonates strangely well with the barren and spectacular beauty of the surrounding countryside: vast red dune systems, punctuated with vegetation, golden plains that stretch to infinity and high sullen mountains in tortuous shapes. The immense villas are on split levels; the sitting room leads out onto a private terrace and the bedroom has a huge bed beneath a star-gazing skylight. Naturally the villas are strong on creature comforts too: air-con, bar, CD system, fireplace, glass-walled bathroom, second outdoor shower and, if the mood takes you, the materials with which to draw your surroundings! The days pass too quickly here: wallowing in the luxury of your villa; savouring delicious meals; going for a morning walk; taking off on game drives into this striking reserve in search of oryx, springbok, zebra and ostrich; enjoying a romantic sundowner at the top of a petrified dune or comfortably seated on one of the decks back at the lodge. In the evenings you might be surprised to discover a very sophisticated observatory where an astronomer can point out the stars for you.

Rooms: 10 villas with split-level sitting area, en-suite bathroom with shower and an outdoor shower.
Price: Depends on season & number of nights. From N$2,205 pp sharing in low season to N$4,235 in high season for 1-3 nights. No single supplement for first 2 rooms & 50% off full rate after that. Scheduled activities in the NamibRand & laundry included.
Meals: 3 meals, soft drinks, house wine, local brand spirits and beers, tea and coffee included.
Directions: About 130km south of Sesriem, accessible from Solitaire, Malthahöhe or Helmeringhausen, on C27. Access also by charter flight.

The Desert Homestead and Horse Trails

Andrew and Melissa Gillies
C19, Sesriem area
Tel: 063-683-103 or 061-246-788 Fax: 063-683-104 or 061-243-079
Email: homestead@africaonline.com.na
Web: www.deserthomestead-namibia.com Cell: 081-127-7161

The owners took their 22 horses, saddles and harnesses, their dogs and their cats, and moved even closer to the Sossusvlei dunes to recreate something of the atmosphere of the former Desert Homestead. The structures all face the superb views over the golden plains and the Zasis Mountains. The restaurant is perched on a promontory and dinner is usually served elegantly on the terrace at individual tables by candlelight under the starry night sky. The menu is written up on a board: the evening I stayed there was green pea soup with delicious rolls straight from the oven, ostrich kebabs with spinach and then cheesecake. The vast semi-circular room with its high ceiling, combining both living area and interior dining room, is full of atmosphere with old farm tools hanging above the stone bar counter and comfortable sofas arranged around a cast-iron fireplace - the grey cat certainly seems to appreciate it. From the dining room, you can see the meal preparation through a large opening to the modern kitchen. I always like that sort of confidence from a kitchen. In the morning, lively conversations among the staff are heard and everyone, from managers to waiters, is smiling and friendly. The bungalows built down below are light-filled and cheerful, with pretty, wooden furniture and designer bathrooms. Excursions to the Sossusvlei dunes 32km away and to the Naukluft can be arranged, as well as nature drives, guided walks, horse-back safaris and sunrise or sunset horse rides.

Rooms: 20: all bungalows with en-suite shower.
Price: From N$1,200 per double room, N$750 singles and N$1,600 triples.
Meals: Full breakfast included. Early morning packed breakfast possible. N$55 light lunch. N$120 dinner.
Directions: Along C19, 32km south east of Sesriem and 3km north of the junction of the C19 and D854.

Zebra River Lodge

Rob and Marianne Field
on D850, Naukluft area
Tel: 063-693-265 Fax: 063-693-266
Email: marianne.rob@zebrariver.com Web: www.zebrariver.com

Some places, and Zebra River Lodge is one, seem to be blessed by the gods! From the road there is no hint of the dramatic beauty of this 13,000-hectare property in the heart of the Zaris Mountains. Having visited several times, I have still not explored all of the hiking trails there; the most spectacular of these crosses a canyon almost as deep as that of Fish River (just 60m less), at the end of which is a spring surrounded by centenary ficus. The limestone mountains are beautifully striated and form terraces where comiphora and moringa trees grow. Not only is this some of the most beautiful landscape in Namibia, but you will also be delighted by the warm and friendly welcome from Marianne and Rob. In the evening, everyone gathers in the living room, filled with a variety of objects, that give it great eclectic charm - antique pine furniture, dishes, old coffee-grinders, bouquets of dried flowers and Rob's own superb photographs of the dunes. You find the same atmosphere in the décor of the rooms. The new suite perched on the hill is particularly special! Marianne's cooking is excellent and it is a pleasure to stay on and chat beside the fire, enjoying the excellent wines chosen by Rob. He has a passion for the fascinating geology and palaeontology of the region. If you ask in advance, Rob will take you to the Sossusvlei dunes or into the Namib Naukluft National Park.

Rooms: 8 double rooms and 1 suite with en-suite bathroom.
Price: N$690 pp sharing in double room. Singles N$750.
Meals: Full breakfast, light lunch and 3-course dinner included.
Directions: Accessible from Maltahöhe, Duwisib, Sesriem, Büllsport. Zebra River Lodge is on the D850, 19km from the intersection with the D854 and 10km from the intersection with the D855. Access also by plane on the brand new airstrip.

Büllsport Guestfarm

Johanna and Ernst Sauber

On C14, Naukluft Mountains
Tel: 063-693-371/63 Fax: 063-693-372
Email: info@buellsport.com Web: www.buellsport.com

In the heart of the Naukluft Mountains, Büllsport is the rallying point for hikers of all nationalities. Numerous excursions are detailed on their website. Don't miss the very scenic Naukluft Plateau Excursion and Quiver Tree Hike. After an early-morning breakfast, a game drive will take you to the top of the plateau – en route you will see moutain zebra, klipspringer, springbok, oryx and kudu. At the top you set off walking for 3 hours along a gorge with quiver trees growing up its steep slopes. The presence of water makes this a magical spot; the river is bordered with fig trees where birds and baboons live and in summer it is a treat to bathe in the crystalline water pools. And, at the end of the gorge there is a 4x4 patiently waiting with cold drinks! Then, in the evening, with everyone reunited at a big communal table, animated conversation takes place with Ernst and Johanna present too. Belonging to the third generation of Saubers living at Büllsport, Ernst is a mine of information on the history and the environment of his region. Johanna is passionate about horses which she rears. Beginners can go riding by the hour, while the more experienced can go on horse safaris lasting several days. The biggest draw here is the amazing natural environment which you can explore in an informal and unpretentious atmosphere with enthusiastic hosts.

Rooms: 6 double rooms, 1 triple room, and 1 family room (sleeping 4) with en-suite bathroom (shower).
Price: N$730 single room; N$1,090 double room; N$1,440 triple room. Naukluft Plateau & Quiver Tree Valley Hike: N$270; Rock Arch: $135; Scenic Farm & Game Drive (2 hrs): N$80. Sossusvlei excursions on request.
Meals: Breakfast and dinner included. N$25 for afternoon coffee and cake. N$75 lunch.
Directions: Accessible from Maltahöhe, Walvis Bay or Windhoek. Büllsport is on the C14 at the junction with D1206 and D854.

Barchan Dunes Retreat

Hannetjie and Willem Van Rooyen
On D1275, Sesriem area
Tel: 062-682-031 Fax: 062-682-031
Email: barchan@iway.na Web: www.barchandunes.com and www.natron.net/tour/barchan-dunes

Barchan Dunes is one of my favourite places in Namibia. Hannetjie, with her natural charm, and Willem, with his sense of humour, are truly great hosts. Their friendly welcome is reinforced by the enthusiasm of their dogs who rush to meet your car; and the dogs are followed in their turn by three cute pet meerkats! The generously-sized cottages, each decorated in a different theme, are built into the crescent-shaped hollow of the dunes that overlook a serene landscape of mountains and rocky outcrops in the distance. In the evening, dinner is served communally in the elegant dining room. This is a highlight, as much for the quality and quantity of Hannetjie's culinary skills (make sure you prepare for this by dieting beforehand!) as for the good conversation. Willem generously serves some excellent wines - you find your glass refilled as if by magic - and it is all included in the price. The retreat merits a stay of at least two nights to appreciate the beauty of the surrounding area and simply to pamper yourself. Don't miss walking in the canyon among the ghostly silver trunks of the moringa trees. Willem can organise excursions into the dunes of Sossusvlei, one hour away (book in advance). Late in the afternoon, Willem takes you on a game drive to see the 40 oryx on his farm or to contemplate the sunset, drink in hand, from a viewpoint on the rose-coloured dunes. "Another boring day ends in Africa!" he concludes with a laugh.

Rooms: 6: 2 rooms inside the main house, 3 cottages and 1 self-catering cottage. All have en-s shower.
Price: N$796 pp sharing full board. N$420 pp sh breakfast included. Self-catering N$650 per unit. No single supplement. Farm drive also included in rate.
Meals: Full board includes breakfast, coffee & cake in the afternoon, 3-course dinner, malt & soft drinks. Or, meals on request at www.kuangukuangu.com
Directions: On D1275. Accessible from Walvis Bay take C14, turn L on D1275 "Nauchas" for 15km; or from Rehoboth take C24, in Nauchas turn R to D1275 to Spreetshoogte Pass. After pass it is 20km.

Lagoon Loge Guesthouse

Hélène and Wilfried Meiller
88 Kovambo Nujoma Drive, Walvis Bay
Tel: 064-200-850 Fax: 064-200-851
Email: french@lagoonlodge.com.na Web: www.lagoonlodge.com.na

Only the street separates the lodge from the lagoon and its flamingos. Walvis Bay is the departure point for a very popular and enjoyable tour by boat or canoe to see dolphins, seals, tortoises and birds. Lagoon Loge itself is bright yellow, doffing the cap to southern France where its proprietors come from. Hélène and Wilfried are both passionate about Africa, having left France without much regret, to move to Walvis Bay, taking with them their beautiful antique furniture and a good stock of cotton fabric. It is obvious from the attention to detail - perfectly coordinated colour schemes, household linens hand-embroidered by Hélène - that the owners have put their hearts into furnishing their lodge. The comfortable rooms are each different in terms of colour, theme and décor. Wilfried, who is also a talented wood-turner, has created many of the decorative objects himself. A roof deck has been added with a wonderful view on the lagoon. Hélène and Wilfried are particularly helpful in spontaneously offering their assistance in giving advice and booking tours. Breakfasts are taken in the dining room and its lovely conservatory. They are delicious, with jams and cakes all home-made by Hélène! The lodge also organises an interesting day tour to Sandwich Harbour through beautiful dunes – they provide you with a small 4x4 and a guide.

Rooms: 8 rooms with en-suite shower.
Price: N$990 doubles. N$650 singles. N$1,220 family room.
Meals: Full breakfast included. Restaurants nearby (for good seafood in a great seafront setting try 'The Raft').
Directions: At the entrance of Walvis Bay follow directions to Sandwich Harbour. Kovambo Nujoma Drive borders the lagoon on your right, and Lagoon Loge is the yellow house just on your left. Secure off-street parking.

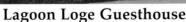

Sam's Giardino

Samuel Egger
89 Anton Lubowski Ave, Swakopmund
Tel: 064-403-210 Fax: 064-403-500
Email: samsart@iafrica.com.na Web: www.giardino.com.na

"Hospitality with a touch of heart" is the slogan of Sam's Giardino. Holding a Swiss diploma in hotel management from Lausanne, Samuel Egger is no newcomer to the world of hospitality and this is immediately apparent. The guests are welcomed by an efficient and smiling team, all of whom are completely interchangeable: each member of staff takes it in turn in a very modern kitchen to cook the 5-course menu no less! A tasting of South African wines is offered in the impressive cellar and dinners are served with flair at individual tables near the new fireplace. Food and drink are an essential part of the experience here! The atmosphere throughout is convivial, the guests gathering in the living room to watch National Geographic CDs, or browsing in a very well-stocked library. There is a cosy lounge on the gallery upstairs with tourist info, where you can organize your visits while having a coffee. Sam will help you with advice on the main points of interest, and book activities and restaurants on your behalf. Sam's Giardino, a comfortable house built in Swiss style with a glass-wall in front, is found in the midst of its own bijou garden with rose trees and a fish pond. The rooms are spread out over two floors and decorated in tones of red and green. Sam's passion, and this you will understand, are his two pedigree bernese hounds: Einstein, whom Sam refers to as the Public Relations Manager, and his new companion Ornella!

Rooms: 10: 9 with en-suite shower and 1 family room with 3-4 beds and en-suite shower.
Price: N$900 double. N$700 single. Dogs and cats also welcome if well-behaved! (by prior arrangement).
Meals: Swiss breakfast included. N$160 for 5-course dinner. N$80 wine tasting at 6.30pm.
Directions: In Swakopmund, from Sam Nujoma turn left into Moses/Garoeb street, then left again into Anton Lubowski Ave. 15 minutes on foot from town centre.

The Stiltz B&B

Danie Holloway and Catharina Hofmeister

Strand Street South, Swakop River, Swakopmund
Tel: 064-400-771 Fax: 064-400-711
Email: info@thestiltz.in.na Web: www.thestiltz.in.na
Cell: 081-127-2111(Danie), 081-127-0868 (Catharina), 081-149-4979 (after hours)

You enter the Stiltz as if through a secret door to a well-guarded kingdom of sea, wind and surrounding dunes, and yet it is just a few minutes' walk to the centre of town. Built high up on stilts on the edge of the dry Swakop River's bed, the wooden, thatched chalets are linked together by walkways. If possible, ask for a chalet facing the sea. The architect, Danie Holloway - who is clearly partial to elevated structures having built The Raft at Walvis Bay, The Tug at Swakopmund and Erongo Wilderness Lodge - has created something magical here. At night, you are lulled to sleep by the sound of the waves and in the morning you wake to contemplate the wild tamarisk bushes as pink flamingos fly overhead. All the chalets are big and bright and are colourfully and stylishly decorated. Wood, sometimes collected from the riverbed, has been used throughout, from the light, twisted wood of the sofas to the large double bed. The bathrooms are made from rosewood, glass, stainless steel and coloured ceramic tiles and you have a wonderful shower with a large showerhead. Breakfasts, served in the honeycomb, polygonal structure of wood and glass, are superb. The new huge luxury Villa is extremely atttractive with an incredible view onto the sea.

Rooms: 10 chalets: 3 twins and 4 doubles, 1 honeymoon, 1 family (sleeps 4) and 1 Villa (sleeps 6). All with en-suite bathroom.
Price: From N$585 - N$700 pp sharing. Singles from N$880 - N$995. Family unit N$1,995 (4 pp). Villa: price on request (2, 4 or 6 persons).
Meals: Full breakfast included. Selection of restaurants, including The Tug (good seafood), 5 mins away.
Directions: In Swakopmund, from Sam Nujoma, turn left into Strand Street (along ocean), pass 'The Tug' restaurant and the aquarium, turn left at Gull's Cry, and The Stiltz is on your right.

Skeleton Coast Safaris

The Schoeman Family
Skeleton Coast Safaris, Windhoek
Tel: 061-224-248 Fax: 061-225-713
Email: scs@iway.na Web: www.skeletoncoastsafaris.com

What a unique and unforgettable experience, to discover the solitary and bewitching beauty of the Skeleton Coast by plane with the Schoeman brothers! What a heady feeling of freedom it gives! On these safaris for small groups lasting several days, the aeroplane serves as your vehicle and allows you to reach extraordinarily out-of-the-way places. Walks on foot and drives in 4x4s are also part of the programme. Skeleton Coast Safaris is a family company created by Louw Schoeman who took a leading role in the creation of the Skeleton Coast National Park. It has been taken over by his four sons, Bertus, Henk, André and Leon, who are all extremely experienced guides and pilots, each with his own speciality – geology, fauna and flora, logistics or art. It's their passion for the desert which they have known since childhood that really motivates them and which they take such genuine pleasure in sharing with you. The beauty of the areas visited will take your breath away; long wild beaches where wrecks run aground, roaring dunes bordering the ocean; the amazing geological formations of the Ugab and Huab valleys; rock paintings and the mythical Hartmann Valley which opens onto the Kunene River. A visit to a settlement of Himba people is on the schedule and with a bit of luck you will meet some of the desert-dwelling animals.... At each stop you stay in a different camp made up of simple but comfortable tents in an exceptional location. This safari is recommended as the privileged way to discover the most secret aspects of Namibia. *Can be combined with Sossusvlei, Etosha, NamibRand Nature Reserve and Lüderitz. See the website for a detailed description.*

Rooms: 4 flying safari itineraries from 4 days/3 nights to 6 days/5 nights. Groups of 2 to 8 people. Skeleton coast accomm in exclusive and privately-owned equipped tented camps. In NamibRand Nature Reserve stay in Wolwedans Dune Camp or similar.
Price: All-inclusive. From US$4,395 pp to US$6,525 pp depending on trip. Details on website.
Meals: All meals & drinks supplied.
Directions: Participants usually start from Windhoek. For pick-up or drop-off to other places ask. Max. 10kg of luggage allowed pp + 2 kg of camera equip't.

Kunene River Lodge

Peter and Hillary Morgan

D3701
Tel: 065-274-300; for reservations call Erika on 061-237-294
Fax: 061-237-295
Email: reservations@exclusive.com.na Web: www.kuneneriverlodge.com

Peter and Hillary, an English couple, came to stay at Kunene River Lodge on a visit to their daughter who was then working in Namibia as a volunteer... and fell in love with the place. In an admirable and dramatic display of free will, six months later they had sold up in the UK and become the owners. They have since infused the place with new energy. At Kunene River Lodge, there is no unnecessary luxury but you feel the serene atmosphere, the magic presence of the Kunene, bordered with magnificent jackalberries, wild jasmine, ficus, mopanes and bamboo. The area is well known to ornithologists because of the endemic species found here, one of which being the Cinderella waxbill. Peter is passionate about birds and has already counted over 230 species. He will take you to watch them by boat, preferably very early in the morning or late in the afternoon at sundowner time. The rooms have been built in a garden of flowers behind the camp sites by the river. So, it is the latter that have the best view, which is very democratic! You will have every opportunity to enjoy the view as well, on the footpaths along the river or on the huge wooden terrace, built on piles, where meals are served. Activities not to miss are bird-watching, rafting on the rapids in the Onduruso Gorge, canoeing, fishing, quad-biking, or a visit to a Himba family.

Rooms: 7 bungalows (5 with 2 double beds and 2 with 3 single beds) and 4 A-frame chalets, all with en-suite shower.
Price: Chalet: N$350 pp sharing and N$440 single. Bungalow: N$520 pp sharing and N$620 single.
Meals: Breakfast included. Lunch and dinner à la carte.
Directions: Via Ruacana towards Swaarbooisdrift or via Opuwo-Epembe (D3700 - D3701). Gravel roads.

Onguma Tented Camp

André Louw
Right before Namutoni gate of Etosha National Park
Tel: 061-232-009 Fax: 061-222-574
Email: onguma@visionsoafrica.com.na; reservations@visionsofafrica.com.na
Web: www.onguma.com

Two leopards crossed our path a little before we arrived at Onguma, a rare sighting indeed and a prelude for our wonderful stay. Bordering the Etosha Park and opposite a waterhole in a depression full of acacia and age-old combretums, we discovered a camp that reminded me of the tents of Berber princes! Conceived by André Louw, this camp mingles a highly original oriental style with African and more modern elements and is devilishly seductive! The living spaces, under cavernous draped tents, in both their materials – canvas, wood and stone – and in their colours – beige, white, black and touches of green – have been perfectly integrated with the camps natural surroundings, exuberant after the rains when I visited. You cannot escape the wonderful natural world that surrounds you... nothing separates you from the outside. The immense tents are a minimalist and sophisticated dream with their huge beds, white feather duvets, mosquito nets and fabulous bathrooms. Here you will find claw-foot baths, ultra-flat circular basins and designer showers with huge handles. The two spaces containing the sitting room and dining room have been harmoniously decorated with extravagant armchairs beaded with white pearls, ultra-modern chairs and fine stools sculpted from wood. Linked by a wooden deck, they open directly onto nature on the water-hole side and only some linen drapes floating in the breeze separate you from the animals that come there to drink. At Onguma you can see all the Etosha game, except the elephants.

Rooms: 7 tents with en-suite shower and bath.
Price: N$1,600 pp sharing (breakfast & dinner) - N$2,310 (all meals and one activity included). Single supplement: N$500. Transfer from Mokuti airstrip included in all rates. N$450 morning game drive & N$350 afternoon game drive.
Meals: Lunch N$105.
Directions: Accessible from Tsumeb, after 73km on B1 turn left direction Namutoni gate. Onguma entrance is right before the gate of the park, on the right. You will drive then 7km on a dirt road.

Mushara Lodge

Mariza and Marc Pampe
8km from Namutoni gate of Etosha National Park
Tel: 067-229-106 Fax: 067-229-107
Email: reservations@mushara-lodge.com Web: www.mushara-lodge.com

I arrived at Mushara with the first rains, an unforgettable moment in Namibia as a heavy perfume of dry grasses and scorched earth fills the air. Mariza and Marc built the lodge ten years ago, naming the lodge after the purple pod terminalia trees, 'mushara' in the local Ovambo language. The immense interior room with its high ceiling, incorporating the reception, bar and lounge, reminds me of a scene from *Alice in Wonderland* with the play of mirrors reflecting the garden and the ostrich egg chandeliers like stars. The wooden screens allow for cosy seating arrangements; leather sofas, kilim carpets, cashmere throws, paintings and drawings collected by Marc's parents and black-and-white photographs of elephants all combine to give the area a refined atmosphere. Under Mariza's supervision, dinner is an elegant affair of candles and white cloths - a pleasure for the eye as well as for the taste buds. The air-conditioned chalets are large and very comfortable, decorated with the same mix of modern and traditional Africa. I couldn't imagine how the two newer "Villa Musharas" could really surpass these already superb chalets, but an involuntary "Ah!" of admiration sprang to my lips as I walked in! A piece of advice: don't plan to do much else than bathe in all the luxury. My desire to hit the hiking trail was quickly subdued by the fact that a lion had been seen there some days before. The luxury of Mushara can make you forget that you're at the entrance of the Etosha Park!

Rooms: 10 doubles, 2 singles and 1 triple, all with en-s sh's. 2 luxury 'Villa Musharas' with living-room, bedroom, en-s bath and sh'r. Family House with living room, two bedrooms and two bathrooms.
Price: N$1,580 per double. N$940 per single. N$2,300 per triple. 'Villa Mushara': N$2,320 pp sh, singles N$3,328. Family House N$3,160.
Meals: Full breakfast included. N$70 lunch or packed lunch N$55. N$150 3-course dinner. Full board included in 'Villa Mushara.'
Directions: Accessible from Tsumeb, after 73km on B1 turn left direction Namutoni gate. Mushara is 8km before the gate of the park.

!Uris Safari Lodge

Charmaine and Anton Voslo
Off B1 about 24km northwest of Tsumeb
Tel: 067-687-060/1 Fax: 067-687-062
Email: info@uris-safari-lodge-namibia.com; reservations@uris-safari-lodge-namibia.com Web: www.uris-safari-lodge-namibia.com

Colourful hanging lanterns were glowing in the dark when I arrived at !Uris, reminding me unexpectedly of a Persian palace from The Arabian Nights. The oriental theme recurs in extravagant and sumptuous interior designs: a wooden antique swing-seat, chests, etched glass vases, clocks, armchairs decorated with rams' heads in silver. All of these treasures were purchased from a South African collector of Indian furniture. The main building with its thatched roof stands on huge, round, wooden piles and opens onto a gorgeous garden and terrace where a centuries-old marula tree stands. In the living room, the enormous mirror above the fireplace reflects the suspended red and blue lights to infinity and sofas have been arranged along the walls in the oriental style. !Uris has several mines, now abandoned, that you can visit on foot, in a donkey cart, by car or by quad, through wonderful wooded countryside of amarula and commiphora. Old photographs above the bar trace the history of the Tsumeb Mine. The former miners' cottages, in the midst of palms and cannas, have undergone a pleasing metamorphosis and are now the guest rooms. Cosy, air-conditioned interiors are decorated with great originality, with beautiful Afghan carpets and light canopies above the beds hung with colourful pompoms. Don't miss a visit to the underground cellar built by the owners, who are great wine enthusiasts.

Rooms: 7 semi-detached chalets (14 rooms) with 7 double rooms and 7 family rooms with a loft.
Price: N$435 pp sharing. N$640 single. Family room from N$1,108 (with 1 child under 12) to N$1,331 (with 2 children under 12). Rates valid until 31 October 2008.
Meals: N$80 light lunch. N$145 dinner.
Directions: From Windhoek take B1 north towards Tsumeb, passing thro' Okahandja, Otjiwarongo and Otavi. At 4-way crossing 3km before Tsumeb turn L to Namutoni/Ondangwa. Continue for c.14km on B1 until sign for !Uris Safari Lodge. Turn L onto dirt road. Follow signs until you reach stone wall & continue for 4.2km till you reach lodge.

Tandala Ridge

Tim & Laurel Osborne
Farm Windpoort, on D2695
Tel: 067-333-408
Email: kori@iway.na Web: www.tandalaridge.com
Cell: 081-124 5202

It is not every day that you have the opportunity to be welcomed by two enthusiastic biologists, ready to share their knowledge with an exclusive group – only one party is accepted at a time – and with such energy! Tim and Laurel, both Americans, have spent 30 years in Africa. After three years at the Etosha Research Centre, studying the Kori bustard, they decided to retire to Windpoort Farm. Tim discovered four new species to science on the farm - a rock mouse, an elephant shrew, an agamid lizard and a gecko - and has counted over 200 bird species. You will be surprised to find yourself as fascinated by the smallest animals, like the rare Welwitchi hyrax and Jameson's rock rabbit, as you are by the 'big ones'. The property also has stromatolites – 650 million-year-old fossil algae – and strange miniature limestone formations, which are extremely sharp. The chalets are set on a hill amongst the commiphoras. Meals are served on the terrace, overlooking a waterhole from where you can observe kudu, oryx, red hartebeest, zebra and eland. There are binoculars for your use. The vegetables come from the garden and I tasted the best cream cheese pie here! And then, Tandala still holds surprises for you: dinner enjoyed to the accompaniment of porcupines; the repertoire of mating calls of Hartlaub's francolins which sometimes attracts a magnificent wild cat; and, during the game drive, a lonely male ostrich might run after the 4x4 to give you his courtship display!

Rooms: 2 double cottages with en-suite bathroom (shower). One party at a time.
Price: N$600 pp sharing. Game drives, walks and night drives included.
Meals: All meals and cool drinks included.
Directions: From Outjo, drive 70km north on C38. Turn west on D2695 and drive 48km. From Anderssen Gate (Etosha NP) drive 25km south on C38 turn west on D2695.

Hobatere Lodge

Steve and Louise Braine
Next to Otjovasandu gate of Etosha west
Tel: 067-687-066 Fax: 067-687-067
Email: hobatere@mweb.com.na Web: www.exclusive.com.na/hobatere.htm

Hobatere, a concession area of 32,000 hectares bordering the Etosha National Park, is blessed with a beautiful undulating landscape of hills, trees, and rocks. During day game drives you have a very good chance of seeing numerous elephants, lions, hyenas, zebras, elands, kudus and giraffes. When we visited, the elephants were right at the foot of the thatched deck at the swimming pool and from the hide overlooking the waterhole 300 metres from the lodge we watched five lions hunting. Later that night we heard them roaring not far from the lodge. On a night game drive, quite rare in Namibia, we encountered the nocturnal wildlife: spring hares jumping from their holes, nightjars landing on the track; we even saw a cheetah and a wild cat. Steve and Louise, who have operated the concession for the past 18 years, are the soul of the place and their kind, informal but attentive welcome assures that, once found (Hobatere means 'find me'), it is a place to which you will want to return. Steve has a great sense of humour and is passionate about nature. No creature is too small or insignificant in his book and he shares his knowledge of birds, butterflies and insects, as well as the larger beasts, with infectious enthusiasm. He also organises birding trips throughout Namibia. The rallying point in the evenings is the stone terrace in front of reception, surrounded by a rock garden, where you dine well under Louise's discreet but watchful eye.

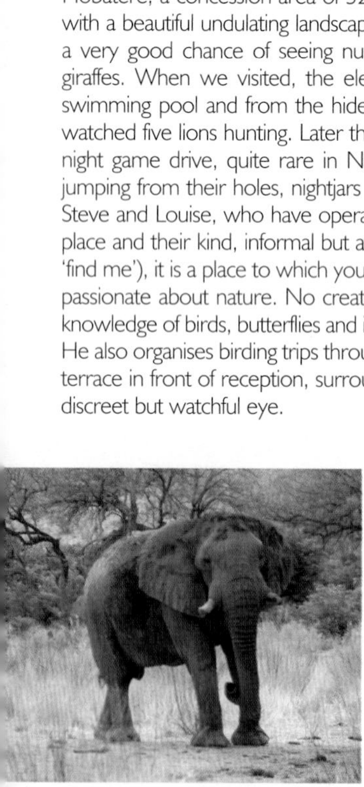

Rooms: 12: 6 chalets and 6 twin rooms, with en-s showers. One rustic tree-house overlooking waterhole.
Price: Dec - Feb & Jun: N$447 pp sh, singles N$487; Mar - May, Jul - Nov N$746 pp sh, singles N$812. Children sadly can't go on guided walks/night drives due to lions. Game drive N$180 pp; night drive N$210 pp; morning guided walk: N$160 pp.
Meals: Full breakfast and dinner included. Lunch from N$40 - N$90; dinner N$130.
Directions: Details on website or faxed/emailed on booking.

Grootberg Lodge

Simonetta and Dominic Du Raan

On C40, Palmwag area
Tel: 067-687-043 Fax: 067-687-044
Email: reservations@grootberg.com Web: www.grootberg-lodge.com

What a vista! The views over the Klip River valley from the lodge, roosting on the edge of the Grootberg Plateau, will delight you no matter where you stand: in the brand-new swimming pool built just on the edge of the mountain; in the restaurant, the living room, your bedroom; or on the terrace furnished with comfortable armchairs… even in your shower! The managers, Simonetta and Dominic, are a wonderful young couple, full of kindness and enthusiasm. Simonetta, who bubbles over with energy and good spirits, ensures that you want for nothing, while Dom is the one who takes you on game drives into the valley in search of the desert elephants, rhino or birdlife he knows so well. You can also walk on the plateau at your own pace. The basalt stone walls of the buildings have the allure of a mountain refuge – by the way, the nights are deliciously fresh up here on the plateau – and the interior décor imparts a feeling of purity and well-being. A symphony of white tones contrasts well with the pretty, rustic Oregon pine furniture. In the vast long room which serves as a living and dining area, tall mirrors at each end reflect the ecru sofas covered with bright plaid throws, individual pine tables, tree trunks and local stone décor as well as a huge bay window which opens out over the valley. Much more than a mere stopping place between Etosha and Palmwag, this is definitely a place worth staying at for a couple of days. *Elephant and black rhino tracking, himba trip and horse rides are also organized.*

Rooms: 12 chalets with en-suite shower (2 of which are family chalets).
Price: N$1,650 double room. N$1,050 single room.
Meals: Full breakfast and 3-course dinner included.
Directions: On C40. Accessible from Kamanjab (97km) and from Palmwag Lodge (25km).

Huab Lodge

Jan and Suzi van de Reep
At the end of D2670 halfway between Khorixas and Kamanjab
Tel: 061-224-712 (reservations) or 067-687-058 (lodge) Fax: 061-224-217 (reservations) or 067-687-059 (lodge) Email: reservations@resdes.com.na
Web: www.huablodge.com Cell: 081-242-7375

Huab is steeped in serenity and what a warm welcome! In 1992, Suzi and Jan, both keen birders and conservationists, began rehabilitating this mountainous, overgrazed farmland of 8,000 hectares. Waterholes were constructed and fences removed so that the harassed desert-dwelling elephant and re-introduced game could roam freely once more... and today their vision has become a reality. Tall grasses sway in the mopane and acacia woodlands and the number of wild animals has exploded. Over 200 bird species occur including nine of Namibia's desert endemics. While the architecture echoes the mountains, flair and imagination are evident in the décor. A natural rock outcrop is integrated into the main building with its soaring thatched roof and open sides. Everyone gathers here for delicious meals, served at the family table and enjoyed together with your hosts; or to spot the stars with the help of various telescopes. The cottages are bright and very comfortable, with huge windows and beautiful bathrooms where you can contemplate nature while you shower. Everything is arranged to encourage relaxation: spaciousness, light, wellness treatments, natural thermal pool, a swimming pool, birding hide, peace. There is no piped music, just the song of the birds, cicadas, barking geckos and frogs. Jan and his team are knowledgeable guides who will captivate your interest for the smaller aspects of nature, what he calls "the bushman newspaper". *Trips with Jan's own registered safari company to Etosha, Etendeka and a Himba settlement can be arranged in advance.*

Rooms: 8 bungalows (16 guests) each with two double beds, large patio, en-suite bathroom and separate en-suite loo. Rustic hide overlooking a waterhole.
Price: N$1,850 pp sharing fully inclusive. Single supplement N$620. Includes 3 activities (morning walk, nature drive & scenic drive) car wash & laundry service (if staying for at least 2 nights).
Meals: English breakfast, lunch, dinner & drinks inc'd.
Directions: Halfway between Khorixas & Kamanjab on C35, turn west to D2670 at Huab sign for 35km.

Mowani Mountain Camp

Andre Louw
Twyfelfontein Conservancy, off D2612, Khorixas
Tel: lodge: 067-697-008; reservations: 061-232-009
Fax: lodge: 067-697-009; reservations: 061-222-574
Email: mowani@visionsofafrica.com.na Web: www.mowani.com

It is the views that first take your breath away. I was instantly captivated by the spectacular yet grotesque forms of the rocky outcrops that cradle Mowani Lodge in their midst: from the tent, from the restaurant, from the swimming pool or from the enormous flat boulder where your sundowners are served, the views are just sensational. The original architectural style allows the structures to blend discreetly into the surrounding landscape. The main buildings with their round cottage roofs and low, ochre, terracotta walls clearly ape the surrounding boulders. The lounge and dining room open directly onto untamed nature and are decorated in rustic elegance with African objects and rattan and wood furniture. The cosy tents are scattered amongst the rocks, with superb raised terraces. On a special occasion, you can treat yourself to the extravagant suite on the edge of the cliff. There are no windows here to separate you from nature and you can enjoy your bath under a starlit sky. If you manage to tear yourself away from this bewitching place, you can go on game drives to search for the desert elephant (4 to 6 hours) or go to admire the Bushman paintings and engravings of Twyfelfontein, about an hour away – no less than 2,500 have been counted. *The Burnt Mountain and the Petrified Forest are also easily accessible from Mowani.*

Rooms: 8 standard tents and 4 view tents, all with en-s shower; 1 luxury room with en-s bathroom; 1 suite with lounge, bedroom, en-s bathroom and bush bath & sh'r, butler service, TV, CD, private dining and bar.
Price: Standard tents: N$1,600 - N$2,310 pp sh; View Tent & Luxury Room: N$1,850 - N$2,560. Suite N$3,700 - N$4,410. Single supp' N$500. Guided nature walk & transport from Twyfelfontein airstrip included. Elephant/nature drive: N$450 pp.
Meals: Full b'fast and dinner incl' in the 1st formula. Rates incl' 3 meals and one activity. Lunch: N$105.
Directions: Details on website or on booking.

Etusis Lodge

Herbert and Monika Lauenroth
On P1954, 35km from Karibib
Tel: 064-550-826 Fax: 064-550-961
Email: etusis@iway.na Web: www.etusis.com

We arrived at Etusis Lodge on Easter Sunday and the large rectangular table, where communal meals are served, was decorated with coloured chocolate Easter eggs, making a rather surreal tableau in the April heat. After our departure, there were distinctly fewer eggs – I am completely, and unfairly, unable to resist chocolate! The owner of Etusis, M. Ledermann, who lives in Germany, fell in love with the Otjipatera Mountains where the lodge was built. He decided to buy the farm and build the lodge to preserve the environment, especially the Hartmann's Mountain Zebra, and to share it all with his guests. The geology of Etusis is very interesting and amateurs will find all the information they need on the website. The tourmaline mine, abandoned today, is open to novice collectors – we tried without success, but even the ordinary rocks you find here are very beautiful! Numerous hiking and escalade trails criss-cross the 12,000-hectare game reserve. You can also explore it on horseback or on a game drive. Tents and charming bungalows with mezzanine floors are independently arranged and well spaced out along the dried river bed which sparkles with pieces of white marble. The pathways that link them together are bordered with lawns punctuated by cactus and yuccas. Meanwhile, the main house, with its thatched roof, is roomy and bright with pink bougainvillaea clinging to the stone walls. The night skies are ideal for star-gazing - telescope provided.

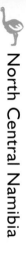

Rooms: 12: 3 double tents with en-suite shower; 2 double tents with shared facilities. 7 bungalows with en-suite shower (sleeps up to 4 persons with additional child's bed available when necessary).
Price: Tents N$550 pp sharing, singles N$650; bungalows N$850 pp, singles N$975. Sundowner game drive in a 4x4 vehicle: N$100.
Meals: Full breakfast and dinner included.
Directions: Turn onto the C32 from Karibib for 19km, then right onto P1954 for 16km.

Erongo Wilderness Lodge

Roger Fusell and Lindy van den Bosch
10km off D2315, Omaruru
Tel: 061-239-199 Fax: 061-234-971
Email: info@erongowilderness-namibia.com Web: www.bigsky-namibia.com
Cell: 081-121-0951

At Erongo Wilderness, the main dilemma is deciding where you will find the most beautiful view: from the verandah of the stilted tents, from the restaurant, from the plunge pool or from one of the surrounding hills. On reflection, I think it must be from the top of the hill where you will be taken for a sundowner, just fifteen minutes' walk from the lodge. Here the view is magical, when the rock glows with the colour of warm amber. The lodge is situated in the Erongo Conservancy and is in complete harmony with the landscape in a valley surrounded by spectacular granite outcrops. Sometimes the rocks are round and smooth while at others they assume grotesque forms with trees emerging from them, as if made of stone themselves. The tents rise in tiers on the hillside, each quite independent but connected to the others by wooden walkways. The bathrooms are partly open to nature. The restaurant is perched on a promontory, accessible by an easy walk and with rest benches provided! Welcoming and informal, the interior is decorated with beautiful, rustic railway-sleeper furniture, basketwork, seeds and African masks. Candlelit dinners with delicious Italian flavours are served stylishly at individual tables. Roger and Lindy are discreet hosts yet attentive at the same time. They work between Erongo Wilderness and an extremely pretty guesthouse, Olive Grove, that they own in Windhoek. Two of the nicest addresses in Namibia.

Rooms: 10: all tents with en-suite showers.
Price: N$895 pp sharing (no single supplement) during low season. N$1,110 pp sharing and N$1,310 per single during high season. All guided walks included in this rate. N$220 pp nature drives.
Meals: Early morning tea/coffee/muffins, full breakfast/brunch, coffee and cake in the afternoon and 4-course dinner included. N$65 light lunch.
Directions: Follow the C33 from Karibib or Otjiwarongo towards Omaruru. 3km on the Karabib side of Omaruru, take the D2315 west. After 10km of gravel road, turn left into the Erongo Wilderness Lodge gate.

Waterberg Guest Farm

Harry Schneider-Waterberg
On C22, at the foot of the Little Waterberg, Otjiwarongo
Tel: 061-237-294 Fax: 061-237-295
Email: reservations@exclusive.com.na Web: www.waterbergnamibia.com

This farm of 42,000 ha located at the foot of the Small Waterberg faces the majestic silhouette of the Waterberg Plateau national. The place is conducive to relaxing. From the dazzling walls to the immaculate quilts covering the soft beds draped with ample mosquito nets, white dominates everything in the bedrooms located in the main house and highlights the basketwork, ostrich egg lamps, photographs of birds and pretty African wooden statues. Four bungalows, hidden in the bush 200m from the house, await those of independent inclination. They are built in traditional Herero method, complemented by the modern African interior design, and have superb views of the Waterberg Plateau. Dinner is served in the welcoming main room with comfortable sofas around the fireplace, coloured kilim carpets, a library filled with books about Namibian wildlife and natural history not to mention the impressive wine collection which occupies almost an entire wall! Harry and Sonja will join you for dinners, and answer your questions about the working farm and the area. There is classical music during breakfast - music being one of the hosts' passions - and at four o'clock, tea, coffee and cakes are served in the lapa amidst bougainvillaea, hibiscus and pink and red impatience. Near the swimming pool there is a small waterhole where game and birds come to drink in the evenings. *Hikes, game drives – with an optional excursion to the Cheetah Conservation – or a drive to the Waterberg National Park, 18km away, are possible.*

Rooms: 6: 4 double rooms, 1 with bath and shower, 3 with shower only and 4 bush bungalows with inside and outside shower.
Price: Main house: N$550 pp sharing and N$600 single. Bush bungalow: N$680 pp sharing and N$770 single.
Meals: Full breakfast included. N$130 dinner. Lunch on request only: N$75.
Directions: Travelling north from Okahandja on the B1, 29km before Otjiwarongo, turn right (east) onto C22, in direction of Okakarara/Waterberg. Travel 30km and find Waterberg Guest Farm signboard on your right.

Wabi Game Lodge

Mark and Christina Egger

Along D2512, Waterberg, Otjiwarongo
Tel: 067-306-500 Fax: 067-306-501
Email: wabi@iafrica.com.na Web: www.wabi.ch

At Wabi, you are right on top of the Waterberg Plateau. After a 20-minute ascent by car, the road follows the edge of the escarpment with its superb views of high, rocky peaks of red sandstone eroded into fantastical shapes and laced with the clinging vines of climbing figs. Don't forget the coolbox to make the most of the spectacular sight of the plateau at dusk with a drink. The game drives allow you to see white rhino, buffalo, roan antelope, sable, waterbuck, nyala, lechwe, giraffe, zebra, black springbok and even hippo among many others. Mark and Christine are filled with enthusiasm for their property and it is fascinating to talk with them at the bar before dinner. Christine is full of energy and is responsible for looking after the needs of her guests and for the preparation of the meals, which are served individually. The park surrounding the house is a verdant delight - the most beautiful garden in Namibia in my opinion! Above carefully-tended lawns, the acacias are filled with the sounds of hornbills, touracos, babblers and glossy starlings while, at their bases, blue plumbago, fuchsia, hibiscus, laurel roses and other roses form colourful flowerbeds. A bougainvillaea-laden arbour leads to the four well-equipped, air-conditioned suites. The two luxury units are independent on the other side of the garden. It is difficult to tear yourself away from the swimming pool, which overlooks the waterhole, but then, why should you? After all, you are on holiday.

Rooms: 8 cottages; each with bedroom, living room and en-suite bath and shower and a porch.
Price: N$895 pp for one night only; for more than one night N$695 pp. Luxury units N$1,195 one night; for more than one night N$995 pp. No single supplement.
Meals: Full breakfast, light lunch, 3-course evening dinner.
Directions: From B1, 23km before Otjiwarongo, turn right to C22, in direction of Okakarara and the Waterberg for 41km, then turn left onto gravel road D2512 direction Waterberg Plateau Park, for 54km. Wabi is well sign-posted on your left.

Gabus Game Ranch

Heidi and Heinz Keuhl
On D3031, 10km from Otavi
Tel: 067-234-291 Fax: 067-234-290
Email: kuehl@mweb.com.na Web: www.natron.net/tour/gabus
Cell: 081-127-9278

"Heinz is for the outdoors and me for the cooking!" Heidi tells us laughing. What she doesn't say, but we quickly discover, is that they both have wonderfully warm hearts. The farm has been in Heinz's family for four generations and he has lovingly constructed a small family museum in a barn. The couple have two children, both with names beginning with H like their parents, and children are most welcome here! On the ranch, wildebeest, giraffe, waterbuck and mountain zebra have been introduced and you can see them during the game drive with Heinz. Behind the now ruined original farmhouse, found at the base of a petrified cascade, the limestone rocks of the Uiseb Mountains are marvels of colour and form. Three varieties of commiphora trees, green, orange and red, grow at the foot of these mountains. Heinz shows us the deep cave of an old leopard that he sees two or three times a year and whose claw-marks are clearly visible on the trunk of a gnarled tree nearby. Heidi is an excellent cook, full of surprises. In a traditional, typically German farm, who would expect to taste a delicious Thai haw moek (fish steamed in banana leaves)? A bougainvillaea-covered portico gives access to a little garden where the dining-room and the air-conditioned rooms, each different in style, are situated. And facing the swimming pool there is a waterhole where the animals come to drink. The Otavi mountains are not only beautiful in their own right, but they are also an excellent stop on the way to Etosha. A special place and extremely friendly hosts.

Rooms: 6: 4 double rooms (3 with en-suite shower and 1 with en-suite bath) ; 1 family room (sleeps 5) with en-suite shower; 1 honeymoon with en-suite shower and outdoor jacuzzi.
Price: N$780 per pp sharing. 1 game drive included. Additional game drives on request N$150 pp.
Meals: Full breakfast, afternoon coffee and cake and 3-course dinner included. Light lunch served on request at N$45.
Directions: In Otavi take C39 direction Outjo, then turn on D3031 (Gabus is well sign-posted). Gabus is 10km from Otavi.

Ohange Lodge

Karla and Justus Brits

On B1, Otavi
Tel: 067-234-031 Fax: 067-234-356
Email: ohangejk@iway.na Web: www.ohange.com
Cell: 081-261-6738

My heart beats faster as we enter the ancient and tortuous tamboti and commiphora woodlands, the ground covered with sharp stones with ferns and lilies growing between them. Let's hope the lodge is at the top of this enchanted place... and there it is, cocooned in the middle of hundred-year-old marulas, a couple of paradise fly-catchers fluttering past and overlooking a waterhole where kudu, oryx, eland, ostrich, impala, blesbok and giraffe come to drink without fear. Behind, the pointed thatched roofs of the little, red-ochre cottages can be glimpsed through the trees. Karla and Justus, who were not expecting us, came forward smiling and immediately offered us coffee. They have made their dream come true recently by buying this property and re-introducing numerous animals to create a little paradise. At the end of the afternoon, during our game drive when the 4x4 begins to climb a steep track to the top of the mountain, Justus laughingly tells us that "the honeymoon is over!" But, at Ohange, the honeymoon is never over: we are offered a surprise sundowner in the bush while admiring a spectacular sunset. In the evening, an excellent braai is served outside, overlooking the illuminated waterhole, followed by a night game drive when we see lesser bush babies, civets and spring hares. No leopards or cheetah that night, but in the morning we could see leopard tracks just behind the lodge.

Rooms: 10 cottages all with en-suite showers.
Price: N$750 pp sharing. N$980 all included (activities as well). N$350 single supplement. Game drive and night drive N$120 pp.
Meals: Full breakfast and dinner included in first formula. Light lunch N$75.
Directions: 30km north of Otavi on B1. 1 hour 15 mins from Etosha (Namutoni gate).

Roy's Camp

Marietjie and Wimpie Otto
Farm Elandslaagte, Grootfontein
Tel: 067-240-302 Fax: 067-240-302
Email: royscamp@iway.na Web: www.swiftcentre.com

And now for something completely different: a journey into the realm of fantasy. At Roy's Camp a leaning towards rusticity in the architecture and the amazing decoration chosen by Wimpie, a passionate craft artist, fuse here into pure poetry. You are welcomed into the lapa through mobiles of seeds, ostrich eggs and bones. You sit on imposing wooden armchairs, with arms fashioned from kudu horns, or at the bar on tree trunks covered in animal hide. The same degree of imagination is found in the thatched chalets, each different of course in both shape and colour, and each with its own braai terrace. The dining room, its roof supported by tree trunks, is highly atmospheric in the evenings when oil lamps and pottered candleholders emit a strange light. Bouquets of dried herbs, antique tools and kitchen implements, jute curtains bordered with seeds, porcupine quills and feathers add further to the tone. The owners live next door but, with young children, have delegated the running of the lodge to very attentive managers. You can hike on two specially laid trails or go on a farm/game drive. Roy's Camp will help you if you want to get involved in other activities (traditional hunting or tracking trips, collecting veld food or making jewellery) at a Bushman village 86km away in the direction of Tsumke. *Transport and guiding could be arranged but need to be book well in advance.*

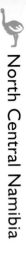

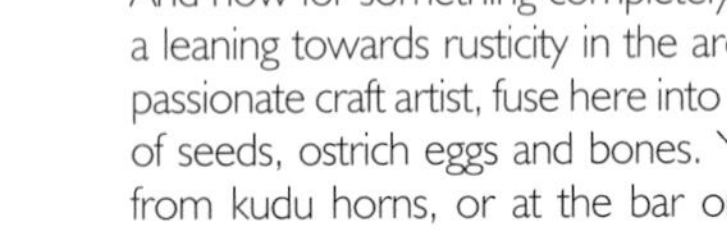

Rooms: 7: all are chalets (2 family chalets) with en-suite showers. Family chalets have 2 bedrooms that share a bathroom.
Price: N$408.25 pp sharing; N$477.25 single; N$327.75 pp in the family chalets.
Meals: Full breakfast included. Lunch and dinner N$120. Light lunch N$70. Braai packs from N$50 to N$80.
Directions: 56km north of Grootfontein on the B8 to Rundu. Turn left just after Tsumkwe turn-off. Roy's Camp is 1km off B8 and well sign-posted.

Susuwe Island Lodge

Tinolla and Craig Collins, managers
In Bwabwata National Park, Caprivi
Tel: +27 11-234-9997 (Johannesburg) Fax: + 27 11-234-0323 (Johannesburg)
Email: info@islandsinafrica.com Web: www.islandsinafrica.com
Cell: + 264-813-064-551 (lodge)

The track plunges into the heart of the Bwabata National Park with its forests and its flood plains. Having arrived at the embarkation point for the island in the middle of the Kwando River, we were intrigued, seeing only a grove of gigantic trees. Our arrival was enchanting when we discovered, buried under a dense cover of vegetation, the romantic soul of the place: a circular wooden platform overlooked by an ancient sausage tree. Decks have been built in the canopy from which to bird-watch – the park is an ornithologist's paradise. The air flashes with blue and red as paradise fly-catchers fly past and squirrels bound about nearby. Here all your wishes – or nearly all – are granted: a friendly and professional welcome from Tinolla and Craig and their team, your choice of numerous activities such as game drives by 4x4 into the park through which herds of elephant travel in season, boat trips on the Kwando, sundowners on a sandbar in the company of hippopotami and excellent dinners on the terrace to the xylophonic sounds of the frogs. The main pavilion is attractively decorated in a fishing theme. The suites, very private hidden in their natural screen of vegetation, all face the Kwando. And what suites they are! The doors - works of abstract art - set the tone… luxury and originality combined. All the rooms – romantic bedroom with enormous bed covered in drapes, superb bathroom and lounge – look through glass bay-windows onto a lovely terrace on stilts with a pool. One of the most romantic addresses in the Namibian chapter.

Rooms: 6 suites with bathroom (bath tub and shower), bedroom, lounge and wooden viewing deck, each with private plunge pool.
Price: US$355 - US$530pp sharing. Single supplement 30%. Rate includes laundry, activities, SOS insurance and park fees.
Meals: All meals, soft, local and house drinks inc.
Directions: Accessible from B8 Katima Mulilo road (132km from KM to Kongola). At Kongola, after bridge, turn L (sand road off opposite Susuwe sign). Drive in park for 10km. Lodge sign on L before Susuwe. Continue to car park facing lodge by river. You will be transferred by boat. Accessible by plane.

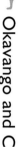

Ntwala Island Lodge

Tinolla and Craig Collins, managers
Ntwala island, Caprivi
Tel: +27 11-234-9997 (Johannesburg) Fax: +27 11-234-0323 (Johannesburg)
Email: info@islandsinafrica.com Web: www.islandsinafrica.com

There is a stunning contrast between the virgin nature of the wooded islet of Ntwala, at the confluence of the Chobe and Zambezi rivers, and the extreme sophistication of its villas. Your arrival on floating walkways through reeds and papyrus in no way prepares you for the mind-boggling luxury of the lodge. A once-in-a-lifetime romantic spot for a once-in-a-lifetime romantic moment.... The villas, completely independent from each other behind screens of vine-strangled trees, are immense and open towards the bush and the rapids through sliding glass doors; the bedrooms are impressive, but even more spectacular are the huge bathrooms with their jacuzzis. Meals can be served on the wooden deck that extends out with the swimming pool embedded in its midst and with tropical white-sand beach on one side. Lower down, on your lapa above the white water, two swing chairs entice you to sit, relax... and just look. And in this position we saw clawless otters swimming in the river and on the opposite bank a group of young male elephants hanging around in the palm trees before crossing the rapids at dusk, trunks and tails held high in the air. The islet is rich in birdlife and in the morning we were woken by giant kingfishers tapping at their reflection in the glass... Craig and Tinolla's welcome was very attentive and yet discreet; they seemed to appear from nowhere - like Jeeves - at exactly the right moment! If you manage to tear yourself away from so much peace – we never managed it ourselves! - you can take an individual boat ride with a guide as far as the Chobe National Park 25 minutes away, or you can go fishing for tigerfish, or bird-watching at sunset.

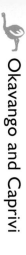

Rooms: 4 ultra-luxury suites with en-s bathroom (double-sized bath with jacuzzi, indoor & outdoor sh'r), a private plunge pool and private sala.
Price: US$405 - US$630 pp sharing. Single supp' 30%. Rates incl' laundry, private guided activities, SOS insurance, boat transfer from Kasane immigration.
Meals: All meals and drinks included.
Directions: If you arrive by car staff of Ntwala will wait for you at Kasane immigration office (near river) & help with formalities & arrange for safe parking for your car. Other arrival details on website.

Ichingo Chobe River Lodge & The Ichobezi Luxury Safari Boat

Dawn and Ralph Oxenham

Impalila Island, Caprivi
Tel: +27-11-706-6242 Fax: +27-11-706-6242
Email: ichingo@iafrica.com Web: www.ichobezi.co.za
Cell: +267-7130-2439 or +27-829-032-490

Impalila Island, in Namibia, occupies a very privileged position near the borders of Zimbabwe, Botswana and Zambia. A crossing on the Ichobezi is a marvellous way to discover this water-logged and fauna-rich region. Comfortably installed on the bridge or in the bay window of your luxurious cabin, you will discover Chobe National Park and its buffalo, elephant, bushbuck, puku, giraffe, waterbuck, lechwe, kudu, impala, hippo, crocodile and more than 400 species of bird. In the early evening, the boat is anchored opposite a river beach where elephants come to drink. The arrival, one by one, of an impressive herd is unforgettable! A small tende boat takes you in to view them from just a few metres away. It is common to see them in the dry season swimming across the Chobe. I recommend spending the first night at Ichingo Chobe River Lodge, a very comfortable tented camp facing the roaring rapids and surrounded by trees and twisting creepers; and then one or two nights on the Ichobezi safari boats. Ralph and Dawn, so full of humour and kindness, are a major part of the pleasure of staying here. Their staff, too, will take great care of you during your stay. The cooking is creative and absolutely delicious. Game-viewing or fishing (tiger fish and bream) by individual motorboats with a guide; tours of Victoria Falls (100km away), or game drives into Chobe National Park can also be arranged. This is a place that you will find difficult to leave!

Rooms: 8 double tents with en-s sh'r; 2 Ichobezi luxury safari boats, each with 4 twin cabins with en-suite sh'r, spacious deck and plunge pool.
Price: Both properties are R2,460 pp sh and R3,360 for singles. Includes transfer from Kasane, all meals, soft drinks, local drinks and activities such as fishing and game-viewing by boat. Special rates & packages at certain times of year on request.
Meals: Full b'fast, lunch and 3-course dinner incl'.
Directions: If you arrive by car staff will wait for you at Kasane immigration office (near the river) and help with formalities & arrange for safe parking for your car. See website for alternative ways to arrive.

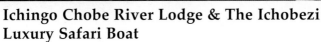

Map Number: 27 & 29

Entry Number: 365

Zambia and Botswana

Introduction

Although there are only seven entries in Zambia and Botswana in this book, they are perhaps the most redolent of what GG is all about. Both countries are littered with lodges but very few of them are independently run… or have that extra character and charm that make a stay so much more than a few animal sightings. This is always down to the management and ownership and I think you will agree, if you do decide to set off on an African adventure in these regions, that you are better off with seven great places than a choice of 60 whose blessings are mixed. Honeymooners take note!

The trail to these new properties was mainly blazed by Sarah Campbell-Pitt on an extended few months of 4x4 adventuring around Southern Africa. Lots of vital extra input for entries has also been provided by Tracy Woodland and Karoline Hanks..

I was contacted by Sarah on her return, still buzzing with all the amazing places she had experienced, and keen to see if GG were going to extend into that area. One conversation was enough for me to offer her the chance to do it herself and she is now the GG editor for the area. If you have any suggestions for next time in any Southern African countries apart for Namibia and South Africa do please send us an email at simon@greenwoodguides.com.

The following introduction to this new area is by Sarah herself.

HOW TO USE THE GUIDE

Almost all the places that we have featured are owned and run by hosts with a deep knowledge of their area. They are for the most part 'old Africa hands', able to bring their wealth of experience to any stay.

There are many ways to approach a visit to these areas. You might choose to jump onto a plane for a long weekend at Victoria Falls or dive into a full 2-week fly-in visit staying with just one of the places featured (that offer lots of variety of accommodation and activities to keep you busy) e.g., South Luangwa, Lower Zambezi, Okavango Delta. Many travellers go for this option as it often comes with the bonus of better rates for a week period than on a nightly rate. Many places also offer specialist safari activities lasting from a few days to over a week: canoe & walking safaris in Zambia or mountain-biking in Botswana. Another option is to fly to a few different places set in a variety of regions, ideally spending 2 to 3 nights at each. With short light aircraft hops you can easily switch between countries.

Another great way of getting to see the 'connecting parts' between lodges is to jump behind the wheel of a car and drive yourself. There are a range of places you can reach by normal saloon car (including northern Zambia) and in some instances where roads become too rough you can leave your vehicle at a safe place and be transferred into different areas – the Tuli Block in Botswana for example.

If you want to venture away from the main national network of roads onto secondary dust roads, the vehicle of choice is a 4x4. Before even thinking of embarking on a 4x4 trip make sure you've read the section on driving tips! Whilst some of the places featured more commonly have guests arrive by air (due to their remote location) it is possible to drive to almost all of them if you have the experience. You can embark on a few weeks' trip using the places in the guide as all your stopping points or, as we did, intersperse nights of 'camping in the wild' with nights of great comfort. Trust me, when you have had a few dust-covered September days in Savuti and Chobe you'll never be so grateful to have someone else do the cooking, laundry, guiding and above all a heavenly bed to flop into.

FLY-IN TIPS

If at any stage on the trip you are likely to transfer on a small light aircraft ensure that you use soft duffel bags not exceeding 12kg per person as hard cases don't fit into the small spaces available for luggage on these planes (or onto the game drive vehicles used for transfers). Light aircraft transfers can usually be arranged by the lodge you are visiting. As you head into the skies make sure you have a camera ready – a flight over somewhere like the Okavango Delta is a spectacular experience on its own!

DRIVING

- Vehicle Requirements

Each country has slightly different vehicle entry requirements. The easiest way of getting the most up-to-date information is from Automobile Association (AA) outlets in South Africa who have details for all Southern African countries. They are able to print out a listing of each country's requirements. If you are hiring a vehicle the hire company should assist you with the correct paperwork (particularly for any border crossings) and extra items such as warning triangles, reflectors etc.

- CHOICE OF VEHICLE & DRIVING TIPS

Botswana and Zambia both have a main network of roads suitable for saloon cars. Conditions of these roads can vary from excellent smooth rides to sections of lumpy pot-holed surprises which with a keen eye are possible to navigate. Plan to do all driving during the day and aim to get to your destination in the early afternoon leaving a few hours of daylight for any unforeseen adventures like taking a wrong turn. All agree that driving at night is hazardous and should be avoided. The other standard piece of advice is: never pass a petrol station that has fuel without filling up. Taking this advice to heart meant that when a temporary fuel shortage took place in Zambia we had sufficient fuel for our journey when many were left high and dry. Doubly satisfying!

When the tar gives way to dust so too should a saloon car be exchanged for a reliable 4x4. Many marked 'dust roads' are nothing more than bush tracks that are kept open by the passage of vehicles and haven't seen a grader in their life.

In Botswana and Zambia dirt roads or bush tracks can be challenging and require real off-road driving skills and experience to handle (especially in the wet season when many become impassable). If you have some experience it is well worth brushing up your skills on an advanced 4x4 course in South Africa before leaving on your travels.

It is also vital not to underestimate the length of time it can take to travel a section of these remote dust roads. A particularly memorable 170km stretch of bush track was a bone-rattling adventurous two-day journey! Do your research before setting off; a great place for first-hand information are the lodges you are visiting who will have up-to-date intelligence on the local road conditions. The dry season is by far the easiest time of year to get around in a 4x4.

It's important to have someone who's mechanically-minded on your trip and able to do repairs along the way as help can be a few hours or days away. Make sure you have the right tools and spare parts and our absolutely top piece of advice is to take a few rolls of duct tape – it's amazing what you can fix with this (we 'taped' our suspension together along a stretch of road till we found an obliging mechanic who could make a more lasting repair!).

All this said if you have the off-road driving experience, a reliable well kitted-out 4x4, you've done your research, got a good GPS, maps, proper supplies of food and water and an excellent sense of adventure there truly is no better way to get the dust of this part of Africa between your toes.

BORDER CROSSINGS

The best advice we were given for border crossings was 'expect them to take a day and when it takes an hour you'll be delighted!' After all our experience in this area we absolutely agree that it's impossible to judge how long it will take so build extra time into your schedule. Some border points are small and efficient, like the crossing from South Africa into the Tuli Block in Botswana; whilst others are used by long lines of trucks and can take hours – such as Kazungula border into Zambia. Border operating hours are usually strictly enforced; keep this in mind as you travel or you could land up spending the night at a border post waiting for it to open.

ROAD-BLOCKS (common in Zambia)

We approached our first roadblock with some trepidation having heard tales of 'officials asking for bribes'. To our joy were only met with the customary vehicle paper questions, big smiles and lots of "how are you enjoying Zambia so far?" Within no time at all we were used to the roadblocks on entering and leaving each town. Best advice we can give - have all your car papers organised ready to present, make sure the vehicle has all the extra 'bits' required in different countries - in Zambia you need two warning triangles in the vehicle and reflectors on the front and back, turn off the radio, take off your sunglasses, roll down the window and be ready to give a big cheery smile. Most importantly remain patient and remember to keep your sense of humour and enjoy the range of experiences that these different countries provide!

CAR HIRE

It is possible to hire a vehicle relatively easily in all three countries from major towns/cities, but which type will depend on the kind of trip you have planned. If you are planning to stick to the main network of tarred roads then a saloon car with high clearance works well. It is vital to do your homework and get as much information as possible about the company and their reputation with vehicles to avoid operators with 'dodgy' cars that are bound to break down in the middle of nowhere. 4x4 hire vehicles need to be properly kitted-out which means long range fuel tanks, extra jerry cans, water tank, recovery equipment, spare tyres etc. Some companies offer a 'back-up' service so if you break down help is available, a really advisable feature if you're on a three-week trip and can't afford to spend two weeks trying to get a spare part! There are also some good companies in South Africa that provide competitive rates for hiring 4x4s.

PRICES

Accommodation rates in the three countries is on average higher than South Africa and Namibia. What you pay for is the opportunity to stay in remote, often quite inaccessible corners of wilderness, which means that behind the scenes lodges face real logistical challenges. Some get supplies by plane, others are only able to operate for part of the year and have to re-build camps each season, which all adds to the costs.

MALARIA

Malaria occurs throughout the region and it is absolutely essential to take preventative steps throughout the year including taking anti-malarial prophylactics and reducing your exposure to being bitten through use of repellents, wearing long sleeves and trousers in the evening and sleeping under a mosquito net. Always seek the advice of a doctor (travel clinics often provide the most up to date information) to make sure you're taking the most appropriate medication for the region and yourself. A top tip is to go on the medication a few weeks before you leave home to check how you react to the drugs – many have side effects and it's better to find out at home rather than in the middle of your dream lodge experience (like I did a few years ago!) so you can change to one that works better for you if necessary. It's also important to find out what immunisations /vaccinations you might need for each country and leave time to have them done before you leave. Some of the jabs left me feeling like I had flu for a few days, so I would advise getting them done in plenty of time.

TIME OF YEAR

The climate falls into two distinctive periods across the three countries. May – November is the dry season where game is plentiful with cooler temperatures in June - August (remember to bring a very warm jacket) and much hotter temperatures from September – November. Top temperatures in October in Zambia's valleys and in Botswana can reach over 40° but the game concentrations around rivers and waterholes provide amazing spectacles that make all the extra sweating worth it. Dec – April is the rainy season (can be hot and sticky) but provides a completely different experience, brilliant for those who have done a few trips into game areas and are looking for something new. Some lodges in Zambia close during this period as roads become impassable quagmires. The lodges that remain open offer different experiences and some offer good 'green season' rates!

WHAT TO PACK

All the places mentioned in the book suggest a similar list of 'what to take' which includes: sun things (sun block, hats, sunglasses), game-viewing things (cameras, film, batteries, binoculars for each person) what to wear (comfy walking shoes, in summer lightweight clothes, swimming costume and waterproof for downpours, in winter light clothing for daytime and very warm jacket for evening time) and toiletries (including personal medication). A torch is an absolute must, particularly for those needing to take a trip to the 'facilities' at night and wanting to avoid stepping on anything that might have scuttled into your room.